BLACK'S NEW TESTAMENT COMMENTARIES

General Editor: Henry Chadwick, DD, FBA

THE EPISTLE TO THE GALATIANS

BLACK'S NEW TESTAMENT COMMENTARY

THE
EPISTLE TO
THE GALATIANS

JAMES D. G. DUNN

HENDRICKSON
PUBLISHERS
PEABODY, MASSACHUSETTS 01961-3473

First published 1993

A & C Black (Publishers) Limited, London

Copyright © 1993 James D. G. Dunn

Hendrickson Publishers, Inc. Edition

ISBN 1-56563-036-X

Reprinted by arrangement with A & C Black (Publishers) Limited.

The mosaic fretwork on the cover comes from the Galla Placidia
Mausoleum in Ravenna and is used courtesy of ITALCARDS, Bologna, Italy.

CONTENTS

To
Martin and Marianne Hengel
in celebration
of our
Durham–Tübingen partnership

PREFACE

Galatians is a document with which I have lived in close communion since the end of the 1970s. I had long been fascinated by the theology of Paul, both in academic terms and for its stimulus to my own theologizing. But it was about then that the significance of Galatians within the collection of Paul's letters became sharply clearer to me. Not only because it is the most pungent and forthright of Paul's expositions of his own understanding of the Christian gospel; that had been common knowledge at least within Protestant circles from Luther onwards. But particularly because it provided insights into the development of Paul's theology and its contextual character which cannot be found anywhere else.

It was about then that the conviction took firm root that the incident at Antioch (ii.11–14) is a key to opening up and understanding the development both of Paul and of Christianity itself which had been insufficiently exploited. The resulting paper was first delivered at the inaugural meeting of the British New Testament Conference in 1980. One study on the opening chapters of Galatians led to another. In all a sequence of six studies was completed in the course of the 80s (see pp. xvi–xvii below). My principal project during that period was a commentary on *Romans*, for which careful study of Galatians was indispensable anyway. But with the latter's publication in 1988 I was able to turn my attention more fully to Galatians in its own right. The following pages have thus been the result of four or five years of detailed research, preceded by eight or so years of specific studies, preceded, I might add, by a lifetime of fascination with Paul and his letters.

As in the commentary on *Romans*, I have attempted as my first priority to grasp the flow and interconnection of thought in the document. Dialogue with other commentaries and specialist studies has been a secondary concern. At the same time I am more than happy to acknowledge the stimulus initially of H. D. Betz's great commentary, whose appearance in 1979 was a factor in my own growing interest in Galatians, and then particularly of E. P. Sanders' *Paul*, as my appreciation of the new perspective which he has brought to Pauline studies was deepened by my own research into particular themes and passages. And, of course, engagement with the grand tradition of Galatian commentators over the past hundred years brought innumerable fresh insights, clarifications and adjustment on many points of detail.

However, the character of the series quite properly discourages detailed engagement with other commentators on particular points. The concern is to expound the text, not to document the endless disagreements of scholars past and present. Having thus noted many points of agreement and disagreement in the second draft, fruit of careful scrutiny of the principal earlier studies, I conformed to the series house style by removing the bulk of these references in the final draft. Those who will wish to engage in detailed study of particular points will have no difficulty in recognizing my dialogue partners (where unnamed) or in amassing supporting or opposing names by their own inquiry. While those who wish simply to make best sense of the text itself will presumably wish the pages of the commentary to be as uncluttered as possible.

For the same reason I have eliminated almost all reference to textual apparatus with its details of manuscripts and versions in which variant readings are to be found. Those who wish further detail will find all they need in Aland[26] or equivalent. Notes on variants in footnotes, however, quite often include comment on the significance of there being such variants in the first place.

As is also the custom with the series, I have used my own translation as the basis for the commentary. In this I have striven for a translation which reflects the emphases of the Greek as closely as possible, including the occasional awkwardness of syntax which is a feature of Paul's epistolary style. Since there has been a recent increase in the number of new or revised translations, it also seemed appropriate to note disagreement (and agreement) with and among these translations, in the hope that readers who cannot deal with the Greek themselves may have some help in deciding between such variations.

In the Introduction I have refrained from including a section which summarizes the theology of Galatians, since the book was already large enough, and since the responsibility of contributing the volume on Galatians in The Theology of the New Testament series (Cambridge University Press) fell to me. The following commentary and *The Theology of Paul's Letter to the Galatians* (also 1993) can thus be seen as companion volumes.

A number of studies of particular relevance to Galatians came to hand too late for me to include reference to them in the following pages. They include the commentaries by F. J. Matera, *Galatians* (Sacra Pagina 9; Collegeville, Minnesota: Liturgical Press, 1992) and by J. Ziesler, *The Epistle to the Galatians* (Epworth Commentary; London: Epworth, 1992). Also the volumes by I.-G. Hong, *The Law in Galatians* (Sheffield Academic, 1993), by H. Hübner, *Biblische Theologie des Neuen Testaments Band 2. Die Theologie des Paulus* (Göttingen: Vandenhoeck, 1993) 57–111, and by P. Stuhlmacher, *Biblische Theologie des Neuen Testaments. Band 1. Grundlegung von Jesus zu Paulus* (Göttingen: Vandenhoeck, 1992) 221–392.

Warm thanks are due to Henry Chadwick for the invitation to contribute the volume on Galatians to Black's New Testament Commentary series and for his various comments on earlier drafts. To join my esteemed predecessor, C. K. Barrett, in contributing the fourth of the Pauline *Hauptbriefe* to the series has been a particular pleasure. Warm thanks are also due to my colleagues at Durham, Sandy Wedderburn and Stephen Barton, for their supportive teamwork and for the stimulus of our ongoing dialogue. Postgraduate seminars at Nottingham and Durham have all contributed to maturing insights, as also Pauline seminars at the annual meetings of the Society for New Testament Studies and the Society of Biblical Literature. The dedication to Martin and Marianne Hengel is token of continuing fruitful interchange in our Durham–Tübingen partnership. Above all my dear Meta has been able to provide just the right mix of support and provocation without which even such an enjoyable task as this might never have been completed.

BIBLIOGRAPHY

Commentaries cited

Becker   J. Becker, *Der Brief an die Galater* (Das Neue Testament Deutsch; Göttingen: Vandenhoeck, 1990).

Betz   H. D. Betz, *Galatians* (Hermeneia; Philadelphia: Fortress, 1979).

Beyer-Althaus   H. W. Beyer, revised by P. Althaus, 'Der Brief an die Galater', *Die kleineren Briefe des Apostels Paulus* (Das Neue Testament Deutsch; Göttingen: Vandenhoeck, 1962).

Bligh   J. Bligh, *Galatians* (London: St Paul, 1969).

Bonnard   P. Bonnard, *L'Épître de Saint Paul aux Galates* (Commentaire du NT; Neuchâtel: Delachaux, 1953).

Borse   U. Borse, *Der Brief an die Galater* (Regensburger Neues Testament; Regensburg: Pustet, 1984).

Bousset   W. Bousset, 'Der Brief an die Galater', *Die Schriften des Neuen Testaments* (Göttingen: Vandenhoeck, 1917).

Bring   R. Bring, *Der Brief des Paulus an die Galater* (Berlin: Lutherisches, 1968) – Eng. tr. *Commentary on Galations* (Philadelphia: Muhlenberg, 1961) of Swedish original (1958).

Bruce   F. F. Bruce, *The Epistle to the Galatians* (New International Greek Testament Commentary; Exeter: Paternoster, 1982).

Burton   E. de W. Burton, *The Epistle to the Galatians* (International Critical Commentary; Edinburgh: T. & T. Clark, 1921).

Cole   R. A. Cole, *Galatians* (Tyndale NT Commentaries; Leicester: Inter-Varsity, 2nd edition, 1989).

Cousar   C. B. Cousar, *Galatians* (Interpretation; Atlanta: John Knox, 1982).

Duncan   G. S. Duncan, *The Epistle of Paul to the Galatians* (Moffatt NT Commentary; London: Hodder, 1934).

Fung   R. Y. K. Fung, *The Epistle to the Galatians* (New International Commentary on the NT; Grand Rapids: Eerdmans, 1988).

Guthrie   D. Guthrie, *Galatians* (New Century Bible; London: Oliphants, 1969).

Lagrange   M.-J. Lagrange, *Saint Paul Épître aux Galates* (Études Bibliques; Paris: Gabalda, 2nd edition, 1925).

Lietzmann   H. Lietzmann, *An die Galater* (Handbuch zum NT; Tübingen: J. C. B. Mohr, 4th edition, 1971).

Lightfoot   J. B. Lightfoot, *Saint Paul's Epistle to the Galatians* (London: Macmillan, 1865).

Longenecker   R. N. Longenecker, *Galatians* (Word Biblical Commentary 41; Dallas: Word, 1990).

Lührmann   D. Lührmann, *Der Brief an die Galater* (Zürcher Bibelkommentare; Zürich: TVZ, 1988).

Metzger   B. M. Metzger, *A Textual Commentary on the Greek New Testament* (London: United Bible Societies, 1975).

Mussner   F. Mussner, *Der Galaterbrief* (Herders Theologischer Kommentar zum NT; Freiburg: Herder, 3rd edition, 1977).

Oepke   A. Oepke, *Der Brief des Paulus an die Galater* (Theologischer Handkommentar zum NT; Berlin: Evangelische, 3rd edition edited by J. Rohde, 1973).

Ramsay   W. M. Ramsay, *A Historical Commentary on St. Paul's Epistle to the Galatians* (London: Hodder, 1900).

Rendall   F. Rendall, 'The Epistle to the Galatians', *The Expositor's Greek Testament*, ed. W. R. Nicoll (London: Hodder, 1917).

Ridderbos   H. N. Ridderbos, *The Epistle of Paul to the Churches of Galatia* (New International Commentary on the NT; Grand Rapids: Eerdmans, 1953).

Rohde   J. Rohde, *Der Brief des Paulus an die Galater* (Theologischer Handkommentar zum NT; Berlin: Evangelische, 1989).

Schlier   H. Schlier, *Der Brief an die Galater* (Kritisch-Exegetischer Kommentar über das NT; Göttingen: Vandenhoeck, 4th edition, 1965).

Sieffert   F. Sieffert, *Der Brief an die Galater* (Kritisch-Exegetischer Kommentar über das NT, Göttingen: Vandenhoeck, 4th edition, 1899).

Zahn   T. Zahn, *Der Brief des Paulus an die Galater* (Kommentar zum Neuen Testament; Leipzig: Deichert, 1905).

Other works cited more than once

Items cited only once have full bibliographical details at the point where they are cited. The author's own publications are listed on pp. xvi–xvii.

Barclay, *Obeying*	J. Barclay, *Obeying the Truth. A Study of Paul's Ethics in Galatians* (Edinburgh: T. & T. Clark, 1988).
Barrett, *Essays*	C. K. Barrett, *Essays on Paul* (London: SPCK, 1982).
Barrett, *Freedom*	C. K. Barrett, *Freedom and Obligation. A Study of the Epistle to the Galatians* (London: SPCK, 1985).
Beker	J. C. Beker, *Paul the Apostle. The Triumph of God in Life and Thought* (Philadelphia: Fortress, 1980).
Betz, 'Spirit'	H. D. Betz, 'Spirit, Freedom, and Law. Paul's Message to the Galatian Churches', *Svensk Exegetisk Årsbok* 39 (1974) 145–60.
Bornkamm	G. Bornkamm, *Paul* (London: Hodder, 1971).
Catchpole	D. R. Catchpole, 'Paul, James and the Apostolic Decree', *NTS* 23 (1976–77) 428–44.
Cosgrove, *Cross*	C. H. Cosgrove, *The Cross and the Spirit. A Study in the Argument and Theology of Galatians* (Mercer University, 1988).
Drane	J. W. Drane, *Paul: Libertine or Legalist?* (London: SPCK, 1975).
Ebeling	G. Ebeling, *The Truth of the Gospel. An Exposition of Galatians* (Philadelphia: Fortress, 1985).
Eckert	J. Eckert, *Die urchristlichen Verkündigung im Streit zwischen Paulus und seinen Gegnern nach dem Galaterbrief* (Regensburg: Pustet, 1971).
Gaston	L. Gaston, *Paul and the Torah* (Vancouver: University of British Columbia, 1987).
Georgi	D. Georgi, *Theocracy in Paul's Praxis and Theology* (Minneapolis: Fortress, 1991).
Hansen	G. W. Hansen, *Abraham in Galatians. Epistolary and Rhetorical Contexts* (Sheffield Academic, 1989).
Hays, *Echoes*	R. B. Hays, *Echoes of Scripture in the Letters of Paul* (New Haven: Yale University, 1989).
Hays, *Faith*	R. B. Hays, *The Faith of Jesus Christ. An Investigation of the Narrative Substructure of Galatians iii.1–iv.11* (Chico: Scholars, 1983).
Hengel	M. Hengel, *The Pre-Christian Paul* (London: SCM, 1991).

Hill	C. G. Hill, *Hellenists and Hebrews. Reappraising Division within the Earliest Church* (Minneapolis: Fortress, 1991).
Holmberg	B. Holmberg, *Paul and Power. The Structure of Authority in the Primitive Church as Reflected in the Pauline Epistles* (Lund: Gleerup, 1978).
Hooker, *Adam*	M. D. Hooker, *From Adam to Christ. Essays on Paul* (Cambridge University, 1990).
Howard	G. Howard, *Paul: Crisis in Galatia. A Study in Early Christian Theology* (Cambridge University, 1979; 2nd edition 1990).
Hübner	H. Hübner, *Law in Paul's Thought* (Edinburgh: T. & T. Clark, 1984).
Jewett	R. Jewett, 'The Agitators and the Galatian Congregation', *NTS* 17 (1970–1) 198–212.
Linton	O. Linton, 'The Third Aspect. A Neglected Point of View', *Studia Theologica* 3 (1950–1) 79–95.
Lüdemann	G. Lüdemann, *Paul, Apostle to the Gentiles. Studies in Chronology* (Philadelphia: Fortress, 1984).
Lütgert	W. Lütgert, *Gesetz und Geist. Eine Untersuchung zur Vorgeschichte des Galaterbriefes* (Gütersloh: Bertelsmann, 1919).
MacDonald	D. R. MacDonald, *There is No Male and Female. The Fate of a Dominical Saying in Paul and Gnosticism* (Philadelphia: Fortress, 1987).
McKnight	S. McKnight, *A Light Among the Gentiles. Jewish Missionary Activity in the Second Temple Period* (Minneapolis: Fortress, 1991).
Martin	D. B. Martin, *Slavery as Salvation. The Metaphor of Slavery in Pauline Christianity* (Yale University, 1990).
Martyn 'Antinomies'	J. L. Martyn, 'Apocalyptic Antinomies in Paul's Letter to the Galatians', *NTS* 31 (1985) 410–24.
Martyn, 'Covenants'	J. L. Martyn, 'The Covenants of Hagar and Sarah', *Faith and History*, P. W. Meyer Festschrift, ed. J. T. Carroll *et al.* (Atlanta: Scholars, 1991) 160–92.
Munck	J. Munck, *Paul and the Salvation of Mankind* (London: SCM, 1959).
Niebuhr	K.-W. Niebuhr, *Heidenapostel aus Israel. Die jüdische Identität des Paulus nach ihrer Darstellung in seinen Briefen* (Tübingen: Mohr, 1992).
O'Neill	J. C. O'Neill, *The Recovery of Paul's Letter to*

	the Galatians (London: SPCK, 1972).
Osten-Sacken	P. von der Osten-Sacken, *Die Heiligkeit der Tora. Studien zum Gesetz bei Paulus* (München: Kaiser, 1989).
Räisänen, *Paul*	H. Räisänen, *Paul and the Law* (Tübingen: J. C. B. Mohr, 1983).
Ropes	J. H. Ropes, *The Singular Problem of the Epistle to the Galatians* (Cambridge: Harvard University, 1929).
Sanders, *Judaism*	E. P. Sanders, *Judaism. Practice and Belief 63 BCE–66 CE* (London: SCM/ Philadelphia: TPI, 1992).
Sanders, *Law*	E. P. Sanders, *Paul, the Law, and the Jewish People* (Philadelphia: Fortress, 1983).
Sanders, *Paul*	E. P. Sanders, *Paul and Palestinian Judaism. A Comparison of Patterns of Religion* (London: SCM, 1977).
Schrage	W. Schrage, *The Ethics of the New Testament* (Philadelphia: Fortress, 1988).
Schmithals, *Gnostics*	W. Schmithals, 'The Heretics in Galatia', *Paul and the Gnostics* (Nashville: Abingdon, 1972) 13–64.
Schürer	E. Schürer, *The History of the Jewish People in the Age of Jesus Christ*, ed. G. Vermes and F. Millar, 4 volumes (Edinburgh: T. & T. Clark, 1973–87).
Scott	J. M. Scott, *Adoption as Sons of God. An Exegetical Investigation into the Background of ΥΙΟΘΕΣΙΑ in the Pauline Corpus* (WUNT 2.48; Tübingen: Mohr, 1992).
Suhl	A. Suhl, 'Der Galaterbrief – Situation und Argumentation', *Aufstieg und Niedergang der römischen Welt* II.25.4 (1987) 3067–134.
Taylor	N. Taylor, *Paul, Antioch and Jerusalem. A Study in Relationships and Authority in Earliest Christianity* (Sheffield Academic, 1992).
Thielman	F. Thielman, *From Plight to Solution. A Jewish Framework for Understanding Paul's View of the Law in Galatians and Romans* (Leiden: Brill, 1989).
Tomson	P. J. Tomson, *Paul and the Jewish Law. Halakha in the Letters of the Apostle to the Gentiles* (Assen: Van Gorcum, 1990).
Watson	F. Watson, *Paul, Judaism and the Gentiles. A Sociological Approach* (Cambridge University, 1986).
Westerholm	S. Westerholm, *Israel's Law and the Church's Faith* (Grand Rapids: Eerdmans, 1988).

Wilckens	U. Wilckens, 'Zur Entwicklung des paulinischen Gesetzesverständnis', *NTS* 28 (1982) 154–90.
Wilcox	M. Wilcox, 'The Promise of the "Seed" in the New Testament and the Targumim', *JSNT* 5 (1979) 2–20.
Williams	S. K. Williams, 'Justification and the Spirit in Galatians', *JSNT* 29 (1987) 91–100.
Wright	N. T. Wright, *The Climax of the Covenant. Christ and the Law in Pauline Theology* (Edinburgh: T. & T. Clark, 1991).

It has been convenient at various points to refer to some of my own publications for fuller treatments of the point treated in the text:

Baptism	*Baptism in the Holy Spirit* (London: SCM/Philadelphia: Westminster, 1970).
Christology	*Christology in the Making* (1980; 2nd edition, London: SCM/Philadelphia: TPI, 1989).
'Gal. i.18'	'Once More – Gal. i.18: *historēsai Kēphan*', in *JPL* 126–8
'Incident'	'The Incident at Antioch (Gal. ii.11–18)' in *JPL* 129–82.
Jesus	*Jesus and the Spirit* (London: SCM/Philadelphia: Westminster, 1975).
JPL	*Jesus, Paul and the Law. Studies in Mark and Galatians* (London: SPCK/Louisville: Westminster, 1990).
'Light'	'"A Light to the Gentiles", or "The End of the Law"? The Significance of the Damascus Road Christophany for Paul', in *JPL* 89–107.
'New Perspective'	'The New Perspective on Paul' in *JPL* 183–214.
'Once More, Works'	'Yet Once More – "The Works of the Law": A Response', *JSNT* 46 (1992) 99–117.
Partings	*The Partings of the Ways Between Christianity and Judaism and their Significance for the Character of Christianity* (London: SCM/Philadelphia: TPI, 1991).
'Paul's Understanding'	'Paul's Understanding of the Death of Jesus as Sacrifice', *Sacrifice and Redemption. Durham Essays in Theology*, ed. S. W. Sykes (Cambridge University, 1991) 35–56.
'Pharisees'	'Pharisees, Sinners, and Jesus', in *JPL* 61–88.
'Pistis Christou'	'Once More, *PISTIS CHRISTOU*', *Society of Biblical Literature 1991 Seminar Papers* (Atlanta: Scholars, 1991) 730–44.
'Relationship'	'The Relationship between Paul and Jerusalem according to Galatians i and ii', in *JPL* 108–26.

Romans   *Romans,* 2 volumes (Word Biblical Commentary 38; Dallas: Word, 1988).

'Theology'   'The Theology of Galatians' in *JPL* 242–64.

Theology   *The Theology of Paul's Letter to the Galatians* (Cambridge University, 1993).

Unity   *Unity and Diversity in the New Testament* (1977; 2nd edition London: SCM/ Philadelphia: TPI, 1990).

'Works'   'Works of the Law and the Curse of the Law (Gal. iii.10–14)' in *JPL* 215–41.

ABBREVIATIONS

ABD	*The Anchor Bible Dictionary*, ed. D. N. Freedman, 6 volumes (New York: Doubleday, 1992).
Aland[26]	E. Nestle, K. Aland, *et al*, *Novum Testamentum Graece* (Stuttgart: Deutsche Bibelgesellschaft, 26th edition, 1979).
BAGD	W. Bauer, *A Greek-English Lexicon of the New Testament and Other Early Christian Literature*, ed. W. F. Arndt and F. W. Gingrich; 2nd edition, ed. F. W. Gingrich and F. W. Danker (University of Chicago, 1979).
BDB	F. Brown, S. R. Driver and C. A. Briggs, *Hebrew and English Lexicon of the Old Testament* (Oxford: Clarendon, 1907).
BDF	F. Blass, A. Debrunner and R. W. Funk, *A Greek Grammar of the New Testament* (University of Chicago/University of Cambridge, 1961).
BZ	*Biblische Zeitschrift.*
CBQ	*Catholic Biblical Quarterly.*
Charlesworth	J. H. Charlesworth, ed., *The Old Testament Pseudepigrapha*, 2 volumes (London: Darton, 1983, 1985).
Dan. Th.	Theodotian's Greek translation of Daniel.
DSS	Dead Sea Scrolls.
ed.	edited by.
EWNT	*Exegetisches Wörterbuch zum Neuen Testament*, ed. H. Balz and G. Schneider, 3 volumes (Stuttgart: Kohlhammer, 1980–3).
GNB	Good News Bible (translation).
h.l.	*hapax legomenon* (sole occurrence).
HR	*History of Religions.*
HTR	*Harvard Theological Review.*
IDB	*Interpreter's Dictionary of the Bible*, ed. G. A. Buttrick. 4 volumes (Nashville: Abingdon, 1962).
JB	Jerusalem Bible (translation).
JBL	*Journal of Biblical Literature.*
JPL	J. D. G. Dunn, *Jesus, Paul and the Law. Studies in Mark and Galatians* (London: SPCK/Louisville: Westminster, 1990).
JSJ	*Journal for the Study of Judaism.*
JSNT	*Journal for the Study of the New Testament.*
LSJ	H. G. Liddell and R. Scott, *A Greek-English*

	Lexicon, revised by H. S. Jones (Oxford: Clarendon, 9th edition 1940; with supplement, 1968).
LXX	Septuagint (Greek translation of the OT).
MM	J. H. Moulton and G. Milligan, *The Vocabulary of the Greek Testament* (London: Hodder, 1930).
NDIEC	*New Documents Illustrating Early Christianity*, ed. G. H. R. Horsley (North Ryde: Australia, 1981–).
NEB	New English Bible (translation).
NIV	New International Version (translation).
NJB	New Jerusalem Bible (translation).
NovT	*Novum Testamentum.*
NRSV	New Revised Standard Version (translation).
NT	New Testament.
NTA	E. Hennecke, *New Testament Apocrypha*, ed. W. Schneemelcher & R. McL. Wilson, Volume 2 (London: Lutterworth, 1965).
NTS	*New Testament Studies.*
OCD	*Oxford Classical Dictionary*, ed. N. G. L. Hammond and H. H. Scullard (Oxford: Clarendon, 1970).
OT	Old Testament.
par., pars	parallel, parallels.
PGL	*Patristic Greek-Lexicon*, ed. G. W. H. Lampe (Oxford: Clarendon, 1961).
REB	Revised English Bible (translation).
RSV	Revised Standard Version (translation).
SB	H. Strack and P. Billerbeck, *Kommentar zum Neuen Testament*, 4 volumes (München: Beck, 1926–8).
SNTSMS	Society for New Testament Studies. Monograph Series.
Sokoloff	M. Sokoloff, *A Dictionary of Jewish Palestinian Aramaic of the Byzantine Period* (Bar Ilan University, 1990).
TDNT	*Theological Dictionary of the New Testament*, ed. G. Kittel and G. Friedrich, 10 volumes (Grand Rapids: Eerdmans, 1964–76).
Th.	Theodotion (Greek version of OT).
VT	*Vetus Testamentum.*
v.l	*Varia lectio* (alternative reading).
WUNT	Wissenschaftliche Untersuchungen zum Neuen Testament.
ZNW	*Zeitschrift für die neutestamentliche Wissenschaft.*

NB In transliterating the Greek of Galatians I have varied between use
of *u* and *y* to transliterate the Greek upsilon (whichever seemed the
more fitting in any case in point).

Books of the Bible with Apocrypha

OLD TESTAMENT

Gen.	2 Chron.	Dan.
Exod.	Ezra	Hos.
Lev.	Neh.	Joel
Num.	Esth.	Amos
Deut.	Job	Obad.
Josh.	Ps. (Pss.)	Jonah
Judg.	Prov.	Mic.
Ruth	Eccl.	Nah.
1 Sam.	Cant.	Hab.
2 Sam.	Isa.	Zeph.
1 Kings	Jer.	Hag.
2 Kings	Lam.	Zech.
1 Chron.	Ezek.	Mal.

APOCRYPHA

Add. Esth.	Additions to Esther
Bar.	Baruch
Ep. Jer.	Epistle of Jeremiah
1 Esd.	1 Esdras
2 Esd.	2 Esdras
Judith	Judith
1 Macc.	1 Maccabees
2 Macc.	2 Maccabees
Sir.	Ecclesiasticus (Wisdom of Jesus the son of Sirach)
Tobit	Tobit
Wisd. Sol.	Wisdom of Solomon

NEW TESTAMENT

Matt.	Eph.	Heb.
Mark	Phil.	James
Luke	Col.	1 Peter
John	1 Thess.	2 Peter
Acts	2 Thess.	1 John
Rom.	1 Tim.	2 John
1 Cor.	2 Tim.	3 John
2 Cor.	Titus	Jude
Gal.	Phm.	Rev.

Other early Jewish literature (usually called OT Pseudepigrapha)

Adam and Eve	Life of Adam and Eve.
Apoc. Abr.	Apocalypse of Abraham.
Apoc. Zeph.	Apocalypse of Zephaniah.
Aristeas	Epistle of Aristeas.
Apoc. Mos.	Apocalypse of Moses.
2 Bar.	Syriac Apocalypse of Baruch.
1 Enoch	Ethiopic Enoch.
2 Enoch	Slavonic Enoch.
4 Ezra	4 Ezra.
Joseph and Asenath	Joseph and Asenath.
Jub.	Jubilees.
3 Macc.	3 Maccabees.
4 Macc.	4 Maccabees.
Odes Sol.	Odes of Solomon.
Ps. Philo	Pseudo-Philo.
Ps. Phoc.	Pseudo-Phocylides.
Pss. Sol.	Psalms of Solomon.
Sib. Frag.	Fragments of Sibylline Oracles.
Sib. Or.	Sibylline Oracles.
Test. Abr.	Testament of Abraham.
Test. Ash.	Testament of Asher (in *T. 12 Patr.*).
Test. Ben.	Testament of Benjamin (in *T. 12 Patr.*).
Test. Dan	Testament of Dan (in *T. 12 Patr.*).
Test. Gad	Testament of Gad (in *T. 12 Patr.*).
Test. Iss.	Testament of Issachar (in *T. 12 Patr.*).
Test. Job	Testament of Job.
Test. Jos.	Testament of Joseph (in *T. 12 Patr.*).
Test. Jud.	Testament of Judah (in *T. 12 Patr.*).
Test. Levi	Testament of Levi (in *T. 12 Patr.*).
Test. Mos.	Testament of Moses.
Test. Naph.	Testament of Naphtali (in *T. 12 Patr.*).
T. 12 Patr.	Testaments of the Twelve Patriarchs.
Test. Reub.	Testament of Reuben (in *T. 12 Patr.*).
Test. Zeb.	Testament of Zebulon (in *T. 12 Patr.*).

Other Jewish Writings

DEAD SEA SCROLLS
CD	Cairo (Genizeh text of the) Damascus (Document).
p	Pesher = interpretation, commentary
Q	Qumran.

1Q, 2Q, 3Q, etc.	Numbered caves of Qumran yielding written material; followed by abbreviation of the book.
1QH	*Hôdayôt* (Thanksgiving Hymns) from Qumran Cave 1.
1QM	*Milḥamah* (War Scroll) from Qumran Cave 1.
1QpHab	Pesher on Habakkuk from Qumran Cave 1.
1QS	*Serek hayyahad* (Community Rule, Manual of Discipline) from Qumran Cave 1.
1QSa	Appendix A (Rule of the Congregation) to 1QS.
4QFlor	Florilegium (or Eschatological Midrashim) from Qumran Cave 4.
4QMMT	Unpublished scroll (*Miqsat Ma'aseh Ha-Torah*) from Qumran Cave 4.
4QpNah	Pesher on Nahum from Qumran Cave 4.
4Qps Dan Aª (4Q246)	Fragment of pseudo-Daniel from Qumran Cave 4.
11QMelch	Melchizedek text from Qumran Cave 11.
11QTemple	Temple Scroll probably(?) from Qumran Cave 11.

PHILO

Abr.	*De Abrahamo.*
Cher.	*De Cherubim.*
Cong.	*De Congressu quaerendae Eruditionis gratia.*
Decal.	*De Decalogo.*
Fuga	*De Fuga et Inventione.*
Heres	*Quis Rerum Divinarum Heres sit.*
Jos.	*De Josepho.*
Leg. All.	*Legum Allegoriae.*
Legat.	*De Legatione ad Gaium.*
Migr.	*De Migratione Abrahami.*
Mos.	*De Vita Mosis.*
Post.	*De Posteritate Caini.*
Sac.	*De Sacrificiis Abelis et Caini.*
Som.	*De Somniis.*
Spec. Leg.	*De Specialibus Legibus.*
Vit. Cont.	*De Vita Contemplativa.*

JOSEPHUS

Ant.	*Jewish Antiquities.*
Ap.	*Against Apion.*
Life	*Life.*
War	*The Jewish War.*

RABBINIC WRITINGS

b.	Before a tractate indicates Talmud.
m.	Before a tractate indicates Mishnah.

Abod. Zar.	*Abodah Zarah.*
Abot	*Pirqe Abot.*
Ber.	*Berakot.*
Ohol.	*Oholot.*
Rab.	*Rabbah,* as in *Gen.Rab.=Genesis Rabbah.*
Roš Haš	*Roš Haššana.*
Sabb.	*Sabbat.*
Sanh.	*Sanhedrin.*
Shemonah Esreh	=the 18 Benedictions.
Sipra	*Sipra.*
Targ. ps. Jon.	*Targum pseudo-Jonathan.*

Early Christian writings

Barn.	Barnabas.	
1 Clem.	1 Clement.	
2 Clem.	2 Clement.	
Did.	Didache.	
Eusebius, *HE*	Eusebius, *Historia Ecclesiastica.*	
Eusebius, *Praep. Evang.*	Eusebius, *Praeparatio Evangelica.*	
Gosp. Thom.	*Gospel of Thomas.*	
Ignatius,	*Eph.*	Letter to the Ephesians.
	Magn.	Letter to the Magnesians.
	Philad.	Letter to the Philadelphians.
	Rom.	Letter to the Romans.
Justin, *Dial.*	Justin Martyr, *Dialogue with Trypho.*	
Ps. Clem.	Pseudo Clementines.	
Epistula Petri	*Epistle of Peter.*	
Clem. Hom.	*Clementine Homilies.*	
Clem. Recog.	*Clementine Recognitions.*	

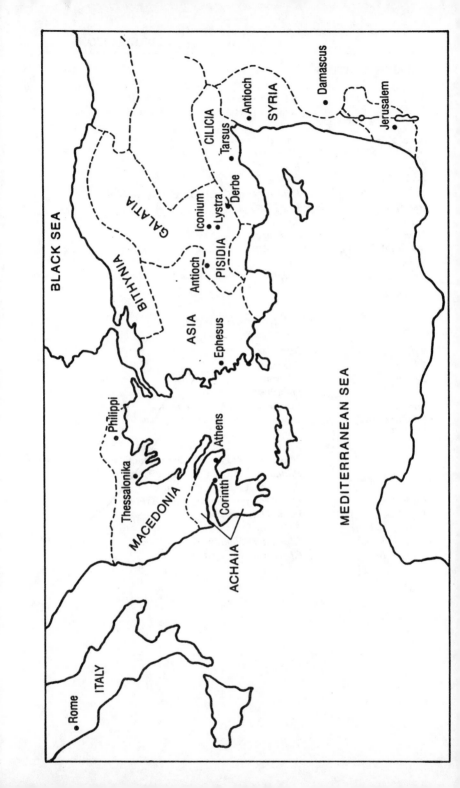

INTRODUCTION

1 The letter

This letter, 'to the Galatians', comes down to us from the earliest days of Christianity. It is an established part of the Pauline corpus in all the major Greek manuscripts containing all or part of the New Testament, that is, from the fourth century onwards. It appears in broken, but almost complete form, in **p**⁴⁶, a papyrus collection of the Pauline epistles, dated to about the year 200.[1] It is cited, with attribution to Paul, the first great missionary to non-Jews, as early as Irenaeus and Clement of Alexandria, that is from about AD 175, and may well be alluded to by earlier second-century writers.[2] So far as we know, no question was ever raised in these early centuries as to its integrity[3] or authenticity.

When modern readers turn to this document, therefore, they may be entirely confident of several things. First, that the letter was written by the Paul who introduces himself in i.1. Second, that it was received by those to whom he sent it and retained by them, so that it was not lost – as appears to have been the case with some of Paul's other letters, for example to Corinth. Third, that it was circulated to other churches and thus became more widely known – how soon, or how quickly we cannot say, nor do we know when the collection of Paul's letters into a single unit began.[4] And fourth, that it was valued more and more widely and its significance seen to transcend the particular historical situation for which it was written, so that its subsequent canonization (as part of the canon of the New Testament) was simply a recognition and acknowledgment of the authority and influence it had exercised more or less from the beginning.

Here then is a letter which takes us right back into the period of Christianity's foundation and initial expansion, a letter which

---

1 The details can be found in the appendices at the back of the Nestle-Aland Greek Testament (*Novum Testamentum Graece*, 26th edition; Stuttgart 1979).
2 Details in Burton lxviii–lxix.
3 O'Neill's suggestion that the current letter comes to us in a substantially redacted and interpolated form has won no support – and rightly so, since it presumes a wooden Paul with an artificially narrow and uniform language, theology and style.
4 Most of the papyri (the earliest texts) contain fragments or parts only of individual NT writings.

1

evidently helped to establish the authority of Paul the apostle, and which thus also helped to shape the character and self-perception of early Christianity, both in terms of its fundamental principles and in relation to the Jewish matrix from which Christianity emerged. H. D. Betz, indeed, calls it 'one of the most important religious documents of mankind'.[1] Familiarity with it, therefore, should not be allowed to dull the sense of excitement and anticipation which may properly be felt by any who begin to read it, and who are interested in the character of Christian beginnings and in the Christian gospel whose exposition and defence were its chief concern.

To 'set the scene', however, we need to know something more of the letter's author, those to whom he wrote, when he wrote, and the issues which caused him to write in the first place. The second, third and fourth of these topics (to whom, when, and why) have been the subject of considerable debate. But the extent to which they hang together, and, in particular, the extent to which they hang together with the first, has not been sufficiently appreciated in this long and often detailed discussion. It will be necessary first, therefore, to let the author introduce himself in the way that he does in the letter. Then, without becoming immersed in the fine detail of the debate on the other topics, it will be appropriate to outline the main options in each case. Only then will we be in a position to offer an integrated reconstruction of what seems to be the most plausible historical context within which this letter emerged and for which it was written. In this way, we hope, we can ensure so far as possible that the evidence of the letter itself is given greatest weight in any attempt at historical reconstruction.

2 The author

Not least of fascination about Galatians is the information which it provides about Paul himself – details which we learn nowhere else – and particularly about the phases of his life. Since he takes care to give his readers such details, and just these details (we shall see in chs. i and ii how carefully he chose them), they provide vital information as to why Paul wrote as he did. Here, uniquely in Paul's letters, the information he gives about himself

1 Betz, 'Spirit' 145.

provides invaluable insights into the occasion and purpose for the letter. The self-image he projects is in service of the message (the gospel) he wants his readers to hear. Paul 'presents his "autobiography" as a paradigm of the gospel of Christian freedom . . . (and) considers himself in some sense a representative or even an embodiment of that gospel'.[1]

From i.13–14 we gain a brief but highly informative picture of Paul's 'way of life in Judaism' before he became a Christian, of his zeal for the law and passionate concern to preserve the distinctive character of Judaism, that is, from defilement by Gentile lawlessness; hence his career as 'persecutor' and destroyer of 'the church of God'. Paul evidently alludes to this period of his life later when he talks about 'building again the very things which I demolished' (ii.18), referring, it would appear, to the actions of Peter and 'the rest of the (Christian) Jews' in Antioch when they withdrew from table-fellowship with the Gentile believers in Antioch (ii.12–13).

Verses i.15–16 give us Paul's perspective on what has traditionally been called his conversion. But in these verses it is evident that Paul saw this encounter with God's Son (on the 'road to Damascus', according to Acts ix) not so much as a conversion, and much more as a commissioning – a commissioning specifically to preach the good news of this Jesus 'among the Gentiles'. If we may speak of the event as a conversion it was not a conversion from the religion of Israel to a new religion, but a conversion from one viewpoint within Judaism, regarding the relation of Israel to the other nations (the Gentiles), to another viewpoint – conversion from suspicion of and antipathy to non-Jews, to concern for their conversion to the gospel of the Jewish Messiah. To what extent this perspective on his Damascus-road encounter (as a commissioning to the Gentiles) was given to Paul there and then, or was the product of later reflection (and thus a case of autobiographical reconstruction), we cannot say. But Paul was evidently anxious in these verses, as in i.1 and 12, to make it clear that his apostolic commission was direct from God and had this character from the first (apostle to the Gentiles).

From i.16c to ii.10 there emerges an intriguing picture of Paul's relationship with the Christian leaders in Jerusalem (the mother church of Christianity).[2] The care with which Paul

1 G. Lyons, *Pauline Autobiography. Toward a New Understanding* (Atlanta: Scholars Press, 1985) 171.
2 Cf. Holmberg 15 – 'the dialectic between being independent of and acknowledged by Jerusalem is the keynote of this important text'; see further my 'Relationship'.

narrates these contacts (particularly in i.16c–17, 18–20, and ii.2, 6, 7–10) indicates a double phase of Paul's ministry. Initially he worked as one not directly dependent on Jerusalem's authority (even though for much or most of the time a missionary of Jerusalem's daughter church in Syrian Antioch, as Acts xiii–xiv attests), but ready to acknowledge the authority of the Jerusalem leadership to pronounce on issues related to the gospel and its proclamation among Gentiles. Paul willingly concedes this degree of recognition, because in the test-case of the Greek Titus (whether as a non-Jew he needed to be circumcised in order to be acceptable as a fellow believer in Jesus the Christ), the Jerusalem leadership backed him, and in face of strong pressure from those whom Paul calls 'false brothers' – an amazing step of faith and foresight on their part, for which they have been too little honoured (ii.2–6). The agreement reached between James, Peter and John, on the one side, and Paul and Barnabas, on the other, regarding the openness of the gospel to the Gentiles (without requiring them to undergo the characteristic Jewish rite of circumcision) is the climax of the section (ii.7–10).

By the time Paul wrote the letter, however, it is clear that there had been a change in his relationship with Jerusalem. This is signalled particularly by the distancing and indeed rather dismissive way he describes the Jerusalem leadership (in ii.2 and 6). But also, more explicitly, by the fierceness of the language Paul uses in ii.11–14, where he attacks Peter in forthright terms, as also, by clear implication, the group whose coming to Antioch 'from James' had disrupted the table-fellowship previously enjoyed between Jewish and Gentile believers. It is obvious that in Paul's view the behaviour of Peter and the other (Christian) Jews at Antioch was in breach of the Jerusalem agreement. From this it also follows, most probably, that it was the incident at Antioch which changed Paul's relationship with the Jerusalem authorities. Moreover, from the way Paul follows through from his description of that incident and leads into the main argument of his letter (ii.15–21), it is also evident that the Antioch incident had particular relevance to the situation in Galatia which the letter was intended to address (see also Introduction to ii.15–21). The very personal language of that section indicates the extent to which Paul's appreciation of how the gospel affected him was inextricably bound up with his perception both of the gospel as for the Gentiles (by faith and not 'works of the law'), and of his authority so to preach.

Paul gives us a little more information about himself when he recalls his actual bringing of the gospel to the Galatians (iv.13–15) and in his peroration (vi.17). But the crucial information which informs the purpose and meaning of the letter is provided in the first two chapters. We do not need, yet, to be more specific about the chronology of the letter – either about the precise sequence of the events described in i.18–ii.1, or about how the letter fits into the 'missionary journeys' narrated in Acts xiii–xvi (see below). Nor is it of any great moment that Paul used an amanuensis (or secretary) to transcribe the letter at his dictation (see particularly Longenecker lix–lxi, and on vi.11). What is more to the point here is the way in and degree to which the letter fits into the theological self-perception and development of Paul himself.

What we see, then, or are given by Paul to see, in summary, is a man who was a Christian Jew, but with a commission from God to take the good news of Christ to the Gentiles. The tension between Paul's past (as a zealot and persecutor) and present (as evangelist and apologist for the church he once sought to destroy) is also the tension of the letter. The tension between Paul's commission as standing within the tradition of Israel's prophet commissionings, but as a commission to the Gentiles, is also the tension of the letter. The tension between Paul and the Jerusalem leadership is also the tension of the letter. It was precisely as a *Jew* who was also apostle to the *Gentiles*, that Paul wrote. It was precisely as a Jew who rejoiced in the blessing and inheritance of Abraham, but who now saw it to be integral to that blessing and inheritance that they are for Gentiles as well, that he pleads and warns so fervently. It was precisely in defence of his own inheritance as an Israelite, its fundamental character and richest blessing, that he fights so fiercely to maintain that character and blessing for Gentile as well as for Jew.

3 The recipients

Here we come to the first major dispute among students of Galatians during the past two centuries. We need not rehearse it in any detail, since the pros and cons have been debated repeatedly over the intervening decades and can be found in any good introduction to the NT or large (particularly English-language) commentaries on Galatians. The basic facts are clear. Paul was writing to the 'the churches of Galatia' (i.2), to

'Galatians' (*Galatai* – iii.1). The name derives from the Gallic tribes (the Gauls, or Celts) who migrated into Asia Minor and settled in its heartland in the third century BC.[1] The uncertainty arises because the name (Galatia/Galatians) can be used both ethnically (to refer to the descendants of these Gallic tribes) and administratively (to refer to the Roman province so designated from 25 BC and its inhabitants). This uncertainty does not affect the question of whether the recipients were Jews or Gentiles; even on the latter alternative (Galatia as the Roman province) a description of the recipients as 'Galatians' almost certainly implies that non-Jews were in view (as iv.8 confirms – 'you did not know God and were in slavery to beings that by nature are no gods'). The issue in fact boils down to whether Paul could be referring to the churches established during 'the first missionary journey' (Acts xiii–xiv) as a missionary of (Syrian) Antioch: (Pisidian) Antioch, Iconium, Lystra and Derbe. These towns lay south of ethnic Galatia, but had been included in the Roman province as its southernmost part.

The whole issue hangs for most to a decisive degree on the relation between Galatians and Acts. Acts speaks of Paul's passing through 'Galatia' on subsequent missionary trips (Acts xvi.6 and xviii.23), and in the former reference the implication is clear that 'Phrygia and Galatia' are distinct from the cities named earlier (Derbe and Lystra at least, referred to in xvi.1–5).[2] That also implies that for Luke (the author of Acts) 'Galatia' refers to ethnic Galatia. If this correlates with Paul's usage, then Paul cannot be referring to the churches established on 'the first missionary journey' and must be referring to those initially established in the mission indicated in xvi.6.[3] For obvious reasons this view is usually named 'the north Galatian hypothesis'.[4]

Alternatively, we need not assume that Paul's and Luke's usages were mutually compatible. 'Galatia' and 'Galatians' were quite proper designations of the towns in the south of the Roman province and of their inhabitants. And it is difficult to see what

1 Details e.g. in Burton xvii–xxi and Bruce 3–5.
2 Zahn 16–17 and Burton xxx–xli, however, question whether the Acts xvi.6 journey was intended as a missionary trip, that is, whether it resulted in the establishment of churches or simply in the gaining of some scattered disciples converted *en passant*.
3 That Paul addresses his audiences as 'Galatians' (iii.1) does not determine the matter, since the address is a rebuke ('foolish Galatians') and may be used for its rhetorical effect – 'you of the province of Galatia who are acting as though you truly were foolish Gauls' (see also on iii.1).
4 So particularly Lightfoot 18–25; J. Moffatt, *An Introduction to the Literature of the New Testament* (Edinburgh: T. & T. Clark, 3rd edition 1918) 90–101; W. G. Kümmel, *Introduction to the New Testament* (London: SCM, 1965) 296–8.

other single designation could embrace all four towns: Iconium, Lystra and Derbe belonged to Lycaonia; but Antioch would be more properly designated as in Pisidia. 'The south Galatian hypothesis' therefore identifies the Galatians with the churches established by Paul in these towns during 'the first missionary journey'.[1]

The only obvious conclusion to draw from all this is that the evidence briefly reviewed is actually decisive on neither side. In particular, the difficulties of correlating Galatians with Luke's account in Acts make it doubtful whether, or at least to what extent, we can use the details of Acts to fill out the picture in Galatians. At each point of contact, indeed, there remain unresolved problems or unanswered questions. How to correlate Luke's record of Paul's visits to Jerusalem with Paul's own account in Gal. i–ii (see below §4)? Why does Luke say nothing whatsoever about the agreement at Jerusalem which Paul evidently saw as of the first importance (ii.7–10), or about the incident at Antioch, to which Paul, in contrast, gives such a central place (ii.11–14) in the build-up to his main theme? Why does Luke give none of the details about Paul's visit to 'Galatia' which made the visit so memorable for Paul (iv.13–15)? Why, not least, does Luke say nothing about the situation which gave rise to the letter to Galatia or about Paul's evidently deep and passionate concern for his converts there, or indeed about the letter itself? Some of this fits with Luke's pattern overall: he draws a veil over most of the discord and disunity which racked much of the early expansion of Christianity; and he makes no mention of any of Paul's letters. But the lack of correlation generally between Luke and Paul in matters relating to Galatians makes it of doubtful wisdom to give Acts the determinative voice on this question.

At all events we should note the vividness with which Paul recalls his first visit to these Galatians (iii.1; iv.13–15), the success of his evangelism, as attested particularly by the powerful experiences of the Spirit which launched the Galatian churches (iii.2–5; iv.6; v.25), and, not least, the depth of his continuing concern for them (iv.19). The most obvious deduction is that the visit took place during the period covered by i.21 (see on i.21).

4 The date

The issue of when the letter was written is problematic in the same measure, since, historically, it has been so much bound up

1 So particularly Burton xxvii, xxix, xliv and Bruce 14–18.

with the issue of destination. On the north Galatian hypothesis, the letter could not have been written till after Paul had evangelized the northern regions of the Galatian province. And if iv.13 refers to two visits (see on iv.13), we would have to allow time for a further trip through north Galatia. That would fit quite neatly with the two trips narrated in Acts xvi.6 and xviii.23. Allowing time for developments following that second visit would put the letter to Galatia quite far down the sequence of Paul's letters – not only after the Thessalonian correspondence, but also, probably, after the Corinthian correspondence, but before Romans. The similarity in tone between 2 Cor. x–xiii and Galatians, on the one hand, and in theme between Galatians and Romans, on the other, can be taken as support, therefore, for a date in the middle of the 50s (so most who accept the north Galatian hypothesis).

The south Galatian hypothesis, however, usually implies a much earlier date. Here again the correlation between Acts and Galatians is given decisive voice. Since Paul insists that the agreement in Jerusalem (ii.1–10) was reached on his *second* visit there, and since Luke records a second visit (for famine relief) in Acts xi.29–30, the suggestion seems attractive that Paul wrote his letter shortly after returning from 'the first missionary journey'. Moreover, the Antioch incident (ii.11–14) would help explain the need for a fuller consultation with the Jerusalem leadership on matters of disagreement regarding missionary work among Gentiles, which accords with the Acts' account of the so-called council of Jerusalem in Acts xv. On the Acts time-scale that would put Galatians *before* the Jerusalem council, usually dated to about 49, and suggests, therefore, a date for Galatians of about 48 or early 49, making Galatians the earliest of Paul's letters.[1]

It is somewhat ironic that it is the correlation with Acts which proves decisive for the *north* Galatian hypothesis on the question of recipients (above §3), and the correlation with Acts which proves decisive for the *south* Galatian hypothesis on the question of dating. That simply adds to the feeling of unease about allowing the correlation with Acts to be decisive on these issues. On balance, the weight of considerations probably favours the view that Gal. ii.1–10 is Paul's account of the Jerusalem council (Acts xv; see on ii.1), but, as we shall see, that conclusion does not tell necessarily against the south Galatian hypothesis, or for a date as late as the mid-50s.

---

1 So, recently, particularly Bruce 55 and Longenecker lxxxviii.

5 The opponents

Here there is greater agreement. Most follow the clear enough hints of the letter itself. Since Paul's last (or only) visit to these little groups of believers in Galatia, others had appeared or arisen who were urging them to be circumcised; this is explicit in v.2–12 and vi.12–13, though already implicit in ii.3–5. That the 'troublemakers' or 'agitators' (i.7; v.10, 12) were *Jews* is also fairly obvious.[1] It is implicit in the very fact that circumcision was their primary demand (v.2; vi.12–13) – circumcision being so much bound up with Jewish identity that Jews could be designated 'the circumcision' (see on ii.3). It is implicit in the fact that central to Paul's concern in i.12–ii.14 is his relationship with the Jerusalem leadership (see above §2), and in the way he integrates talk of 'Judaism', 'Jews' and 'judaizing' into this biographical build-up to the main theme (i.13–14; ii.13–15).[2] It is implicit in the fact that descent from Abraham dominates chs. iii–iv, and from the way Paul describes the purpose of the 'troublemakers' in terms of 'zeal' (cf. i.13–14), and as 'wishing to shut you out' (see on iv.17) and to 'boast in your flesh' (see on vi.13). And it is implicit, not least, in the prominence of the (Jewish) law, the Torah, in the whole discussion – particularly in the key phrases, 'works of the law' (see on ii.16), and 'under the law' (iii.23; iv.4–5, 21; v.18).[3]

Moreover, it is equally clear that the 'troublemakers' were also *Christians*, or at least saw themselves as such. Or if the term 'Christian' imports a sharpness of definition which is anachronistic, we should simply say that the 'troublemakers' saw themselves as believers in Messiah Jesus and followers of his 'way' (cf. Acts ix.2; xxii.4; xxiv.14, 22), and, presumably having been baptized in Jesus' name, were regarded by others as fellow believers. This is implicit in the fact that 'gospel', or indeed

1 Munck, particularly 130–4, argues that it was some of Paul's own (Gentile) converts who reached the conclusion that circumcision was necessary on the basis of their own reading of the (Jewish) scriptures. But this 'fanciful attempt at reconstruction' (Mussner 17) relies too heavily on vi.13 (see on vi.13) and hardly accords with the evidence reviewed below or with the fact that Paul always refers to 'the troublemakers' in the third person, whereas he addresses his converts directly in the second person (e.g. iii.1–5).

2 The opponents should, however, *not* be called 'Judaizers', as is still common today. A 'judaizer' in the terminology of the time was one who 'lived like a Jew' (see below n. 21 and on ii.14), *not* one who tried to get others to judaize.

3 Gaston 29–30 argues, most implausibly, that 'under the law' refers to Gentiles; but in the context of the argument from iii.17 onwards that is virtually impossible.

'gospel of Christ' is common language between them and Paul; Paul himself questions the validity of the terms in their case (i.6–9), but it is obvious from the way Paul labours the point in these verses that he is contesting a claim already made by them or for them. A similar implication attaches to Paul's description of those who insisted on Titus' circumcision in ii.3–4 as 'false brothers': evidently they thought of themselves as 'brothers' and were so accepted by those who admitted them to the Jerusalem consultation – Paul's designation ('false brothers') obviously attempts to undermine a status claimed and recognized by others; and the 'for you' of ii.5 relates the episode of the 'false brothers' directly to the crisis confronting the Galatians. Not least, it is clear enough from the main thrust of the letter that faith, that is faith in Christ, is a common denominator between Paul and those whom he criticizes (see e.g. on ii.16 and iii.6). It is the *corollary* to that faith which provided the bone of contention between Paul and those against whom Paul writes: whether that faith must be supplemented or delimited by works of the law like circumcision, food laws and Jewish feast-days (ii.3–6, 12–16; iv.9–10), or whether 'faith operating effectively through love' is sufficient (v.2–6); whether a beginning with faith (in Christ) is made complete, or rather undermined by allowing such fleshly (ethnic) considerations to determine faith's scope and working out (iii.3). And above all, only of Christians could it be said that they were seeking 'to avoid being persecuted for the cross of Christ' (vi.12).[1]

The inference is also fairly strong that these Christian Jews had come to Galatia some time after Paul's last visit and that they had come as 'apostles' or *missionaries* 'preaching the gospel'. This is implied in Paul's insistence on the independence and immediacy of *his* commissioning (i.1, 11–12, 15ff.); presumably the others had come claiming the authorization of respected Christian leaders, such as James of Jerusalem. This is suggested also by the prominence given to Jerusalem in the opposite column in iv.25, and by the emphasis on festivals in iv.10 whose correct dating (in the case of the new-moon festival especially) would probably need to be determined from Jerusalem (see on iv.10). It is implicit also in Paul's repeated talk of 'gospel' and 'preaching the good news' in ch. i–ii (i.6–11, 16, 23; ii.2, 5, 7, 14). Hence the frequent designation in the following pages of

---

1 Mussner 29 notes the importance for subsequent history of the conclusion that Paul was not attacking Jews as such, far less the Jews, but only Christian Jews, fellow Christians of Jewish origin.

them as 'the other missionaries'.[1] We need not doubt that these other Jewish-Christian missionaries had (at least some) support among the Gentile Galatians. But it is very unlikely that the issues and challenges to Paul's gospel in Galatia had arisen purely by spontaneous internal combustion. On the contrary it is difficult to see how such a comprehensive challenge to Paul's gospel, and of such a clearly Jewish-Christian character could have arisen without input of a fairly determined and purposeful kind (see also on v.7).

That Paul was also battling on a 'second front' has been argued by some,[2] on the basis particularly of the alteration of focus and thrust at v.13, and of the charge in vi.13 that 'they do not themselves keep the law'. But that is an unnecessary hypothesis, as the great majority agree (see opening remarks on v.13–15 and on vi.13). Still more idiosyncratic and unconvincing is the argument of W. Schmithals (*Gnostics* 13–64) that the whole letter is directed against Jewish-Christian Gnostics, which assumes that Paul was ill informed on the situation in Galatia and thus has to read more into the letter than it reads out. J. Drane, in contrast, somewhat influenced by Schmithals, argues that 'Paul's teaching in Galatians could be construed almost as an open invitation for Gnosticizing influences to enter the first-century church' (p. 114). R. Jewett ('Agitators' 209–12) tries to steer a difficult middle course in hypothesizing a pneumatic liberalism which was being attracted by 'works of the law' understood as giving access to higher perfection. But v.13ff. is adequately explained as Paul's warning of potential dangers for those who give the Spirit the emphasis Paul desires, dangers he was no doubt already aware of (not least if he was writing from Corinth), but not yet necessarily already part of the Galatians' experience; otherwise there would have been more description of the situation reported to Paul, and less guarded comments at iii.2–5, and the final summary vi.12–16 would not have reverted so completely to the single major issue of circumcision.

In short, the letter makes clearest and fullest sense if we see it as a response to a challenge from *Christian-Jewish missionaries* who had come to Galatia to improve or correct Paul's gospel and to 'complete' his converts by integrating them fully into the heirs of Abraham through circumcision and by thus bringing them 'under the law'.

1 Cf. particularly J. L. Martyn, 'A Law-observant Mission to Gentiles: the Background of Galatians', *Scottish Journal of Theology* 38 (1984) 307–24 – 'a law-observant mission to Gentiles' *independent* of Paul's; but he ignores the clearly implied critique of Paul's apostolic authority by the other missionaries.
2 Particularly Lütgert, and Ropes.

6 *The situation reconstructed*

We are now in a better position to reconstruct the situation which called forth this passionate letter from Paul. In so doing it seems wisest to make first and fullest use of the letter itself and of the hints it provides so fully. Where they correlate with other evidence from outside Galatians, all the better. But where they clash with other evidence it will have to be a matter of judgement as to whether to give more weight to an integrated and coherent picture drawn from Galatians or to the other evidence. We have already cautioned against a too straight-forward reliance on Acts; though equally we must remember that Paul's account of affairs will hardly be unbiased and wholly objective. And as for correlation with other Pauline letters, the shortness of the time span covering the main letters (at most less than ten years), and our lack of knowledge of the circumstances which called them forth, and therefore of the degree to which Paul's argument in each letter will have been conditioned by these circumstances, should make us wary of drawing firm conclusions regarding their chronological relationship and the development of Paul's theology from one to other. At all events, the indications gleaned from Galatians should be given first consideration.

6.1 We best start from the point at which Paul breaks off his autobiographical narrative and defence and begins to turn to address the Galatians directly — that is, the confrontation with Peter in Antioch (ii.11–18). It is evidently at that point that Paul's previous history ceases to be of positive value in the defence and plea he wishes to make to the Galatians. Presumably it was the issues posed most sharply by that episode which most fittingly led into the main argument of chs. iii–iv.[1]

This is all the more important when we further realize that the most obvious deduction to draw from this section is that Paul was defeated in his confrontation with Peter. Had Peter and the other (Christian) Jews backed Paul on that occasion, he could hardly have failed to draw attention to and underline that fact since it was of first importance to his Galatian readers (as he had in the earlier confrontation — ii.6; see further on ii.14). This is again confirmed by the way Paul's thought moves from ii.11–14

---

1 'It cannot be accidental that at the end of the *narratio* in Gal. ii.14, when Paul formulates the dilemma which Cephas is in, this dilemma is identical with the issue the Galatians themselves have to decide: "why do you compel the Gentiles to judaize?"' (Betz 62).

through ii.15–21 to the main thrust of his argument and appeal, since it strongly suggests that Paul saw the issue confronting him in Galatia as a re-run of the battles fought in Jerusalem and Antioch. The battle won in Jerusalem, its fruits in danger of being lost as a result of the Antioch fiasco (from Paul's perspective), had to be fought afresh in Galatia for the same reasons (hence ii.5 – 'in order that the truth of the gospel might remain for *you*').

The confrontation with Peter, and behind him the shadowy figures 'from James', is the most likely explanation for the change in Paul's relationship with the Jerusalem leadership (reflected in his language in ii.2 and 6 in particular; see above §2). That is to say, the consequences of Paul's defeat at Antioch almost certainly included a breach between Paul and Jerusalem, and also, by implication, with Barnabas. This ties in to the account of Acts, (a) that soon after the Jerusalem council Paul and Barnabas split up (Acts xv.36–41), and (b) that thereafter Paul in effect became an independent missionary, using first Corinth (Acts xviii.11) and then Ephesus (Acts xix.10) as his centre of operations. That is, from having been a missionary (apostle) of Antioch (Acts xiii.2–3; xiv.4, 14, 26–7), and therefore under Jerusalem's authority (Antioch being a daughter church of Jerusalem – hence Paul's trepidation in ii.2, and the evident readiness of the Antioch believers to respond positively to the 'men from James' in ii.12), Paul had come to a clearer understanding of himself as simply apostle to the Gentiles, with direct legitimation and authority from God, and to insist on this point with the fervour of i.1 and 11–12.

How much of all this Paul explained to the (south) Galatian churches on his second visit (Acts xvi.1–5) is not clear. Verse i.9 certainly suggests that Paul sought to restate in clear terms the essential character of his gospel on that second visit. But he may not have been too anxious for these churches, since, despite the outcome of the Antioch confrontation, they lay beyond the territory of Antioch's natural administrative oversight, with the Taurus mountain range intervening. At any rate, if Acts is correct, Paul seems to have been relaxed enough to circumcise Timothy (son of a Jewish mother and Greek father), in order to include him in his team (Acts xvi.3) – an action which quite possibly lies behind the retort in Gal. v.11.

However, the fact remained that 'the first missionary journey' (of Acts xiii–xiv) had been carried out under the auspices of Antioch (and so of Jerusalem), and it would be understandable (from the perspective of the dominant group at Antioch) that the churches founded during that mission must forthwith be drawn within the circle of the practice established (or re-established?) at Antioch as a result of those who came 'from James' (ii.12). That is, those who understood the gospel in terms similar to that of the 'men from James' would presumably try to extend their victory at Antioch to all the daughter churches of Antioch. The so-called 'apostolic decree' of Acts xv.20–9 may provide some confirmation here. For, according to Acts it was sent at James' bidding (xv.20–1), and explicitly to 'the Gentiles in Antioch and Syria and Cilicia' (xv.23), that is, to the region administered from Antioch, and so to churches which would most naturally come under the oversight of the church in Antioch. Paul himself, it will be recalled, presumably includes the south Galatian churches in 'the regions of Syria and Cilicia' in i.21. To that extent, Luke confirms an attempt made from Jerusalem to bring about a conformity of practice within the churches most likely to look to Antioch as their mother church.

6.2 This in fact provides an obvious, probably the most obvious occasion for the letter. That is to say, the crisis in Galatia was probably caused by the arrival in the Galatian churches of a group equivalent to the 'men from James' (ii.12), anxious to press home their success at Antioch and to establish the Jewish way of life ('judaizing' – ii.14) as the norm for all churches founded as a result of the expansion from Antioch. In the wake of Paul's defeat at Antioch they could readily exploit the ambiguity of his earlier relation with the Jerusalem leadership (see above §2), and emphasize their own authority, while at the same time undermining his (as implied in i.1 and 11–12). That they should (now) be demanding circumcision as well, or rather, above all (see above §5), may simply indicate that the pressure brought in Antioch (ii.11–14) had already marked something of a retreat from the liberalism of the agreement made in Jerusalem (ii.6–10). The considerations which weighed so heavily with Peter and Barnabas in ii.12–14 (see on ii.12 and 13) would have weighed all the more heavily with those less sympathetic to a mission to Gentiles in the first place. The parallel between ii.12 and vi.12 suggests that similar motives were operative in both cases – that is, fear lest being seen to accept Gentiles on equal terms as full members of the covenant people (made so by the cross of Christ – iii.13–14), without requiring them to judaize and be circumcised, would be seen by Jewish zealots (like Paul of old – i.13–14) as an unacceptable adulteration and abandonment of Israel's covenant status and obligations (see particularly Jewett, 'Agitators'; also on ii.12 and vi.12). As parallel episodes of the period indicate, circumcision was the natural correlate and climax of any judaizing process for most Jews.[1]

Moreover, it is quite possible that Paul won the day at Jerusalem (ii.1–10) because the status of the Gentile adherents to the new movement had been ambiguous: without circumcision they could be regarded simply as God-fearing Gentiles. But once the question of their full status as members of the covenant and full heirs of its promises was raised, that would be a different story. Once the question of sonship of Abraham became an explicit issue and a central factor of identity (see below §6.3) – then circumcision was almost bound to reappear on the agenda of any devout (Christian) Jew (not least in the light of Gen. xvii.9–14). We may therefore have to recognize that between Antioch and Galatia the stakes were increased – from the open question of the ill-defined character of a God-fearer judaizing, to the explicit issue of full proselyte status.

Alternatively, and more threateningly, 'the other missionaries' may have been representatives of the 'false brothers' defeated in Jerusalem (ii.3–6), who, in the wake of Paul's defeat at Antioch, saw their chance to undo the mischief they thought Paul was doing. Certainly we should not underestimate the spectrum and diversity of views on this matter (the acceptability of Gentiles as Gentiles) within the earliest Christian groups, or the passion with which divergent views were maintained. In a context of sharp factional rivalry (cf. the language of ii.4, 13–14; v.12), talk of 'defeat' and 'victory' is hardly inappropriate, and shifts of emphasis and policy would depend on which viewpoint was most influential in a given situation. Either way the authority of Jerusalem could be claimed in some degree or other. And either way Paul's own position and the authority of his version of the gospel were vulnerable to disparagement, given the ambiguity of his earlier relationship with the Jerusalem leadership and the way he had evidently been isolated and 'left out in the cold' by the united Christian-Jewish front at Antioch.

6.3 In any attempt to reconstruct the 'gospel' and rationale of the other missionaries there are two crucial features to be

1 Esther viii.17 LXX – 'many of the Gentiles were circumcised and judaized for fear of the Jews'; Theodotus in Eusebius, *Praeparatio Evangelica* ix.22.5 – Jacob would not give Dinah to the son of Hamor 'until all the inhabitants of Shechem were circumcised and judaized'; Josephus, *War* ii.454 – Metilius (commander of the Roman garrison in Jerusalem) 'saved his life by entreaties and promises to judaize and even to be circumcised'; Josephus, *Antiquities* xx.38–46 – Izates, king of Adiabene, having been converted by a Jewish merchant, without circumcision being required, was thereafter persuaded that circumcision was essential.

observed in the letter.[1] The first is indicated in the terms of the main section (ch. iii–iv) – that sonship of Abraham and share in his promises and inheritance were what was at stake. We do not know why this became the central ground of dispute. Traditionally Gentiles who adopted a Jewish way of life ('judaized') without circumcision were acceptable as adherents to Jewish synagogue communities ('God-fearers'; see on ii.12). That may well indicate a willingness on most diaspora Jews' part to recognize that the righteous Gentile could have a share in the world to come even without becoming a Jew; this is certainly an accepted view within later rabbinic Judaism.[2] But in this case at least the talk is all of sharing in Abraham's blessing. For traditionally minded Jews that must mean more than simply 'fearing God': to share in Abraham's inheritance was open only to those descended from Abraham; and for others to enter that heritage was impossible without circumcision; Gen. xvii.9–14 surely put the question beyond dispute. We may well imagine 'the other missionaries' so arguing and attempting so to persuade the Galatian believers (though see on iii.9). Whether it was they who first introduced the topic (sonship of Abraham), or Paul previously, we need not try to determine at this point. What is clear enough is that the topic once seized on by the other missionaries was almost bound to polarize the range of Christian views regarding acceptability of Gentiles and to bring the issue of circumcision inescapably to the fore (despite the earlier Jerusalem agreement).

The other crucial feature is the degree to which the whole argument in Galatians focuses on what we might call the 'second phase'. It is most explicit in iii.3: what follows from the beginning once made by the Galatians? how do they think the completion of God's saving work will be achieved?[3] The answer of the other missionaries is clear – by 'works of the law'. Faith in Christ must be complemented and demonstrated by the observances laid down in the law (see on ii.15–16). The grace of

---

1 Cf. Burton liv–lv; Barclay, *Obeying* 60–74, sums up the issues at stake in the Galatian crisis as 'the identity' of the Galatian Christians and 'their appropriate patterns of behaviour'. For the pitfalls and possibilities in 'mirror reading' as a means of deducing the opponents' views, see particularly J. M. G. Barclay, 'Mirror Reading a Polemical Letter: Galatians as a Test Case', *JSNT* 31 (1987) 73–93.

2 See e.g. P. Fredriksen, *From Jesus to Christ* (New Haven/London: Yale University, 1988) 149–51; and the material collected e.g. by C. G. Montefiore and H. Loewe, *A Rabbinic Anthology* (New York: Schocken, 1974) ch. 29.

3 Perhaps also, How should they live appropriately, determine patterns of behaviour, settle disputes (Barclay, *Obeying* 71)? but that is more to be deduced from v.13ff. than here.

God was displayed pre-eminently in the past in the giving of the law, and obedience to the law is the proper and necessary corollary or response to that grace (ii. 21; v.4). To which Paul responds by insisting that the role of the law was temporary and primarily for Israel's benefit in the period before Christ (iii.15–24), and that faith is not only the beginning of relationship with God but the sole continuing basis for it on the human side (ii.16, 20; iii.2–5, 7–9, 12–14, 22–6; v.5–6). In so far as Paul also recognizes the importance of believers' response to divine grace in ethical terms (v.16–vi.10) and is willing to speak of that responsibility by reference to the law (v.13–14), his position is not so far from that of his opponents; but that should not be allowed to obscure the fact that for Paul faith is the only and only continuing basis for relationship with God.[1] So when it was asserted that faith's obedience necessitated circumcision and that God's acceptance of Gentiles was dependent on their assuming Jewish identity, Paul saw the heart of the gospel and its character of grace as under direct threat.[2]

All this speaks strongly in favour of the south Galatian hypothesis. On the Acts schedule, only those churches established during the first missionary journey would naturally be regarded as falling within Antioch's jurisdiction. Moreover, the natural implication of ii.1, 9 and 13 is that Barnabas was well known to the Galatians; but according to Acts, Barnabas accompanied Paul only during that first missionary journey; prior to the missionary trip through north Galatia Barnabas and Paul had parted company. So far as Galatians is concerned, the implication of the sequence ii.11 through to ch. iii is that the Antioch incident and its issues led directly into the crisis in Galatia.[3] Which strongly suggests that the other missionaries pursued Paul some little time after he had left Antioch and had struck out for western Asia Minor by way of the churches in Lycaonia and Pisidia (Acts xvi.1–6). That the time-scale was short certainly fits with (even if not required by) the 'so quickly' of i.6 (see on i.6).

6.4 In the meantime, if we follow the Acts itinerary, Paul had continued on the so-called 'second missionary journey', through

---

1 This point is obscured by Sanders' suggestion that Paul distinguished between 'getting in' (not by works of law) and 'staying in' (by keeping the law) – *Law* 10 (better 46).

2 For the theology of Galatians see further my 'Theology' and *Theology*.

3 This feature tells strongly against the central thesis of Howard, *Crisis* 2, 9, that the opponents thought they were on Paul's side. So too does i.9 (Paul had already warned the Galatians against alternative versions of the gospel), the fact that this other gospel 'troubled' the Galatians (i.7; v.10), and the clear implication of i.1–ii.6 that the opponents had attacked Paul's authority.

northern Galatia (Acts xvi.6) and subsequently through Macedonia into Greece (xvi.11–xviii.1). By the time the other missionaries had reached Galatia, travelled through the (south) Galatian churches, explaining their understanding of what participation in Abraham's inheritance involved and sowing their seeds of confusion, and the news of this development reached Paul (messengers would not know where to find him and would have to follow in his footsteps), he had probably been settled in Corinth for some time. As soon as he heard the news he evidently called for some papyrus and a scribe and began to compose his letter in the full flood of his dismay and anger.[1] As he perhaps had feared, the incident at Antioch had undermined the crucial agreement reached earlier at Jerusalem, and steps must be taken at once to set the record straight and to prevent the collapse of all that he had worked for; his fears of ii.2 were being realized all too fully.[2]

The possibility of being a little more precise is given by a comparison with the Thessalonian correspondence. We can be confident that it was despatched from Corinth during the same period, and early in the same period (cf. particularly 1 Thess. ii.17; iii.1–2, 6). The most notable differences between the Thessalonian correspondence and the rest of Paul's (undisputed) letters is that in the former there is no talk of justification and righteousness (themes which are prominent in all of Paul's other main letters), and that Paul does not introduce himself as an apostle (as almost every time thereafter). Paul's normal practice of beginning by mentioning his apostleship must have started after he wrote to Thessalonica. And Galatians gives us the obvious starting point. It is clear enough from Gal. i.1 and 11–12 that Paul perceived his status and authority to have been called in question by the other missionaries (explicitly or implicitly). It was the Galatian crisis, in other words, which convinced Paul of the need to assert his apostolic status and thus almost certainly established the pattern of his self-introduction thereafter (see on i.1).

Likewise it was the Galatian crisis which brought the themes of righteousness and justification to the forefront of Paul's theology, and which ensured that thereafter he usually made a point of drawing them in, even when the topic did not require it. The Thessalonian correspondence could imply, by way of contrast, either that these themes had not previously received

1 Verse vi.11 implies that only one copy of the letter was sent and was intended to be taken round to each of the Galatian churches.
2 The lack of reference to Timothy in Galatians (Longenecker lxxi) may be simply explained by his absence from Corinth on one of the trips on which Paul seems regularly to have sent him (see also on i.2).

such prominence in Paul's preaching, or that he had shifted or varied the thrust of his original preaching in Thessalonica. In the former case the corollary would be that Paul's initial preaching in Galatia had not emphasized the themes of justification and righteousness and could imply that the centrality of 'justification by faith' first emerged as a consequence of the confrontation at Antioch and its sequel in Galatia. Either way, the crisis in Galatia reinforced the importance of justification by faith as central to the gospel and the ongoing relations between Jewish and Gentile believers.

All this suggests that the letter was sent from Corinth some time (not necessarily very long) after the Thessalonian correspondence, and therefore also before the Corinthian letters and the still later Romans. The degree of closeness in tone between 2 Cor. x–xiii and Galatians hardly tells against this, since we can neither assume that Paul sustained a very high level of indignation over a lengthy period, nor that he was thus indignant on only one occasion during a three- to five-year period. Nor does the closeness in theme between Galatians and Romans tell against such a dating since the modifications in presenting his Abraham exposition (see for example on iii.6 and 15) must indicate some interval for further reflection on these matters on Paul's part, and there is no obvious reason why that interval should not have extended across a five-year rather than, say, a two-year period.

In short, the most plausible hypothesis is that Paul wrote Galatians from Corinth to the churches of south Galatia in the early 50s, or, to be more precise, during the period from late 50 through the first half of 51,[1] and that he wrote to meet the threat posed to his gospel to the Gentiles by Jewish-Christian missionaries from Antioch or Jerusalem. The fact that the letter was retained by at least some of the Galatian churches and evidently cherished, so as to be integrated into the subsequent process whereby Paul's letters were collected into a single corpus, strongly suggests that Paul won a significant victory in Galatia (cf. also 1 Cor. xvi.1; and from the Pauline circle, 2 Tim. iv.10 and even 1 Pet. i.1). Although he had lost at Antioch he was able to hold the line on the more fundamental issue of Gentile circumcision and thus to maintain the fundamental faith (rather than ethnic) structure of the household of God (see on vi.10).

---

1 Betz 12 and Watson 58–9 prefer the combination of the north Galatian hypothesis and an early date (Betz – 50–5; Watson, before 1 Corinthians).

7 *The structure of the letter*

Considerable attention has been given in recent years to the letter within the setting of ancient epistolary and rhetorical conventions. For full treatments in these terms see particularly Betz 14–25 and Longenecker c–cxix. It is certainly the case that such comparisons shed light on various features of the letter and of the form and ordering of its contents. More important, they shed light on the conventions by which any reasonably well educated among Paul's readership or audiences would have appropriated the letter and recognized both its high points (not least, the way the *narratio* leads up to the Antioch incident – i.12–ii.14) and any significant departures from convention (e.g. the omission of an opening thanksgiving in the Introduction – see on i.6).[1] Beyond that, however, attempts to label Galatians as a particular kind of letter or to determine its structure from conventional parallels are of questionable value. It is clear that Galatians does not accord closely with any ideal type,[2] and there is a danger that analysis of the letter will be too much determined by fitting it on to a grid drawn from elsewhere rather than by the natural flow of the argument. More important, there is a danger that too much emphasis on rhetorical considerations may blur the extent to which the letter is driven by theological logic and passion. It is the theological issues and logic which are likely to have determined the main line and structure of the argument, particularly in the central section (chs. iii–iv), more than anything else, though we will find plenty of evidence of Paul's rhetorical skill in pressing home his case.

---

1 Hansen 56 quotes E. A. Judge's observation that 'Paul would have had the opportunity of a Greek education even in Gamaliel's school at Jerusalem'; see further Hengel, *Pre-Christian Paul* 57–61.
2 See particularly the critique of Betz by Longenecker cxi–cxiii; Longenecker 185 posits a 'mixed rhetorical genre'; see also Introduction to iv.12–20.

ANALYSIS OF THE EPISTLE

A *Introduction*   i.1–10
    1 Greeting   i.1–5
    2 Rebuke   i.6–10

B *Paul's defence of his gospel*   i.11–ii.21

    1 Summary statement   i.11–12
    2 Paul's previous life in Judaism   i.13–14
    3 Paul's calling   i.15–17
    4 Paul's first visit to Jerusalem   i.18–20
    5 Between visits   i.21–4
    6 The consultation at Jerusalem   ii.1–10
    7 The incident at Antioch   ii.11–14
    8 Paul's restatement of his case   ii.15–21

C *The main argument – the testimony of experience and of scripture*   iii.1–v.12

    1 The appeal to experience: continue as you began
      iii.1–5
    2 The appeal to scripture (1): the blessing of Abraham – to
      faith   iii.6–9
    3 Despite the curse of the law   iii.10–14
    4 Because given by promise   iii.15–18
    5 Whereas the law's role was interim   iii.19–22
    6 Until the coming of faith   iii.23–5
    7 Conclusion: all sons in Christ through faith   iii.26–9
    8 The corollary: the danger of reverting to the old
      status   iv.1–11
      iv.1–7   No longer children and slaves, but sons and
             heirs
      iv.8–11   So why return to the old status?
    9 A personal appeal   iv.12–20
   10 The appeal to scripture (2): the two covenants
       iv.21–31
   11 Conclusion: do not abandon your freedom   v.1–12
       v.1–6   Submission to circumcision is contrary to
       freedom in Christ
       v.7–12   Those who advocate it are only trouble-makers

TRANSLATION AND COMMENTARY

A Introduction

i.1–10

1 GREETING

i.1–5

(1) Paul, apostle – not from human beings[1] nor through a human being,[1] but through Jesus Christ and God the Father[2], who raised him from the dead – (2) and all the brothers[3] with me, to the churches of Galatia. (3) Grace to you and peace from God our[4] Father and the[4] Lord Jesus Christ, (4) who gave himself for[5] our sins, in order that he might rescue us from the present evil age, in accordance with the will of our God and Father; (5) to whom be glory for ever and ever, amen.

1 Paul introduces himself in accordance ·with the normal courtesies of letter writing of the ancient world – usually in the form, 'X to Y, greeting' (as in 1 Macc. xii.6 and Acts xxiii.26). As was also customary, the single name was sufficient means of identification, partly because it would be accompanied by a title,

1 The Greek here denotes 'man' in contrast to God, not 'man' in distinction from 'woman'; the word (*anthrōpos*) could indeed be used as a feminine (LSJ, *anthrōpos* II). I follow NJB in opting for the more inclusive language, even though the more cumbersome expression somewhat weakens the force of Paul's point and the terseness of his expression (cf. NEB, REB).

2 '. . . and God the Father': this phrase was omitted by Marcion, since, presumably, he took it to refer to the God of the OT. But the consequent clause, 'who raised himself from the dead', is completely unPauline.

3 Unlike the word translated 'human being' in verse 1, 'brother' is gender specific. It is probably better, therefore, to give a straight translation, in order not least to retain the familial metaphor, rather than to follow NEB/REB in rendering it as 'friends'; see also comment.

4 Important manuscripts read 'from God the Father and our Lord . . .'. But the text is in accord with Paul's almost unvarying practice in his other (undisputed) letters; whereas the Pastorals consistently use the 'our' in reference to Jesus. Both variants can be explained as scribal slips or conscious emendations and it is hard to decide between them. See Metzger 589.

5 The manuscript evidence is almost equally divided between *huper* ('on behalf of') and *peri* ('concerning'), but the range of meaning of each merges into that of the other. The use of *huper* in Gal. iii.13 and 1 Cor. xv.3 may be taken as an indication either of Paul's preferred usage, or of the reason why an original *peri* was assimilated to that usage.

and here too because he was well known to his addressees. Since the title in this case ('apostle') was not one which would be used in face-to-face conversation, it would mean that there was an element of what we today would call 'first-name terms' about the relationships which Paul enjoyed with his converts from the beginning. To be sure, Acts xiii.9 may indicate that 'Paul' was his second name ('Saul Paul'), for 'Paul' was a Roman surname which does not occur as a praenomen (first name) in writing of the time. But Paul never uses 'Saul' for himself in any of the letters bearing his name, not even the most intimate (Philemon). So Acts xiii.9ff. probably indicates a shift in the familiar name Paul wished to be known by, rather than a shift from more friendly to more formal.

On the other hand, the shift evidently happened during the 'first missionary journey', and Luke's account implies that it coincided with the emergence of Paul to the role of acknowledged leader of the missionary team (cf. Acts xiii.1–2, 7 with xiii.9,13). So perhaps the decision to be known as 'Paul' rather than 'Saul' reflects a new sense of status on Paul's part. And also, quite likely, a growing conviction about or understanding of his calling to missionary work among the Gentiles (hence the shift from Jewish to Greco-Roman identity?). At all events, the Galatian churches to whom he thus introduces himself were the easternmost and probably the earliest of the Pauline foundations whose correspondence from Paul has been preserved. Which means that already, before the beginning of the effective missionary work attested by his letters, it was the identity of 'Paul' (apostle to the Gentiles) rather than 'Saul' (a Hebrew of Hebrews – Phil. iii.5) by which Paul wished to be known. In discussion of the continuities/discontinuities between Paul's past as a Pharisee and his new Christian identity, or even between his earliest thought as a Christian and the maturer theology of his letters (his 'Paul' period?), such considerations should not be forgotten.

The fuller means of identification is provided by the title, **apostle** (bibliography in Bruce 72). Although not common in the Greek of the day, *apostolos* would be readily understood in the sense 'messenger, envoy, or ambassador' (LSJ), that is, one sent out to represent and with the authorization of those represented. Paul himself uses it in this sense in 2 Cor. viii.23 ('apostles of the churches') and Phil. ii.25 (Epaphroditus, apostle of the church at Philippi). But in Christian vocabulary it was to have more specific reference and more theological weight, as 'apostle of Christ Jesus' (1 Cor. i.1; 2 Cor. i.1; Eph. i.1; Col. i.1; 1 Tim. i.1; 2 Tim. i.1; Tit. i.1; 1 Pet. i.1; 2 Pet. i.1) – that is, as one sent, commissioned by Jesus, for the work of mission. Hence its usage in Matthew and Mark exclusively in the context of the twelve's being 'sent out' by Jesus to preach and heal (Matt. x.2; Mark iii.14(?); vi.30). The primary impulse for this usage, however, seems to have come from the recognition that the risen Christ had appeared to a number of people, individually or in groups, and had given them a special (life-long) commissioning or responsibility to bear witness to the good news of his life, death and resurrection and of the new possibilities of salvation thereby given (Acts i.15–26; 1 Cor. xv.7–11). Certainly Paul believed that he had been so commissioned (1 Cor. ix.1–2; xv.8; see also on iv.14), though this claim and the significance Paul attached to it became a matter of some contention, as we shall see.

However true to normal form Paul's opening had been so far, the next phrase would certainly have caught his audience's attention when it was first read to them by Paul's emissary – **not from human beings nor through a human being, but through Jesus Christ and God the Father**. It was unusual enough for a writer to interrupt the opening greeting of his letter. But the abruptness with which Paul does so here, indicates a degree of agitation and sense of urgency on his part (see also on i.4). It was evidently a matter of concern and of priority that his addressees should understand what his claim to apostleship meant. The whole phrase, in fact, hangs together as a single concept – 'apostle-not-of-men-nor-through-man-but-through-Jesus-Christ- . . .'.

The fact that Paul puts the negative part of the definition first strongly suggests that he was rebutting and rebuking an alternative way of defining his apostolic status. Paul had evidently heard that there were those among the Galatian churches (presumably those referred to in i.6–9) who affirmed what he here denies – that his apostleship *was* 'from men and through man'. What they would be referring to, no doubt, was the fact that Paul had been commissioned as a missionary by the church of Antioch (Acts xiii.1–3). It is certainly significant that the only time Luke describes Paul as an 'apostle' is during his 'first missionary journey', on which he embarked precisely as a missionary (=apostle) of Antioch, and indeed during his mission among the towns of southern Galatia (Acts xiv.4, 14). This is the first of a number of points at which Luke's account in Acts may reflect something of the views of Paul's *opponents* (Linton). In other words, we have a strong hint already that the authority of Paul's original preaching to the Galatians was being subtly undermined – not by means of an outright denial of his claim to be an 'apostle', but by the argument that his commissioning and its consequent authority were less weighty than Paul claimed. If he was simply an 'apostle' of the church at Antioch, then his message and its authority were subject to the higher authority of those commissioned by Jesus himself (at Jerusalem), just as the church at Antioch itself was subject to the authority of the church in Jerusalem (see below; also Introduction §2 and §6.2).

It is also relevant to note that in what are probably his two earliest letters Paul does *not* introduce himself as an 'apostle' (1 Thess. i.1; 2 Thess. ii.1), whereas, as we have already seen, it became his almost unvarying practice thereafter to describe himself as 'apostle of Christ Jesus'. If Galatians is the third (or second) of his extant letters, the implication is obvious: that a claim to authority as 'apostle of Christ', which was unquestioned before (1 Thess. ii.6), became a matter of some sensitiveness for Paul and something he felt it important to assert from the first in all dealings with his churches from then on (see also Introduction §6.4). This shift in emphasis was almost certainly occasioned by the crisis in Galatia, and by the fact that his message was being challenged there by means of a challenge to his apostolic status.

The double denial (not **from human beings**, nor **through a human being**) probably indicates that the critique of Paul's apostleship was two pronged: his apostleship *originated* with the leaders of the church at Antioch (Acts xiii.3); and/or it was *mediated* through an individual – presumably Peter (Gal. i.18), or possibly Barnabas. Either way, it implies that the commissioning of an apostle was understood to include the communication of the message which the apostle was to transmit (since it was not a 'bare' authority or authority to act without restraint which was thus transmitted). Paul does not dispute that. His claim is rather that the apostolic authority of his message did not depend on human authorization, but only on divine: the gospel which he had been commissioned to preach to the Galatians came 'through Jesus Christ and God the Father'.

The double name **Jesus Christ** was obviously already well established by the time Paul wrote Galatians. The loss so quickly of the titular reference of 'Christ', as the Greek translation for the Hebrew 'Messiah', is somewhat surprising (not 'Jesus, the Christ'), since the defence and explanation of Jesus' messiahship were evidently, as one might expect, a major element in the earliest apologetic of the infant Christian movement as a sect within second-Temple Judaism (e.g. Acts ii.31, 36; iii.18; xvii.2–3; cf. 1 Cor. i.23; Luke xxiv.26, 46). The titular reference is retained in Christian writings where the Jewish identity or heritage of the new movement was a continuing issue (e.g. Matt. i.17; ii.4; John i.41; xx.31; Rom. ix.3, 5; xv.3, 7), but in writings more directed to Gentile readership as such the title was soon transformed into something more like a proper name. However, the fact that the epithet 'Christ' became so quickly established, and so firmly attached to Jesus that it could function as in effect a proper name in Greek translation, is a reminder both of how important the claim that Jesus did fulfil the chief messianic expectations of his people was for the first Christians, and of how speedily they felt able to take that claim for granted (see also on i.22).

The idea of **God** as **Father** was deeply rooted in all the religious traditions of the Mediterranean world (*TDNT* v.951–8). It was bound up, of course, with the belief in an ultimate begetter of the cosmos, and use of that epithet carried with it the implication that the world had been created by a personal God, however much the metaphor might be depersonalized in more sophisticated systems. By implication also it indicated the equivalent of a blood-tie between God and those begotten by him, with all the overtones of family solidarity and obligation to kin thus involved. At the same time we should recall the reality of the ancient patriarchal society, where the head (father) of a household had full power and authority over wife and children, however much that legal authority might be tempered by the tenderness of human relationship (*TDNT* v.949–51). That Paul would be thinking in terms of the God and Father of Israel in particular need hardly be doubted (cf. e.g. Deut. xxxii.6; Isa. lxiii.16; Jer. xxxi.9), but he would not have wished to limit his assertion to that point here. His concern was rather to call on the authority which both words so powerfully evoked. His appeal was to nothing less than the highest authority conceivable, the God who is Father (of all). *That* was the source of his authority as apostle.

The conjunction of the two names is also noteworthy — **through Jesus Christ and God the Father**. We might have expected '*through* Jesus Christ and *from* God the Father', which would have made the antithesis more balanced, and accorded more with the implication of 'father' — that the one so called is the source and seat of the authority claimed, with Jesus Christ as the mediator of that authority. Paul would probably not have wished to be understood otherwise, but his primary concern was evidently to emphasize that even the *mediation* of his apostolic authority was direct from heaven. Clearly he had his experience on the Damascus road already in mind (i.15–16); this fact, and the emphasis on mediation, is probably sufficient to explain the unusual feature of naming 'Jesus Christ' *before* 'God the Father'. The effect of thus linking both 'Jesus Christ' and 'God the Father' together in a single prepositional phrase was to underscore his conviction that all the authority of the God who is over all was behind and in that revelation and in the authorization it gave him. That is the force of Paul's formulation. There is no thought of 'father' as a distinction *within* the Godhead, or as a means of distinguishing God the Father from Jesus. 'Father' here defines God's relationship to creation and humankind (note again the contrast with 'men/man'), not his relationship specifically to Christ.

Paul however does qualify his description of God as Father by adding, **who raised him** (Jesus) **from the dead**. This is the 'Father God' to whom he is referring, not simply as creator of all, but also as re-creator after death has done its worst. As distinct from the wider concepts of the supreme God as Father, Paul defines him precisely by his action in reference to Jesus, and as the God whose will for creation will reach its fulfilment in a final triumph over death. In distinction even from, or better within, the more traditional Jewish understanding of the one God, God had defined himself (as Paul might have said) by already raising Jesus from the dead. The relationship between God and Jesus is thus clarified to some extent. Although in the previous clause Paul had not broken up the single prepositional phrase ('through . . .'), by adding this relative clause he does indicate clearly enough that the source of Jesus Christ's authority (at least in commissioning for apostleship) was God's action in raising him from the dead. The action was revelatory in regard to the authority it accorded to Jesus, but also in what it unveiled of the God who thus committed this authority to Jesus.

The language is formulaic and Paul is clearly echoing what was probably the earliest credal-type affirmation of the first Christians (cf. particularly Acts iii.15; iv.10; Rom. viii.11; x.9; 1 Thess. i.10; 1 Pet. i.21; see further W. Kramer, *Christ, Lord, Son of God* [London: SCM, 1966] 20–6). As such it reflects the foundational character of the belief in Jesus' resurrection for the first Christians. Here it is the *only* qualifying or defining clause; there is, for example, no mention of Jesus' earlier life or of his death. That which really marked out God for Paul, in relation to his other and older beliefs regarding God, was the fact that he had raised Jesus from the dead. Of course Paul was looking to undergird the authority of the risen Christ (in appointing Paul as apostle!), and perhaps in distinction to those whose claims were rooted more or as much in their relationship with Jesus during his earthly mission (cf. Acts i.21–2; Gal. ii.6). Nevertheless the hope for the effectiveness of his claim rested firmly on the fact that this was the most fundamental belief shared by all believers, the very core of their common confession and baptism (Rom x.9).

The fact that Paul makes no further mention of Christ's resurrection in this, his most polemical letter, is proof enough that it was part of the foundational creed which united himself and his readers.

As such it also served to underline another feature of earliest Christianity – the apocalyptic outlook which those who confessed belief in resurrection from the dead thereby attested. For 'resurrection from the dead' as a category stems from such an outlook (as expressed most typically in such passages as Dan. xii.2; *1 Enoch* li.1–2; *Apoc. Mos.* xiii.3; xxviii.4; xli.3; xliii.2; *2 Bar.* l.2; not to mention Matt. xxvii.52–3). To be noted particularly is the disjunction implied between the present age/history, which ends in death, and the belief in a new age and recreated life the other side of death, over which death has no more hold (Rom. vi.9–10). The point here then is the conviction that Jesus had already experienced this 'resurrection'; in his case it had not awaited the end of world history (as preliminary to final judgment); nor had he simply been taken to heaven; and what had happened to him could not simply be translated into the more typically Greek conception of 'the immortality of the soul'. In Jesus' resurrection a new age had dawned. And, by implication, those to whom the resurrected Christ revealed himself could share some of the power of that new age, some of the life which had defeated death, even though their full deliverance from 'this present evil age' (i.4) was not yet (cf. vi.14).

2 The unexpected parenthesis of verse 1 now gives way to the normal form of epistolary introduction – **and all the brothers with me**. As usual, Paul associates others with his greeting (1 Cor. i.1; 2 Cor. i.1; Phil. i.1; Col. i.1; 1 Thess. i.1; 2 Thess. i.1; Phm. i.1). Unusually he does not name any of them. This could be simply because he wrote in some haste and agitation. Elsewhere he adds the greeting from '(all) the brothers' at the end (1 Cor. xvi.20; Phil. iv.21). But the immediate mention of '*all* brothers' here, at the very beginning, is probably a not too subtle attempt to underscore the support Paul had for the position he was going to maintain in what followed. Although he was making strong claims for himself and his authority as apostle, claims disputed at least in their implications by some among the churches in Galatia, he was writing with the *unanimous* support of those among (or along with) whom he was now ministering.

'Brother' was in common use for members of religious associations in the Greek-speaking world (e.g. BAGD, *adelphos*;

NDIEC 2.29–50), but was equally common among Jews (as in Exod. ii.11; Deut. iii.18; Neh. v.1; Isa. lxvi.20; Tobit i.3; 2 Macc. i.1 is a nice parallel here), including not least the Essene sectarians at Qumran (e.g. 1QS vi.10, 22; CD vi.20–vii.2). So it was the natural word in the circumstances. In the light of this general usage, it must be considered doubtful that Paul would intend his readers to recognize a reference only to his missionary colleagues, thus distinguished *from* the rest of his present Christian company; though, of course, an appeal to *all* his fellow missionaries would be equally, if not more effective here; and conceivably Paul was on one of his missionary excursions with a team of helpers when the news from Galatia (which occasioned the letter) reached him (Duncan 9). Since Paul uses the term even when addressing women as well as men (cf. Rom. xvi.3, 6–7, 12, 15, 17; Phil. iv.1 and 2; Col. iv.15) the term was probably regarded as appropriate for a mixed company, and within a patriarchal society would have been accepted as such.

The second part of the normal epistolary address was the name of the recipients for whom the letter was intended – here **the churches of Galatia**. 'Churches' might be better translated 'assemblies'. For the Greek word (*ekklesia*) would have been well known to his readers in this sense, as denoting the gathering of a political body, or sometimes the business meeting of a club (LSJ). But it is also the regular LXX word to describe an assembly, particularly the assembly of the Lord's people (as in Deut. xxiii.1–2; Judg. xx.2; 1 Chron. xxviii.8; Mic. ii.5). The word could therefore serve as an emerging technical term for the Christian movement (and taken over as such by Latin-speaking Christians in the west): its meaning was easily understood by any Greek-speaking audience; but the overtones from LXX usage implied that the assemblies so designated were continuous with 'the assembly of Israel' in the Jewish scriptures (see also on i.13 and 22).

The discerning eye, however, might note two differences from traditional Jewish usage. One was the fact that Paul was using the term for predominantly *Gentile* assemblies; whereas a not untypical concern within Jewish writings was to preserve the purity of the assembly of Israel (Neh. xiii.1; Lam. i.10; 1QSa ii.3–4; CD xii.3–6). The other was the fact that in the LXX the usage is almost always singular; whereas Paul addresses many (or at least several) assemblies (obviously local gatherings) in Galatia alone. There is no implication that Paul saw this as a regrettable or unwelcome state of affairs; the idea of a single or universal church does not appear in the Pauline corpus before Ephesians (see again on i.13). Rather Paul seems simply to have assumed that each gathering of those baptized in the name of the Lord Jesus was 'the assembly of the Lord' in that place (Rom. xvi.1, 4, 5, 16, 23 – 'the whole church' in Corinth, as in 1 Cor. xiv.23; 1 Cor. i.2; iv.17; vii.17; etc.). The question of who 'the churches of Galatia' were is discussed in the Introduction §§3 and 6.

The bareness of his reference to his addressees, in contrast to his more normal, more fulsome description (cf. particularly Rom. i.7; 1 Cor. i.2), would have served as a further preliminary indication to those of his audience who knew him well that Paul was far from satisfied with their present condition and of the storms to come (i.6ff).

3 Paul completes the typical form of epistolary introduction by adding the third element, the greeting itself – **grace to you and peace from God our Father and the Lord Jesus Christ**. This is his normal greeting (Rom. i.7; 1 Cor. i.3; 2 Cor. i.2; etc). His readers would probably recognize that Paul has here amalgamated and adapted the two most characteristic greetings of Greek and Jewish etiquette: where the Greek speaker would write 'Greeting' (*chairein* – as in 1 Macc. xii.6, Acts xxiii.26, and, somewhat surprisingly, Acts xv.23 and James i.1), Paul writes 'grace' (*charis*); where the Jew would say 'Peace' (*shalom* – as in 1 Sam. xxv.5–6), Paul simply uses the Greek equivalent (*eirene*). He had almost been anticipated in this in 2 Macc. i.1 – 'Greeting . . . and good peace' (see also on vi.16); but 'grace' is Paul's own distinctive and characteristic touch. The closeness in sound between 'Greeting' and 'grace' (*chairein* and *charis*) must have been sufficient excuse for Paul to replace the limpness of the former by the richness of the latter.

In so doing Paul brought to immediate prominence one of the key words in his understanding of the gospel – 'grace'. It would have been a word well enough known to his readers in the sense particularly of 'favour', felt or shown (LSJ). But they must have been familiar with it on Paul's lips too. For Paul was to make it one of the great words in the Christian vocabulary (it occurs a hundred times in the Pauline corpus), as the word which more than any other encapsulates the attitude and activity of God as expressed in the gospel – God's outreaching, redeeming, sustaining concern for a fallen humanity, God's 'favour to men contrary to their deserts' (Burton 424). To be noted is the fact that in Paul's usage it is not merely a disposition in God, but something dynamic, the generous output of his power to achieve what is best for his creation. The occurrences in the rest of Galatians give a fair sample of Paul's wider usage (i.6, 15; ii.9,

21; v.4; vi.18; see also on i.6 and ii.9; and for fuller details see my *Jesus* 202–5).

In this combination ('grace and peace'), even recently converted Gentile hearers would recognize that Paul was not using 'peace' in the more typically Greek sense of 'absence from war' (LSJ, *eirene*). As the 'Jewish' part of the greeting, it retained the much more positive sense of the Hebrew word (*shalom*). For Hebrew speakers from of old, *shalom* embraced all that makes for well-being, for wholeness and prosperity, both 'material' as well as 'spiritual', and social more than individual – that which makes for productively harmonious relationships (e.g. Deut. xxiii.6; Pss. lxxxv; cxlvii.14; Zech. viii.12) (see further *TDNT* 2.400–20). The two words together form as rich a greeting as can be imagined: a prayer which recognizes God as the source of the enabling ('grace') to live in mutually productive and beneficial harmony ('peace'). Such a greeting itself was a precious contribution which infant Christianity made to human discourse, a token of the still richer potential in the blending of Jewish and Greek resources which constituted Christianity in the beginning.

The second reference to God as Father personalizes the relationship indicated – **from God our Father**. If this is the original reading (see p. 23 n. 4), it shifts the focus in the thought of God from that of his supreme authority as creator and recreator to that of his personal relationship with people, with its overtone of protective care as well as of paternal authority. For Paul's Christian readership the sense of the intimacy of this relationship would not be far distant (see on iv.6). The switch to first-person plural constitutes a tacit appeal to the fact that Paul and his readers shared the same relationship with the supreme source of authority.

With 'God our Father' Paul conjoins **and the Lord Jesus Christ**. If the double name 'Jesus Christ' was, somewhat surprisingly, already so firmly fixed in Christian vocabulary (see on i.1), the fuller form was equally common – '(our) Lord Jesus Christ' – appearing as an established formula in every NT epistle (apart from Hebrews). The addition of 'Lord' is directly attributable to the resurrection: in raising Jesus from the dead, the first Christians believed, God had also exalted him to his right hand and given him the title 'Lord' (*kyrios*). This conviction is clearly expressed in what is probably one of the earliest baptismal formulae (Rom. x.9) and one of the earliest Christian hymns (Phil. ii.11), as well as in the widespread use made of Ps. cx.1 ('The Lord said to my Lord, "Sit at my right hand . . ."') in earliest Christian apologetic (e.g. Acts ii.34–6; Rom. viii.34; 1 Cor. xv.25; Heb. i.13; 1 Pet. iii.22). Implicit in this regular use of the larger formula is the fact that the claim of Jesus' Messiahship was quickly absorbed within the more potent claim (for Greek audiences) of Jesus' Lordship; with the corollary that it was not Jesus' Messianic status as such which provided the growing point for Christian faith, but, once again, the impact of his resurrection; without the epithet 'Lord', the epithet 'Christ' would almost certainly have been insufficient to sustain a new movement, at least as anything more than a Jewish sect. This may help explain why it is that 'Lord' is Paul's most favoured title for Jesus (nearly 230 times in the Pauline epistles).

The title itself signified the rights of domination and disposal of superior to inferior in a range of such relationships, from that of master in relation to slave, to that of god(s) in relation to their devotees. In conjunction with 'God our Father' the status thus accorded to Jesus Christ clearly was closer to the latter than to the former. Thus it was used of the divinities worshipped in the various cults which were such a feature of ancient societies (the 'lords many' of 1 Cor. viii.5) (BAGD, *kyrios*; *TDNT* 3.1041–58). But where they typically would refer to a mythical figure (like Sarapis), the Christians referred it to one who had been crucified less than two decades earlier.

More striking is the fact that it was the title used for the sacred name of God, when the Jewish scriptures were read out in diaspora synagogues in Greek translation, and that the first Christians, if Paul is any guide, were prepared to apply some of these scriptural passages to the exalted Christ as Lord (Rom. x.13 applying Joel ii.32 to Jesus as Lord; Phil. ii.11 echoing Isa. xlv.23). This is probably less significant than is often thought, since both Greek and Jewish societies were not strangers to the idea of humans' being apotheosed to heaven, and since Jewish thought could embrace the idea of such as Enoch and Abel being given share in divine functions (of judgement) without any sense that it was thereby infringing the traditionally strong Jewish monotheism (*1 Enoch* xc.31; 11QMelch; *Test. Abr.* xi and xiii). Moreover, the frequent amalgamation of Ps. 8.6 with Ps. 110.1 in earliest Christian apologetic (see my *Christology* 108–10) strongly suggests that Paul saw Jesus' Lordship also in terms of the dominance over the rest of creation which God had intended for Adam (as in 1 Cor. xv.25–7). In fact, Paul regularly takes care to juxtapose talk of Jesus' Lordship with more traditional talk of God – including the formula, 'the God and Father *of* our *Lord* Jesus Christ' (Rom. xv.6; 2 Cor. i.3; xi.31; Col. i.3), and the powerful assertion that God's exaltation of Jesus as Lord has in view the supreme Lordship of God (1 Cor. xv.24–8; cf. Phil.

ii.11 – '. . . to the glory of God the Father'). In other words, for Paul the confession that 'Jesus is Lord' did not detract from the older confession, 'God is one' (1 Cor. viii.6) (see further my *Partings* §10). At the same time that such assertions could be made of the crucified Nazarene within such a short time remains an astonishing fact – here in particular the conviction that this 'Lord Jesus Christ' could be so linked with 'God our Father' as the source of the 'grace and peace' which summed up Paul's basic hope for his converts.

4 In every other letter of the Pauline corpus the preceding greeting closes the introduction to the letter, giving way most typically to a prayer of thanksgiving on behalf of the people to whom he writes. Here, however, he immediately adds, **who gave himself for our sins**. This further departure from characteristic courtesy is another indication of the agitation Paul clearly felt as he dictated this letter (see also on i.1). Presumably he intended the appended clauses as something of a rebuke to his readers: any thanksgiving is solely for what God has done – the implication being that they had forgotten the significance of Jesus' death, and its character as unselfish giving, and were acting as those who still belonged to 'the present evil age'. Thus is struck the first chord in a theme which reappears at various points thoughout the letter (ii.19–20; iii.1; iv.3, 9, 25–6; vi.8, 14–15). At the same time, the continued use of first-person plural ('for *our* sins') is itself an appeal for reconciliation on the basis of their common participation in Christ's rescue act.

The thought of Jesus given, or giving himself to death, is one which keeps recurring in the Pauline corpus – whether with this verb (*didōmi* – also in 1 Tim. ii.6 and Tit. ii.14) or its compound, 'hand over' (*paradidōmi* – Rom. iv.25; viii.32; Gal. ii.20; Eph. v.2, 25); whether as a voluntary act of self-sacrifice as here (Gal. ii.20; Eph. v.2, 25; 1 Tim. ii.6; Tit. ii.14), or as an act of God (Rom. iv.25; viii.32; cf. 1 Clem. xvi.7; Barn. xvi.5). The variety of formulation indicates that the substance of what was being claimed was more important than any particular form of words. The compound form could also embrace the thought of the (human) betrayal which resulted in Jesus' death (1 Cor. xi.23); the version expressing self-sacrifice echoed the passionate commitment of martyrdom (1 Macc. vi.44; cf. ii.50); and, of course, Paul would not wish to make any distinction between the act as willed by God and the act as one of Jesus' self-giving.

By adding 'for our sins' (as in Rom. iv.25; cf. Rom. v.8) and not just 'for us' (as in Rom. viii.32; Gal. ii.20; Eph. v.25; Tit. ii.14) Paul indicates clearly enough that he was thinking in sacrificial terms (so explicitly Eph. v.2; cf. Rom. iii.25; 1 Tim. ii.6). In an age when sacrifice was almost universal as a means of retaining the goodwill and blessing of the gods such overtones would not have been missed. The long-established and sophisticated Jewish system emphasized that the sacrifices were provided by God as a means of atonement, covering over and obliterating the sins which injured individual and community (for the 'logic' of the theology of sacrifice see my 'Paul's Understanding'). And in Jewish martyr theology, the self-sacrifice was effective precisely as being a sacrifice (2 Macc. vii.37–8; *4 Macc.* vi.28–9; xvii.21–2). Hence the ease with which Paul could vary his formulation. When Jesus' death was first expressed in these terms is a matter of some dispute, but Paul himself might well have been aware of a tradition going back to Jesus himself (Mark x.45 par.; Matt. xxvi.28; Luke xxii.19); he cites a similar formula in 1 Cor. xv.3, which he must have learned at or soon after his conversion; the early influence of Isa. liii is hard to dispute behind the formula Paul uses in Rom. iv.25, as also the influence of Jewish thought about the sacrifice of Isaac in Rom. viii.32; and the plural 'sins' (rather than the more characteristically Pauline singular) also points behind Paul to an earlier Jewish Christian formulation (see further my *Partings* 70).

That Paul should mention both the resurrection of Jesus and his sacrificial death within the opening sentence of the letter is a reminder of how fundamental and central these two elements were to the Christian gospel from the first. Presumably too he did not see them as having distinct and separable significance: it was as the *crucified* Christ that Jesus had been raised; his death was not an end in itself but could only be recognized in its significance (as a sacrifice accepted by God) by virtue of the *resurrection.* At the same time the double formulation allowed Paul to achieve a certain balance between the act of God 'who raised Jesus from the dead' and the act of Jesus 'who gave himself for us'.

This self-giving of Jesus had as its purpose **to rescue us from the present evil age.** Paul is primarily dependent on his Jewish heritage at this point. The verb (*exairein*) is not much used in Greek writing in the sense of 'rescue, deliver from', but occurs frequently in the LXX in this sense, particularly as a physical act of release from enemies and troubles (regularly in the idiom, 'rescue from the hand of . . .'). Since this is the only time in his writings that Paul uses the word, he may have been quoting a form of words known to his readers, although the near synonym (*ruesthai*) would have done as well, since it is used as an alternative to *exairein* in the LXX, and Paul uses it elsewhere. So too 'the present evil age' presupposes the Jewish apocalyptic schema which saw world history as divided into two ages, the present age and the age to come, and the present age as one dominated by evil, in contrast to the glories of the future age. The contrast comes to explicit expression only in the two classic examples of Jewish apocalyptic, *4 Ezra* and *2 Baruch* (4 *Ezra* vi.9; vii.12–13, 50, 113; viii.1; *2 Bar.* xiv.13; xv.8; xliv.11–15; also *2 Enoch* lxvi.6), which were written after AD 70. But it was a natural outworking of such seminal passages as the visions given in Dan. 2 and 7, and was implicit in Qumran's talk of 'the time of wickedness' (CD vi.10, 14; xii.23; xv.7; 1QpHab. v.7), as in various sayings recalled in the Jesus tradition (Matt. xii.32; Mark x.30; Luke xx.34–5). Paul certainly had no doubts that the present age was marked by corruptibility, superficiality, folly, and blindness (1 Cor. i.20; ii.6, 8; 2 Cor. iv.4; Eph. v.16 is a close parallel), or that humankind as heirs of Adam were caught under the reign of sin and death (Rom. v.12–21; 1 Cor. xv.20–2).

In earliest Christian understanding, Christ's death was the key to deliverance from the seductive and corrupting introversion of this age's self-delusion, since by his death he broke both the power of sin and the power of death. For those who identified with this Jesus as their Lord the spell was broken: the evilness of this age, its goals and values, could be the more clearly discerned and resisted, in the light of 'Christ crucified' as 'the wisdom of God' (1 Cor. i.20–5); with the confident hope that he who had defeated the power of death in the case of Jesus would do so in theirs too. The formulation catches the ambiguity of the Christian situation nicely: as a purposed rescue operation, begun but not yet completed; as still within 'the present evil age', but no longer identified with it or ultimately dependent on it.

All this is happening, Paul rounds off his extended opening, **in accordance with the will of our God and Father**. That all things should happen 'through, or in accordance with God's will' is a regular expression of hope in the Pauline literature (e.g. Rom. i.10; xv.32; 1 Cor. i.1; 2 Cor. viii.5; Eph. i.5; Col. iv.12), though here with apocalyptic overtones. We may presume that for Paul it was not a pious platitude, as the quite frequently occurring phrase 'God willing' may have been then, as today. In Paul's case, however, it was a heartfelt expression of his conviction that God had a purpose for his creation, that it should be as he intended it to be, free from its present futility and decay (Rom. viii.19–21); and a purpose of salvation for those caught within 'the present evil age', that they too should share in the fullness of that liberty (Rom. viii.17–23). Christ's death and resurrection were evidently the keystone of that plan. For that purpose to be fulfilled, therefore, it was necessary for those who named his name to be aligned to that purpose and to the character of Christ's self-giving. It will have been no accident, then, that Paul thus rounds off his opening paragraph with his focus once again on God and with a third reference to God as Father in the same sentence. It is his way of underscoring his conviction to his Galatian readers that what was at stake in their dispute was nothing less than the will and purpose of God for his world, and that Paul's gospel looked to no other source and no other validation.

5 The thought of God's will as the ultimate factor in the ordering of human affairs draws from Paul the appropriate human response – **to whom be glory for ever and ever, amen**. In the use of the word 'glory' Paul may have been consciously bringing together the different characteristic emphases of the concept in Greek and Hebrew. The native Greek speakers among his mainly Gentile readers would understand it primarily in terms of 'good reputation', the honour accruing from the good opinion in which one was held by others (*TDNT* 2.233–7); Paul echoes this usage elsewhere (Rom. ii.7, 10; 1 Cor. xi.14–15; 2 Cor. vi.8; 1 Thess. ii.6). But the greater influence on his thought would again be from the Hebrew side, where 'glory' denotes the visible 'splendour' as of kings, and so also the 'honour or reverence' due to such majesty (BDB, *kabod*). Hence the OT talk of the honour due to Yahweh which Paul here makes his own (e.g. 1 Sam. vi.5; Pss. xxix.1–2; xcvi.7–8; Isa. xlii.12; Jer. xiii.16; Mal. ii.2), as also elsewhere (particularly Rom. xi.36; Phil. iv.20). Still more characteristically Jewish is the conception of time involved, as consisting in a sequence of 'ages' (literally 'to the ages of the ages') (BAGD, *aiōn* 1b; *TDNT* i.198–200). The conviction is that God has so intended and supervised the outworking of human history, that when his human creatures recognize this, the acknowledgment of his majesty will last through all the ages, that is, for ever. The essentially theocentric (and Jewish) character of Paul's theology is thus again brought out. The 'Amen', though formal, nevertheless constitutes Paul's heartfelt confirmation of and commitment to this conviction and hope (*TDNT* i.335–7; elsewhere in Paul, Rom. 1.25; ix.5; xi.36; xv.33; etc.). Since the normal epistolary introduction had been disrupted by lifting his readers' eyes from the immediacy of their own situation to the eternal purpose of God, no more fitting conclusion could be found.

2 REBUKE i.6–10

(6) I am astonished that you are so quickly turning away from the one who called you in the grace (of Christ)[1] to another gospel, (7) which is not an other,[2] except that there are some who are disturbing you and wanting to turn the gospel of the Christ into something else. (8) But even if we or an angel from heaven preach to you[3] a gospel[4] contrary to[5] what we preached to you, let him be accursed! (9) As we said before, I now also say again: if anyone preaches to you something contrary to what you received, let him be accursed! (10) For am I now trying to persuade[6] men,[7] or God? Or am I seeking to please men? If I were still trying to please men, I would not be the slave of Christ.

6 If Paul's audience had failed to note the lack of the usual courtesies in the opening paragraph, they could hardly fail to do so now. For the normal convention was to continue the opening greeting with a word of thanksgiving and prayer on behalf of those addressed (the *exordium*; see Betz 44). And this indeed is

1 The absence of 'of Christ' from p[46] and some Western witnesses is hard to explain and may well indicate that the majority reading (which includes 'of Christ' or alternatives) is a scribal addition made at an early stage (see Metzger 589–90). Without 'of Christ' we could translate '*by* grace' (NEB, REB).

2 I have attempted to indicate the use of different words for 'another' in vv. 6 and 7 by writing the second one as 'an other'. It would be possible to translate either one of them as 'different', but it is probably better to keep to two very similar renderings. The fact that they are interchangeable is indicated by Paul's use of both of them in the closely similar passage 2 Cor. xi.4; also 1 Cor. xii.9–10 (see BDF §306; the older discussion looked for a clearer distinction – see e.g. Ramsay 261–6; Burton 420–2, 424).

3 'To you' is omitted by some important manuscripts, but even if Paul expressed himself in more general terms the force of his comment is obviously directed to the situation in Galatia.

4 The verb translated here 'preach a gospel' is the verbal form of 'gospel', meaning basically 'to bring or announce good news'.

5 The preposition has the basic sense of 'alongside', but can have comparative force, 'more than, beyond, to the exclusion of', or adversative force, 'against, in contrast to'.

6 The verb 'persuade' is in the present indicative (literally 'Am I persuading . . .?'), but the present can denote an attempted but incomplete action=conative present (BDF §319, citing as examples John x.32; xiii.6; Gal. v.4; vi.12).

7 Here again (as in verse 1) the translator has the problem of how best to render the word denoting a human being without reference to gender. Since English does not have an adult equivalent to 'child' (rendering a choice between 'boy' and 'girl' unnecessary), the choice is between a cumbersome rendering like 'human beings', or the misleading 'persons' or 'people', or (what appears to be) the gender-specific 'men', or a paraphrase such as REB fails to carry through consistently.

Paul's normal practice in his other letters (Rom. i.8ff.; 1 Cor. i.4ff.; Phil. i. 3ff.; Col. i.3ff.; 1 Thess. i.2ff.; 2 Thess. i.3ff; Phm. 4ff); thus, already in 1 Thess., probably his earliest letter, the typical pattern had been set – 'We give thanks to God always for you all, making mention of you in our prayers, constantly remembering your work of faith . . .' (1 Thess. i.2–3). But in this case Paul had little time for such niceties. There was nothing to give thanks for in what he had heard of the Galatian churches. Having restrained himself so far, evidently with some impatience, Paul could hold back no longer, and turns abruptly to his primary concern in writing – **I am astonished that you are so quickly turning away . . . .**

The opening word ('I am astonished') sets the tone. It denotes surprise or wonder at some unexpected and amazing utterance, or deed, or turn of events. Elsewhere in the NT it occurs most frequently as the response of the onlookers to a miraculous act (Matt. viii.27; ix.33; xv.31; xxi.20; Mark v.20; Luke viii.25; ix.43; xi.14; John vi.21; Acts ii.7; iii.12). It is, however, not part of Paul's regular vocabulary (elsewhere in the Pauline letters only 2 Thess. i.10); although he was no stranger to miracles in his ministry (see on iii.5), he was not a 'wonder' worker and did not depend on the effect of such miracles for the success of his ministry. Nor can it be explained simply in terms of typical epistolary or rhetorical style (as Betz 47 and Hansen 33–4), otherwise we might have expected it to be a more typical feature of Paul's letters. Given the agitation evident in these verses, there would seem to be more passion than artifice at work at this point. Paul's use of the word here, therefore, is probably an expression of the genuine sense of shock which the news from Galatia had brought him. It was not the grace of God and its effect which caused him surprise, but the perversity of human response to that grace.

The charge he lays before his audience is put without frills and without qualification: they were betraying their calling as Christians. Again the word (*metatithesthai* – 'turn away') is not part of Paul's regular vocabulary (only here in his letters, and little used elsewhere in the NT). But its sense of 'change one's mind, turn away, desert' was well enough known in Greek usage, and Paul's readers would not mistake it (BAGD, *metatithemi* 2b, who note that '*ho metathemenos* means a turncoat who leaves one philosophical school for another one'). In view of the probable Palestinian origin of those who were causing the trouble in Galatia (see Introduction §5), it is a poignant irony, and one on which Paul may have played, that the same language was used in 2 Maccabees to describe the apostasy of the hellenistic Jews from their covenant faith (='Judaism'; see on i.14), during the Maccabean crisis two centuries earlier (2 Macc. iv.46; vii.24; xi.24). The surprise and unnaturalness of the crisis confronting him thus forced from Paul what was an unusually harsh and hurtful accusation. The charge would no doubt have caused surprise in turn to the Galatians, since they must have thought they were doing something very different.

The surprise would have been all the greater if they had caught an overtone of passages such as Exod. xxxii.8 and Deut. ix.16 (cited by Mussner 53): they were making the very mistake of the first Israelites in abandoning the covenant almost before it had been ratified. The 'so quickly' could denote either the brevity of the time which had passed since Paul had left the Galatian churches ('so soon'), or the speed with which they had capitulated ('so easily'). If a decision could be made between these two we would be in a better position to decide the date of writing (see Introduction §§4, 6); but while the meaning of the text would of course have been clearer to his readers it remains ambiguous to us (GNB's 'in no time at all' catches the ambiguity well). At the same time it will be significant that Paul chose the present tense rather than the aorist (past) tense for the verb. They had begun the process of apostasy, but not yet completed it. The report had presumably been sent to Paul by a well-wisher soon after the first signs that the gospel he had preached to them was being abandoned. Hence the urgency of the letter and of its tone. He still had hopes of preventing or undoing the damage that was being done before it became too serious (see also iv.9–10 and on v.2).

The seriousness of what they were doing in Paul's eyes is indicated in the next few words – they were turning away **from the one who called you in the grace of Christ to another gospel**. It was not simply that they were abandoning Paul, or the message Paul had brought them. They were being unfaithful to *God*; 'the charge is transgression of the first commandment' (Ebeling 47). Or, in alternative terms, they were failing to appreciate the essential character of their own experience of faith and grace. The word 'call' is another characteristically Pauline term. In everyday speech it denoted an invitation (to a meal) or summons (to court). But once again the weightier influence on Christian usage derives from the OT – particularly the striking language of Second Isaiah, where it becomes closely equivalent to 'choose' (and commission) (Isa. xli.8–9; xlii.6; xliii.1; xlv.3–4; xlviii.12; xlix.1; li.2). It is with this force that Paul uses the word. So here he reminds the Galatians that their conversion was a compelling summons they had been unable to deny (cf. Rom.

viii.30; 1 Cor. i.9; vii.17–24; Gal. v.13; 1 Thess. iv.7; 2 Thess. ii.14), as had been his own (see also on i.15).

Still more to the point is the character of this summons, the grounds on which and means by which God puts his summons into effect – 'in grace' (see on i.3 and ii.9). 'Of Christ' can be added (see above p. 38 n. 1) since for Paul, and his Christian readership, there would be no doubt that 'the grace of God' had come to its supreme focus and most effective expression in Christ (as already implied in i.1 and 4). But it is the gracious character of this calling which was of first importance for Paul, particularly in the dispute he was about to engage in; whether he was thinking in terms of the means by which it was accomplished, or of the state into which it had brought them, need not be decided (the language would have been as ambiguous to his first readers as it is to us). For it was essential that those who were urging circumcision on the Galatians, as well as the Galatians themselves, should recognize that Israel's own election was an expression of the same calling, also in grace (cf. Rom. ix.7–11; xi.5–6), and by virtue of that same character (grace) open also to Gentiles as well as Jews (cf. Rom. ix.24–6). For Paul, God is always the one from whom the summons comes, 'he who calls' (Rom. iv.17; ix.11; Gal. v.8; 1 Thess. ii.12; v.24; see also on v.8) – a further reminder that Paul saw God as the moving source of and force in salvation, with Christ as the main expression and facilitator of his call.

What it was that the Galatians had done which had brought this charge of apostasy against them becomes clear in the next phrase: they have turned away **to another gospel**. 'Gospel' is a still clearer example of how the infant Christian movement was developing its own technical vocabulary to express the wonderful new thing that had come to them. The word was used elsewhere in the plural ('joyful messages'), particularly in the Caesar cult (*EWNT* 2.176–86). But the uniform use of the singular in the NT, the regularly explicit understanding that it is 'good news' from God (Rom. i.1; xv.16; 2 Cor. xi.7; 1 Thess. ii.2, 8, 9), and the echo of the characteristic language (once again) of Isaiah which we find in early formulations (see on i.8) are sufficient indication that the word was chosen to express the conviction that the message of and about Jesus Christ was *the* good news from God. It is, of course, precisely because of its character as *the* good news that Paul was so concerned lest his Galatian converts were in process of abandoning it for something else.

The fact that Paul uses the Christian technical term for 'the gospel' also is clear indication that those whom he was about to attack were also Christian missionaries. He calls their message '*another* gospel' because it was significantly different from his own; but he calls it '*gospel*' because that was the term they no doubt also used in their capacity as missionaries like Paul (see further Introduction §5).

7 Having granted his opponents' status, as Christian missionaries who also claimed to preach the 'gospel', Paul immediately qualifies himself – another gospel **which is not an other**. The point is plain: whatever their status as Christian missionaries, whatever the authorization to which they laid claim, the message they actually preached was so 'different' (see above p. 38 n. 2) as no longer to deserve the title 'gospel'. The message of God's calling in (the) grace (of Christ) *was* the gospel, and there was no other. However much his opponents might justify their message as the 'gospel' and therefore equal in validity to Paul's, presumably as a supplement or corrective to Paul's, so far as Paul himself was concerned it failed the acid test: it did not adequately express or uphold God's calling in grace. It is not immediately apparent how this 'gospel' relates to 'the gospel of the circumcision' (ii.7): either it was the same, and Paul had hardened his attitude to it, presumably in the light of how it had been interpreted at the Antioch incident (ii.14–21); or the incoming missionaries in Galatia represented a more traditional understanding of the gospel, a more strongly 'judaized' version of the gospel agreed at Jerusalem (see Introduction §§5–6 and on ii.7).

The true state of affairs, so far as Paul saw the situation in Galatia, was not that other missionaries of equal status had brought a message of equal validity to his converts, **except that there are some who are disturbing you and wanting to turn the gospel of the Christ into something else**. The conjunction ('except that, but only') does not make entirely clear what the qualification of the preceding phrase is (NIV abandons any attempt to show the connection). It indicates that, whereas what was now being preached in Galatia was being called 'gospel' and put forth as an exposition of 'the gospel', the reality was otherwise. Needless to say, this is Paul's perspective on the situation in Galatia. The other missionaries, identified here only cryptically and dismissively as 'some' (Paul's usual way of referring to his opponents – Rom. iii.8; 1 Cor. iv.18; xv.12; 2 Cor. iii.1; x.2; Phil. i.15), would no doubt have seen things differently! But Paul's attitude was objectively rooted at least to the extent that some of his Galatian converts had been 'disturbed' by the events there (presumably the ones who had sent to inform Paul of what had transpired since his departure); and there were clear

enough differences of emphasis in what was now being asked of
them (what Paul later sums up under the phrase 'the works of
the law' – see on ii.16). The metaphor ('disturb') is of water
shaken or the sea stirred by waves (cf. John v.7), and was used
frequently for political agitation (cf. Acts xvii.8, 13) (LSJ, *tarassō*)
– hence NJB's translation, 'troublemakers'. As such, it well
describes the state of (some of) Paul's converts, into which the
other 'gospel' had thrown them, as one of troubled confusion. It
is another word which Paul uses only in this letter (again in
v.10). And there is the important parallel in Acts xv.24 (the only
other occurrence in Acts) which suggests that Luke's source
shared Paul's view of such teaching. The syntax Paul uses
indicates a long-drawn-out and continuing state of affairs.

Paul also attributes to the other missionary teachers a desire
'to turn the gospel of Christ into something else'. The
identification of the 'gospel' now as 'the gospel of Christ' is
largely stylistic (cf. Rom. i.1 and 9; xv.16 and 19; 1 Thess. ii.9
and iii.2). It is the same good news from God (i.6), but with
Christ so much at the centre (cf. already i.1, 3–4, 6(?)), it can
equally be described as 'the gospel of Christ' – that is, probably,
the gospel concerning Christ, rather than the gospel of which
Christ is the author; but the ambiguity of the genitive
construction allows both senses. The variation, however, does
further underline the degree to which Paul could associate God
and Jesus together in the process of salvation, and regard Jesus'
death and resurrection as giving definitive expression to the good
news of God's gracious call. The definite article with 'Christ' may
also indicate a continuing titular force for word: it is precisely
when confronted with those whose roots are more firmly
embedded in Jerusalem than his own that he reminds his readers
that his gospel is 'the gospel of the Messiah'.

The verb 'turn into something else' is another word which
Paul uses only here in his writings – once again stretching his
vocabulary to find language with which to address this untoward
situation. It is a forceful word, denoting a radical change, as of
water into blood, or fresh water into salt, or feasting into
mourning, or daylight into darkness (Ps. lxxviii.44; Joel ii.31;
Amos viii.10; Sir. xxxix.23; 1 Macc. ix.41). Its frequently negative
force is well illustrated by Pss. lxxviii.57, cv.25, Sir. xi.31 and
Test. Ash. i.8 ('turning good into evil'). Once again the
attribution by Paul of desire on the part of the other Galatian
preachers so to 'pervert the gospel of Christ' has to be seen as
Paul's account of the matter. But we may presume that their
desire to counter Paul's gospel or to change it for the better (in
their eyes) was conscious and actively pursued.

8 The depth of Paul's feelings, already evident in his talk of 'deserting' God and 'perverting the gospel', now comes to full expression: **but even if we or an angel from heaven preach to you a gospel contrary to what we preached to you, let him be accursed.** So convinced was Paul that the gospel as he had preached it in Galatia was the gospel from God, the gospel of Christ, that he was prepared to maintain it as the norm by which all other claims to revelation from heaven might be judged. This was not merely to put one claim to such revelation (i.15–16) over against another – the one as convincing (or as unconvincing) as the other to the onlooker. To be sure, so far as securing validation for his understanding of the gospel was concerned, Paul's claim to a special revelation from God and Christ (i.1) did put him in a vulnerable position on this score, especially when compared with those whose credentials in the gospel of Christ were the more obviously soundly based (hence the lengthy attempt at self-defence which dominates the first section of the letter – i.11–ii.21). But implicit also in what he had already written was the claim that his preaching of the gospel was in full accord with the gospel shared by all Christians (hence the deliberate use of the already established formulae in i.1 and 4); and as part of his defence he would be able to point also to the transformation of his own life (i.23) and the manifest effectiveness of his gospel in the lives of his converts (ii.7–9 – recognized by the pillar apostles), not to mention the lives of the Galatians themselves (i. 6; iii.2–5). So his claim for the normative status of his gospel was not based simply on the fact that it had prior claim on his Galatian converts, as being the first to reach them. It was rooted much more in the effective reality of their own (his and their) experience, and ultimately in the character of God, of his call and of the grace by which he brought that call to effect. It was because the issues were so fundamental (not just a question of a change of emphasis) that Paul wrote with such passion.

To show that it was not simply a matter of *who* were the preachers, Paul puts the alternative as strongly as he could: 'Even if we ourselves were to preach another gospel . . .'. He takes care by using the first person *plural* to remind his readers that the gospel as they first received it came not through him alone, but through a missionary team; the 'we' should not be taken as equivalent to 'I'. It was *not* a matter of his *own* prestige and authority or that of his fellow missionaries who with him had brought the gospel to Galatia. Had it been so he could have written with more effect, 'Even if Cephas or James . . .'. Had it been so he would have had to safeguard the possibility that in different circumstances he himself might well preach with a different emphasis (cf. 1 Cor. ix.19–23; Gal. v.11). Once again, the *gospel itself* provides its own norm (i.1, 4, 6).

Even if it was 'an angel from heaven . . .'. Within the apocalyptic mind-set which the first Christians shared, in at least some measure (see on i.1, 4, 15–16), this was no slight alternative to put forward. For the angelic interpreter was a standard element in Jewish apocalypses – the heavenly messenger (the word is the same in Greek) who gave the stamp of heavenly authority to the message he delivered (Ezek. viii.2ff.; Dan. x.5ff.; *1 Enoch* i.2ff.; *2 Enoch* i.4ff.; *Apoc. Zeph.* ii.1ff.; *4 Ezra* ii.44ff.; iv.1ff.). But even such a messenger and any message he brought had to be judged by the touchstone of the gospel. What is implied, of course, is that in comparison with such an awe-inspiring messenger, the people to whom the Galatians were giving ear were far less weighty in authority. If even what an angel from heaven said as 'gospel' had to be so discounted in relation to the gospel they had already experienced so richly, how much less should they listen to ordinary human messengers. Paul may already have been thinking forward to the argument to be made in iii.19: they *were* accepting something, the law, on the basis of angelic revelation.

Once again Paul uses language which acknowledges the Christian standing of those who preached the 'other gospel' in Galatia. He uses the verb ('bring or announce good news') which, like the noun derived from it ('gospel' – see on i.6), had already become a Christian technical word for the preaching of the good news which characterized the first Christian missionaries (see e.g. Acts v.42; viii.4; x.36; xi.20; 1 Cor. i.17; xv.1–2; 1 Thess. iii.6; Heb. iv.2; 1 Pet. i.12). The terminology was certainly influenced by the striking use of it in Isaiah (Isa. xl.9; lii.7; lxi.1; note Luke iv.18 and Rom. x.15), as were others in the preceding period (*Pss. Sol.* xi.1; 11QMelch.), but the line of influence in this instance probably came through Jesus himself (note particularly Matt. xi.5/Luke vii.22) and is reflected already in the early formulation in Acts x.36–8. Paul's repeated use of it in the present chapter (i.8–9, 11, 16, 23) shows how important a word it was for Paul as summing up the character of the Christian message as 'good news', the good news predicted by Isaiah. But once again, as in i.6–7, having conceded the Christian terminology to the other missionaries in Galatia, he makes it plain that by the standard of the 'good news', what they were preaching went beyond, stood in contrast to the gospel. Not even Paul himself, not even an angel from heaven could validate such a 'preaching of the gospel'.

The fierceness and depth of Paul's concern explode in the abrupt dismissal of such an alternative – **let him be accursed!** 'Die ganze zornmütige Kampfesnatur des Paulus flammt auf' (Bousset 36). Once again Paul uses a word whose force depended wholly on its Hebrew equivalent. To be sure, it would be known in Greek speech in the sense 'something dedicated' (LSJ and BAGD, *anathema*), and it does occur in a pagan curse from Megara dated to first or second century AD (MM; see also Betz 50–2). But it was the LXX sense of 'devoted to God in order to be destroyed' (see particularly Lev. xxvii.28–9; Deut. vii.26; Josh. vi.17–18; vii.1, 11–13) which dominates Pauline usage here and elsewhere (Rom. ix.3; 1 Cor. xii.3; xvi.22). Paul presumably could assume, either on the basis of his own preaching in Galatia, or from the fact that the problems in Galatia stemmed from an over-attraction to distinctively Jewish practices, that his readers would feel the full negative force of the word.[1] At the same time, the fact that he called the curse upon his own preaching team and an angel from heaven as possible preachers of the different gospel, rather than upon those actually active in Galatia at that time, constitutes something of a softening in Paul's otherwise unrelenting hostility to these missionaries, and reflects a characteristic Christian unwillingness to curse others (Luke vi.28; Rom. xii.14; Did. i.3). Even so his attitude is clear and uncompromising: so to distort the gospel of Christ as he believes them to be doing deserves a destruction which is complete (though in view of 1 Cor. v.5 NIV's 'eternally condemned' and GNB's 'may he be condemned to hell' go too far). This is the other side of the gospel (cf. Rom. i.17–18), equivalent to the tension between the blessing and curse of God in iii.8–14 (Osten-Sacken 122–4).

The fierceness of Paul's language strikes a discord with modern sensibilities; though it is somewhat rhetorical (and therefore hyperbolic) in character, the polemic of those days was much more robust than we would think fitting (cf. v.12; 2 Cor. xi.13–15), and elsewhere Paul expresses his own willingness for *himself* to be accursed if it would help his kinspeople (Rom. ix.3). At the same time we should recall that the force of such a dedication to God was to separate the thing from all human contact and use. So what Paul had in mind, probably even more strongly than the thought of destruction, was the desire to remove the preachers of the 'other gospel' away from the

---

1 P. Trebilco, *Jewish Communities in Asia Minor* (Cambridge University, 1991) ch. 3 notes that Jewish tomb inscriptions in Asia Minor evoke the curse of Deut. xxx.7 as something well enough known to protect the tombs from abuse and robbery.

Galatians and keep them separate, so that they could do no more harm (cf. 1 Cor. xvi.22; NEB – 'outcast'; REB – 'banned'; talk of 'excommunication', however, is anachronistic, as Lightfoot 78, long ago pointed out). Leave them to God! At all events the language should remind us of just how crucial the issues were to Paul.

9 Lest there be any doubt as to Paul's seriousness on the point, he repeats with slow and measured solemnity – **As we said before, I now also say again: if anyone preaches to you something contrary to what you received, let him be accursed!** Quite what Paul means by 'we said before' is not clear. The verb strongly suggests something said on a previous occasion (2 Cor. xiii.2; 1 Thess. iii.4; iv.6; so also Gal. v.21). And presumably the use again of the first-person plural ('we') must refer back to what had been said during the initial evangelizing mission (i.8), or on the follow-up visit probably implied in iv.13 (see also on iv.13). That Paul should have had such foreboding would be explained by the fact that his last (or first) visit to them had been in the wake of the incident at Antioch (ii.11–14), which had resulted in a confrontation between Peter and Paul and a parting of the ways over what the gospel actually required of Gentile converts (see on ii.16). That Paul had left Antioch concerned to warn his converts (new or old) of the dangers of succumbing to a misinterpretation of the gospel, as had been the case at Antioch, would be wholly understandable (see also Introduction §6.1; there is another reference to his earlier teaching in v.21). The fact that he had given precisely such a warning previously would make his agitation and anger over what had happened among the Galatian churches all the stronger. The switch back to first-person singular ('I now say again') simply underlines the extent to which he had taken upon himself to write this letter – in his own name and authority (cf. vi.11).

The curse formula of verse 8 is repeated with only two variations. One broadens out its scope – 'if *anyone* preaches to you another gospel' – us, an angel, or anyone. No missionary is exempt from being measured against the gospel. The other replaces the previous repetition of the word 'preach' with the normal word to denote the reception of a message or tradition (as in Mark vii.4; and consistently in Paul – 1 Cor. xi.23; xv.1, 3; Phil. iv.9; Col. ii.6; 1 Thess. ii.13; iv.1; 2 Thess. iii.6; also Gal. i.12). Paul appeals not only to what he and his fellow missionaries had first preached to them, with the implication that the message was not theirs alone but already traditional, but also to what they could well recall as having *received*, with all that their reception had meant for them in lives changed.

10 For am I now trying to persuade men, or God? Or am I seeking to please men? The present tense of the first question has the force of 'attempting to' (conative present – BDF §319), thus balancing the 'seeking to' of the second question. Why Paul should ask these questions is not immediately clear. But there are at least four clues. (1) The 'for' may simply be a linking conjunction without much weight, the appropriate idiom in such a question (BAGD, *gar* 1f; BDF §452); but what weight it has suggests a causal connection. The questions, in other words, follow on more directly from what Paul has just said than the majority of modern commentators allow when they make verse 10 the beginning of a new or separate section (but see Burton 20–1, 33). That in turn suggests that the strong emphasis of verses 8 and 9 already had verse 10 in view: that in verses 8 and 9 Paul was refuting a Yes answer to the questions of verse 10. It is the force of verses 8 and 9 which allows the form of the questions (see point (3)).

(2) The 'now', quite unusually, stands first in the sentence, indicating a place of emphasis – 'Am I *now* trying to persuade . . .?'; note also the 'still' of verse 10c. The implication is of a previous occasion to which these questions looked back or which gave rise to these questions (cf. John xvi.31; 1 Cor. xiii.12b).

(3) The form of the questions (in the first question, the first part at any rate) invites the answer No! (and note again verse 10c). Paul was evidently trying to rebut a possible inference, drawn not from verses 8 and 9 (see point (1) above), but from an earlier statement of the gospel which verses 8 and 9 were attempting to defend.

(4) The language ('persuade', 'please') has strongly negative connotations. The idea of using persuasive language to achieve an improper end was familiar in the ancient world (BAGD, *peithō* 1b; Lüdemann 51). 'Since Plato philosophers and others have regarded the "art of persuasion" as something rather negative and unfitting. Rhetoric became identified with deception, slander, and even sorcery' (Betz 54–5). Paul shared this view (v.7–8; 1 Cor. ii.4; Col. ii.4) and could assume his readers would not mistake the point. Likewise the idea of being a mere 'man-pleaser' was well enough known in the ancient world (*TDNT* 1.456; Betz p. 55 nn. 112, 113; the compound word 'man-pleaser' is only found in Ps. liii.5; *Pss. Sol.* iv.7, 8, 19; Eph. vi.6; Col. iii.22; but the noun from the verb, *areskeia*, regularly had a bad sense, 'obsequiousness'). Paul elsewhere with equal

firmness denies that his preaching had such an object in view (1 Thess. ii.4).

None of these points on their own would be decisive. But taken together they strongly suggest that Paul here was attempting to refute criticisms made of his earlier preaching by those whom he now saw as troublemakers in Galatia. We could properly translate: 'for am I now "trying to please men . . ."?' or 'am I "seeking to please men"?' Or to bring out the force in paraphrase: 'In view of the strength of the curse just pronounced, in view of my willingness to be accursed myself, how can anyone say I am merely playing with words or seeking merely to flatter?' If this is correct it would help explain the degree of obscurity which modern readers find in the verse: Paul did not need to make himself any clearer, since his readers would have known well enough what he was referring to. Such allusions often cause difficulties for later readers, precisely because they can assume what therefore does not need to be said. In such cases particularly, the meaning of the text cannot be read off from the text immediately, but only from the text-set-in-context, whereby the allusions can be recognized and the full meaning of the text 'heard'.

We can also have a fair idea of why such a criticism would be levelled against Paul. His readiness to accept Gentiles into the Jewish sect of the Nazarenes, that is, into the covenant people of Israel (on Paul's reckoning), without requiring them to observe the obligations of the covenant, the works of the law — particularly food laws, feasts and above all circumcision (see ii.12; iv.10; v.2) — was obviously regarded as intolerable by the incoming missionaries (see Introduction §§5–6). Moreover, we know that such peculiarly Jewish practices were usually looked down on by the Greco-Roman intelligentsia, with circumcision in particular regarded as mutilation (e.g. *TDNT* vi.78–9; Schürer iii.615; Philo begins his treatment of *The Special Laws* [*Spec.Leg.*] by recognizing that circumcision is 'an object of ridicule among many people' and proceeds to defend it; see also v.12). It would be quite natural, then, for missionaries, who were themselves devout Jews, to draw the conclusion that someone who was preaching faith in the Jewish Messiah Jesus, to Gentiles, but without making clear the covenant obligations of that faith, was guilty of softening or cheapening the gospel. We can easily imagine the charges and jibes: 'he dresses it up for them in fancy language and ignores the hard demands; he makes it easy for them by leaving out the bits they don't like'. Similar complaints in not too dissimilar circumstances are found in Philo, *Migr.* 92, and Josephus, *Ant.* xx.44–5; the charge itself may be echoed in *Clem. Hom.* xviii.10 (Bruce 86). Paul's point, in response, is that what he has just said (verses 8 and 9) proves that such rebukes are simply unjustified; what was at issue was not a question of rhetoric or even of a covenant status compromised, but the very character of the gospel, of God's call in grace.

The only phrase not covered by the above is the second half of the first question: 'Or (am I trying to persuade) God?' It is unlikely that Paul meant to pose the two halves of this question as alternatives – implying the answer, 'It is God I am trying to persuade' (so NEB, REB, GNB). The negative force falls not on the nouns ('Am I trying to persuade *men* or *God*?' – cf. NJB), but much more on the verb ('Am I trying to *persuade* men or God?'), as we saw above (4). Had it been Paul's intention to imply that he was trying to persuade God, he would have completed the second question in the same way ('Am I seeking to please men, or God?'), since 'pleasing God' is a wholly positive ambition (1 Cor. vii.32; 1 Thess. ii.4, 15; iv.1). It is more likely that the 'or God' was part of the criticism made of Paul by the other missionaries and reported to him by his supporters. The implication would be that Paul's 'cut-down' gospel was an attempt to 'persuade God' to take Gentiles on easier terms (than those laid down in the covenant law) (cf. *TDNT* vi.2). Alternatively, it could be Paul himself who drew out this corollary – 'No, I am not "trying to persuade men" – nor God either'. The suggestion of Betz 55, that the question amounted to a charge of magic or religious quackery, fits less naturally into the context envisaged, unless the miracles alluded to in iii.5 were a factor (cf. the charge made by Paul in iii.1).

The clear implication of the questions, that a negative answer was expected, is confirmed by the final sentence – **if I were still trying to please men, I would not be the slave of Christ**. The inference is again strong that this was a charge laid against Paul's original preaching of the gospel in Galatia. Hence again we may translate, 'If I were still "trying to please men" . . .'. The apparent concession (that he previously had 'tried to please men') is simply a way of sharpening the antithesis. For 'slave of Christ' is one of Paul's favourite self-designations and descriptions of the Christian state (Rom. i.1; xii.11; xiv.18; 1 Cor. vii.22; Eph. vi.6; Phil. i.1; Col. iii.24; iv.12). And his readers would know well that a slave owed absolute and exclusive loyalty to his master; as a mere chattel of his master he could have no obligations to another. 'Enslavement of outsiders and their conversion into property meant *ipso facto* deracination: loss of name . . ., of all the normal ties of kin and "nation", even of gods, replaced by new focuses of attachment provided by the master and his society' (*OCD* pp. 994–5). Paul implies, clearly, that his commitment to Christ as his Lord was so complete, his obligations to Christ so absolute, that his actions as an apostle of Christ were directed by him alone, and that any other course would be unthinkable to him (see further my *Romans* 7–8). At the same time to be slave of an important figure carried a certain status with it, so that 'slave of Christ' could also function in some degree as a claim to leadership (Martin, *Slavery*, ch. 2).

B   Paul's defence of his gospel   i.11–ii.21

1   SUMMARY STATEMENT   i.11–12

(11) For[1] I want you to know, brothers,[2] that the gospel preached by me is not of human origin. (12) For it was not from a human being that I received it, neither was I taught it, but through a revelation of Jesus Christ.

Having caught his audience's attention with the language of his introduction and indicated beyond doubt the gravity of the issues at stake, Paul can now begin his self-defence, or rather, the defence of his gospel. The atmosphere in the congregations in Galatia when the letter was first read out to them must have been electric. Their own astonishment and upset at the charges already levelled against them would ensure careful attention to and careful scrutiny of what he was about to say. The tactic was no doubt deliberate. Paul was a practised public speaker, and in thus gaining his audience's attention he was following the simple techniques which all successful orators have known how to use.

He begins with a thematic statement (i.11–12), which he then proceeds to elaborate and defend in the following paragraphs (i.13ff.). Contrast Betz 46 and 56, whose insistence on identifying clear rhetorical patterns and precedents leads to a division of the text which fails to respect its natural rhythm, though his identification of the following section (i.12–ii.14) as equivalent to the *narratio* provides a better 'fit' (pp. 58–62). J. Jeremias,

1 A weaker connective, *de*, is equally strongly attested, allowing a translation like 'Now', and is preferred by Longenecker 22.
2 See above p. 23 n. 3.

'Chiasmus in den Paulusbriefen', *ZNW* 49 (1958) 152–3, on the other hand, sees the rest of the letter as a chiastic working out of the claims made here: 'not from a human being' – i.13–ii.21; 'not in human terms' – iii.1–vi.10 (he is followed by Mussner 77 and Beker 44–5; but see Longenecker 21).

11 The **For** indicates the connectedness of thought (though see above p. 51 n. 1). At no point did Paul want the issue to become reduced to a mere clash of human opinions or styles (i.10): the origin and authority for the gospel lie solely in God. **I want you to know, brothers**, is a formula Paul used elsewhere when he wanted to express something with solemnity and as worthy of fullest attention (1 Cor. xii.3; xv.1; 2 Cor. viii.1). In view of his departure from his usual etiquette in i.6–10, the use of 'brothers' here strikes a conciliatory note. 'To make known' was also typically used of the revelation of heavenly mysteries in apocalyptic thought (so regularly in Dan. Th. e.g. ii.23, 28–30, 45; v.7–8, 15–17; vii.16; also 1QpHab. vii.4–5; 1QH iv.27–8; vii.27; and in the later Paulines Col. i.27; Eph. i.9; iii.3–5, 10; vi.19 – 'the mystery of the gospel'), so that Paul was already looking forward to verse 12 ('revelation of Jesus Christ'). Its effect, therefore, is to reinforce the strength of the assertion which it introduces: **that the gospel preached by me is not of human origin**. For 'gospel' see on i.6, 'preach' see on i.8, and 'preached by me' see ii.7. The tense used (aorist) does not limit the assertion to the occasion when Paul preached in Galatia; rather it embraces the whole of Paul's past preaching as seen from his present perspective and sums it up as stamped by the same consistent character (hence he can say '*is* not of human origin'). Whereas in verses 8–9 he had made a point of linking others with the preaching ('we'), here it begins to become clear that it is Paul's own defence of this gospel which is at issue. 'Not of human origin' is the briefest of the several statements Paul makes to this effect (verses 1, 12), underlining its summary and thematic character. The phrase was a familiar idiom in Greek speech, 'in a human way, from a human standpoint', and 'emphasizes the inferiority of man in comparison with God' (BAGD, *anthrōpos* 1c; see also on iii.15); so elsewhere in Paul (Rom. iii.5; 1 Cor. ix.8; Gal. iii.15). In slightly different language, but making the same basic point as here, 1 Cor. ii.4–5 and 1 Thess. ii.13.

12 Lest the degree of ambiguity, inescapable in such a brief formula, cause any to mistake his meaning, and to ensure that no one miss the key point of his self-defence, Paul restates it in slightly fuller form – **for it was not from a human being that I**

received it, neither was I taught it, but through a revelation of
Jesus Christ. The claim is complementary to the one made in
verse 1, since, in Paul's eyes at least, apostleship and preaching of
the gospel were inextricably bound together. His use of the word
'received' so soon after he used it in verse 9 would help make
Paul's point: whereas they had 'received' the gospel as a tradition
conveyed to them by Paul himself (see on i.9), Paul himself had
not so received it. It did not come to him as human tradition, on
human authority. Corresponding to the 'by me' of verse 11, the
'I' is emphatic – 'I also', like the first apostles, or, more likely, 'I'
in contrast to the other missionaries in Galatia, who are more
probably in view. By adding 'nor was I taught it' Paul was not
simply being tautologous; nor was he denigrating the idea of
teaching. Rather he was seeking to cover all loopholes: he had
neither been converted by human agency (cf. i.9), nor had he
been taught the gospel in the basic catechesis in which no doubt
already all new converts to the new faith were instructed (cf.
Rom. vi.17; xii.7; xvi.17; 1 Cor. iv.17; Col. ii.7; 2 Thess. ii.15; Acts
ii.42). It is precisely this basic denial which he will fill out and
defend in the following verses (see on i.16 and i.18).

The denial is balanced by the positive assertion – **but through
a revelation of Jesus Christ** – with a verb like 'it came to me'
(RSV, NJB), or 'I received it' (NEB/REB, NIV) understood. The
choice of word ('revelation' = *apokalypsis*) is striking. It is a
predominantly Pauline word in the NT (13 out of 18
occurrences) and denotes a disclosure given from heaven, with
heavenly authority, usually of heavenly secrets (1 Cor. xiv.6, 26;
2 Cor. xii.1, 7; Gal. ii.2), and regularly with eschatological
reference, that is reference to the future consummation – coming
of Christ, completion of salvation, final judgement (Rom. ii.5;
viii.19; 1 Cor. i.7; 2 Thess. i.7). Here Paul uses the word clearly
with reference to the appearance of Jesus Christ to him on the
Damascus road, as the forward look to i.16 makes clear. To
describe this event as an 'apocalypse' not only underlined its
heavenly authority but also implied that it had eschatological
significance, that is, as the key which unlocked the mystery of
God's purpose for his creation, the keystone of the whole arch of
human history (cf. Rom. i.17; xvi.25; 1 Cor. ii.10; Eph. iii.3, 5;
and see also on Gal. iii.23). The forward reference to i.15–16 also
indicates that 'Jesus Christ' is not thought of as the source of the
revelation (GNB, NIV), but as its content (see particularly Burton
41–3); the point is important, as we shall see (see on i.16); the
only feature common to the Acts accounts of Paul's conversion
and Paul's own allusions to it is that it centred on an appearance
of Christ to Paul (Acts ix; xxii; xxvi; 1 Cor. ix.1; xv.8; 2 Cor.

iv.4–6). This also is what makes the difference with verse 8, and explains why Paul can speak dismissively of an angelic revelation (see on i.8), while basing his own claim on 'a revelation of Jesus Christ': the gospel is not simply 'from Christ' but *is* Christ. Since this apparently was not at issue with the other Galatian missionaries (cf. ii.16–17; v.2; vi.12), Paul could be sufficiently confident that his readers would accept that the 'revelation of Jesus Christ' had normative force. It was what that revelation meant, and how it was spelt out in the gospel which caused the differences between Paul and the others. Subsequently the attempt was made to downgrade Paul's experience from the status of an authentic 'revelation' to that of a mere vision or dream by the Jewish Christians who remained unreconciled to Paul to the end (*Clem. Hom.* xvii.13–19 – cited by Betz 332–3).

The assertion made with repeated force in these two verses stands in even more marked contrast with another of Paul's assertions, closely parallel in form – 'I want to make clear to you, brothers, the gospel which I preached to you, which you also received . . . For I passed on to you as of first importance what I also received . . .' (1 Cor. xv.1–2). Here Paul seems to admit what he so fiercely denies in Gal. i.11–12. The difference is not so sharp, however, as at first appears. For even in Galatians Paul has already by implication acknowledged his dependence on more established or shared formulae (i.1, 4). The point then is not the form of the tradition, the central statements regarding Jesus' death and resurrection in which the gospel was enshrined. It was what these statements meant, how they were interpreted in the differing concrete situations addressed by the gospel, which gave rise to the disagreements tackled by this letter. And particularly what this gospel meant for Gentiles who wished to accept it. It was on this subject most of all that the Damascus-road encounter came to him with the force of 'revelation', as the opening of his eyes to something which had up till that time been hidden from him, however well he may have known the claims made by those whom he was persecuting. See also my *Unity* 66–7; and further literature in Mussner 66–7, n. 116, who properly warns against reading out too much of Paul's theology from this 'revelation', as though it was all given to him there and then (see again below on i.16).

2   PAUL'S PREVIOUS LIFE 'IN JUDAISM'   i.13–14

(13) For you have heard of my way of life previously in Judaism, that in excessive measure I persecuted the church of God and tried to destroy[1] it; (14) and that I progressed in Judaism beyond many[2] of my contemporaries among my people, being exceedingly zealous for my ancestral traditions.

Having stated the thesis he is seeking to defend (i.11–12), Paul turns to the first part of the defence itself – his conduct prior to his encounter with the risen Christ. He evidently thought it important that he should start there. His readers needed to be reminded that he knew Judaism from inside, and indeed was a prime exponent of it. He knew therefore what were its attractions and appealing strengths. It is notable also that he focuses on praxis: it was not his beliefs, whether those of Judaism itself or about Jesus which were relevant to the Galatian crisis; it was his conduct. This emphasis reflects both the character of Judaism, as laying out a way of life, and presumably also the points at issue in Galatia. In other words, already we have a hint that what was at issue in Galatia was not such credal statements as are echoed in i.1 and 4, but what they meant in practice in the lives of those who confessed their faith in such statements.

13   Paul starts then by reminding his audiences of what they already knew – **for you have heard of my way of life previously in Judaism**. He could assume such knowledge, presumably, because either he had told them about his earlier life in one of his visits to Galatia – in which case, we may imagine, his own testimony would have been part of his preaching – or the facts were generally known among the churches (cf. i.23). Alternatively he knew from his informants that the incoming missionaries had informed his converts about his previous way of life – in which case, we may imagine, they may have tried to use it as a weapon against Paul (perhaps suggesting that Paul had over-reacted against his zealous past).

The word translated 'way of life' was well known in Greek, both as a noun and in verbal form, to denote 'conduct, behaviour' (BAGD and MM, *anastrophē* and *anastrephō*). More significant

---

1 This is another example of the 'conative imperfect', as in i.10 (BDF §326). So again in i.23.
2 The positive 'many' can also stand for the comparative 'most' (cf. BAGD, *polus* 2aβ); so NJB, REB, GNB.

here, though, is the fact that the verb was sometimes used to translate the Hebrew *halakh*, 'walk' – the word which more than any other characterizes the Jewish understanding of the obligations laid upon the devout (hence the technical term 'Halakhah' in rabbinic Judaism – see Schürer ii.339–46; see also on v.16). Here we may note 1 Kings vi.12 ('walk in all my commandments'), Prov. xx.7 ('one who walks blameless in righteousness'), *Test. Ash.* vi.3 (taking the law as your way of life), and the quite close parallel in 2 Macc. vi.23, which speaks of 'the excellence of the way of life from childhood' of the Maccabean scribe and martyr Eleazar (cf. also James iii.13; *TDNT* vii.715–16). Paul thus speaks here with the authentic voice of Judaism, and not of some straw man erected only to be overthrown, and not as one whose memory of his past had been distorted by an over-reaction to it.

More striking here is Paul's use of the word 'Judaism' (only in these two verses in the NT). It was a word which only came into currency with 2 Maccabees, where its first appearance indicates why the word had to be coined or brought into use: ii.21 – 'those who strove eagerly on behalf of Judaism'; viii.1 – 'those who had continued (faithfully) in Judaism'; xiv.38 – Razis, one of the Jerusalem elders who, earlier in the revolt, 'had been accused of Judaism, and had risked body and soul for Judaism with all diligence'; also *4 Macc.* iv.26 – Antiochus 'tried to compel everyone in the nation to eat foods defiled with blood and to renounce Judaism'. 'Judaism' clearly received its distinctive emphasis as the antithesis to 'Hellenism' (2 Macc. iv.13). That is to say, the word 'Judaism' began to be used in order to distinguish those who were being faithful to their heritage as Jews, from others (including other Jews) who were giving way to the syncretistic pressures coming from Hellenistic Antioch and 'adopting foreign ways' (2 Macc. iv.13). 'Judaism', we may say, as a description of the religion of Jews, only emerged in the Maccabean revolt, a fact which stamped its character as fiercely nationalistic and loyal to the law, in reaction to those who attempted to eliminate its distinctiveness (as expressed particularly in its sacrificial system, its feasts, circumcision and food laws – 2 Macc. vi; similarly in rabbinic use – *TDNT* iii.363); 'the word carries connotations which hint at those *practices* which separated Jew from Gentile' (H. Räisänen, 'Paul's Call Experience and his Later View of the Law', *Jesus, Paul and Torah, Collected Essays* [Sheffield Academic, 1992] 23).

Given the fuller description of this 'way of life in Judaism' in the following clauses (i.13b–14), it can be no accident that Paul chose to use just this word at just this point. The implication is that in his younger days he had seen Judaism as a heritage to be maintained with whole-hearted commitment and to be defended with vigour. The phrase 'in Judaism' also implies a sense of being 'inside' a well-defined area; so also 2 Macc. viii.1, and a funerary inscription from Italy which praises a woman 'who lived a gracious life inside Judaism' – Judaism understood as 'a sort of fenced-off area in which Jewish lives are led' (Y. Amir, 'The Term *Ioudaismos*: A Study in Jewish-Hellenistic Self-Identification', *Immanuel* 14 [1982] 35–6, 39–40), Jewish life as regulated by the halakhah (Osten-Sacken 153–6; see further my *Romans* lxix–lxx; and below on ii.14).

Does Paul's use of the word here imply that 'Christianity and Judaism were already separated' (Oepke 57)? The answer must be Yes, but only in the sense that 'Judaism' constituted a particular claim to and interpretation of Israel's covenant and heritage which Paul had once embraced but now questioned, 'Judaism' as characterized by the attitudes and life-styles documented in verses 13 and 14. In fact, however, it was precisely the identity of the 'Jew' which was at issue (Rom. ii.28–9) – as still today in modern Israel. If Paul's use of 'Judaism' here indicates a certain distancing of himself from the characteristic self-understanding of most of his fellow Jews, he still regarded himself as a Jew (ii.15; i.14 – 'my people'); and his description of the sect of Jesus Messiah as 'the church of God' (see below) indicates a firm claim that the new movement with which he now identified was wholly part of and continuous with the Israel of old. It would be more accurate, then, to say that Paul converted from one Jewish movement, the Pharisees, to another, the Christians (see particularly A. F. Segal, *Paul the Convert. The Apostolate and Apostasy of Saul the Pharisee* [New Haven: Yale University, 1990]; and further my *Partings*, ch. 8). The explicit contrast between 'Judaism' and 'Christianity' is first drawn in Ignatius, *Magn.* x.3 and *Philad.* vi.1. In the light of this importance attaching to the word 'Judaism', and the important issues its use raises, it is regrettable that NEB/REB have obscured the point by using paraphrases ('a practising Jew', 'our national religion').

Paul explains what he meant by 'his way of life formerly in Judaism' in two clauses. The first is **that I persecuted the church of God in excessive measure and tried to destroy it**. The verb meaning 'pursue, chase' quite naturally can be extended to the non-legal sense 'persecute' (as distinct from the legal sense, 'prosecute') and seems to be predominantly Jewish and Christian in usage (LSJ, BAGD, *diōkō*). Here it may be significant that the word is used in 1 Maccabees to describe the faithful Maccabees' pursuit of 'the sons of arrogance' (including the apostate Jews) and the 'lawless' (1 Macc. ii.47; iii.5). It was certainly burned into Paul's memory of his past – 'I persecuted the church of God' (1 Cor. xv.9; Gal. i.13, 23; Phil. iii.6), and his resort to the word consistently in this sense in Galatians, and more frequently than anywhere else, shows how deeply the memory affected him (iv.29; v.11; vi.12). The same inference follows from the adverbial phrase he uses, 'to an extraordinary degree, beyond measure, extravagantly, in excess'; he now regards his ardent defence of Judaism as excessive (the well-known idiom, however, is characteristically Pauline – Rom. vii.13; 1 Cor. xii.31; 2 Cor. i.8; iv.17).

He had even 'tried to destroy' the church (LSJ, *portheō*; conative imperfect – BDF §326) – a word, which, since it occurs only in Gal. i.13, 23 and Acts ix.21, all with reference to Paul's persecuting activity, indicates a strong historical connection between the two accounts at this point (cf. Acts viii.3). P. H. Menoud notes that the verb when elsewhere applied to things or people always conveys the idea of material assault (destroying and ravaging cities and territories), or even more violent physical or mental destruction, but then deduces that since Paul was never accused of murder, his attack must have been more spiritual (to undermine their faith) than physical ('The Meaning of the Verb *porthein* (Gal. i.13, 23; Acts ix.12)', *Jesus Christ and the Faith* [Pittsburgh: Pickwick, 1978] 47–60). However 'the use of brute force' (Hengel, *Pre-Christian Paul* 71–2) can hardly be excluded. It is true that the legal powers of Jewish authorities over their own people were limited, but they did include severe disciplinary floggings (up to 39 lashes; cf. 2 Cor. xi.24), and, as we shall see, the imagery of the 'zealot' evoked in i.14 is one associated with physical violence. So physical destruction must be in view here too, however exaggerated the language may be at this point.

Even more poignant is Paul's description of the objects of his persecuting zeal as 'the church of God'. For he now realized that those whom he had persecuted so ardently were none other than 'the assembly of God's people' (see on i.2). The very actions aimed at preserving the purity of the assembly of Israel (see again on i.2 and on 'zealot' in i.14) had actually been directed against that assembly itself! This reference to the regular OT usage ('assembly' of God) is sufficient explanation of why Paul here uses the singular (the consistent LXX usage). It was not because he had a concept of the Christian assembly as a single universal church (as subsequently in Ephesians); his consistent usage is otherwise (see again on i.2; in 1 Cor. xii.28 the 'church' is each church with its founding 'apostles'); here note the variety of formulations – 'church of God', 'churches of God', 'church of God in Corinth' etc. (1 Cor. x.32; xi.16, 22; xv.9; 2 Cor. i.1; Gal. i.22; 1 Thess. ii.14; 2 Thess. iv.1). The language was determined rather by this revelatory realization that all those he had been persecuting, each group of believers in Jesus Messiah, were 'the church of God', in direct continuity with the congregation of Israel; though if Paul's persecution had been largely limited to Jerusalem (Acts viii.3) the title would be particularly appropriate in that case (cf. 1 Cor. xvi.1 – 'the saints'; but contrast 1 Thess. ii.14 – 'the churches of God in Judea'). Presumably Paul had in mind the 'Hellenists', whose persecution in the wake of Stephen's martyrdom 'scattered' them from Jerusalem (Acts viii.1, 4; xi.19).

14 The other aspect of Paul's life formerly within Judaism on which he focuses is his memory of how **I progressed in Judaism beyond many of my contemporaries among my people**. The verb is neutral ('progress, advance'), but it can easily carry the overtone of improvement and resultant superiority, as particularly in Philo (*TDNT* vi.704, 709–11). Here, with the imperfect tense, which can be rendered as 'made constant progress', defined as 'progress in Judaism' (see on i.13), and linked with the preposition 'beyond' (BAGD, *huper* 2), the sense of superiority is strong. It fits well with what we know of the factional character of second-Temple Judaism since the Maccabean revolt, where the concern to progress in righteousness often resulted in the corollary that the 'righteous' regarded those fellow Jews ('among my people') who disregarded or disputed that understanding of righteousness as 'sinners' (see my 'Pharisees'). Whether Paul's attitude at that time was overt or conscious or not, the effect was to downgrade in religious status those who had not progressed so far. Such is always the danger of a spirituality of 'progress'. To those in Galatia who thought that their positive response to the other missionaries was an advance on the gospel as preached by Paul it was a timely reminder: Paul had not abandoned such ideas because he had been a failure in his own response to them; on the contrary he had outdone most of the rest of his contemporaries, including, by implication, these very same missionaries who now preached this message to the Galatian churches. This is a consistent claim by Paul (particularly Phil. iii.4–6; but also Rom. xi.1 and 2 Cor. xi.22; so too Acts xxii.3; xxiii.6; xxvi.4–7). Not least of significance here is the fact that Paul recollects no pangs of conscience or Luther-like agonizings for peace of conscience prior to his conversion. The talk of 'my people' confirms that Paul's audience consisted (predominantly) of Gentiles, but constitutes a further reminder that he spoke as an insider to those attracted by that status (cf. 2 Cor. xi.26; Phil. iii.5).

In terms specifically of his Pharisaic past Paul probably had in mind the *akribeia*, 'scrupulousness, exactness, strictness' which both Josephus and Acts pick out as characteristic of the Pharisees (Josephus, *War* i.110; ii.162; *Ant.* xvii.41; *Life* 191; Acts xxii.3; xxvi.5): the emphasis on the importance of the 'ancestral traditions' (see below) is the same (*Ant.* xvii.41; *Life* 191; Acts xxii.3); and the note of comparative excellence is consistent (e.g. *War* i.110 – 'more exact exponents of the laws'; *Ant.* xvii.41 – 'priding themselves on their strict observance'; *Life* 191 – 'reputed to be superior to the rest in their strictness'; Acts xxvi.5 – 'the strictest sect of our religion'). The picture Paul here paints is of a dedication to excellence and to the most careful exposition of and living in accordance with the law, as interpreted within the sect of the Pharisees, which outstripped most even of his fellow Pharisees. Such evidence concerning his Pharisaic past, from the only Pharisee writing in the period before AD 70 from whom we have first-hand reports, should be more highly regarded in any attempt to build up a picture of the pre-70 Pharisees than has usually been the case.

This 'progress in Judaism' is further explained in terms of Paul's **being exceedingly zealous for my ancestral traditions**. Although the last phrase has a wider resonance, Paul here certainly recalls a further characteristic Pharisaic concern – to live in accord with and to defend as necessary the traditional explanations and rulings (the oral Halakhah), which drawn from the Torah, had already gained, in Pharisaic eyes at least, the same status as the Torah itself. So again in Josephus and Acts, the same slightly different word is used for 'ancestral': *Ant.* xiii.408 – 'regulations which the Pharisees introduced in accordance with the ancestral tradition'; Acts xxii.3 – 'instructed in accordance with the strictness of the ancestral law, being a zealot for God'; note also Josephus, *Ant.* xiii.297 – 'the Pharisees had passed on to the people certain regulations handed down from the fathers'; and Mark vii.5 – the Pharisees and scribes ask Jesus why his disciples 'do not walk in accordance with the tradition of the elders' (cf. 2 Macc. vi.1; vii.2.30; *m. Abot* i.1). The reference is probably sufficient confirmation that Paul had received instruction from a Pharisaic teacher in Jerusalem (so Acts xxii.3).

In this context the word 'zealot' could not but have had strong overtones for anyone knowledgeable about contemporary Judaism. For 'zeal' was a powerful ideal for many Jews of the time – 'zeal for God' (Rom. x.2; *Test. Ash.* iv.5), 'zealots for the law' (Acts xxi.20; 1QS iv.4). Moreover, Jewish history had produced several ideal types of such 'zeal', which exercised a powerful influence on the piety of the devout. Simeon and Levi had embodied such zeal when they expunged the defilement of their sister Dinah by destroying the Shechemites (Judith ix.2–4; *Jub.* xxx.5–20). So too particularly Phinehas, when he killed the Israelite who had taken a Midianite woman (Num. xxv.6–13; Sir. xlv.23–4; 1 Macc. ii.54; *4 Macc.* xviii.12). Similarly Elijah when he slaughtered the defeated prophets of Baal (Sir. xlviii.2; 1 Macc. ii.58). And Mattathias, when he first raised the sword of rebellion and called on others to join him (1 Macc. ii.19–27; Josephus, *Ant.* xii.270–1). The Maccabean rebels prized highly this 'zeal for the law' and themselves epitomized it (1 Macc. ii.26, 27, 50, 58; 2 Macc. iv.2). And 'Zealots', of course, was the name taken by those who led the revolt against Rome which exploded some fifteen years after this letter was written (see Schürer ii.598–606). Philo bears witness to the same attitude when he warns that 'there are thousands, who are zealots for the laws, strictest guardians of the ancestral customs, merciless to those who do anything to subvert them' (*Spec. Leg.* ii.253). In the same spirit are the rulings preserved in the Mishnah: 'If a man . . . made an Aramean woman his paramour, the zealots may fall upon him. If a priest served (at the altar) in a state of uncleanness his brethren the priests did not bring him to the court, but the young men among the priests took him outside the Temple court and split open his brain with clubs' (*m. Sanh.* ix.6).

This is precisely the attitude which Paul recalls himself as sharing. He could have made the words of the Qumran hymnist his own – 'I am full of zeal against all evil-doers and men of falsehood' (1QH xiv.14). Two features of this 'zeal' are particularly relevant if we are to understand what it was that Paul felt so deeply and what it was in turn that he reacted against. One is that such zeal was characteristically directed towards the preservation of Israel's purity and distinctiveness – from intermarriage which breached Israel's ethnic identity, and from syncretistic influences which diluted Israel's dedication to Yahweh alone and the purity of the cult. This is the same attitude which comes to definition in 'Judaism' itself (see on i.13), the desire to maintain the boundaries on which self-definition depends. To be noted is the fact that such zeal was directed more against fellow Jews who were seen as such a threat, than against outsiders as such. It was presumably because Paul saw the new Jesus movement as just such a threat that he had taken up the task of persecution.

The other relevant feature of this zeal is that it was consistently expressed in violent activity — typically in taking the sword against those who were seen as breaching these boundaries. Against this background, the violence of Paul's actions against the early Christian movement, or the Hellenists in particular, should not be wondered at. In this too Paul was simply expressing his excess of zeal, as he now saw it (the adverb is typically Pauline — 9 out of its 11 NT occurrences in Paul). That it was this zeal which had made him a persecutor of the church was also something sharply etched in his memory (Phil. iii.6), a connection also well preserved in Acts xxii.3–4. It is of all this that he reminds his Galatian audience. It is a regrettable feature of 'religious zeal down through the ages that it has expressed itself in and been able to justify such violence and persecution. Characteristic of a less tender age is the fact that Paul's regret indicated here is not that he persecuted and destroyed, but that he persecuted and destroyed *the church of God*.

3 PAUL'S CALLING i.15–17

(15) But when it pleased the one[1] who set me apart from my mother's womb, and called me through his grace, (16) to reveal his Son in me, in order that I might preach him among the Gentiles, I did not consult immediately with flesh and blood, (17) nor did I go up to Jerusalem to those who were apostles before me, but went away into Arabia and returned again to Damascus.

15 The dominance of the first-person reference of the preceding verses ('my way of life', 'I persecuted and destroyed', 'I advanced' . . .) is broken by the intervention of God — **But when it pleased the one** . . . The reference to God is not explicit, but unmistakable (see also n. 1; and cf. particularly 1 Cor. i.21). The verb has the sense of 'consider good', and so 'determine, resolve' (BAGD, *eudokeō*). The readers would take the point that the transformation in Paul's understanding and way of life (from that just described — i.13–14), was not accidental or fortuitous, but the work of God; nor was it arbitrary as such, but an expression of the same good pleasure in his people and land of which the Psalmist often spoke (particularly Pss. xliv.3; lxviii.16;

1 Although 'God' has some strong support among the textual witnesses, it is almost certainly a scribal addition to make explicit the otherwise unnamed subject of the verb (Metzger 590).

lxxxv.1; cxlvii.11; cxlix.4). This sense of God's supervening
purpose in decisive events of personal history is the source and
heart of predestination teaching.

The possibility that Paul may have intended to evoke such
overtones is strengthened by the next phrase – **who set me
apart from my mother's womb**. For it may contain a deliberate
echo of Jer. i.5 ('Before I formed you in the womb I knew you,
and before you were born I consecrated you; I appointed you a
prophet to the nations'); with the implication that Paul's
appointment to 'preach God's Son among the nations' was of the
same order, inspiration and authority as Jeremiah's commission
(see also next phrase). In addition, in view of the preceding
verses, with their description of his past as a Pharisee, it is
possible that he was consciously playing with the (likely) original
meaning of 'Pharisee' as 'separated one'; if 'Pharisee' did first
emerge as such a nickname (Schürer ii.396) Paul would surely
have known this, even though his Greek-speaking readers would
hardly have recognized the allusion (there may be a further
allusion in ii.12). The point would then be that his attempt at
'separatism' within Judaism had been superseded by God's
separating him for the gospel (Rom. i.1) – and from before his
birth, so that his time as a Pharisee (i.13–14) had been merely
an interlude between the major phases of God's purpose (cf.
iii.15–24). Here again it may be possible to see Paul countering a
view of his 'separation as an apostle' which traced it back to his
commissioning by the church at Antioch, as again preserved in
Acts (xiii.2) (see also above on i.1).

When we include the next phrase, **and called me through his
grace**, the evocation of prophetic language becomes still stronger
(see also K.O. Sandnes, *Paul – One of the Prophets?* [WUNT 2.43;
Tübingen: Mohr, 1991] ch. 5). For in Second Isaiah the Servant
of Yahweh says, 'The Lord called me from the womb', before
being sent 'as a light to the nations' (Isa. xlix.1, 6); and Paul
shows elsewhere that this passage influenced his thinking about
his calling as an apostle (Rom. i.1; 2 Cor. vi.1–2; Phil. ii.16; see
my *Romans* 8; bibliography in Mussner 82, nn.26, 28). On 'call'
see on i.6; and on 'grace' see on i.3 and i.6. To be noted is the
fact that Paul always speaks of his entry into Christianity as a
call or commissioning; he never speaks of it as a 'conversion', and
would almost certainly have disputed the use of that word (in
the modern sense) in reference to his Damascus-road experience,
since he saw it *not* as a conversion from one religion to another,
but as a recall to a proper understanding of the grace-character
of Israel's calling (see again on i.6 and on i.13). The grace-
character of his own commissioning was one of its most

important features for Paul (see on ii.9). As the calling of an opponent of his Son it was an expression of God's unconditional generosity from start to finish.

16 The separation and call of God were 'from my mother's womb', but they came to effect when God enacted his good pleasure **to reveal his Son in me**. Paul undoubtedly had in view here the event of the Damascus road, which he describes elsewhere in terms of 'seeing' Christ, or of Christ's 'appearing' to him (1 Cor. ix.1; xv.8; cf. 2 Cor. iv.6 – 'the face of Jesus Christ'). Here he describes it as an act of 'revelation', as an unveiling of the heavenly reality which is Christ as God's Son 'raised from the dead' (see further on i.12). This ties in with the records in Acts of Paul's seeing the exalted Christ as a 'heavenly vision' (Acts xxvi.19); that there was an auditory as well as visual identification of the exalted Christ (the most constant element in all three Acts accounts) is not excluded by what Paul says here. At the same time he says 'in me', which presumably indicates Paul's awareness of the subjectivity of such a vision (however 'objective' the reality thus seen). Several argue that the phrase should be read as equivalent to the dative – 'to me' (e.g. BDF §220(1); RSV, GNB), but when Paul wanted to use a dative with the verb 'reveal' he did so (1 Cor. ii.10; xiv.30; Phil. iii.15). The implication is rather that he wished at this point to express the personal transformation effected by this revelation from heaven (cf. 2 Cor. iv.6 – 'in our hearts'; Gal. ii.20 – 'Christ in me') (see further my *Jesus* 104–7), but as a transformation not so much of person as of purpose and commitment (no longer 'to destroy the church', but now 'to preach Christ among the Gentiles'); hence, presumably, REB's 'in and through me'.

Sonship is one of the principal motifs of this letter – 'son(s) of God' (i.16; ii.20; iii.26; iv.4, 6–7) and 'sons/seed of Abraham' (iii.7, 16, 19, 29; iv.22, 30). The question in effect was how the two were related. Could one be a son of God only if one was a son of Abraham? Paul's answer would be that only in and through Christ, *the* seed of Abraham (iii.16), *the* Son of God (iv.4), could others benefit from and participate effectively in the relationships thus denoted (iii.29; iv.6–7). Here the first reference to Christ's sonship presupposes that his relation to God had a unique character which marked it off from other relationships with God where the same imagery of sonship was quite common and acceptable – whether of angels or of kings, of Israel as a whole or of the righteous within Israel (e.g. Job i.6; ii.1; Ps. lxxxix.26–7; Jer. xxxi.9; Wisd. Sol. ii.13, 16, 18; see also on iii.26 and further *TDNT* viii.335–62 and my *Christology* 14–15). It is not the case that divine sonship was seen as something quite unique in reference to a human being, and that the application of such language to Jesus was what gave him that unique status. On the contrary, it appears to have been the particular appropriateness of this more diffuse metaphor to the distinctive ministry, death and resurrection of Jesus which resulted over the course of time in its being accorded to him in a unique and qualitatively distinct degree. That this process was already well under way is indicated here by Paul's talk of Christ simply as 'his (God's) Son', with no further qualification or description needed. The stimulus for this 'take over' of such a more general category was probably given in the memory of Jesus' own characteristic prayer language (see on iv.6) and in the already established association of the royal Messiah as God's Son (2 Sam. vii.14; Ps. ii.7; 1QSa ii.11–12; 4QFlor. i.10ff.; 4QpsDan A^a=4Q246; Mark xiv.58–61) (see further my *Romans* 12; and on iv.4).

The objective of this 'revelation of God's Son' was **that I might preach him among the Gentiles**. For the verb see on i.8. The word translated 'Gentiles' means 'nations, peoples' (=Latin, *gentes* or *gentiles*). But it was quite common in Greek to speak of 'the nations' meaning 'the other nations' (BAGD, *ethnos* 2), and so it was the natural translation for the Hebrew *goyim*, commonly used in the OT to denote nations other than Israel. Hence also in the NT it can easily be taken for granted that 'the nations' are distinct from 'the Jews' (as e.g. in Acts xiv.5; xxi.11, 21; Rom. iii.29; ix.24; 1 Cor. i.23; Gal. ii.15), so that 'the Gentiles' is the appropriate translation (see also *TDNT* ii.367–72).

There are several features of Paul's claim here which were bound to strike his audiences, as he no doubt intended. (1) The characterization of his Damascus-road encounter as a commissioning to preach. Paul did not think in his case of a conversion, followed by a period of preparation, followed by a different and distinct commissioning to mission; that, in fact, would probably be closer to the views of some of Paul's opponents, which may, once again, be reflected in Acts (xxii.12–21). Paul's argument, however, runs in quite the opposite direction (as the 'immediately' of verse 16 confirms): the force of the syntax is that the revelation of Christ had no other purpose than this preaching; he does not think of a 'conversion', *only* of a commissioning. The point is no doubt polemically oriented (i.1, 11–12), but it accords with Paul's understanding of all believers as baptized into the body of Christ to be functioning members (1 Cor. xii.12–27): baptism is also vocation; initiation is also ordination.

(2) More to the point here, it was a commissioning to preach Christ *among the Gentiles*, that is, the nations other than Israel; though the formulation does not exclude Paul's preaching to other than Gentiles, the thought is not of a commission to a delimited area but of a commission freed from previous limitations. This was clearly integral to Paul's sense of apostleship (Rom. i.5; xi.13; xv.15–16; Gal. ii.7–9; also Eph. iii.7–9) and cannot be separated from it, so that we may regard it as implicit also in 1 Cor. ix.1–2 and xv.8–10. According to Paul, this was his conviction *from the first*, or at least he had no doubts in tracing it back to that initial encounter (so also consistently in the three Acts accounts of his conversion – Acts ix, xxii, xxvi). Indeed, apart from seeing Christ himself, this was for Paul the main point of and *reason for* the revelation of Christ to him – 'in order that I might preach him among the Gentiles'.[1]

The significance of this becomes more evident when we recall Paul's description of his previous way of life in Judaism (i.13–14), where we saw clearly implicit the zealous concern to maintain Judaism in its distinctiveness against Hellenistic/Gentile encroachment and to defend the purity of its self-identity and the integrity of its boundaries with the sword if necessary. Central to his conversion, properly speaking, therefore, was this change in his perception regarding the Gentiles in God's purpose and the resulting transformation of his previous 'us-and-them' (Jews and Gentiles) attitude. The Gentiles from being outsiders, 'strangers to the covenants of promise, having no hope and without God in the world' (Eph. ii.12), had moved to the centre of God's purpose. So that all the previous effort to maintain 'the assembly of God' as something distinct and separated from the Gentiles by definition had now to be abandoned. If we may speculate further, we may presume that the language and vision of Isa. xlix.1–6, already echoed in verse 15, played a part – 'I will give you as a light to the nations, that my salvation may reach to the end of the earth' (xlix.6; alluded to at the climax of the third account of Paul's conversion, in Acts xxvi.23, and quoted by Paul and Barnabas in Acts xiii.47). The 'revelation of Jesus Christ' meant that with Christ's resurrection the new age of eschatological hope had dawned, which in turn meant that the climactic phase of God's purpose for the Gentiles (as well as for Israel) had also begun (cf. Rom. xi.13–15; xv.19; 1 Cor. iv.9), and that old priorities simply had to be revised accordingly.

---

1 Paul's emphasis thus runs directly counter to Watson's thesis that 'the presupposition of Paul's mission to the Gentiles was that the Jewish people as a whole had been hardened by God, so that preaching to them was useless' (p. 53).

(3) In the same connection, the fact that Christ was the content both of the 'revelation' to Paul and of Paul's consequent preaching is bound to be significant – 'to reveal his Son in me in order that I might preach him among the Gentiles'. The implication clearly is that it was a new perception of Christ which made the transformation (from zealot within Judaism to 'apostle to the Gentiles') both possible and necessary. This is also implicit in the important motif of sonship noted above: Christ as the one who eliminates the boundary between 'sons of Abraham'/'sons of God' and 'Gentiles', so that the boundary no longer exists for those 'in Christ' (v.6), for those who belong to him (iii.29). Just how 'the revelation of Jesus Christ' brought this home to Paul is not immediately clear, but we may infer that it was not only the eschatological implications which struck Paul down, but also the recognition that God had acknowledged as indeed his Son the very one whom the law had consigned, like the Gentiles, to the status of an outsider. This is different from the oversystematized claim that Paul's conversion was itself his choice between the Either-or of the law or Christ (see e.g. those cited in Mussner 85–6, n. 42; but on both the above points see my 'Light', and further on iii.13). That Christ is the content of the gospel is a characteristic Pauline emphasis (Rom. i.3–4, 9; xv.19; 1 Cor. i.23; ii.2; 2 Cor. i.19; Gal. iii.1; Phil. i.15, 27; 1 Thess. iii.2; see also on i.2, ii.2 and iv.14).

But Paul was not finished. It was precisely this claim regarding his 'gospel to the Gentiles' which he thought necessary to defend against the imputations that apostolic authority had to be transmitted or validated through human channels (i.1, 11–12). So he continues, in an unbroken sentence which shows how tightly tied together in his thinking were the several points being made in these verses: **I did not consult immediately with flesh and blood**. The point is obscure until we realize the significance of the verb used. For it evidently had a technical meaning of consulting with someone who was recognized as a qualified interpreter about the significance of some sign – a dream, or omen, or portent, or whatever. For example, Diodorus Siculus relates an odd incident from the life of Alexander and goes on to tell how he 'consulted with the seers regarding the sign' (xvii.116.4 – further details in my 'Relationship' 109–10). So the force of the word is not simply 'consult', but 'consult in order to be given a skilled or authoritative interpretation'.

The implication which Paul must have intended, therefore, is that he did not consider it necessary to go to anyone else to be told what the 'revelation of Jesus Christ' meant; its significance was clear enough in itself – its significance, in particular, as a commissioning to preach Christ and the gospel concerning Christ to the Gentiles. This understanding of the gospel was given him directly by God, and did not require ratification by any human being; 'flesh and blood' being chosen obviously, as in Matt. xvi.17, to contrast with God-given revelation (cf. *TDNT* vii.124, 128). Perhaps the other missionaries in Galatia would not have regarded an authority stemming from Damascus very highly themselves, so that no more specific rebuttal was required by Paul. The obvious tie-in here with i.1, 11–12 is sufficient confirmation that it was Paul's understanding of Christ and the gospel as *for the Gentiles* which was the main bone of contention between Paul and those now challenging his authority. To be noted also is the fact that the word 'immediately' is in a place of emphasis, so indeed as to govern all three of the clauses following ('immediately I did not . . . nor did I . . . but I . . .'). It was *not* the case that gaining such an authoritative interpretation from others was first priority for him, or that he was unable to act upon the revelation of Christ until such an interpretation had been given. The Acts accounts are not at odds with Galatians here since they make no claim that Paul was instructed by Ananias or the Damascus believers.

17 The disclaimer continues: **nor did I go up** (immediately) **to Jerusalem to those who were apostles before me**. The point is the same. Paul is presumably responding to some report or suggestion that he had received the gospel from the Jerusalem apostles. Of all who might have claim to be able to provide an authoritative interpretation of 'the revelation of Jesus Christ', the apostles in Jerusalem certainly had the best. Who precisely these 'apostles' were is not immediately clear. Paul will certainly have meant Peter and presumably the rest of 'the twelve', who together headed the list of witnesses of the resurrected Christ which Paul 'received', presumably at or immediately after his acceptance into the new movement (1 Cor. xv.3, 5), and who therefore must have been counted the primary authorities for the 'resurrection appearances'. Whether Paul also included 'all the apostles', whose appearance-commissioning certainly preceded his (1 Cor. xv.7–8), is less clear. The implication of the word's earliest use is that integral to the concept of 'apostle' was the idea of being sent out on some mission (see on i.1). But here Paul has in view the apostles in Jerusalem, and the thought of representation is more to the fore (the one sent going with the authority to represent the sender). The nuances here are important for our grasp of Paul's argument: he acknowledges that the apostles in Jerusalem had, inevitably, a pre-eminent claim to represent and thus to speak for Christ – this much he concedes to his Galatian critics; but the point he really makes is that he did *not* consult their authority – since the God-given meaning of the revelation to him was clear in itself he did not need to depend on those whose apostleship took precedence over his (the prepositional phrase, 'before me', could have this overtone too).

Such nuances suggest that Paul was conscious of the danger of resting his authority in what others could regard as a delusion, 'visions wrought by demons' (*Clem. Hom.* xvii.16.6). This is presumably part of the explanation for the somewhat curious dialectic which is such a feature of Paul's description of his relationships with the leadership of the Jerusalem church throughout these two chapters – the dialectic between acknowledging their authority and maintaining his own independence of that authority (see also Introduction §2). It was evidently important to him to acknowledge that authority, for in the event they had exercised that authority in his favour: they had ratified his gospel (ii.1–10); and that ratification was crucial both to his own understanding of Jerusalem as the symbolic focus of the gospel (iv.26), and to the success of his own mission (see on ii.2). But they were not the source of his gospel, and having once ratified it (ii.1–10), they or their emissaries could not now deny it (see further my 'Relationship'). Such was the narrow tightrope on which Paul walked between maintaining the unity of the Christian churches and the freedom of the gospel.

Instead of immediately looking for some authoritative ruling regarding 'the revelation of Christ' to him, Paul **went away into Arabia**. Both where he went and the reason why are unclear and the subject of some dispute. The word ('Arabia') itself could refer to anywhere west of Mesopotamia, east and south of Syria and Palestine, including the isthmus of Suez (cf. iv.25 – the Sinai peninsula). But the proximity to Damascus (implied by the next clause) points most naturally to the kingdom of Nabatea, immediately to the south of Damascus; and this fits best with our other evidence, including the reference in 2 Cor. xi.32 to King Aretas who would be the Nabatean king Aretas IV (see fuller details in BAGD, *Arabia*; Betz, *Galatians* 73–4; the precise limits of Nabatean rule during this period are unclear – see Schürer i.578–82).

More difficult to resolve is the question why Paul went there. It should not be assumed that 'Arabia' meant for Paul desert or semi-desert land. To be sure, some parallel with the tradition of Jesus' forty days in the wilderness is inviting. It would accord with the much more widely attested practice in the history of religions of a period of withdrawal into an uninhabited region, following a revelatory or visionary experience, in preparation for some prophet-like or shamanistic role. And the psychological need for such a 'retreat' and reconstruction of his theology can well be imagined (see especially Burton 55–7 and Duncan 29–30). It would also fit Paul's emphasis throughout this passage on the independence of his calling from all human resource – 'I did not consult with flesh and blood but went away into Arabia' (Lightfoot 90). But at this time Arabia/Nabatea was a prosperous region with a number of large cities, probably including at least some of the Decapolis, so that it is also quite possible that Paul went to Arabia 'in order to preach Christ among the Gentiles' (so e.g. Bornkamm, *Paul* 27; Betz 73–4; Barrett, *Freedom* 8). This too would have served Paul's purpose in his statement of defence: the implication being that the gospel preached by him was thus firmly established from the first (cf. Acts ix.20). However, Paul has left the point unclear and further clarity is not possible. It is idle, for example, to speculate whether his silence on the success (or otherwise) of this earliest mission indicates a relative failure on his part, causing some re-evaluation of his mission and gospel. The only point Paul chooses to make is that his time in Arabia further underlines his independence from the Jerusalem leadership; in Arabia there was no one whom he could consult ('The meaning is: he was in Arabia and consequently not in Jerusalem' – Linton 84). And with that we must be content.

Following an unspecified period in Arabia Paul **returned again to Damascus**. Paul has given no indication of the intervals of time at this point, since that information was irrelevant to his main concern (his relationship with Jerusalem). The talk of 'return' to Damascus clearly implies that the initial period following his conversion was spent in that city; though if the 'immediately' of verse 16 does govern the previous clause, he cannot have spent long there before going off to Arabia. But presumably he was there long enough to be baptized and received into the church in Damascus (cf. Rom. vi.3–4; 1 Cor. xii.13; otherwise Taylor). All this is sufficient confirmation of the basic outline of Paul's conversion itself as given by Luke (Acts ix.3–19). Nor do we know how long he spent in Arabia before his return to Damascus; it could have been quite a short period; the aorist tense probably excludes any implication of repeated visits to Arabia, using Damascus as a base. To put the same point from the other angle, we do not know how much of the three years between his calling and his first visit to Jerusalem (i.18) was spent in Damascus itself; it could have been the bulk of the three-year period. If we add in the evidence, once again, of

2 Cor. xi.32–3, it would appear that Paul's activities were sufficient to cause unrest in Damascus, presumably among the large Jewish community primarily (cf. Acts xviii.12–17; Suetonius, *Claudius* xxv.4; Josephus, *War* ii.559–61), to such an extent that his liberty (or life) was in danger and he had to make a humiliating escape. This again makes quite a plausible 'fit' with Acts ix.23–5 and strengthens the case for the latter's historical value. But of this Paul says nothing, since, once again, it was not relevant to the primary purpose of defending his gospel. For further details on Damascus see Schürer ii.127–30.

4 PAUL'S FIRST VISIT TO JERUSALEM i.18–20

(18) Then, after three years, I did go up to Jerusalem to get to know Cephas,[1] and I stayed with him fifteen days. (19) Other of the other apostles I did not see, but only James the Lord's brother. (20) What I write to you, please note, before God, I am not lying.

18 Paul was evidently concerned to give an orderly account of his *cursus vitae*. So having described the earliest phase of his adult life as a zealous Pharisee (i.13–14), and his commissioning, its independence from Jerusalem and its immediate sequel (i.15–17), he begins to describe his actual relationship with Jerusalem. **Then** in verse 18 is the first of three (i.18, 21; ii.1), which are obviously intended to mark out in chronological sequence the most relevant events which followed his encounter with the risen Christ and his time in Arabia and Damascus; though most think that Paul reckoned the three years from the Damascus-road encounter itself.

After three years is expressed in the normal Greek idiom (BAGD, *meta* B.II). It could denote an interval of fully three years; but since the year from which counting began would be reckoned as the first year, the period could be anything from not much over two years. To be sure, Paul was evidently anxious to record the different stages of his relationship with Jerusalem with some care, lest there be any possibility of misunderstanding.

---

1 The Aramaic 'Cephas' is read by the most important witnesses, but the more familiar 'Peter' was evidently substituted at some stage and became the established reading of later manuscripts.

However, the point would be sufficiently safeguarded so long as there had been a substantial gap between the 'revelation of Jesus Christ' and his first visit to Jerusalem (contrast the 'immediately' of verse 16). And however lengthy the period denoted, 'after three years' provided a sufficient time buffer. The point, which is clearly implicit, is that Paul's understanding of the revelation of Christ, 'to preach him among the Gentiles', was already firmly established before he ever went near Jerusalem. Paul's recollection fits not too uncomfortably with the account of Acts ix.23–6 at this point, since Acts ix.23 speaks of Paul's spending 'many days' in Damascus. Depending on the other dates which we can fix within a limit of two or three years, Paul was looking back here to a period probably some time between 35 and 38 (see also Introduction §4).

The main part of the principal clause could be translated simply 'I went up to Jerusalem' (the words are exactly the same as in verse 17). But the emphatic denial of verse 17 ('I did *not* go up to Jerusalem'), the fact that two of the 'then' conjunctions refer to visits to Jerusalem (i.18; ii.1), and the disclaimer of i.22 ('I was not personally known to the churches of Judea'), all make it clear that it was his relationship with Jerusalem and the Jerusalem leadership in particular (i.18–19; ii.2, 6–9) which was Paul's primary concern. In a c.v. extending over probably as much as seventeen years (see on ii.1), he passes over the events of the intervals, between commissioning and first Jerusalem visit, and between first and second Jerusalem visit, in order to focus attention on the specific connection with Jerusalem. Hence the translation, 'After three years **I did go up to Jerusalem**'. The reason for this sustained and narrow focus within Paul's c.v. must be that his relationship with Jerusalem and the Jerusalem leadership had become a matter of some controversy among his Galatian readers. And when we add in the disclaimers of i.1, 11–12 (the thematic statement heading this whole section), and i.16–17, the only obvious deduction is that what was at issue in the controversy was the independence of Paul's apostleship and gospel. Evidently there were those in Galatia who were claiming that Paul's apostleship did come through human beings, and that his understanding of the revelation of Christ must have been provided or at the very least validated by the Jerusalem apostles – with the obvious corollary, that Paul should continue to acknowledge Jerusalem's continuing authority on any points at which Paul's current preaching was distinctive. Paul's response is that his gospel to them is the gospel he received on the Damascus road, established by divine revelation well before he made direct contact with Jerusalem.

It follows that Paul would have taken great care in his choice of language to describe this first crucial visit to Jerusalem. And so we find: 'I went up to Jerusalem **to get to know Cephas'** – using a verb which occurs only here in the NT. The precise weight of the verb is in some dispute, a dispute reflected in the current translations – 'visit' (RSV, JB), 'meet' (NJB), 'get to know' (NEB/REB), 'get acquainted with' (NIV), 'obtain information from' (GNB). The basic meaning is 'to inquire into, or about, or from' (LSJ, *historeō*) (so e.g. Herodotus ii.19; iii.77; Polybius iii.48.12; Plutarch, *Moralia* 516C; cf. 1 Esd. i.33, 42 – 'report'). And though the sense can be eroded towards that of a traveller's mere 'sight-seeing' (MM), the element of 'inquiry' in the 'visit' is usually hard to exclude (e.g. Josephus, *Ant.* i.203). And when the object is personal it is equally hard to exclude the idea of a getting to know which includes getting to know *about*, a knowledge which enables an informed opinion or judgement about the person and his significance (Josephus, *War* vi.81; *Ant.* viii.46) (see more fully my 'Relationship' and 'Gal. i.18'; BAGD, *historeō* – 'visit for the purpose of coming to know someone or something').

Paul was evidently concerned neither to claim too much nor to deny too little. He did not wish to be understood as admitting that he had gone up to Jerusalem, however laggardly, in order to be instructed by Peter on the meaning of the revelation and commissioning given him on the Damascus road. He avoided any word which might be taken to mean that he had been commissioned by Peter or that Peter was the real source or authority for his gospel to the Gentiles. He went up as an equal, an apostle like Peter, to make his acquaintance. At the same time he had already acknowledged that the Jerusalem apostles had been appointed 'before him' (i.17), his singling out Peter constitutes an acknowledgment of his key position, and he had every interest in maintaining the continuity of his gospel with his fellow apostles (as implied by the very talk of a recognized 'gospel' and the echo of already traditional formulae in i.1 and 4). The word 'get to know' therefore served his purpose well: it put the emphasis on the development of a personal relationship with Peter; and it implied that getting to know Peter would have included learning about Peter what made him so important for the first Christians, including no doubt his time as one of Jesus' first disciples. Certainly the implication of the next clause – **and I stayed with him fifteen days** – must be that the 'getting to know' was extensive, especially as it is followed by a firm denial that during this period he saw any of the other apostles (i.19). It is true that the 'fifteen days' is set over against the 'three years' of the previous period; even so, the point is that it was long enough to get to know Peter well, but not long enough to be thoroughly instructed in his new faith. It is no abuse of historical imagination to envisage many hours of conversation between Cephas and Paul during the fortnight (both part days at either end of the period of the visit are included to make 'fifteen' – BAGD, *deka*) when Paul was Peter's guest.

Some commentators, however, prefer to press for the weakest possible sense of the verb ('visit'), since otherwise they cannot make sense of Paul's insistence on the independence of his gospel (i.11–12) (e.g. Betz 76, n. 196). But Paul elsewhere does freely acknowledge his dependence on the traditions which he received from others, including kerygmatic formulae (particularly 1 Cor. xv.1ff). Unless we are prepared, therefore, to accuse him of a blatant twisting of the facts, we must allow that his early encounters with those in the new movement before him had a fairly substantive level of 'information content', to supplement or correct the picture he had gained as a persecutor. The word 'get to know' strikes just the right balance. It makes no concession on the chief point of Paul's concern – that the understanding of the gospel given him in the 'revelation of Christ' was validated by the direct authority of heaven. But it acknowledges that his getting to know Peter would, of course, have helped fill him in on such matters as background to the beginnings of the movement with which Paul had now identified himself, supplementary information about Jesus and particular formulae in which the gospel was already being framed.

The use of the Aramaic 'Cephas' here rather than the Greek 'Peter' (see p. 71 n. 1) may be significant. This is the name Paul normally uses for Peter (ii.9, 11, 14; as well as 1 Cor. i.12; iii.22; ix.5; xv.5; 'Peter' only in Gal. ii.7–8; for bibliography see Betz 77; for Aramaic usage see Bruce 98); the name 'Peter' itself was not known in Greek (BAGD, *Petros*). It is possible, however, that he preferred the Aramaic form as a gentle acknowledgement of Peter's status within the Jewish-Christian congregations, as the one named 'the rock' by Jesus (Mark iii.16 pars). And he may have preferred the Aramaic form also because it symbolized Peter's commitment to take the gospel to Jews (ii.7–8), just as Paul's switch from the Hebrew 'Saul' to the Greek 'Paul' may have symbolized his commitment to the Gentiles (see on i.1).

19 Paul's apologetic concern is even more evident as he continues – **Other of the apostles I did not see**. As to who 'the apostles' were, see on i.17; presumably the twelve were included. Once again the negative formulation has the ring of a denial –

that is, presumably, of a claim or interpretation of Paul's visit to Jerusalem which was being put about in Galatia (cf. i.1, 7, 11–12, 16–17). Once again the inference would have been that Paul's time in Jerusalem was when he received the authoritative version of the gospel and the validation of his apostleship from those who were apostles before him. And once again Acts ix.27 seems closer to the account which Paul was evidently anxious to deny. In this connection the choice of verb here will again be significant – 'to see' being a much less weighty word than 'to get to know'. It is precisely the connotations of learning about and from, so hard to escape in the latter, which are quite lacking in the former: he 'got to know' Peter; he did not even 'see' any of the other Jerusalem apostles. He does not say why, but one plausible inference could be that as 'apostles' they may have been absent from Jerusalem on mission (ministering perhaps among 'the churches of Judea'); or were they simply fearful of Paul (Acts ix.26)? or was it Paul who was fearful of retribution from his previous colleagues and kept out of sight (cf. Acts ix.29)? or since Paul had just come from a Hellenist congregation (Damascus) is there an indication here of some of the tension between 'Hebrews' and 'Hellenists' (Acts vi.1) which Stephen's work and martyrdom may have aggravated? Bruce 104 suggests that the other apostles may not yet have returned to Jerusalem because of the persecution; but the indications are that Paul himself was the main instigator of the persecution (cf. i.23; Acts viii.1–3; ix.1), so that it may well have slackened following Paul's own about-face. Alternatively, Paul's language may indicate not so much their absence as Paul's lack of interest in them (Mussner 95).

There was only one qualification necessary: he saw none of the other apostles, **but only James the Lord's brother**. Jesus is called simply 'the Lord' in a way which shows that the title had become completely natural to Paul and his fellow Christians (see on i.3). It would appear that James was the eldest of Jesus' brothers (named first in the list of Mark vi.3). That could mean the elder brother of Jesus (son of Joseph by a previous marriage), or, more likely, the eldest after Jesus (by Joseph and Mary) – there being no hint anywhere in the NT that James and the others mentioned in Mark vi.3 were anything other than full brothers of Jesus. The implication of what is said about him during Jesus' ministry is that he was unsympathetic to what Jesus was doing (Mark iii.21, 31–5; John vii.5). But his inclusion among the first witnesses of the resurrection (1 Cor. xv.7), and among the early disciples after Easter (Acts i.13), is usually taken to mean that he was won to discipleship either by or in connection with that appearance of his brother risen from the dead. He is not mentioned again in Acts till xii.17, the implication being that he was then a leading member of the Jerusalem church, perhaps the leading member in Peter's absence.

By the time of his next appearance in our records (Gal. ii.9 and/or Acts xv.13) James is clearly understood to be the leader of the Jerusalem church, being named ahead of Peter (Gal. ii.9), and given the decisive summing-up speech at the Jerusalem council (Acts xv.13–21). Thereafter there is no question as to his being at the peak of the Jerusalem leadership (Gal. ii.12; Acts xxi.18; Josephus, *Ant.* xx.200; Eusebius, *E.H.* II.i.2–5; xxiii; VII.xix), probably on the model of the 'ruler of the synagogue', and in anticipation of the subsequent emergence of the monarchical episcopate (James is regarded as 'bishop' in the pseudo-Clementine literature – *Epistula Petri* i.1; *Recognitions* i.43). In a middle-eastern society, where the line of inheritance is horizontal (to a brother) rather than vertical (to a son), it is readily understandable that the earliest Jerusalem community should look to 'the brother of the Lord' for leadership. Nevertheless, James must have been a considerable personality, who stamped his authority on the Jerusalem church, and one whose growing status Paul cannot have been unaware of on his first visit to Jerusalem, even though Peter still seems to have been regarded as the principal apostle, to whom Paul naturally devoted his almost exclusive attention. And certainly James would have been regarded very highly by the Galatians, or at least by the incoming missionaries; even the most fleeting of contacts on that first visit, therefore, could not be omitted. (See also on ii.9; for bibliography on James see Betz 79; also R. Bauckham, *Jude and the Relatives of Jesus in the Early Church* [Edinburgh: T. & T. Clark, 1990]).

There is, however, a question as to the status Paul accords to James at this point. The conjunction (*ei mē*) introduces an exception, and should be translated 'except' or 'but only', rather than as a straight contrast ('but') (Lightfoot 76; see the brief discussion in my *JPL* 212). The question is whether the exception relates to the clause as a whole: 'I did not see any of the other apostles (that is other than Cephas), the only one I did see was James'; that is, James is *not* to be counted as one of the 'other apostles'. Or whether the exception relates only to 'other of the apostles': 'I did not see other of the apostles, except James'; that is James was the only other apostle Paul did see. Despite Lightfoot 84–5 (followed by Bruce 101), the issue is not settled on syntactical grounds, since the 'other' can be fully explained by reference back to Cephas, and the same construction in i.7 indicates that the relation of the clauses thus linked need not be precise. Nor is the question resolved by any other NT passage (cf. 1 Cor. ix. 5; xv.7), though Borse 67 notes that the conjunction is used inclusively in 1 Cor. i.14 and Phil. iv.15. Yet, since Paul was laying claim to apostolic status despite his not being one of the twelve, the matter may have been one of greater sensitivity than the text indicates. If, for example, the essence of apostleship for Paul was a missionary commissioning by the risen Christ (i.16 – '. . . reveal his Son in me in order that I might preach . . .'; 1 Cor. ix.1–2; xv.8–11; see on i.1), Paul may have been dubious about calling 'apostle' one who apparently remained centred in Jerusalem throughout his period of leadership. But others might have reckoned apostleship more in terms of representing one absent rather than in terms of going somewhere to do so.

The point however, is that Paul has *not* made himself clear, and may have chosen to be deliberately ambiguous; commentators need to bear this possibility in mind and not force modern readers into an either-or choice of meanings. That is to say, Paul may have wished to drop a hint of doubt regarding the apostleship of James, without being openly discourteous to one whom others did call 'apostle'. This at any rate would chime in with the distancing phrase Paul uses for the Jerusalem leadership in ii.2 and 6 (see on ii.2). It would also fit well into the contrast between Paul's relationship with Cephas during this visit and his relationship with James: he came to Jerusalem in order to get to know Cephas, and stayed with him for a whole fortnight; he only 'saw' James. Does that mean Paul did not share table-fellowship with James during his visit? Or simply that in a church with numerous house groups Paul was involved only with the one led by Peter? The implications for our understanding of the earliest Jerusalem church and its manner of functioning and organization would be fascinating, were we able to tease them out more than is in the event possible.

20 Somewhat surprisingly Paul pauses at this point to give his immediately preceding statements the weight of testimony sworn on oath – regarding **what I write to you, please note, before God, I am not lying**. The last phrase ('I am not lying') on its own has the force of a formula of affirmation (Job vi.28; xxvii.11; Ps. lxxxix.35; *4 Macc.* v.34; Plutarch, *Moralia.* 1059A) (BAGD, *pseudomai*; *TDNT* ix.601); Paul uses it on other occasions (Rom. ix.1; 2 Cor. xi.31; also 1 Tim. ii.7); for the seriousness of lying within the Jewish tradition see *TDNT* ix.598–600. The addition of 'before God' gives the affirmation the force of an oath, indicating that Paul was willing to stake his whole standing before God on the veracity of what he had just written (see further J. P. Sampley, '"Before God, I Do Not Lie" (Gal. i.20): Paul's Self-Defence in the Light of Roman Legal Praxis', *NTS* 23 [1977] 477–82). Most translations make no attempt to translate the Greek word meaning literally, 'Behold!', here rendered not very satisfactorily as 'Please note'. Like the frequently occurring Hebrew *hinneh* in the OT, its purpose is to arouse the attention of the readers and to signal that something important is being said (BAGD, *idou*). The stiltedness of the Greek indicates that Paul's syntax could not fully cope with the strength of his feeling on the point at issue.

The full force of the statement is confirmation that Paul felt the need to defend himself at this point. His version of what had happened on his first visit to Jerusalem was evidently under attack or threat (cf. again Acts ix.27); and Paul must have been aware that his claim to have met only two of the Jerusalem leadership during a fortnight's visit sounded thin. He evidently felt it necessary therefore to insist that the report just given was wholly accurate. He had to convince the Galatians that he had only gone to Jerusalem to get to know Peter and that he had seen no one else of significance (so far as the Galatians were concerned) except James, and that only in passing. The alternative being put about in Galatia can readily be imagined (cf. again 1.1, 11–12, 16–17, 18–19). For a comparison between Gal. i.18–20 and the Acts reports of Paul's first visit to Jerusalem after his conversion see particularly Borse 68–70.

5   BETWEEN VISITS   i.21–4

(21) Then I went off into the territories of Syria and of[1] Cilicia. (22) I continued to be unknown by sight to the churches of Judea which are in Christ. (23) The only thing they kept hearing was that 'Our former persecutor now preaches the faith which once he tried to destroy'. (24) And they used to glorify God because of[2] me.

1 The article before 'Cilicia' is omitted in some manuscripts, probably because 'Syria and Cilicia' formed a natural unit (see on i.21).
2 Literally 'in me'; but *en* can have the force of 'because of, on account of' (BAGD, *en* III.3); perhaps 'with reference to me' (cf. Schlier 63), 'for what had happened to me' (REB).

Having stated the facts about his first visit to Jerusalem as he wanted them understood, Paul moves on to the next phase of his personal history. But since it had little bearing on his present concerns he passes over it with almost indecent speed. Despite its covering some fourteen years (ii.1), a period of very active and successful missionary work (i.23; ii.2, 8), during which Paul's theology and expression of the gospel must have developed significantly in at least some degree, the only thing that interested Paul about it at this point was that throughout it he had been far away from Judea and the Jerusalem leadership. The lack of detail must also indicate that the other Galatian missionaries had made nothing of this period, nothing at least which required rebuttal by Paul.

21 The **Then** indicates once again a concern to provide an orderly record; nothing intervened between his time with Cephas and his trip to the north-east quadrant of the Mediterranean. **I went off into the territories of Syria and Cilicia.** This fits sufficiently closely to Acts ix.30 as to require only a little further discussion. Paul's account does not indicate whether he went to or via Antioch, but he does mention Syria first and since Antioch was the largest city in Syria and seat of the imperial power in the whole region (BAGD, *Antiocheia*) it would have been a logical move; the Acts report of a trip directly to Tarsus may be at least partly determined by the fact that Luke has completed this section of the Paul narrative prior to his account of the establishing of the new movement in Antioch (Acts xi.19ff). However, Paul may have mentioned Syria first simply because of its greater importance in his own work. The two Roman territories adjoined each other (folded round the north-east corner of the Mediterranean), and eastern Cilicia had been united with Syria as a single province administered from Antioch some sixty years earlier (Ramsay 275–8; Bruce 103; the two were quite often mentioned together – BAGD, *Syria*). Given the barrier formed by the Taurus mountains to the north, it was natural that Cilicia should be linked more with Antioch than with the hinterland of Asia Minor. Indeed, the implication of Acts xv.23 (the letter sent to Antioch, Syria and Cilicia) is that Antioch was the base for missionary work in these two adjoining regions. And this also fits with Acts 13.3ff. at least to the extent that it confirms that Antioch provided a strategic centre for expanding missionary work in the regions close by. On the other hand, Paul's account is so much abbreviated that he could simply be using the natural way of speaking of the two regions without implying that he went to one before the other. And if the description covers much or all of the fourteen years (as the tenses of the following verses imply) we could well imagine a period when he was first based in Tarsus at the west end of the Cilician plain, and began evangelistic work in that region, before transferring to Antioch and using it as his base (more or less as Acts xi.25–6 indicates).

The suggestion, most recently by Lüdemann 59–61, that the period included extensive missionary work much further west (Macedonia and Achaia = Paul's so-called 'second missionary journey') can hardly be fitted into the language here without either forcing the sense or implying that Paul was after all, despite his protest, trying to hide something (so rightly, Longenecker 40; also lxxv–lxxvii). On the other hand, it is probable that Paul includes his first missionary journey (more properly so called – Acts xiii–xiv) within this period, including the conversion of many of his readers (see Introduction §6.1), since he could be confident that any personal knowledge of his activities during this period shared by his readers would confirm or, at least, not gainsay the primary claim here made (Paul's independence from Jerusalem). Whatever the work included, however, it was evidently very successful (Gal. ii.7–9).

22 The one point which Paul wanted to make about this lengthy period of his early missionary work was that **I continued to be unknown by sight to the churches of Judea**. The phrase translated 'by sight' means literally 'by face' (dative of respect – BDF §197). Since a person's face was the feature by which he or she could be most easily identified, the 'face' could denote the person's personal presence in both Greek and Hebrew (*TDNT* vi.770–2; in the NT cf. Acts xx.25, 38; Col. ii.1; 1 Thess. ii.17; iii.10). Paul's point is that he was personally unknown to the Judean churches (not just unknown as a Christian), and that he continued to be so throughout the period (the periphrastic verbal form emphasizes duration – BDF §353). Presumably he mentions just these churches not because they were the only churches then established, but because, as the churches of Judea, they could be ranked with the mother church of Jerusalem, as together the oldest assemblies of the new Jesus movement; and quite probably also, because the opposition in Galatia stemmed from there (for the status and extent of Judea see Burton 435–6 and Schürer i.240, 360; ii.13). The implication once again is clear: he could not have been dependent in any way (for his gospel or apostleship) on those who did not even know him personally. The whole narrative is still controlled by the thematic statement in i.11–12. Since Paul must have been 'seen' by at least a few of the (non-leading) Jerusalem believers, 'the churches in Judea' presumably were not intended to include Jerusalem with which he had already dealt (cf. Matt. iii.5; iv.25; John iii.22; Acts x.39; xxvi.20; Josephus, *Ant.* x.184) (for the plural see on i.2).

The verse is quite often used as evidence against the claim by Acts that Paul had been involved in the persecution in Judea following Stephen's martyrdom from the first (Acts viii.1, 3; ix.1) (e.g. Bousset 40–1; Bornkamm, *Paul* 15; Becker 18). Its effectiveness as such evidence depends on a number of assumptions: particularly the assumption that Paul's persecution, if based in Jerusalem, either extended beyond Jerusalem, or that at least some of those whom he persecuted stayed in Judea. So far as the former is concerned, the evidence, such as it is, suggests a Jerusalem-focused persecution (Acts viii.3; xxvi.10), and speaks of a mission beyond Jerusalem only in terms of Paul's projected journey to Damascus (ix.1; xxii.4–5) or to 'foreign cities' (xxvi.11). As for the latter, Acts viii.1 does speak of the persecuted Nazarenes being 'scattered throughout Judea . . .'. Paul's primary targets, however, were probably the Greek-speaking Hellenists (cf. Acts ix.29). And it is by no means out of the question that Paul simply assumed that they all fled well beyond Judea (the territory attached to the Temple) where they would be most at risk from those who had been outraged at the Hellenist views of the Temple; this likelihood is given some strength by the account of those who were so scattered (Acts viii.4ff; xi.19ff.) and by the fact that Paul evidently saw the next logical target as Damascus. At the very least we may observe that those churches, who are here cited because an association with them could be invested with as much significance as his trips to Jerusalem itself, were likely to be more traditionally Jewish in their view of the new sect and therefore all the less likely to have been the target of the persecuting zeal Paul described in i.13–14; 'if the Jewish Christians of Judea were obeying the Torah, Paul would have had no reason to persecute them' (Betz 81, n. 234). The testimony of 1 Thess. ii.14–16 may be relevant, but it may equally apply to a period well after Paul's conversion when the Jewish zeal was directed against his own efforts to preach to the Gentiles (ii.16). On the other hand, Acts xxvi.20 ('throughout all the country of Judea') once again looks like the sort of report about Paul's earliest period as a Christian which this verse attempts to counter. That apart, however, it is by no means clear that Gal. i.22 counts against the broad sweep of the narrative of Acts at this point. See also Hengel, *Pre-Christian Paul* 23–4, 72–9; Niebuhr 58–9.

Paul makes a point of adding the descriptive phrase, 'the churches of Judea **which are in Christ**'. The phrase ('in Christ') is one of Paul's favourite phrases, and distinctively his within earliest Christian vocabulary, occurring more than eighty times in the Pauline corpus, and in a wide variety of uses (see e.g. BAGD, *en* I.5d; elsewhere in the NT only 1 Peter). As such it clearly denotes a fundamental perception of Paul's regarding the position of members of the new movement: as a result of their belief in and regarding Jesus as Christ and Lord, they were now 'in Christ' ('in the Lord' is also popular with Paul, but not so common). It is remarkable that 'Christ' could have been so quickly transformed from simply a title ('the Christ' = the Messiah), to serve not only as an identifying name ('Jesus Christ'; see on i.1) but also in such a formula as already a technical term for Paul.

The theological rationale of the phrase is surprisingly hard to unpack. But certainly so far as this letter is concerned, it is the 'in Christ' which marked the difference between Paul's pre-Christian standing ('in Judaism' − i.13−14) and the freedom he now rejoiced in (ii.4, 17), which made it possible for Gentiles to inherit the blessing of Abraham (iii.14), and which rendered insignificant the old distinctions between circumcised and uncircumcised (v.6). It is therefore bound up with Paul's understanding of Christ as himself transcending that old boundary − as the 'seed of Abraham' so central to the covenant (iii.16, 19), who was also put under the law's curse, outside the covenant (iii.13), and who therefore could represent both Jew and Gentile and provide a transformed definition of what inheritance of the covenant and its promises involved (iii.23−iv.7). In other words, it is difficult to avoid a 'locative' sense for the 'in' (C. F. D. Moule, *The Origin of Christology* [Cambridge University, 1977] 56; see also on iii.27; and further Longenecker 152−4). This also means that Paul replaces one bounded system (Judaism bounded by the law) with another (Christ); not a completely different one (Christ is the seed of Abraham), but one enlarged by relativizing the significance attached to the old boundary markers like circumcision. It is not clear from Galatians whether Paul had developed his full Adam christology yet, but certainly in his later letters the 'in Christ' was the answer not only to being 'in the law' (Rom. ii.12; iii.19), but also to being 'in Adam' (1 Cor. xv.22; cf. Rom. v.12−vi.6). Quite how he envisaged Christ's own continuing personal existence is difficult for us to conceptualize, but the experiential note present in so many of his 'in Christ' formulations (see my *Jesus* 324, 326−38) implies at least a shared consciousness of

Christ as a personal accepting presence which formed a primary bond for the first Christians and basis for their fellowship, and Paul himself does not seem to have explored this aspect of the phrase and its theological logic any further. See also on ii.17 and v.6.

In the present passage the phrase could almost be translated 'Christian' (REB – 'the Christian congregations in Judaea'), so much of a Christian identification formula has it become for Paul (cf. e.g. Rom. xvi.7; 2 Cor. xii.2; 1 Thess. iv.16). Elsewhere he does speak of his churches as 'in Christ', though never quite using this formula (cf. 1 Cor. i.2; Phil. i.1; Col. i.2; 1 Thess. i.1; 2 Thess. i.1). But here, as in 1 Thess. ii.14, the closest parallel, the application of the phrase to 'the churches of Judea' may have an added overtone – that their continuity with 'the assembly of Israel' (see on i.2 and i.13) was not their most important or determinative feature, but the fact that they were 'in Christ'. Once again the implication presumably is that it was their relation to Christ which was the key element in their identity, not their Jewishness.

23 The **only** thing ('only' given the place of emphasis) **they kept hearing** (again the periphrastic verbal form indicating that the action of the main verb covered a lengthy period – BDF §353) **was that 'Our former persecutor now preaches the faith which once he tried to destroy'**. Paul was evidently able to quote, or effectively summarize as a quotation what was said of him in the Judean churches during this period; and there is no reason to doubt that such reports did reach him of the surprised reaction among the Judean churches to his about-face and transformation; though to see here 'one of the oldest theological statements of Christianity' (E. Bammel, 'Galater i.23', *ZNW* 59 [1968] 108–12) probably puts more weight on the words than the text indicates. 'Our former persecutor' (literally 'he who persecutes us formerly') indicates an established way of referring to Paul among the churches, ('the persecutor'). Since these were churches which must have missed out on the persecuting activity of Paul (they had never seen him – see on i.22), the nickname ('the persecutor') must have been widespread throughout all the churches. The fact that they called him 'our persecutor' also implies a strong sense of solidarity on the part of those who escaped the worst of the persecution with those members of the new sect who bore its brunt. The nickname also suggests that Paul was the leading persecutor during that earlier period ('the one who persecutes us'). For 'preaches' see on i.8; and for 'tried to destroy' see on i.13.

The description gives us no further help in clarifying the extent of Paul's preaching ministry during this period (see on i.21 and ii.1). At this point Paul is content simply to record the Judean churches' acknowledgement of his preaching ministry: it does not imply that they knew, far less accepted Paul's preaching of a 'law-free gospel', though he would want the Galatians to know that the gospel he preached to them had been acknowledged by the Judean churches as 'preaching the (common) faith'; the question of gospel and law, however, evidently did not come to the fore as an issue for some time (ii.1–14), and Paul would be happy thus to imply that opposition to him and his gospel was relatively recent.

This is the first occurrence of a word which is central to Paul's theology and to the argument of this letter in particular – 'faith' (142 of the 243 references in the NT are in the Pauline corpus, and the 22 references in Galatians mean that, in proportionate terms, Paul makes greater use of it in this letter than anywhere else). Its significance will require fuller treatment later (see on ii.16). Here we should note its objective force – 'the faith' – in some contrast to the regular subjective sense ('faith, trust'). This is remarkable at such an early stage of the Christian movement (see also iii.23–5 and vi.10; but otherwise only later in Jude 3; the other references in BAGD, *pistis* 3 are questionable; cf. *TDNT* vi.213). Such a sense has no immediate parallel either in Paul's Jewish background, where the characteristic usage of the most closely related concept denotes rather 'faithfulness' (see BDB, *'emunah* ; in LXX *pistis* mostly translates *'emunah*), or in the wider Greek usage of the time, which could readily speak of both 'faith' (trust) and 'faithfulness' (LSJ, *pistis*; *TDNT* vi.176–7, 182).

All this strongly suggests that for Paul at least 'faith' had become so characteristic of the new movement to which he now belonged, that it could function as an identity marker, an identification which was sufficiently distinct to denote and define the movement itself – as equally the talk of 'preaching Christ' (2 Cor. i.19; iv.5; Phil. i.15; Gal. i.16). Moreover, it was this 'faith' which Paul had tried to destroy: already at that even earlier period, 'faith' in Messiah Jesus (ii.16) was what marked out the new Jewish sect; and it was precisely this faith, presumably as that which most threatened 'Judaism', which had aroused his persecuting zeal. The implication is that 'faith', in the preaching of many of the Hellenists at least, had already come to be perceived as a significant threat to the traditional identity markers of Judaism by a zealous Jew like Paul (see on i.13–14). How far Paul had already thought through the ramifications of all this at such an early stage is unclear; but his object in this whole section is precisely to demonstrate how these ramifications became clearer for the new movement, and as they became clear became more controversial (ii.1–14; see also on v.22).

24 Paul cannot resist adding, **And they used to glorify God because of me.** 'To glorify God' is to give him the 'reverence' due to his 'glory' (see on i.5; elsewhere in Paul cf. particularly Rom. i.21). In the NT it is a natural reaction to an amazing or unexpectedly good outcome or report (e.g. Mark ii.12; Luke xxiii.47; Acts iv.21; with Acts xi.18 and xxi.20 more immediate parallels). Here Paul is making the not too subtle point that during this lengthy fourteen-year period (the tense is past continuous), the only response the churches of Judea made to his work as a missionary was to praise God for him! Also implied, once again, is the fact of an established missionary work, independent of Jerusalem, and yet thus acknowledged by the mother churches.

6   THE CONSULTATION AT JERUSALEM ii.1–10

(1) Then after fourteen years I travelled up once again to Jerusalem with Barnabas, taking Titus also with me. (2) I travelled up in accordance with a revelation. And I laid before them the gospel which I proclaim among the Gentiles, but privately to those held in repute, lest somehow I was running or had run in vain. (3) But not even Titus who was with me, though a Greek, was compelled to be circumcised. (4) But because of the false brothers smuggled in, who sneaked in to spy on our freedom which we have in Christ Jesus, in order that they might enslave us, (5) to them[1] not

---

1 'To them' has been omitted by a scatter of witnesses, to reduce the awkwardness of the wording (anacoluthon). Translators today still have the same problem: whether to reflect the awkwardness of the Greek at such a point (as RSV and NJB) or to smooth it over (as rather effectively by NEB/REB and GNB).

even[1] for an hour[2] did we yield submission, in order that the truth of the gospel might remain for you. (6) But from those reputed to be something – what they once were makes no difference to me, God shows no partiality – for to me those of repute added nothing. (7) But on the contrary, when they saw that I had been entrusted with the gospel for the uncircumcision, as Peter with the gospel for the circumcision, (8) for he who worked with Peter for the apostleship of the circumcision worked also with me for the Gentiles, (9) and recognized the grace given to me, James, Cephas[3] and John, those reputed to be pillars, gave to me and Barnabas the right hand of fellowship, in order that we should be for the Gentiles, and they for the circumcision; (10) with the one qualification that we should remember the poor, the very thing which I have eagerly done.

Paul could skate over the intervening years very quickly (i.21–4) because they had been spent far away from Jerusalem, with no contact, beyond the third-hand reports of his exploits which had circulated among the churches of Judea. Even his earlier visit to Jerusalem could be passed over briefly (i.18–20) since it had been so inconsequential for the matter of present moment – he was prepared to swear to that. But now the pace slows. Paul begins to go into more detail. His second visit to Jerusalem was obviously of greater importance. His narrative testimony is about to reach a

1 'Not even', sometimes the whole phrase ('to them not even'), has been omitted by a number of Western witnesses, but only the one major Greek MS (D). The most obvious reason is the recognition on the part of some Western scribe(s) of a possible contradiction. Acts xvi.3 reports that Paul did circumcise Timothy; so, on the basis of his own stated policy of accommodation (1 Cor. ix.20–3), it would be natural to assume that Paul *had* circumcised Titus. Such an admission, however, would be completely contrary to the tone and thrust of the language Paul uses here. Besides which, the fuller text is read by the great majority of witnesses, including all the most important Greek MSS apart from D (Metzger 591–2; Bruce 114–15).

2 Since the hour was the smallest serviceable unit of time (twelve hours of daylight and of dark), 'not even for an hour' could be expressed today as 'not for one moment' (NJB, NEB/REB, NIV); cf. John v.35 and 2 Cor. vii.8. But the more literal translation helps underline the implication that the confrontation was more drawn out with Paul under sustained pressure, an implication which could be obscured by the more idiomatic translation.

3 Several, mainly Western witnesses, read 'Peter' instead of 'Cephas', indicating that for them 'Peter' had become the established name, rather than 'Cephas' as for Paul. Most of them also read 'Peter, James and John', presumably on the assumption that this was the regular threesome of the Gospels (Mark v.37; ix.2; etc.), and failing to recognize that the 'James' must be 'James, the Lord's brother' (i.19; see also above p. 71 n. 1 and on ii.9).

critical juncture (as was recognized by those who made the chapter division at this point). But his theme is still the same: 'a gospel not of human origin or from a human being' (i.11–12).

1 Once again the **Then** indicates a careful sequential record; nothing of significance for the defence being offered has been omitted. The time span was no less than **after fourteen years,** again using a regular Greek construction to indicate an interval of time (BAGD, *dia* II.2). Here again it has to be remembered that the year on which counting began would be included in the calculation (and with the *dia* formula probably also the final year), so the gap Paul had in mind would be something over twelve years. Paul does not make it clear whether he began his counting from the Damascus-road revelation (the previous 'after three years' included within the fourteen), or from the previous visit to Jerusalem ('after three years' *plus* 'after fourteen years'; so most), or from his time in Syria and Cilicia (3 + ? + 14). The *dia* makes the second most probable, as denoting the period *through* and so beyond which he had been absent from Jerusalem. But uncertainty on this point cannot be wholly removed and makes calculation of Pauline chronology very imprecise. The gap between Paul's conversion-commission and the Jerusalem consultation could be anything from something over twelve to nearly a full seventeen years or even more. Added to the uncertainty of the date of Jesus' crucifixion and our ignorance as to the gap between that and Paul's conversion-commission, the date now in view could be anything from the early 40s to the early 50s. Despite Borse's recent advocacy (pp. 74, 76), the 'fourteen years' here most probably has nothing to do with the 'fourteen years' of 2 Cor. xii.2: Paul was no stranger to 'revelations' (2 Cor. xii.7); the content was quite different; and the early dating for the second Jerusalem journey thereby entailed (43 AD – Borse) lies towards the less probable end of the possible timescale (see also Bruce 107).

I travelled up once again to Jerusalem – presumably from Antioch. This is Paul's second visit since the Damascus-road revelation. The debate as to how Paul's account here squares with the record in Acts continues unabated and produces no new evidence or arguments. There is no need therefore to review it at length and reference can be made to fuller discussions, for example in Borse 93–100 and Fung 9–28 (bibliography in Betz 83). The problem can be simply stated. According to Acts, Paul's *second* visit took place at an unspecified date in order to deliver famine relief from the church of Antioch to the church in Jerusalem (Acts xi.29–30). But also according to Acts the *issue* discussed in the visit of Gal. ii.1–10 was not discussed until a third visit, again from Antioch as the base (Acts xv.2–29). The problem thus posed has found two major resolutions.

(1) Bruce 43–56 and Longenecker lxxvii–lxxxiii are the most prominent current proponents of the first alternative: that the Gal. ii visit is the same as the Acts xi visit (Gal. ii = Acts xi). The decisive consideration in this case is the basic reliability of the Acts record. This can be maintained since Acts also speaks of Paul (Saul) as going up to Jerusalem with Barnabas (Acts xi.30; cf. Gal. ii.1), and since Gal. ii speaks of the discussion with the Jerusalem leadership as 'private' – that is, unlike the public debate of Acts xv. But it points almost inexorably to the conclusion that Galatians was written *before* the Acts xv council (making it the earliest of Paul's letters), and suggests the likelihood that the council was called to resolve the issue raised at Antioch (Gal. ii.11–14). The problem with this is that if the issue of circumcision was resolved as decisively as Gal. ii.1–10 indicates, with the full and formal approval of the Jerusalem leadership (ii.3, 6–9) in the face of strong internal pressure to the contrary (ii.4–5), it is difficult to see how it could have become an issue once again in Acts xv. In order to preserve Luke's reliability it seems necessary to impugn the good faith of the Jerusalem leadership.

(2) The majority of commentators favour the second alternative: that the Gal. ii visit is the same as the Acts xv visit (Gal. ii = Acts xv). The decisive consideration is that the central issue, key participants and principal agreement are so close that the two accounts must be variant versions of the same episode (see further e.g. Schlier 115–16). Most of the variant details can be accounted for in terms of the different perspectives of Luke and Paul in their writings. This also allows a later date for Galatians, subsequent to the Thessalonian epistles which show little evidence of the theological concerns which came to the fore in Paul's theology with Galatians (see Introduction §6.4). The problem with this view is the degree to which it puts the historicity of Acts in question, not just with regard to the Acts xi visit, but also with regard to the 'apostolic decree' in Acts xv.20, 29. At worst, however, it may be sufficient to allow that Luke has tidied up his account: inserting a tradition of a visit to Jerusalem from Antioch for famine relief, which was not correlated very precisely with other events in the recollection of his informants, and which, inserted at the end of ch. xi, made an effective dramatic link back to Jerusalem; and assuming that the Jerusalem council of Acts xv agreed to a larger compromise package whose formal agreement and implementation came only

later. See also Introduction §§4 and 6; Catchpole; Barrett, *Freedom* 91–108; Hill 107–15.

At all events, our primary concern is to understand Galatians in its own terms, and while the second alternative carries the greater weight, the exegesis of Gal. ii is not greatly affected either way. But points of relevance to the issue will be noted as we proceed.

Paul makes a point of noting that he went up **with Barnabas**. This is the first mention of one who evidently played a major role in earliest Christianity. He is recalled as (probably) the first (significant) landowner in Jerusalem to contribute to the common fund (Acts iv.36–7). As a native of Cyprus (iv.36) he may have belonged to the 'Hellenists' (Greek speakers) of Acts vi.1, which, in view of the problems arising on that front over the distribution from the common fund (vi.1), may indicate a deeper significance in his initial act of generosity than Luke has recounted. He was evidently a conciliatory figure (Luke notes that his name meant 'son of encouragement' – iv.36), who was able to act as intermediary between Hellenists and the Jerusalem leadership (ix.27; xi.22–4). He presumably settled in Antioch where he became an established member of the church's leadership: he was responsible for bringing Saul/Paul from Tarsus to Antioch, according to Acts (xi.25–6), and is subsequently named first among its leadership (Acts xiii.1). It was from there that he and Saul were commissioned as missionaries of the Antioch church and embarked on the 'first missionary journey' (Acts xiii.1–3, 4ff). His association with Paul is equally attested by Paul himself, the implication of the three references in Gal. ii (1, 9, 13) being clearly that he was recognized to be responsible along with Paul for the mission to the uncircumcised. That a breach took place between Paul and Barnabas is attested by Acts xv.36–40 and implied by Gal. ii.13 and its aftermath (see on ii.14); but the implication of 1 Cor. ix.6 and Col. iv.10 is that the breach was not long lasting.

It is no doubt significant that Paul says 'I went up with Barnabas', rather than 'Barnabas and I went up'. The language may reflect the fact of the subsequent breach: Paul was conscious that the criticisms he had to meet among the Galatian churches were directed against himself alone, since Barnabas was no longer associated with his missionary work (see again on ii.14). It may also be the case that Paul was attempting to distance himself from his previous association and status: on that second visit he and Barnabas probably went to Jerusalem with the blessing or at the behest of the Antioch church and as spokesmen for the gospel as proclaimed and practised at Antioch. This inference drawn from Galatians is confirmed by *both* of the relevant Acts accounts – Acts xi.30 (Barnabas and Saul sent by the Antioch disciples) and Acts xv.2 (Paul and Barnabas appointed by the Antioch church to go to Jerusalem to resolve the question of Gentile converts being circumcised). The difference with Acts xi.30 is that there Barnabas is still the dominant figure in the partnership and no mention is made of Titus. The difference with Acts xv.2 is that there Paul and Barnabas are leaders of a larger delegation ('Paul and Barnabas and some of the others'). Neither difference is of sufficient substance to provide much help in resolving the issue Gal. ii = Acts xi, or Gal. ii = Acts xv. The reference seems to indicate that Barnabas would be well known to the Galatians, which adds support to the view that the churches addressed are those of the 'first missionary journey' (southern Galatia), since in Paul's next expedition in that region he was not accompanied by Barnabas (Acts xv.40–xvi.6); see further Introduction §§3 and 6.3.

Paul adds that he went **taking Titus also with me**. Again the use of first-person singular is significant, as though the decision was solely Paul's and that Barnabas had no say in the matter (see discussion of preceding paragraph). The verb probably has the force of 'take along as assistant or helper' (LSJ, *sumparalambanō*), and is used elsewhere in the NT, curiously enough, only in reference to Paul and Barnabas's association with John Mark (Acts xii.25; xv.37–8); in addition to which, issues raised in connection with each seem to have been factors in the breach between Paul and Barnabas (Acts xv.39; cf. Paul's silence regarding Barnabas in Gal ii.3–8 with ii.13ff). But that is hardly ground enough for thinking there may have been some confusion on Luke's part between Mark and Titus, even though Luke's silence is surprising on the latter since he became one of Paul's chief assistants, particularly as go-between with the Corinthian church (2 Cor. ii.13; vii.6, 13–14; viii.6, 16, 23; also 2 Tim. iv.10; Tit. i.4). Nor is it necessary to explain Luke's silence by following Borse (80–5) in the implausibly forced attempt to identify 'Titus' as the diminutive of 'Timothy'. A better explanation for Luke's silence is that Titus was too closely associated with the Jerusalem collection, over which Luke evidently chose to draw a veil of silence, Acts xxiv.17 apart (Longenecker 46). As with Barnabas, the way in which Paul speaks of Titus implies that at least his name would be well known to the Galatians (perhaps as a result of the events about to be described). When their association began is not clear; but we may assume that he became attached to Paul during the latter stages of his decade or so of missionary work in Syria and

Cilicia (i.21). Paul was probably on the look-out for promising younger men to train as part of his team (cf. Acts xvi.1–3), and Titus' role may not yet have developed much. Whether Paul took him to Jerusalem as a helper or as test case is also uncertain, but we should certainly allow that Paul had both motives in mind (see further C. K. Barrett, 'Titus', *Essays* 118–31).

2 And I went up in accordance with a revelation. For 'revelation' see on i.12; despite Howard, *Crisis* 38, the lack of a definite article ('the revelation') almost certainly rules out a reference back to i.12. Here it retains its basic sense of a disclosure from heaven with heavenly authority, but the heavenly secret revealed was simply God's will that Paul should go up to Jerusalem. Whether it came through prophecy (cf. 1 Cor. xiv.6, 26, 30), or through a vision or dream (cf. 2 Cor. xii.1ff.; Acts xvi.9–10; xviii.9), or through a God-given conviction (cf. Phil. iii.15; Acts xvi.6–7; xx.22) is not made clear (see my *Jesus* 212–25). The point is that he went at heaven's behest, not at Jerusalem's, nor even Antioch's; though the claim does not diminish the likelihood that Paul went to Jerusalem as a representative of the church in Antioch (cf. again both Acts xi.29–30 and xv.2). He was not answering a summons, or going 'cap in hand'. The Galatian readers could be expected to pick up the point, just as they would find no difficulty in accepting that an apostle could receive direct 'revelations' from God and act upon them as his primary or sole authority. Of course Paul could make the claim without fear of exposing that authority to question in this case, since, in the event, his course of action and the position he defended on the basis of his 'revelations' had been so signally supported by the Jerusalem leadership.

Such nuances are part and parcel of Paul's carefully framed narrative, as his next statement confirms – **and I laid before them the gospel which I proclaim among the Gentiles**. Once again, as in i.16 and 18, the verb he uses to describe his relationship with Jerusalem has been judiciously chosen for its weight. For *anatithesthai* means 'to declare, communicate, refer (with the added idea that the person to whom a thing is referred is asked for his opinion), lay something before someone for his consideration' (BAGD). The point is, however, that its use tells us nothing about the relative competence or status of the parties involved. So, for example, it can be used of communication between friends (Plutarch, *Moralia* 772D; Alciphron iii.23.2), or in describing the action of those with *greater* power and status than the one to whom the report is given or from whom an opinion is asked (2 Macc. iii.9; Acts xxv.14). Here again the implication is clear: Paul has chosen a verb which would give no ground whatsoever to those who might have argued that Paul went up to Jerusalem in order to refer his gospel to the Jerusalem leadership and to ask them for an authoritative ruling on it. The language implies that Paul counted their opinion on the matter referred as something he valued (were they not the first to receive the gospel?), but not as something which determined the truth or otherwise of his gospel. It was more an act of courtesy, an expression of regard and fellowship to ensure that they were indeed of a common mind on 'the gospel which he preached among the Gentiles'. See further my 'Relationship' 113–14.

The echo of the phrasing used in i.16 ('preach . . . among the Gentiles'; see on i.16) will not be accidental: the implication is that it is the very gospel he had received direct from God in and through Christ – confirmed, in effect, by a second 'revelation' – which he continues to preach (present tense). The verb 'proclaim' (*kērussein*) is for Paul a near synonym for 'preach the gospel' (*euaggelizesthai*; see on i.8). Here the first-person-singular usage is probably significant (as in v.11), since elsewhere he characteristically uses it in the plural (Rom. x.8; 1 Cor i.23; xv.11; 2 Cor. i.19; iv.5; xi.4; 1 Thess. ii.9): Paul again indicates a sensitivity that it was *his* understanding of the gospel which was specifically under attack; Barnabas's support at the time of the Jerusalem visit had, at least in Paul's view, been called into question by the incident at Antioch (ii.13, 15ff). For 'gospel' see on i.6. That 'Christ' (i. 16; cf. 1 Cor. i.23; xv.12; 2 Cor. i.19; iv.5; xi.4; Phil. i.15) can be interchanged with 'gospel' (Col. i.23; 1 Thess. ii.9) as the object of the verb is a reminder of the extent to which the infant Christian movement focused its identity and message on Christ, his life, death and resurrection (see again on i.16).

So far Paul has not identified the 'them' to whom he referred his gospel, but now he begins to fill out the picture, and once again with careful choice of words – **but privately to those held in repute**. Who were 'the men of repute'? Almost certainly James, Cephas and John, since they are specifically described in ii.9 with a similar formula ('held in repute as pillars'; also ii.6); but a larger group is possible. More significant is the formula itself. The phrase means literally, 'those who are influential, recognized as being something, have a reputation' (BAGD, *dokeō* 2b). Paul has evidently chosen it in acknowledgment of the high standing in which the 'pillar' apostles were held, by others, without indicating whether he himself fully endorsed that

opinion (see further ii.6; cf. particularly Betz 86–7 and
Longenecker 48). In other words, it has the character of a
distancing formula – an acknowledgment of authority which
includes a certain degree of personal questioning of that
authority (cf. Mark x.42). Like the verb ('laid before'), then, it
serves well the nuanced account which Paul is offering.

Were 'the men of repute' the same as the 'them' of the
preceding clause? The 'them' could be the church in Jerusalem as
a whole, or, more likely, in representative session (we can hardly
assume that all the Jerusalem disciples could gather in a single
house, even if such figures as Acts iv.4 and xxi.20 are greatly
exaggerated), to which Paul explained his understanding of the
gospel (cf. Acts xv.12). And the report to 'those of repute' could
have been a separate private meeting, either before, or during, or
after the larger gathering. The facts are unclear; but the meeting
with 'those of repute' seems to have been the decisive one, in
which the issue was fought out and determined. It is quite
possible, however, that the matter was referred by a larger
meeting of the church to a small, more private meeting of its
senior members, and the 'sneaking in' to which Paul refers in ii.4
was actually the more traditionalist faction of the Jerusalem
church 'gate-crashing' the private meeting to ensure that
concerns and fears roused at the larger gathering were properly
safeguarded.

Given the care Paul has taken thus far to ensure a degree of
distance and independence from the Jerusalem leadership, his
next words are even more revealing – **lest somehow I was
running or had run in vain**. As elsewhere in Paul's letters, the
'lest somehow' indicates a real not merely hypothetical possibility
(1 Cor. viii.9; ix.27; 2 Cor. ii.7; ix.4; xi.3; xii.20; Gal. iv.11; 1
Thess. iii.5); genuine anxiety is expressed here (BDF §370;
Burton 72–5). The metaphor is of a foot race in the stadium, and
carries with it the note of disciplined exertion towards a goal –
as in Paul's other uses of it (1 Cor. ix.24–6; Gal. v.7; Phil. ii.16).
To run 'in vain, to no purpose' is to fail to achieve the goal.
Elsewhere in Paul that means failure of his converts to remain
faithful to the gospel and to persevere to the end (2 Cor. vi.1;
Phil. ii.16; 1 Thess. iii.5). Here the fear seems to be partly lest
both his earlier and current converts abandon the gospel Paul
preached to them (was he picking up language used by his
opponents – as in Ps. cxix.32?). But even stronger is the
implication that Paul saw the Jerusalem leadership's approval of
his gospel as vital to the success or failure of his missionary
effort (Holmberg 27–8; Osten-Sacken 129). The nuance is again
important. It was not that he cherished any lingering doubts as

to the truth and authority of his gospel; he had emphasized that point sufficiently by now. It was rather that his gospel made claims regarding its continuity with Israel's promise and hope which Jerusalem's effective disclaimer would render a dead letter. His gospel would still be 'the power of God to salvation' (Rom. i.16), but the Gentiles converted by it would be out of communion with the Jewish believers centred in Jerusalem. The oneness of the gospel, its character as the climax of Israel's promise and hope, and consequently the communion of all in Christ, and so in Israel, would have been effectively destroyed from the start. The unity of the gospel was Paul's immediate concern, as that on which the unity of the churches depended. See further my 'Relationship' 115.

In this verse, then, we see still more clearly that Paul was attempting to steer a careful middle course between according the Jerusalem apostles too much authority and according them too little authority in relation to his missionary work. On the one hand, it was important to acknowledge the authority of the Jerusalem apostles (1) since it was an authority widely recognized by others, (2) since they were 'apostles before him' (i.17), (3) since without their formal recognition of his gospel the claims and character of his gospel would be rendered *ineffective*, and not least (4) since in the event they had exercised their authority in his favour at the Jerusalem consultation (ii.6–9), thus reassuring Paul that he had *not* been running in vain. On the other hand, it was important to distance himself from that authority, since his gospel had come to him direct from God with the full sanction of revelation, so that (1) the *authority* of its claims *vis-à-vis* the Gentiles was not dependent on their approval, and (2) any claims to supersede or supplement his gospel citing Jerusalem's authority, as in Galatia, could find no precedent or justification in any of his previous dealings with the Jerusalem apostles.

3 Having stated the purpose of his second visit to Jerusalem, Paul turns at once to the central issue which was fought out there – **but not even Titus, who was with me, though a Greek, was compelled to be circumcised.** Paul maintains the use of the singular, as though Barnabas played no role in the whole matter. This contains no suggestion that Barnabas failed to back him at this point; the surprise and hurt at Barnabas's defection come only at ii.13 ('even Barnabas'). It may simply be because Paul himself had been the main advocate in the dispute at Jerusalem, or that Barnabas's subsequent defection made his earlier support of doubtful value in relation to the Galatians (see further on ii.1).

The description of Titus as a 'Greek' would pose the issue at once both for any Jewish readers and for Gentile converts desirous of 'judaizing'. For since the spread of Greek culture through the conquests of Alexander the Great and the subsequent Maccabean crisis, 'Greek' not only could indicate the pervasiveness of Greek culture in the eastern Mediterranean, but also could stand in contrast to 'Jew' as a way of categorizing the whole civilized world from a Jewish perspective (2 Macc. iv.36; xi.2; *4 Macc.* xviii.20). Hence Paul's regular formulation – 'Jew and Greek' (Rom. i.16; ii.9–10; iii.9; x.12; 1 Cor. i.22, 24; x.32; xii.13; Gal. iii.28; Col. iii.11). 'Titus, being a Greek', meant, 'Titus, being not a Jew' (Lietzmann 10). 'Not even Titus' makes the point even more forcefully: Titus was so obviously a Greek and not a Jew; if Paul could successfully defend his position in relation to Titus he could sustain it for all Greeks.

The issue clearly implicit for Paul's readership was that of circumcision, as is confirmed by the next words. For in Jewish perspective the 'Jew/Greek' classification could be readily translated into 'circumcision/uncircumcision' (Rom. ii.25–7; iii.30; iv.9–12; Gal. ii.7–8; Col. iii.11; Eph. ii.11); circumcision and lack of circumcision so summed up the difference between Jew and Greek that the world could be divided simply into 'circumcision' (not 'the circumcised') and 'uncircumcision' (not 'the uncircumcised') – 'circumcision' providing the fundamental principle of classification (see also on ii.8). Here again it was the Maccabean crisis which had brought this distinctiveness of Jew from Greek to the fore (1 Macc. i.15, 48, 60–1; ii.46; 2 Macc. vi.9–10; Josephus, *Ant.* xii.241 – 'they concealed the circumcision of their private parts in order to be Greeks even when unclothed'). Circumcision was also widely regarded by Greco-Roman writers as a distinguishing mark of Jews, and since other peoples were known to practise circumcision (Herodotus II.104.2–3; Strabo XVII.2.5), such close identification between circumcision and Jewishness must be a reflection of sustained Jewish insistence on circumcision as marking out Jew from Greek – as Tacitus confirms: 'They adopted circumcision to distinguish themselves from other peoples by this difference' *(Hist.* V.5.2). Similarly Josephus, *Ant.* i.192: God commanded Abraham to practise circumcision 'to the intent that his posterity should be kept from mixing with others'.

The reason why Jews should regard circumcision as such an important distinguishing mark would also be obvious to many if not all of Paul's readers. It had been commanded by God as 'a sign of the covenant' between Yahweh and Abraham (Gen. xvii.9–14 – 'So shall my covenant be in your flesh an everlasting covenant. Any uncircumcised male who is not circumcised . . . shall be cut off from his people; he has broken my covenant'). The Maccabean crisis simply reinforced the teaching of Genesis that circumcision was a 'make or break' issue for Jews; insistence on circumcision was integral to the emergence of 'Judaism' (see on i.13). Hence the forced circumcision of all uncircumcised Jews during the Maccabean revolt (1 Macc. ii.46) and of the males in the surrounding territories when they were incorporated into Judea by the Hasmoneans (Josephus, *Ant.* xiii.257–8, 318; see also xx.139, 145). The position, then, was simple for most Jews: only the circumcised were Jews; only the circumcised were members of the covenant; only the circumcised belonged to the people chosen by God to be his own (see also Schürer iii.169; J. Nolland, 'Uncircumcised Proselytes?', *JSJ* 12 [1981] 173–94; McKnight 79–82).

This is clearly the logic lying behind the struggle indicated in the final phrase – 'was not compelled to be circumcised'. Clearly implied is an attempt made by some (identified in ii.4) to have Titus circumcised, on the grounds no doubt that he could not be a member of the people to whom the promise of Abraham had been made without it. But Paul does not say simply, 'Titus was not circumcised'; he says, 'was not *compelled* to be circumcised'. Again the implication is fairly clear. *Not* that Paul gave way gracefully – he did not need to be compelled, he exercised his Christian liberty; such a response would have wholly undermined Paul's argument and made his disavowal in ii.5 a piece of shameless self-apologetic. Rather the implication is that the *Jerusalem apostles* did not exert the compulsion. Again the nuance should not be missed: the Jerusalem apostles had tried to persuade Paul to accede to the demand, but did not insist; they were sympathetic to the demand, but recognized the force of the reasons Paul gave for refusing and did not press the point (Lightfoot 105–6 – 'The counsels of the Apostles of the Circumcision are the hidden rock on which the grammar of the sentence is wrecked'; Howard, *Crisis* 28–9). The implication is that they could have done so: their authority within the Nazarene movement was such that they could have compelled other members to maintain the traditional distinguishing mark of the covenant. Whether Paul would have gone along with them we will never know (perhaps he did not know either). All we can say is that Paul's resistance won the day on this occasion, and that when a closely related issue came to a head later on Paul stood his ground (ii.11ff).

4 The reason why the issue of circumcision arose was because of pressure exerted during the private meeting – **but because of the false brothers smuggled in**. Paul here begins a sentence which he fails properly to complete (anacoluthon) – a not uncommon Pauline trait (BDF §467). This may have been by design: allusions to unsavoury activities, dark hints of skullduggery, implication of dishonourable motives and things left unsaid (leaving the readership to fill out the unfinished sentence) would serve Paul's polemic better than explicit details which could be the more directly challenged and refuted; Paul shows himself at this point to be the master of political propaganda. But equally it could have been simply a case of Paul's thought running ahead of his dictation, or of his strength of feeling overcoming his ability to express himself clearly (Ebeling 84 cites Luther appositely: 'Anyone who is inflamed while speaking cannot at the same time observe the grammatical rules').

The 'because of' strengthens the impression (see on ii.3) that pressure was exerted on Paul by the Jerusalem 'pillars' as well, 'because of' the presence and views of the 'false brothers'. This makes much better sense (infiltration into a private meeting to exert pressure in reference to Titus) of the admittedly fractured train of thought than the suggestion (Lagrange 32; Schlier 71; Bruce 115–17; Watson 50–1; Fung 91–2) that the infiltration of 'the false brothers' took place at Antioch (Acts xv.1) before the Jerusalem consultation. It is difficult to imagine a traditionalist pressure in Antioch which was not more resolutely applied and more difficult to resist in Jerusalem; Titus was too blatant a 'case in point' to be ignored. Still less convincing is Munck's contorted attempt to take the sentence as a reference to the 'Judaizers' in Galatia (pp. 97–8).

Who 'the false brothers' were is not clear. The designation clearly implies a group who regarded themselves as 'brothers', who presumably were so regarded by the Jerusalem leadership (otherwise they could not have gained admittance to the private meeting), and who may well have been known to the Galatians (not 'certain false brothers' – contrast ii.12). In calling them 'false *brothers*' Paul treats them as he treated the 'other *gospel*' of i.6 (cf. 2 Cor. xi.13 – 'false apostles'). That is to say, he recognized that they claimed to be brothers (and the acceptance of that claim by others), but he disputed its validity: either they did not realize what being a 'brother' in the new movement meant, just as the other Galatian missionaries had failed to appreciate the real character of the gospel (i.7); or they were deliberate counterfeits through and through, whose claim to

Christian faith and discipleship was a sham from start to finish. Either way, a degree of polemical exaggeration (to put it no more strongly) has to be discounted; this was hardly an unbiased or objective assessment by Paul. Nor should we disguise the degree of personal animosity Paul's language betokens.

The indications, then, are that 'the false brothers' were members of the Jerusalem (or Judean) church (for 'brother see on i.2), and recognized as such (having been baptized in the name of Jesus); but they belonged to that section of the Judean church who viewed the increasing recruitment of Gentiles with suspicion, and who insisted on the movement's maintaining its distinctive Jewish character, with all that that involved in terms of circumcision (see on ii.3). The identification of this group with those described by Luke as 'some believers who belonged to the sect of the Pharisees' (Acts xv.5) is most natural. Paul of course had belonged to this sect prior to his own conversion-commission (see on i.14), which may well provide a further reason for the fierceness of his response here: whereas baptism in Christ's name had meant a complete about-face in Paul's understanding of God's promises and purpose, for the 'false brothers' it had meant simply an extension of their faith and halakhah as Pharisees.

Why 'the false brothers' should raise the issue now, when mission work among the Gentiles had been having considerable success for years, is also unclear; but it may indicate both the increasing success of the mission in Judea and the increasing religio-political tensions in Palestine. Certainly it must be judged improbable that this was the first time that the Jerusalem apostles became aware that a circumcision-free gospel was being preached among the Gentiles (as argued by Howard, *Crisis* 21, 38–9); more likely it was the extent of the success of this gospel which made them aware that an anomaly was getting out of hand. See further my *Partings* 124–30, and below on ii.12.

The 'smuggled in' does not add much clarification. It is a rare word, meaning 'secretly brought in' (see Betz 90, n. 305). It probably indicates an action initiated by some other(s), but its time reference is uncertain. It could refer to their being brought into the Jesus movement itself, or to their introduction to the private meeting. Either way it suggests that among the established members of the Jerusalem church were some (James?) who acted as sponsor for these more traditionalist Jewish believers and who saw them as a means of maintaining a more traditional Jewish identity for the new movement in the face of Gentile incomers. All this still leaves us unclear as to whether Paul deliberately engineered the confrontation by bringing Titus with him; or whether the presence of the uncircumcised Titus among the Antioch delegation was seized upon by the 'false brothers' and their sponsor(s) as a test case.

Even less clear is what sort of communion was practised in the Jerusalem church during their visit. Did the Antioch delegation worship and share table-fellowship only with the (presumably) small group of Hellenists still left in Jerusalem (friends of Barnabas; Mnason, also of Cyprus – Acts xxi.16)? Would the 'false brothers' have refused table-fellowship with Titus? Or did the Antioch delegation attempt to avoid bringing such a question to the fore by maintaining the sort of unspoken conventions and compromises which any large movement must observe if it is to hold the diversity of its membership together? Such behaviour, of course, would be likely to engender just the sort of suspicion and surreptitious scrutiny from the 'false brothers' which Paul describes in these verses.

Whoever the 'false brothers' were and whenever they were 'smuggled in', Paul had no doubt as to their motives – **who sneaked in to spy on our freedom which we have in Christ Jesus, in order that they might enslave us**. The main verb is also not widely used, but has the sense of 'carefully insert', 'enter surreptitiously', 'intrude', 'infiltrate', and here clearly with the overtone of unworthy motives (BAGD, *pareiserchomai* 2). If 'smuggled in' may refer to their earlier entry into the Jesus movement itself, 'sneaked in' is best taken as referring to their part in the Jerusalem consultation. The infinitive ('to spy out') occurs only here in the NT, but again its meaning would be clear (LSJ, *kataskopeō*; *TDNT* vii.417; cf. 2 Sam. x.3; 1 Chron. xix.3; 1 Macc. v.38). The implication is that they would have given Paul's account of his missionary work a suspicious hearing, with the intention of subverting it. The piling up of such language ('false brothers', 'smuggled in', sneaked in', 'spy out') indicates Paul's total lack of sympathy towards this group (the concentration of military metaphors is striking; cf. iii.23 and iv.17); but, once again, it is the language of polemic, which should not be regarded as an objective account. Expressed in their own terms, the concerns of this group's members would be quite other: to ensure that the new movement within Judaism remained true to the principles and practices of the covenant clearly laid down in the Torah (even as interpreted by Jesus), reinforced by the Maccabean crisis, and promoted particularly by the Pharisees. The argument used by Eleazar to Izates, king of Adiabene, who round about this very time became a proselyte without being circumcised, may well be like the arguments used by the 'false brothers': 'In your ignorance, O king, you are guilty of the greatest offence against the law and thereby against God.

For you ought not merely to read the law but also, and even more, to do what is commanded in it. How long will you continue to be uncircumcised? If you have not yet read the law concerning this matter, read it now, so that you may know what an impiety it is that you commit' (Josephus, *Ant.* xx.44–5).

The sharpness of Paul's polemic and the crucial nature of the issues involved are evident in Paul's contrast between 'our freedom in Christ Jesus' and the motive he imputed to the 'false brothers' ('that they might enslave us'). For a Greek readership this was a most emotive chord to strike, since the distinction between slave and free was fundamental in Greek thought and the idealization of freedom was axiomatic in Hellenistic self-perception (*TDNT* ii.261–4; see also on i.10). So too for most Jews, the idealization of the golden age of independence under David and the memory of the success of the Maccabean freedom fighters must have given Paul's language a similar resonance. Paul himself clearly experienced his new faith in Christ as a 'liberation'; this is one of the most consistent notes in his major letters, often with a similar depth of feeling expressed (Rom. vi.17–22; vii.3; viii.2, 21; 1 Cor. vii.22; ix.1, 19; x.29; 2 Cor. iii.17), and is a central emphasis of this letter in particular (Gal. iv.7, 26, 30–1; v.1, 13). That is not to say that he had experienced his previous life 'in Judaism' as an enslavement; far from it (Gal. i.13–14; Phil. iii.5–6). But as he looked back to that way of life he could only see it as a form of slavery; in what sense will become clearer later (see on iv.1–3). Worse still, he saw the 'false brothers' as enforcing that status on his converts, forcing them to exchange their *freedom* (from the law as traditionally understood) for *slavery* (that is, for a dependence on the law rather than directly on God's Spirit; see also v.22–3, 25); Paul was himself enough of a Greek to recoil in horror at the very thought. Needless to say, Paul's opponents would certainly not agree with such an antithetical juxtaposition of law and freedom (contrast James i.25; ii.12); and Paul himself would qualify it later (Rom. viii.2; see my *Romans* 416–19). For the 'in Christ Jesus' see on i.22, though here it has a more dynamic sense – 'brought about through and made possible by being in Christ Jesus'.

5   Paul did not complete the sentence, but allowed himself to be distracted by the memory of the episode and of the stand he had to take, which may have swept over him even as he dictated – **to them not even for an hour** (see p. 86 n. 2) **did we yield submission**. The verb means 'to give way', regularly with a negative implication (yield to passion or impulse, withdraw from

a battle; LSJ, *eikō*). 'Submission' in Paul's vocabulary was not a negative concept. On the contrary, it is what the creature owes the Creator (Rom. viii.7; x.3; even Christ – 1 Cor. xv.28); and a proper response to legitimate authority (Rom. xiii.1, 5; 1 Cor. xvi.16). The issue here, of course, was that Paul thought the authority being exercised (but not insisted on) was illegitimate: not in the sense that the Jerusalem leadership could not exercise such authority; but rather in the sense that such authority exercised on this matter would have to be counted illegitimate in relation to the gospel, an illegitimate perversion of the freedom of the gospel. Here Paul reverts to the plural ('we') to remind the Galatians that in this stand Barnabas was wholly at one with him.

Paul states his motivation clearly – **in order that the truth of the gospel might remain for you**. 'Truth' is a word which as used in the NT regularly reflects both a Greek and a Hebrew background. In Greek thought 'truth' characteristically is defined as 'reality' in antithesis to (mere) appearance (LSJ, *alētheia*). In the LXX, however, *alētheia* is often used to translate the Hebrew *'munah* ('faithfulness'; see also on i.23), particularly in the Psalms. In Romans Paul speaks of 'the truth of God' to denote both the reality which is God (Rom. i.18, 25) and the faithfulness of God to his covenant promise (Rom. iii.3–4, 7; xv.8) (see my *Romans* ad loc.). In Galatians the key concept is rather 'the truth of the gospel' (so also ii.14; but with similar effect, v.7; elsewhere cf. particularly Col. i.5; 2 Thess. ii.12–13). Linked as it is here with the thought of the liberty of the gospel, Paul's meaning is clear: he appeals to the reality of his readers' own experience as an experience of liberation (see on ii.4), and contrasts it with the alternative offered by the other missionaries which, by implication, gives only the appearance of freedom; he appeals also to the trustworthiness of the gospel, that its promise of participation in the blessings given through Abraham (note particularly iii.8) is firm and secure, requiring, by implication, no supplementation by circumcision. That Paul says 'might remain for you', 'remain continually with you' (BAGD, *diamenō*), does not mean that he had the Galatians in mind when he took his stand at Jerusalem (as would be possible on the 'south Galatian' theory and a very early dating), or that he was speaking throughout verses 4 and 5 only of the current confrontation (see on ii.4), but that he took his stand for the sake of Gentile converts in general, including the Galatians. The rhetorical touch (like the 'our freedom' of ii.4) is an effective way of gaining his readers' sympathy and a fresh reminder that the issue at Jerusalem was the same issue which confronted them, and that the stand he took in Jerusalem was, therefore, in the event, precisely for their benefit.

6 The ones who really mattered in this confrontation in Jerusalem, however, were the leading Jerusalem apostles. It was their decision which made all the difference then, and which should still carry most weight for the Galatians. So, having made his forceful side-swipe at the 'false brothers', Paul returns to the key point – **But** (in contrast to the outright opposition of the 'false brothers') **from those reputed to be something**. The distancing note already present in the earlier use of the same formula (see on ii.2) rings more clearly here in the lightly depreciatory 'reputed (that is, by others) to be of account' (but of what account Paul does not bother to specify). It was the esteem in which others held them, including, no doubt, the other missionaries in Galatia, which made their decision so important for Paul. By using this formula Paul can attest their authority without implying that he himself was necessarily bound by it.

That Paul was walking a narrow tightrope between affirming the Jerusalem apostles' authority and disowning it is confirmed by the parenthesis he immediately adds, **what they once were makes no difference to me – God shows no partiality**. The phrase 'it makes no difference, does not matter to me' would be familiar Greek usage, including its reference to specific persons (BAGD, *diapherō* 2c; *TDNT* ix.62). The first two words (*hopoioi pote*) could be translated 'what sort of people' (BAGD, *hopoios*; BDF §303). But that would not give enough weight either to the context or to the *pote* ('once'). The 'what (kind of)' must qualify the immediate antecedent – 'those reputed to be of some account': it was the kind of reputation they had among others which Paul treats so dismissively. And together with the imperfect ('were'), the *pote* would most naturally be understood as strengthening the backward look – 'what they once were'. The words therefore indicate the reason why Paul too might have been expected to hold them in esteem. Presumably the 'once were' refers to the fact that two of the three (Cephas and John) had been Jesus' closest and leading disciples, and James was 'the brother of the Lord', and that they had been leading figures of the mother church, the church of God in Judea, from the first. In addition, the conjunction of the past tense ('what they once were') with the present ('makes no difference to me') probably indicates that there was a time when Paul himself shared that esteem (both journeys to Jerusalem attested it), but that now he wished to discount it drastically. (All these nuances are lost by

NEB/REB's 'not that their importance matters to me', and NJB's 'whether they actually were important or not').

The balancing act is spectacular: Paul had admitted in so many words (ii.2) that the decision of the Jerusalem leadership had been critical for him; he wished to place the full weight of that authority behind the decision actually made at Jerusalem; he was more than ready to appeal to that authority because of the weight it carried for others; but at the same time he wanted it to be clear that he no longer recognized that authority over himself or his mission. Evidently something had happened between the Jerusalem consultation and the writing of the letter. It takes no great insight to guess that the 'something' was the incident at Antioch (ii.11–14) and the sequel attempt to subvert Paul's work in Galatia. It is particularly striking, then, that in the very verse where he indicates most clearly the crucial decision taken at Jerusalem (implying his dependence on it – cf. ii.2) Paul made a deliberate point of denying that the authority of those who made that decision (now) counted for anything with him (see again my 'Relationship').

As the reason for the indifference to the Jerusalem apostles which he now professed, Paul cites a fundamental Jewish conviction – **God shows no partiality** (e.g. Deut. x.17; 2 Chron. xix.7; Sir. xxxv.12–13; *Jub.* v.16; *Pss. Sol.* ii.18; 1 *Enoch* lxiii.8; Rom. ii.11; see further my *Romans* 89). Here it has a potentially slighting overtone, since the metaphor is primarily that of God as judge and could imply some attempt to bribe him or to gain his favour by improper means. That is not necessarily the case here; Paul implies simply that such esteem as human beings bestow on others is an improper ground for assuming that the latter are regarded as highly by God. That Paul was willing to use such dismissive language is a further indication of the degree to which he had become disillusioned with the Jerusalem leadership (which is not the same as to say that he was disillusioned with his Jewish heritage or identity).

The key point in Paul's defence is thus reached: **for to me those of repute added nothing**. The linking 'for' (resuming the construction broken by the parenthesis), together with the fact that the 'to me' is in the place of emphasis at the beginning,   • implies that Paul's thought was running on from the parenthesis to give a further explanation of his current attitude to the Jerusalem leadership. Whatever his apprehensions at the time he made his trip to Jerusalem (ii.2), and the fierceness of the struggle during the period of consultation (ii.3–5), the key factor was that the figures of acknowledged authority had not contributed anything to Paul himself, to his standing (as apostle) or to his gospel (i.11–12). That meant that they could take nothing away from him (hence he could be indifferent to them). But more important for the success and maintenance of his continuing missionary work, that meant that no additional claim could be made on his converts on the authority of the Jerusalem apostles. It should also be noted that Paul does not say '*We* agreed that . . .', but '*They* added nothing'. At that point it was not a resolution reached by equals. Paul won the argument. But 'those of repute' made the critical ruling.

The precise weight of the verb is difficult to compute, since the usage here lacks any close parallels (including its only other NT usage – i.16!). In such a case we may imagine that Paul intended a sense which would be sufficiently obvious from the structure of the compound itself ('to be understood literally' – Lietzmann 12) – 'to put something on in addition' (*tithēmi* – 'put'; *pros ana* + dative – 'on besides'). What precisely he meant is not clear from the clause itself. But the context clearly implies that the 'something in addition' must have included circumcision at least, though whether any more was spelled out must be doubtful in view of the subsequent incident in Antioch (ii.11–14). Hence Burton's 'teach in addition to what I had already learned' (pp. 89–91) is probably too weak; though 'laid no further requirement on me' comes closer to the sense and authority implicit in Paul's earlier talk of a 'compulsion' which might have been but was not exercised (ii.3). Whether Paul had the 'apostolic decree' (Acts xv.24–9) specifically in mind (D. Georgi, *Die Geschichte der Kollekte des Paulus für Jerusalem* [Hamburg: Reich, 1965] 19–20; Bring 70–1; Lüdemann 72) depends on its origin (see further on ii.12). On the whole clause see further my 'Relationship' 116–17.

We should not underestimate how astonishing a decision was here made: that Jews, leaders of a movement focused on Messiah Jesus, should agree in considered and formal terms that circumcision need no longer be required of Gentiles wishing to be counted full members of what was still a sect of second-Temple Judaism – and that, despite the plainest possible teaching of scripture (Gen. xvii.9–14)! Anomalies like god-fearing adherents to diaspora synagogues, or even exceptional cases like Cornelius (Acts x) or Izates (Josephus, *Ant.* xx.38–42), could be winked at so long as they did not become a public issue or point of principle. But Paul had had the temerity to make Titus a test case, whether by design or under pressure from the 'false brothers'. And the Jerusalem leadership had given him their backing, however unwillingly. That is to say, clear scriptural teaching and historic practice had been set aside – presumably on the grounds that Paul's interpretation of agreed confessional formulae could claim not only heavenly authority (i.15–16), but also the validation of successful missionary work (ii.8–9; iii.2–5). No wonder Luke gave the decison such prominence in his own account of the expansion of Christianity (Acts xv).

Nor should we miss the fact that the ruling reached here was one of the most important ever made in Christianity. On the outcome of the Jerusalem consultation hung the whole future of the infant faith: whether Paul's mission would become an independent movement, or whether it would remain in fellowship with the Judean churches; whether the Nazarenes would remain a sub-sect within Judaism or be able to retain within the same body divergent emphases, both traditional and liberalizing; whether the Jewish covenant heritage was to be maintained unquestioningly, abandoned altogether, or retained as a critical factor in Christianity's own make-up. Even allowing for subsequent setbacks, the decision here probably prevented a ruinous schism within Christianity ('Fortunately the "authorities" dealt more wisely with Paul than their successors dealt with Luther and Wesley' – Duncan 54); but at the same time, it substantively increased the rent in the seam which still bonded the new movement to second-Temple Judaism, even though the determinative rupture between Christianity and Judaism was still some decades in the future.

7 The victory secured by Paul was not merely a negative one ('nothing added'), **but on the contrary, when they saw that I had been entrusted with the gospel for the uncircumcision, as Peter . . . for the circumcision . . .** 'They saw', presumably from other reports (cf. i.23) as well as Paul's (ii.2; cf. Acts xv.12), and presumably with at least some reference to observable signs of the Spirit's presence among Paul's converts (ii.8–9; iii.2, 5; Williams, 'Justification' 98); perhaps also in the presence of Titus himself. For 'gospel' see on i.6; and for the distinction 'uncircumcision/circumcision' = 'Gentile/Jew' see on ii.3. Only in these two verses (7 and 8) does Paul use the name 'Peter'; elsewhere always 'Cephas' (see on i.18). This fact, together particularly with the unusual Pauline formulation, 'the gospel for the uncircumcision as . . . for the circumcision', has been used as evidence for the hypothesis that Paul here was citing or echoing an agreed statement which emerged from the consultation (details and discussion in Betz 96–8). But why the Grecized form of Cephas's name should be used in such an agreement produced in Jerusalem, when *Kēphas* itself was quite acceptable Greek (i.18; ii.9), is less clear. And the idea of having been 'entrusted with the gospel' is characteristically Pauline (cf. 1 Cor. ix.17; 1 Thess ii.4; 1 Tim. i.11; Tit. i.3; see also BAGD, *pisteuō* 3).

More important, whether he composed the phrasing himself or echoed a formulation of others, Paul would presumably not have quarrelled with talk of 'the gospel for the uncircumcision', or of an implied distinction between that and the gospel 'for the circumcision'. The point is that it was one and the same gospel (i.6–7; cf. 1 Cor. xv.11); but as preached in the different contexts of the mission among Gentiles and that among Jews, its emphases were bound to differ. Hence Paul's talk of 'the gospel preached by me' (i.11) – that is, both *'the gospel'*, but also *'as preached by me'*. Implicit is the important recognition that one and the same formula is bound to be heard differently and to have different force in different social and cultural contexts. Since the Jerusalem apostles had agreed that Titus need not be circumcised, while James at least continued living in close conformity with traditional practices, this point must have been taken at least to that extent. That continuity of identity involves development and transformation through space and time is an indispensable lesson for any young movement to learn. It is precisely this oneness which is the basis of Christian unity, precisely as unity in diversity (see further my *Unity*, ch. 2). Which means also that unless unity of form can embrace diversity of interpretation and application, consciously and without producing constant identity crises or the abrasive and mutually enervating criticism of suspicion, it will be a dead and not a living unity.

8 What was it that had convinced the Jerusalem apostles? Paul explains: **for he who worked with Peter for the apostleship of the circumcision worked also with me for the Gentiles**. The verb, *energeō*, meaning 'work, be in action, operate, be effective', is characteristically used in the NT of effective divine action (Mark vi.14; 1 Cor. xii.6, 11; Gal. iii.5; Eph. i.11, 20; Phil. ii.13; Col. i.29; 1 Thess. ii.13). In several of these references experiential overtones are evident: this activity of God was experienced as a divine 'energizing' (see also on iii.5). Paul took care to repeat the verb in both halves of the sentence. What was evidently decisive in the consideration of the Jerusalem leadership was the recognition, or perhaps inability to deny, that Paul's missionary work was having precisely the same results among the Gentiles as Peter's among their fellow Jews (Luke makes the same point in his equivalent test case – Acts x.47; xi.15–17; xv.8–9). They could not question the source of Paul's success without questioning also Peter's. That Peter was active and successful in ministry beyond Jerusalem is attested also by Acts viii.25 and ix.32ff.

The variation in the terms distinguishing their respective fields of operation (circumcision/uncircumcision – ii.7; circumcision/Gentiles – ii.8) confirms both that circumcision was the most obvious ethnic, ritual and theological identifying feature of the 'Jew' (see on ii.3), and that it was circumcision which was at the heart of the dispute resolved in Jerusalem. The variation of 'Gentiles' for 'uncircumcision' has no significance; it simply reflects that the formulation was a Jewish composition. Whereas they were prepared to affirm themselves as 'the circumcision' in distinction from 'the uncircumcision', as expressing their own sense of identity and distinctiveness, to call themselves 'the Jews' was not so natural since it was a term used more by others to identify them from 'outside' (see on ii.15).

Whether the other difference in the two halves of verse 8 is significant (the failure to repeat 'apostleship') is less clear. Paul uses the term for himself elsewhere without making a particular point of it (Rom. i.5; 1 Cor. ix.2). But it is possible that Paul was echoing an agreement reached in Jerusalem (see on ii.7) in which the term 'apostleship' was deliberately withheld from the description of Paul's missionary work (so particularly Betz 98) – leaving a similar ambiguity, ironically, with regard to James (apostleship is attributed only to Peter; cf. i.19). In recalling such a formula Paul could have thought it wiser to cite it without comment, since all that he meant and claimed by 'apostleship' had been agreed to in effect, whether or not the title itself had been used. On the other hand such considerations may reflect subsequent sensitivities on this front more than Paul's; that is to say, at this stage the term 'apostle' may well still have had more of a functional than a titular significance (cf. REB which translates 'apostleship' as 'mission'). This would explain why Paul could claim the title of 'apostle' so emphatically at the time of writing Galatians (i.1), even if it had not been formally used of him in the Jerusalem agreement. What mattered was the effectiveness of God's working, that the equivalence of the commissions, to Paul as to Peter (ii.7), was proved by their mutual effectiveness; besides that, questions of title or status were relatively unimportant.

9 The sentence becomes uncomfortably long (ii.6–10 is a single sentence), but it is important to show that the train of thought from ii.6 through ii.9 is unbroken, since verses 7–9 constitute an elaboration of the crucial decision made in Jerusalem, of its positive side and the reasons for it. The flow of thought, then, is:

'. . . added nothing, but on the contrary, when they saw that I had been entrusted with the gospel . . . **and recognized the grace given me . . .**'. The point is that they did not only 'see' the effect of Paul's preaching, they 'understood' that this was 'the grace' of God at work, they 'acknowledged' it, 'recognized the grace given me for what it was' (BAGD, *ginōskō* 3a, 7). The thought of 'grace given' is characteristic of Paul: particularly the grace he himself had received ('the grace given me' – Rom. xii.3; xv.15; 1 Cor. iii.10; Eph. iii.2, 7; cf. Rom. i.5; 1 Cor. xv.10; Phil. i.7); but also the grace experienced by believers generally (Rom. xii.6; 1 Cor. i.4; 2 Cor. vi.1; viii.1; ix.14; also Eph. iv.7; 2 Tim. i.9). The thought is of the divine commissioning as an actual empowering (i.15), whose effectiveness was not of himself; at this point 'grace' (*charis*) approaches the sense of 'charism' (*charisma*) – charism as the expression and embodiment of grace in word or action. As ever with this key word in Paul's vocabulary, the consciousness of utter dependence on the enabling of God's Spirit is close to the surface (see also on i.3 and i.6). The language, then, is thoroughly Pauline, but there is no reason to doubt that the recognition on the part of the Jerusalem three was genuine and that the agreement reached (ii.9) was simply a ratification of what was already happening.

Those who recognized this grace were **James, Cephas and John**. 'James' here will certainly be 'the Lord's brother' (i.19), since James the brother of John had been killed by Herod Agrippa by this time (Acts xii.2; Herod reigned from 41–4), and since there is no reason to link this 'James' with any other (including the 'son of Alphaeus', one of the twelve – Mark iii.18; Acts i.13). It is striking that he is named first, which must indicate that he was already regarded, by the Judean Christians at least (cf. ii.12–13), as the principal leader of the Jerusalem church. That he should have acknowledged Paul to the extent that he did, particularly if he was as traditionalist as ii.12–13 implies and later tradition suggests (Eusebius, *EH* II.xxiii.4–7), says a good deal for him; we must allow him not least an openness and a generosity of spirit which are usually denied him by modern historians (so also Acts xv.13–21). As the leading figure present he may have allowed himself to be swayed by the others, but must have given his assent in good faith. It was particularly important for Paul that James had been party to the agreement, since he would have been very highly regarded by any missionaries who looked to the Jerusalem church for their authorization (cf. again ii.12). For a sympathetic portrayal of James see Munck 112–19. For Cephas see on i.18. Why Paul reverts to 'Cephas' after using 'Peter' in ii.7–8 is unclear (see on ii.7). Why James had taken over from Peter as the leading figure in Jerusalem is also unclear, but it may simply reflect the fact that Peter had been active in missionary work (ii.7–8), away from Jerusalem, while James had remained in Jerusalem and had thus been able to consolidate his position (*TDNT* vi.109; see further on i.19).

John must be the son of Zebedee, brother of the martyred James. As well as being one of the inner circle of Jesus' disciples (Peter, James and John), he is recalled by Luke as a regular companion of Peter in the early days of the new movement (Acts iii.1, 3–4, 11; iv.13, 19; viii.14). He always appears in a secondary role, and though his presence in the list of 'pillar' apostles indicates his stature and influence, he has left much less impact on the earliest decades of Christianity than the other two. Later tradition placed him in Ephesus (Eusebius, *EH* III.i.1; xxiii) and linked him with the Johannine writings of the NT as author (III.xxiv). And while his influence on the earlier stages of the Johannine Gospel tradition is at least probable, theories regarding his specific connection with John's Gospel and the Johannine epistles have to depend more on guesswork than hard evidence.

For the fourth time in eight verses Paul uses the same distancing formula, this time describing the three Jerusalem leaders as **those reputed to be pillars**. The image of a person as a strong support (pillar) was natural and quite familiar (see e.g. Longenecker 57). But the word 'pillars' appears most frequently in the LXX in reference to the supports of the tabernacle and pillars of the temple. Particularly notable are the twin pillars set up in front of Solomon's temple (1 Kings vii.15–22; 2 Chron. iii.15–17), named Jachin and Boaz, which evidently had a covenant significance (2 Kings xxiii.3; 2 Chron. xxxiv.31) about which we know nothing (see *IDB* ii.780–1). It is likely then that the reference here is to the three as 'pillars in the temple' (as in Rev. iii.12); of what or where else would they be 'pillars'? C. K. Barrett is probably correct in the further suggestion that the reference was eschatological ('Paul and the "Pillar" Apostles', *Studia Paulina*. J. de Zwaan Festschrift, ed. J. N. Sevenster [Haarlem: Bohn, 1953] 15–19): there was speculation in second-Temple Judaism about the destruction and reconstitution of the Temple in the new age (Ezek. xl–xlviii; *Jub.* i.17, 27–8; *1 Enoch* xc.28–9; 11QT; *2 Bar.* xxxii.3–4; *Test. Ben.* ix.2); Jesus was recalled as being caught up in it also (Mark xiv.58; John ii.19; Acts vi.14); and Paul himself thought of members of the Jesus movement as 'God's temple' (1 Cor. iii.16–17; 2 Cor. vi.16; note also Heb. iii.6; x.21; 1 Pet. ii.5) (see further my *Partings*, chs. 3–5). In short, James, Cephas and John were probably regarded

THE EPISTLE TO THE GALATIANS

by the Jerusalem church as pillars of the eschatological temple of God's people, that is, as the main support on which their own community was built, 'the church of God' (i.13; 1 Cor. xv.9). The distancing formula ('those reputed to be') has the same function as in its earlier usage (ii.2, 6) – to indicate their important status, and the significance therefore of the backing they gave Paul on this occasion, while leaving the question open as to whether Paul himself (now) shared that estimate of their importance.

Paul now reaches the main point of this long sentence. Having explained the reasons for the pillar apostles' recognition of his authority and work, with suitable qualifications, Paul continues, they **gave to me and Barnabas the right hand of fellowship**. 'Right' had a similar connotation of what is favourable or honourable as in English (with 'left' denoting ill-omen – Latin, *sinister*). Hence the custom of giving the right hand as a sign of assurance or in pledge, and particularly at the conclusion of an agreement or treaty (as in 1 Macc. vi.58; Josephus, *Ant.* xviii.328–9 – 'No one would ever prove false when he had given his right hand, nor would anyone hesitate to trust one that he suspected might harm him, once he had received that assurance of safety'; see further *IDB* iv.79–80; LSJ, BAGD, *dexia*; *TDNT* ii.38). The action thus indicates a formal agreement, clearly set out, and not simply a private arrangement or vague expression of good will (see particularly J. P. Sampley, *Pauline Partnership in Christ* [Philadelphia: Fortress, 1980], ch. 3). This is confirmed by the formal naming of each of the parties to the agreement: on the one side, James, Cephas and John; on the other, Paul and Barnabas (the latter here mentioned for the first time since ii.1, but again as second to Paul). Even if some suspicions were still entertained on either side, the giving of the right hand would provide assurance that the agreement thus sealed would be honoured.

The addition of 'fellowship' further strengthens the point. Although it is characteristically Pauline in the NT (13 out of the 19 occurrences), its use in Acts ii.42, Heb. xiii.16 and 1 John iii.3, 6–7 is sufficient evidence of its familiarity elsewhere in earliest Christianity. From Paul's usage in particular it is clear that its basic meaning was the act or condition of sharing something, including the Holy Spirit (2 Cor. xiii.13/14; Phil. ii.1) and the gospel (Phil. iii.10). Here the thought is of the hand-shake as an expression of what the pillars and Paul and Barnabas already shared in common, which here must include their common faith in Messiah Jesus and their agreement regarding the gospel, as the basis of the specific agreement on division of responsibility (as between 'the Gentiles' and 'the circumcision'). This again is

110

important: the agreement was not simply a working arrangement between diverging interpretations of the gospel, far less a cloak to conceal radical divisions; it expressed a genuine sense of a shared experience and common message, and again a degree of recognition on the part of James in particular which has been insufficiently acknowledged in modern study of the period. Where most of the subsequent emphasis, not least in this letter, is on the disagreements between Paul and the Jerusalem authorities, it is necessary at this point to highlight the extent of their 'fellowship'.

The specific agreement thus sealed was **that we should be for the Gentiles, and they for the circumcision.** This is generally taken to indicate a division of missionary responsibility, with the main debate being as to whether it was a geographical or ethnic division (for the Gentiles/circumcision distinction see on ii.8). However, neither makes much sense, since there were more Jews in the diaspora than in Palestine, and since Paul's regular missionary tactic was probably to preach first to those Gentiles who attended the diaspora synagogues (as many did; see e.g. my *Romans* xlvii–xlviii). The interpretation is certainly encouraged by what Paul says in ii.7–8. But the absence of a verb in *both* parts of this final-purpose clause may well point in a slightly different direction: for there is no verb indicating movement in the preceding clauses which would encourage Paul's readers to supply it here; and in such a case the verb 'to be' is the one which would normally be supplied to complete the sense. This suggests in turn that the preposition is intended here (both times) in the quite common sense of 'for', equivalent to a dative of advantage, or 'with reference to', as appropriate after talk of an agreement (BAGD, *eis* 4g, 5). In that case the agreement would be rather more general than a division of missionary responsibility – an agreement between representatives of Antioch and Jerusalem respectively, that Paul and Barnabas should represent, or act for, or be responsible for the Gentile converts, while the pillars should represent, or act for, or be responsible for the Jewish disciples. Since all five were parties to the agreement, that would also make better sense: James and John are not particularly remembered for missionary work. This was indeed a division of responsibility, and could readily be understood and applied as a division of missionary responsibility; but its wider reference is probably confirmed by Paul's subsequent concern to bring the collection from the Gentile churches personally to Jerusalem (Rom. xv.25–8). It would also help explain the vehemence of Paul's language in ii.11ff. – while James was exercising his role as acting for 'the circumcision' (ii.12), Paul's agreed role as representing and having responsibility for Gentile converts was being disregarded and set aside.

Whatever the precise sense, it is important again to recognize that the agreement was in effect a ratification of what was already the case (ii.3–5, 7–8). The responsibility towards the Gentiles was not first given to Paul and Barnabas by the Jerusalem leadership. It had been given by God and signally approved by God. As with the parallel breakthrough in Acts (x.44–8; xi.15–18), ecclesiastical approval and administration followed upon and conformed to the grace of God already evident, rather than attempting to dictate to that grace and determine its working.

10 The only qualification which Paul recalled agreeing to was **that we should remember the poor**. The verb 'remember' can readily embrace the connotation of continuing solicitude (present tense) for those remembered (as in 1 Macc. xii.11; Col. iv.18). In itself it indicates a consideration for others which is larger than financial (Taylor, *Paul* 116–22), but since 'the poor' is explicitly the object, the primary or major thrust of the request must include financial help. 'The poor' was hardly intended as a title (see e.g. the data in Longenecker 59), but as a reference to those lacking resources to maintain life even at subsistence level, and particularly those at Jerusalem itself (cf. Rom. xv.26). The counsel reflects the strains which the system of 'poor relief' in the Jerusalem church soon ran into (cf. Acts vi.1; xi.29), partly through some imprudence (selling off capital possessions – Acts ii.45; iv.34), but principally it would appear, because their numbers expanded so quickly, with few of their leaders (Galileans) having financial resources in Jerusalem, and because of the severe famine which afflicted Palestine in the period 46–8 (Schürer i.457). Assuming the Acts xi = Gal. ii identification, NIV translates 'that we should continue to remember the poor'.

Active concern for the poor was a particular and distinctive feature of Jewish law and tradition (e.g. Deut. xxiv.10–22; Pss. x.2, 9; xii.5; xiv.6; etc.; Isa. iii.14–15; x.1–2; lviii.6–7; Amos viii.4–6; see further *IDB* iii.843–4). More to the point, however, almsgiving was widely understood within Judaism as a central and crucial expression of covenant righteousness (Dan. iv.27; Sir. iii.30; xxix.12; xl.24; Tob. iv.10; xii.9; xiv.11); 'almsgiving' and 'righteousness' indeed could be regarded as synonymous (*TDNT* ii.196; see further K. Berger, 'Almosen für Israel: Zum historischen Kontext der paulinischen Kollekte', *NTS* 23 [1976–7] 183–92). This, together with the cultic overtones not far away in talk of 'remembering' (*TDNT* iv.682), suggests that the 'only' qualification added to the agreement in Jerusalem was of particular significance, for the traditionalists at least. What the 'pillars' asked for was that an obligation characteristically understood as a primary expression of Jewish covenant piety should be given high priority by Paul and Barnabas. And if they were indeed being treated as responsible for the Gentiles (see on ii.9), that would also imply that Paul and Barnabas should ensure that their Gentile converts shared the same concern. It would appear then that the 'pillars' sought to win what they regarded as an important concession from Paul and Barnabas: that the principle of covenant obligation on those claiming membership of the assembly of God's people should be safeguarded and affirmed at least to this, significant extent. Having conceded the specific issue of circumcision, they sought still to maintain the principle of 'covenantal nomism' (see on ii.16). Despite their compromise over Titus, their mind-set was still the same: that those who share the righteousness of the covenant (the standing with God which the covenant makes possible) must continue to attest and maintain that standing by acts of righteousness.

Somewhat surprisingly, in the light of these overtones, Paul immediately expresses his acceptance of the recommendation – **the very thing which I have eagerly done**. The reference could possibly be to Paul's activity already demonstrated (Acts xi.30); but why then did he revert to the singular 'I', since, according to the Acts account, Barnabas was equally responsible for delivering the 'famine relief'? Tense and number are more naturally understood as Paul's affirmation that he had eagerly embraced the obligation with immediate effect and that this had been a singular concern of his work since then (in the latter phases of which Barnabas had played no part). If this is so, then Paul cannot have regarded the obligation as 'something added to him', which would run too sharply counter to ii.6. Either he did not regard this one qualification as compromising the principle established in the case of Titus: almsgiving was a moral obligation which followed naturally from and was in no way at odds with faith in Messiah Jesus; he was as keen as the 'pillars' to maintain this characteristically Jewish principle of social justice in a less caring Greek world. Alternatively, he might well have recognized its significance, but in the event realized that such a compromise was unavoidable if agreement on his primary objective was to be achieved. This may also be the explanation of why Paul uses no verb here: the most obvious, and historically accurate verb might reveal all too clearly that Paul had accepted 'something added'. Either way the actual agreement was something of a compromise, depending on the way the qualification was understood. Certainly there were seeds of potential misunderstanding which bore fruit all too soon in the Antioch incident (ii.11–14). Paul may well have assumed that he had established a decisive precedent which determined the principle at stake. James on the other hand may have ended the consultation with the stronger impression that an exception had been granted rather than a principle conceded. Whereas Paul probably saw it as a request made and accepted by equals, James may well have thought in terms of an obligation (albeit a compromise) imposed by legitimate authority.

It is unclear whether Paul at this stage envisaged the collection which features so much in his later letters (cf. Acts xxiv.17 – bringing alms). Too much was to happen in between, and the extent of the Gentile mission was perhaps not yet fully foreseen. But we can say that Paul subsequently pursued the objective of the collection in the spirit and with the eagerness he expressed here. This is indicated by the high priority Paul gave to it (particularly Rom. xv.22–32) and by the language he used for it – as an expression of that very 'fellowship' (Rom. xv.26; 2 Cor. viii.4; ix.13) which was sealed with a handshake at Jerusalem, as of the 'grace' (1 Cor. xvi.3; 2 Cor. viii.4, 6–7, 19) which the 'pillars' thereby acknowledged. The Galatians themselves may already have been caught up in the project and so have recognized an allusion (1 Cor. xvi.1); absence of instructions and exhortations on the subject in the letter itself could mean simply that Paul's mind was dominated by the current crisis in Galatia to the exclusion of every other concern. Since the collection could be understood as the Gentiles' acknowledgement of Israel's prerogatives (e.g. Isa. xlv.14; lx.5–17; Tobit xiii.11; 1QM xii.13–15) it was equally fraught with possibilities of misunderstanding and diverse interpretation (see also my *Romans* 873–4). That Paul persevered with it despite such possibilities is an indication that the handshake in Jerusalem meant a tremendous amount for Paul and that, despite the subsequent rupture, the continuity of covenant and salvation-history which Jerusalem symbolized remained fundamental for him (Rom. xv.27). See further Taylor, *Paul*, particularly 197–204.

The fact that Paul does not describe the ending of this second visit to Jerusalem or indicate the length of time he spent there (contrast i.18, 21) implies that this second visit was the crucial one for him, and that the agreement just described was, for Paul, the point both of the visit and of his present defence. Having described the agreement, he need say no more about that visit. This is confirmed by the absence of a fourth linking 'then' in ii.11, which suggests in turn that the following episode had a slightly different function: no longer to assert the independence of his gospel from Jerusalem (i.11–12), but to describe how he had to defend it against the 'hypocrisy' of the believers who still looked to Jerusalem for leadership.

7 THE INCIDENT AT ANTIOCH ii.11–14

(11) But when Cephas[1] came to Antioch I opposed him to his face, because he stood condemned. (12) For before certain individuals[2] came from James,[3] he used to eat with the Gentiles. But when they came,[4] he gradually[5] drew back and separated himself, because he feared those of the circumcision. (13) And the rest of the Jews also joined with him in playing the hypocrite, so that even Barnabas was carried away with their hypocrisy. (14) But when I saw that they were not walking straight towards the truth of the gospel, I said to Cephas[1] in front of everyone: 'If you, a Jew, "live like a Gentile and not like a Jew",[6] how is it that you compel the Gentiles to judaize?'

Paul has now made his chief point in the exposition of the thematic statement in i.11–12: the gospel which he preached (in Galatia as elsewhere) was not derived from the Jerusalem leadership, nor did it owe its authority to them; on the contrary, they had formally recognized in the Jerusalem consultation that God had commissioned Paul and had signally honoured his preaching. That point having been made, Paul turns at once to the sequel: despite this agreement on the gospel, it had not been

1 As in i.18, there is a strong tradition which replaced 'Cephas' with the better-known 'Peter'; but the former is certainly the earlier reading.
2 One of the most important papyrus manuscripts (p^{46} about AD 200) reads the singular here, but with hardly any other support of any weight.
3 We could translate 'When certain individuals from James came' (so NJB), but the difference in degree of attribution of authority for what these individuals evidently demanded is small. REB, however, is over precise: 'some messengers came from James'.
4 The singular is very strongly attested here ('when he came'), but the sense almost certainly requires the plural (though see n. 2), and the confusion in copying is understandable.
5 'Gradually drew back and separated' is an attempt to give the force of the imperfect tenses of the two verbs (Burton 107).
6 The quotation marks indicate that the phrase is probably a quotation from statements made by the 'individuals from James' (see on ii.14).

honoured subsequently in the incident at Antioch.[1] In other words, the Antioch incident is not simply a third example of the independence of Paul's gospel, but derives its significance directly from the Jerusalem agreement as safeguarding 'the truth of the gospel'. The juxtaposition of the two events is abrupt. Paul takes no time to set up the scene. He wanted to set the contrast between the amicable picture of ii.9 and that at Antioch as sharply as possible: the Cephas who had shaken his hand in ii.9 was the very same whom he had had to face down in ii.11. In that sense Bligh is correct to regard the Antioch incident as the climax of Paul's defence: 'all through the autobiographical section i.10–ii.10, St Paul is setting the scene for the Dispute at Antioch' (p. 173). For Paul evidently regarded the Antioch incident as the real test of the Jerusalem agreement. His claim in effect is that, whereas he had remained faithful to that hard-won agreement, Peter and the others had gone back on it. It was to make this very point clear to the Galatian churches that Paul had written the letter itself, to justify the stand he had taken at Antioch. 'His manner of narrating it shows that they have already heard another version, from the Judaizers' (Bligh 175; see also Introduction §§2 and 6.1; also Introduction to ii.15–21).

11 But when Cephas came to Antioch. This is the first mention of Antioch (see on i.21; Betz 104–5 with bibliography; Longenecker 65–71). But it is clear that the account, with its sequence of 'he came' and 'they came', is written from the perspective of Antioch. Paul writes as one who had up to that time been a representative of Antioch, and who had been recognized at Jerusalem as a spokesman for the missionary work among the Gentiles which the Antioch church had sponsored (see on ii.9). Paul implies therefore also that Peter, in coming to Antioch, had entered more into the realm of authority of the Gentile mission, which he, Paul, represented. The equivalence in commissioning and success between Peter and himself, which he had stressed in ii.7–8, was therefore even more significant in Antioch than in Jerusalem. This difference in tone is reflected in the following account, where it is Paul who takes the initiative and speaks with authority, and Peter is represented as following the lead given by others. Why Peter left Jerusalem and came to Antioch is not clear (cf. Acts xii.17), but presumably the presence of a large Jewish colony there (Schürer iii.13) was a major factor.

---

1 The suggestion of some (most recently by Lüdemann 75–7) that the Antioch incident *preceded* the Jerusalem consultation has nothing to commend it; see e.g. Bligh 178–80; Betz 105 n. 436; Bruce 128.

The same change in tone is reflected also in the way the account develops. Whereas in recounting the consultation at Jerusalem, Paul had taken care to build up to the key point (ii.6ff.), here he cannot wait to denounce Cephas – **I opposed him to his face**. The use of the idiom in Jewish history (Deut. vii.24; ix.2; xi.25; Josh. i.5) may suggest a sense on Paul's part that the issue was of epochal significance and its outcome dependent on God's being with him. For his own part, Paul had no doubt that right was on his side – **because he** (Cephas) **stood condemned**. The usage was familiar enough (BAGD, *kataginōskō*), but what precisely Paul meant is less clear. Possibly that all right-thinking people would acknowledge Peter's inconsistency; or that he was condemned before the bar of God's judgement (*TDNT* viii.568, n.51); or that Peter was '*self*-condemned' (cf. LSJ, MM), that is, by the (in Paul's eyes) blatant retreat from the agreement just recorded (ii.6–10); or indeed that Peter knew (or should have known) the condemnation of his own heart and conscience (cf. Sir. xiv.2; *Test. Gad* v.3; 1 John iii.20–1 – the only other use in the NT). The abruptness and forthrightness of Paul's language indicate a depth of feeling and outrage which the rest of his account makes no effort to conceal.

12 Having thus already stated his verdict on Peter's conduct, Paul only now explains what it was that was so reprehensible! – **for before certain individuals came from James, he used to eat with the Gentiles**. The time scale is unclear: how long was it after the Jerusalem consultation that 'Cephas came to Antioch', and how long did he practise table-fellowship with the Gentiles (that is, Gentile Christians) before the 'certain individuals from James' followed ('perhaps weeks and months' – Mussner 137). Also unclear is how long the Antioch church had practised such table-fellowship prior to Peter's coming; Burton 105 thinks a freer practice can only have been a consequence of the Jerusalem consultation, otherwise it would have attracted more attention before this.

Behind this simple description much is also hidden from us which would have been familiar or obvious to the readers. In particular we need to recall the sacred obligation of hospitality to the stranger deeply rooted in all these ancient societies, and the importance of the shared meal as an expression of acceptance. The popular legend of Philemon and Baucis (Ovid, *Metamorphoses* viii.613–70) characterized the ideal, and in Judaism Abraham especially was extolled as the model of hospitality (Gen. xviii; Philo, *Abr.* 107–14; Josephus, *Ant.* i.196) (see further *TDNT* v.17–20). In Jewish thinking table-fellowship had what we might call a sacramental character: the meal beginning with the host speaking a blessing over the bread and then passing it to the others at the table so that all in eating of the bread might share in the blessing spoken over it.

Jewish eating, however, was governed by the food laws and the various traditions which had grown round these. (1) The laws of 'unclean' foods – that various animals etc. were forbidden to them as food, not least pigs (Lev. xi; Deut. xiv). (2) The laws of ritual slaughter requiring that the blood be properly drained from the body (e.g. Lev. xvii.10–14; Deut. xii. 16, 23–4); diaspora communities needed official permission at this point (cf. Josephus, *Ant.* xiv.261). (3) Added to these clear regulations was the fear of being contaminated by the abomination of idolatry by eating meat from animals sacrificed in the pagan temples (*4 Macc.* v.2; 1 Cor. 8–10; probably implied in Josephus, *Life* 13–14; Tomson 230–6 finds the explanation for the policy of the men from James in this fear). (4) The designation of various foods as 'unclean' brought table-fellowship very much within the realm of purity, where further rulings (as in Mark vii.2–4) would be an obvious way to safeguard still more effectively the purity of the meal table. The full panoply of purity rulings appropriate within Palestine (the 'holy' land) is hardly in view, of course, but devout diaspora Jews were purity conscious (Philo, *Spec. Leg.* iii.205–6; *Sib. Or.* iii.591–2), and the policy of 'separation' from table-fellowship is clearly motivated by the same fundamental purity concerns (see below; also my 'Incident' 137–41).

The importance of these laws and traditions within second-Temple Judaism should not be underestimated. Uncleanness was a relative matter (prohibition from participating in the cult during the period of impurity); but disregard of the blood taboos entailed being 'cut off from the people'; and anything which gave scope to idolatry infringed Israel's loyalty to the one God. As with circumcision, the Maccabean crisis made the food laws a test case of national loyalty and religious faithfulness (1 Macc. i.62–3; 2 Macc. v.27). Typical of the period between the Maccabees and the first century CE was the glorification of various heroes and heroines, distinguished consistently by their loyalty and faithfulness in refusing to eat 'the food of Gentiles' (Dan. i.8–16; Tobit i.10–13; Judith x.5; xii.1–20; Additions to Esther xiv.17; *Joseph and Asenath* vii.1; viii.5); to be noted is the fact that four of these examples depict Jews in diaspora settings. At this time the Pharisees were already noted for their concern to erect a purity hedge round their table-fellowship (see again Mark vii.2). And the Qumran Essenes were known to be even stricter (Josephus, *War* ii.138–9; 1QS vi; 1QSa ii). In this context it is no surprise that Jesus was remembered as causing no little surprise and offence by the fact that he evidently ignored at least some aspects of these various rulings and traditions (e.g. Mark ii.16; Matt. xi.19; Luke xiv.12-24) (see further my *Partings* §6.3).

The evidently provocative feature of Peter's table-fellowship, however, was that 'he ate with the Gentiles', that is, obviously, Gentile Christians. What is envisaged here is clearly the practice of table-fellowship, of eating meals together with other believers. Given the importance of guest-friendship in the ancient world, and the prominence of table-fellowship in Jesus' ministry, this was a natural way for the first followers of the Nazarene's 'way' to express their common faith, as had been the case from the beginning, according to Acts ii.42, 46 (cf. 1 Cor. v.11). Peter's habit here, therefore, need not have been 'extraordinary' (Betz 106); though no doubt it did indeed reflect Paul's interpretation of the Jerusalem agreement more than that then current in Jerusalem, as is certainly indicated by the sequel. That the remembering Jesus' death in the shared bread and wine would be a central expression of their oneness and their fellowship we need not doubt (how regularly we do not know), but the issue here does not focus on the Lord's Supper as such, which anyway still consisted in a complete meal (beginning with breaking the bread and with only the cup 'after supper' − 1 Cor. xi.25).

Why would this be so provocative to 'the group from James'? Why was it that **when they came, he** (Peter) **gradually drew back** (BAGD, *hupostellō*) **and separated himself**? Paul gives his own answer: **because he feared those of the circumcision.** But what was the problem? The answer obviously lies in the fact that 'he ate with the Gentiles' and that this was unacceptable to 'the James' people'. But why?

Some would argue that the general practice of Jews was to refrain from all such social contacts with Gentiles, since Gentiles as a whole were 'unclean': note the strong statements to this effect, for example, in *Jub.* xxii.16 ('Eat not with them . . . for their works are unclean') and *m. Ohol.* xviii.7 ('the dwelling-places of Gentiles are unclean'); from a Roman viewpoint Tacitus scornfully describes Jewish 'hate and enmity' towards other peoples − 'they eat separately . . .' (*Hist.* v.5.1-2). The Cornelius episode reflects how deeply felt were such attitudes also within the earliest Christian movement (Acts x.14; xi.3, 8). The mistake here, however, would be to assume that 'Jews' and 'Gentiles' in this discussion were uniform and monolithic blocks which did not touch or overlap at any point. As recent studies have underlined, the real-life situation was more diverse (S. J. D. Cohen, 'Crossing the Boundary and Becoming a Jew', *HTR* 82

THE EPISTLE TO THE GALATIANS

[1989] 13–33; E. P. Sanders, 'Jewish Association with Gentiles
and Galatians ii.11–14', *Studies in Paul and John: In Honor of J.
L. Martyn*, ed. R. T. Fortna & B. R. Gaventa [Nashville:
Abingdon, 1990] 170–88; Hill 118–21). The case is
straightforward.

(1) Jewish legislation had from early times taken account of
the fact that non-Israelites lived in their midst ('resident aliens').
The extension of the same blood taboos and purity regulations to
include them implies that they could share the same meal table
(Lev. xvii.10–13, 15; xviii.26; xix.34; xxiv.22 – 'one law for the
resident alien and for the native') (see also my 'Incident' 142–4).

(2) Post-Maccabean Judaism was riven with factionalism.
There were evidently degrees of strictness in the observance of
the rulings and traditions, not least regarding table-fellowship:
the Pharisees 'separated' themselves from the less scrupulous (see
on i.14 and 15); the Essenes were even more rigorous; Jesus
himself was criticized for not being strict enough (see again my
Partings §6.3). As we shall see, within this intra-Jewish polemic,
those who regarded themselves as 'the righteous' did not hesitate
to describe other Jews as 'sinners' (see on ii.15; and my
'Pharisees'), or to castigate their Jewish opponents as acting like
Gentiles (see on ii.14). *Jubilees* was itself a factional document
and the Mishnah contains the traditions of the faction which
subsequently was to dominate Judaism. Since they also contain
criticisms of other Jews, it cannot be assumed that their attitude
to Gentiles was shared in equal measure by other Jews either.
Judaism then was probably no different at this point from
Judaism today – where the meal table was a sensitive issue, and
some group would eye the practice of another group with
suspicion to see what level of observance they maintained, but
where the non-Jew would be a welcome guest at many an
observant Jews' table where the hospitality was on the host's
terms (cf. even *m. Ber.* vii.1; *m. Abod. Zar.* v.5).

(3) Neither were Gentiles uniform in their attitude to
Judaism. And while the hostility of Tacitus was not untypical of
the Roman intelligentsia's scorn of eastern 'superstition', the fact
is that there were many Gentiles who were greatly attracted to
Judaism and its customs, including its food laws. Philo and
Josephus both attest this attractiveness, even if in exaggerated
terms (Philo, *Mos.* ii.17–20; Josephus, *Ap.* ii.282); and Roman
writers attest it no less clearly (e.g. Suetonius, *Domitian* xii.2;
Juvenal xiv.96–106; see further my 'Incident' 145–6). The
phenomenon of 'god-fearing' Gentiles who adopted a Jewish way
of life in varying degrees can hardly be denied (see e.g. Schürer
iii.160–71; see also on ii.14 – 'judaize'). Particularly noteworthy

is Josephus' report that in the period prior to the Jewish revolt (less than twenty years ahead) the Jewish community in Antioch was 'constantly attracting to their religious ceremonies multitudes of Greeks' (*War* vii.45), and that these Gentiles became 'mixed up' (*memigmenon*) with the Jews (*War* ii.463), where the verb elsewhere denotes social intercourse including guest friendship.

In short, though there were clear boundary lines between Jew and Gentile, marked out, not least, by the food laws and the complex of traditional attitudes and practices gathered round them, there were many Gentiles who were eager to cross these boundaries, to at least some extent, and who were welcomed by Jews when they did so.

What then was it which upset the 'certain individuals from James'? Two possibilities are open to the exegete. (1) That Peter and the other Jewish believers had totally abandoned the food laws in their entirety; they were 'living like Gentiles' (ii.14), like 'Gentile sinners' (ii.15). They would then be requiring Peter and the others to return to at least a minimal level of law observance. (2) The other chief possibility is that Peter and the other Jewish believers were sharing table-fellowship with Gentile believers on less clearly defined Jewish terms – that is, not only welcoming Gentiles to their table, but accepting invitations to Gentile tables without asking too many questions (cf. 1 Cor. x.27), though presumably on the assumption that the Gentile believers would have been mindful of the basic food rules. The James' people, having come to Antioch to visit primarily the Jewish believers (cf. ii.9), would then have been shocked at the degree of laxness being shown by these Jewish believers and criticized them accordingly.

The balance of considerations seem to count more in favour of the second alternative. (a) It is unlikely that *all* the Jewish Christians would have abandoned so completely their whole religious heritage on this crucial point, so important in their history and for their identity; or that having done so, it could have failed to cause considerable comment, not to say uproar at the complete defection of so many Jews in a strong Jewish colony, long before this. (b) Given the readiness, just noted, of so many Gentiles to 'judaize', and assuming that many or most, if not all of the early Gentile converts in Antioch came from the ranks of proselytes and God-fearing Gentiles, it would have been unnecessary for the Jewish-Christians to abandon the food laws so completely. The tradition of table-fellowship on more overtly Jewish terms was well established. (c) The talk of 'Gentile sinners' and 'living like Gentiles' was probably the language of intra-Jewish polemic – more scrupulous Jews condemning those who were relatively less scrupulous as unfaithful to their common heritage (see again on ii.14 and ii.15). (d) Here also may lie the significance of Paul's description of Peter's conduct in terms of 'separating himself', since this was precisely what Pharisees and Essenes did in their table-fellowship – separated themselves from others, in order that they might maintain a greater purity and fidelity to the covenant than the others, despite the fact that the latter also understood themselves to be members of the covenant. Paul, indeed, might have been making a deliberate pun: Peter 'played the Pharisee' (see also on i.15; cf. 2 Cor. vi.17). (e) The previous experience of Peter according to Acts x–xi may point in the same direction, since the table-fellowship he enjoyed with Cornelius was precisely with a God-fearing Gentile (Acts x.2, 22, 35), noted not least for his pious almsgiving (Acts x.2, 4, 31). And unless Titus ate his meals while in Jerusalem in splendid isolation, we may suppose that during that visit he had readily conformed to Jewish practice and scruples in his eating habits. See also my 'Incident' 151–6.

Unfortunately, the relation of the Jerusalem agreement (ii.6–10) to the Antioch incident is less than clear, but some deductions are possible. Presumably the issue of the food laws had not been raised explicitly and was not explicitly part of the agreement, otherwise the differences between James and Peter, let alone between Peter and Paul, would be hard to explain. This leaves us three possibilities. (1) There were simply a number of misunderstandings among the parties to the agreement, or differences in interpretation. We have already noted that, whereas Paul may have thought that a principle had been established, James may have seen the case of Titus more as an exception (see on ii.10). In addition, where Paul saw the agreement as safeguarding the rights of Gentile believers, James may have seen it equally as safeguarding the rights of Jewish believers to continue living as Jews. Such a difference in interpretation could readily explain the ambivalence of Peter and the other Jewish believers: should they not be living more on Gentile terms since they were in the headquarters of the Gentile mission? or should they be living as Jews wherever they were? The James people were able to persuade them that by treating the food laws so casually they were dishonouring the agreement. Such considerations show how unnecessary it is to conclude with Watson 54 that Paul's account of the Jerusalem agreement 'makes the behaviour of James, Peter and Barnabas, as described in Gal. ii.11–14, incomprehensible'.

(2) Moreover, we should perhaps allow also for a shift in power in Jerusalem: now that Peter had left Jerusalem, the

authority of leadership seems to have focused principally and perhaps exclusively on James (we do not know where John was). The hints which we have of his character (see on i.19 and ii.9) suggest that he would have been a good deal more amenable to the 'false brothers' of ii.4–5 than Peter. And the influence clearly brought to bear in his name at Antioch (ii.12; cf. Acts xv.24) points in the same direction: had the 'individuals from James' been misusing his name that fact would sooner or later have become apparent; and the less 'authorized' they were, the less ground Peter would have to 'fear the circumcision'. The difference between James and Peter, therefore, may simply have been that between a 'hard' interpretation of the Jerusalem agreement and a 'soft' interpretation.

(3) A further factor which cannot be ignored, at least as a potential influence, is the current political situation. The fact was that throughout this period the political situation was fairly volatile, marked by a sequence of weak procurators in Palestine and intermittent outbreaks of nationalist violence (Schürer i.455ff; my 'Incident' 133–6). In such circumstances, as in the Maccabean period two centuries earlier, a natural reflex was for loyalists to attempt to mark out and maintain the boundary markers which distinguished their nation. Such pressure could very well lie behind Paul's criticism of Peter that he acted 'out of fear of those of the circumcision'; whether the criticism was justified or not, Peter's action might well appear to be stimulated by fear of those who, like Paul before (see on i.13), had been prepared to use violence to maintain Jewish ethnic and religious distinctiveness (cf. Jewett, 'Agitators' 204–6; for Peter's own attitude see on ii.13). 'Those of the circumcision' (cf. Rom. iv.12; Col. iv.11; Tit. i.10) signifies a group whose self-identity was bound up with circumcision, that is, here at least, with maintaining the distinctive markers of Jewish identity which circumcision itself most clearly expressed (see on ii.3); Peter could well have shown some trepidation at confronting such zealous Jews, believers included (cf. Acts xi.2; 2 Cor. xi.26; Rom. xv.31).

(4) These considerations also cover in some degree the question of whether and where the apostolic decree (Acts xv.29) might fit into all this. For those who date Galatians before the Acts xv meeting, of course, there is no problem (Bruce 129–30). The problem arises from the Acts xv = Gal. ii identification (see on ii.1), since Gal. ii.6 seems to exclude any explicit agreement on obligations 'laid upon' Gentile believers. (a) One possible solution is that James had gone back on the Jerusalem agreement and subsequently issued the 'apostolic decree' unilaterally, and

that this is what the emissaries from James brought with them, which caused the crisis at Antioch (e.g. Catchpole). But it may not be necessary to accuse James of such bad faith (see on ii.6 and ii.9); the above considerations (1–3) are sufficient to explain any apparent shift in James' position. (b) Another possible solution is that the substance of the 'decree' (whatever the precise terms of the original) was already common ground between the earliest Jewish and Gentile missions – the taken-for-granted Jewish heritage of morality and minimal food laws which were among the features of Jewish life-style which attracted Gentiles both to Judaism and to the Jesus movement (cf. P. Borgen, 'Catalogues of Vices, the Apostolic Decree, and the Jerusalem Meeting', *The Social World of Formative Christianity and Judaism*, H. C. Kee Festschrift, ed. J. Neusner *et al.* [Philadelphia: Fortress, 1988] 126–41). The James people would then be pushing for more than that minimal requirement; while Paul would presumably regard any such spelling out of a 'requirement' as contrary to the Jerusalem agreement. Luke, in recording the decree as a matter of formal agreement at the Jerusalem consultation, would then be simply spelling out what had been common ground at that time, and crystallizing it as the actual ground of compromise between Paul and James. Further discussion on this topic belongs more to the study of Acts; see e.g. S. G. Wilson, *Luke and the Law* (Cambridge University, 1983), ch. 3.

13 Whatever the reasons behind the action of the 'individuals from James', the result was that not only Peter but **the rest of the Jews also joined with him in playing the hypocrite**. The church at Antioch was by no means exclusively Gentile (cf. Acts xi.19–21); but we do not know how big the church was and the proportion of Jews to Gentiles. It is striking that Paul speaks simply of 'the other Jews'. Although he obviously has Jewish believers in mind, he characterizes them not as 'those who believe' (cf. iii.22), but simply as 'Jews'. 'Jew' was by now the common name to denote people from Palestine (or more specifically Judea), an identification which presupposed (naturally in the ancient world) that those of the same national stock would share the same religious loyalty and practices (*TDNT* iii.369–71), and which could therefore be used simply to mark off this people from other peoples – Jews from Greeks, Jews from Gentiles (as almost always in Paul (Rom. i.16; ii.9–10; iii.9, 29; etc.; note particularly Gal. ii.14–15; see further on i.13 and ii.3). It is on the Jewishness of the other Jewish believers that Paul focuses therefore. The implication obviously is that the issue was posed in terms of their being Jews, that is, as distinct from Gentiles, which constituted an appeal to their national and national-religious identity as Jews.

Paul charges them with joining in Peter's deception. In Greek metaphorical usage the word meant simply 'play a part' (as also in *Aristeas* 219, 267). But in Jewish usage it gained a regularly negative note – 'pretend, deceive' (as in Sir. xxxii.15; xxxiii.2; *Pss. Sol.* iv.20, 22); a particularly poignant parallel is the memory of the Maccabean martyr, Eleazar, who refused to pretend to eat pork and food sacrificed to idols in order to escape execution (2 Macc. vi.21, 24; *4 Macc.* vi.15, 17) (see further *TDNT* viii.563–5; Betz 109–10). The accusation was presumably not that they pretended to the James people, to deceive them into thinking they were still as faithful to the food laws and traditions as the James people wanted (Betz 108 notes that the word 'withdraw' in ii.12 could indicate a tactical manoeuvre), with the implication that after their departure the Jewish believers resumed their previous practice of eating with the Gentiles; would Paul have been quite so fiercely critical of that? Nor probably did Paul intend to accuse Peter of being consciously insincere (so most, e.g. Fung 109 – 'conduct which masked and belied Peter's genuine convictions'); that does not seem to make enough allowance for the obviously polemical character of the reference (though the imperfect tenses of ii.12b could indicate a certain degree of hesitation on Peter's part). Rather, the clear implication of ii.14 ('not walking straight towards the truth of the gospel') is that Paul saw the conduct of Peter and the others as inconsistent with 'the truth of the gospel' which had been secured in Paul's understanding by that agreement (ii.5) (*TDNT* viii.569). Peter *should* have seen the inconsistency, but evidently did *not* (Mussner 143 points appropriately to the 'knowing' of ii.16).

If that was Paul's view of the matter, no doubt Peter's was quite different (as was that of later Jewish-Christianity – *Clem. Hom.* xvii.19, citing Paul's words in Gal. ii.11 at 19.6). Peter, we may properly assume, had very good reasons for his action – good enough to carry with him all the other Jewish believers, including even Barnabas, who had been on Paul's side of the agreement at Jerusalem. These reasons would probably include: (1) a recognition of the logic of the demand made by the James people, that the Jerusalem agreement required a Jewish believer to continue practising as a Jew; Peter was convinced by the James people that they had been right to criticize him; the 'fear' of which Paul speaks (ii.12) could have been simply Peter's concern not to cause scandal to his fellow Jewish believers. (2) As

'Jews' they would feel the force of any appeal to retain national and religious identity in face of any threatened encroachment from Gentiles: the Maccabean literature demonstrates how powerful that appeal was all through this period; and it would have been strengthened by the recurring crises on the national political front. (3) As 'apostle of the circumcision' Peter's credibility, not to say even the possibility of effective outreach, would have been seriously jeopardized if the charge, presumably put by the 'individuals from James', gained currency that he was now 'living like a Gentile' (see on ii.14). (4) And since the tradition of Gentiles 'judaizing' in order to have a share in the treasures of Jewish heritage was so well established, it was not too much to ask that the Gentile believers in Antioch 'judaize' to a further extent sufficient to satisfy the concerns voiced by the people from James. (see further on ii.14 – 'judaize'; and my 'Incident' 156–7). Thus could the principled and pragmatic action of one Christian seem to another like hypocrisy. Paul himself was later to encourage similar compromises – in predominantly Gentile churches (1 Cor. viii.7–13; Rom. xiv.13–xv.4). But in a Gentile church it could be presented as a proper self-chosen limitation in the exercise of legitimate liberty. In contrast, in the situation at Antioch, the attempt by Jewish believers to impose such a limitation was, in Paul's view, an infringement of the gospel itself. The line between exercise of gospel liberty and defence of gospel liberty is exceedingly narrow.

There is a note of shock and sadness in Paul's further recollection **that even Barnabas was carried away with their hypocrisy**. Barnabas, after all, had been Paul's partner both, it would appear, in the earlier missionary work among Gentiles and in the Jerusalem agreement on division of responsibility (ii.9). That Barnabas should so act must have been a tremendous blow to Paul (see further on ii.1). At the same time the charge against him is not so fierce ('*their* hypocrisy', not Barnabas's). And Paul's choice of verb probably implies (cf. 1 Cor. xii.2) that the action of the Jewish believers as a whole created a wave of fervour (to maintain Jewish identity) which Barnabas could not resist. The charge of 'hypocrisy' of course is polemical: in polemic a genuine disagreement can easily be represented as hypocrisy by those who see the issues differently or more sharply (cf. Matt. xxiii.28; Mark xii.15; Luke xii.1; 1 Tim. iv.2; 1 Pet. ii.1).

14 Paul however had no doubts as to the real nature of Peter's action and about the issues at stake – **but when I saw that they were not walking straight towards the truth of the gospel, I said to Cephas in front of everyone . . .** Although all the Jewish believers were involved ('they'), Paul singled out Cephas (see on i.18) as the one who had given the decisive lead. That Paul should charge him 'in front of everyone' (not just the Jewish believers), without, evidently, having tried to reason with Cephas privately earlier, indicates the urgency and seriousness of the crisis in Paul's eyes. The confrontation presumably took place at one of the larger (representative?) gatherings of Jewish and Gentile believers in Antioch. It may have been a gathering for worship and/or business, but not for a common meal or Lord's Supper. Burton deduces that Paul must have been absent from Antioch when the defection occurred, otherwise he would surely have acted sooner (pp. 101, 109–10).

The recurrence of the same phrase ('the truth of the gospel') which Paul had used in ii.5 is sufficient indication that Paul saw the issue in terms of the agreement at Jerusalem, and that he understood that agreement as safeguarding the reality of the gospel as one of liberation and its trustworthiness as ensuring participation in the blessing of Abraham without requiring Gentiles to judaize (see on ii.5). The Jewish believers were playing false by that agreement. The word 'walk straight or upright' is unattested elsewhere at this time, but its imagery is obvious and Paul may have coined it as being self-explicit. It implies no sense of 'orthodoxy' as yet, simply that in this case they were departing from the, to Paul, obvious truth of the gospel which he thought had been agreed at Jerusalem. Once again, no doubt, Peter saw things differently (see on ii.13). The force of the prepositional phrase following the verb is unclear: after a verb denoting movement it would most naturally mean 'towards'; but it could mean something like 'in reference to' (so English translations). In the former case the image would imply a conviction on Paul's part that the Jewish believers generally still had some way to go before they entered fully into the liberty of the gospel, and that their conduct in Antioch was a serious divergence from that goal (see BAGD, *orthopodeō*; Mussner 144).

Paul recalls the actual words he used on that occasion: **'If you, a Jew, "live like a Gentile and not like a Jew": . .'.** As before, the point is the distinctiveness of Jew from Gentile, and thus the boundary markers which distinguished the two from each other, including, but not only, those drawn round the meal table (see on i.13–14, and ii.3, 12). 'To live like a Jew' was obviously to live in accordance with Jewish customs (as in Philo, *Legat.* 159, 170, 256); 'to live like a Gentile' was to live in a way which marked it out as different from 'the Jewish way of life' (cf. i.13). It is important to recognize here that these are relative terms: 'to live like a Gentile' does *not* necessarily mean that they had wholly abandoned everything that would normally mark out a Jew ('Cephas' total emancipation from Judaism' – Betz 112); the contrast is primarily with 'live like a Jew' and is determined by what 'live like a Jew' was understood to mean in that context.

In fact, we should probably recognize here the tones of *intra*-Jewish polemic, of Jewish factionalism (as already suggested on ii.12). In the factionalism of the Maccabean and post-Maccabean period there were those who saw themselves as 'righteous' and other Jews as 'sinners'; that is to say, they regarded themselves as alone faithful to the covenant obligations laid on Israel, and dismissed other Jews (or at least their Jewish opponents) as effectively outside the covenant ('sinners' equivalent in effect to 'Gentile sinners') (see on ii.15). Thus *Jubilees* condemns not only the sons of Israel who failed to circumcise their sons as 'making themselves like the Gentiles', and who thus had left the covenant and for whom there was no pardon (xv.33–4). But it also condemns those Jews who used a different calendar to calculate the feast days as 'forgetting the feasts of the covenant and walking in the feasts of the gentiles, after their errors and after their ignorance' (vi.35). And the *Psalms of Solomon* condemn in even stronger terms their (probably Sadducean) opponents: 'Their lawless actions surpassed the gentiles before them' (i.8); 'there was no sin they left undone in which they did not surpass the gentiles' (viii.13). It is not correct, therefore, to say that 'it would be quite impossible to describe existence under the (apostolic) Decree as living like a Gentile' (Catchpole 441). On the contrary, for one Jew to accuse another Jew of 'living like a Gentile' was wholly of a piece with the language of intra-Jewish sectarian polemic. When group boundaries are (perceived to be) under threat, a natural response is to castigate those who threaten those boundaries as polar opposites in order to strengthen the group's own identity and distinctiveness (e.g. all those to the 'left' of a 'right-wing' party castigated as 'communists').

Here, then, we should probably recognize that Paul was using not his own language (by that time Peter had ceased 'living like a Gentile'), but the language used against Peter earlier by the 'individuals from James'. That is to say, Paul was probably echoing the accusation made by those from James against the practice of 'eating with the Gentiles' (hence the quotation marks in the text); for the James group, what Peter was doing when they arrived was 'living like a Gentile and not like a Jew' (see also on ii.15). If so, that tells us something about the pressures under which James and his group felt themselves, to demonstrate their faithfulness and loyalty as devout Jews, and about the nationalistic, religious and emotional pressure ('group loyalty') they in turn were able to exert on Peter and the others in Antioch.

If the first half of Paul's charge echoes the language of the 'individuals from James', the terms of the second half are probably Paul's own – . . . **how is it that you compel** (or, are trying to compel – conative present, BDF §319) **the Gentiles to judaize?** 'To judaize' was a quite familiar expression, meaning 'to adopt a (characteristically) Jewish way of life'. The fact that many Gentiles in the ancient world 'judaized', that is adopted Jewish customs, attended Jewish synagogues, identified themselves in some measure with Jews, is well attested (Plutarch, *Cicero* vii.6; Josephus, *War* ii.463; see further on ii.12). Many think that Paul had in mind circumcision in particular, that he was accusing Peter of compelling the Gentile believers to be circumcised. But the usage elsewhere distinguishes 'judaizing' from 'being circumcised' and indicates that the former could embrace a range of degrees of assimilation to Jewish life-style, with circumcision as the climax, but without necessarily including circumcision (Esther viii.17 LXX; Eusebius, *Praep. Evang.* ix.22.5; Josephus, *War* ii.454 [cited in Introduction §6.2 n. 21]). Nor is it likely that Peter and Barnabas had so completely reneged on the central point of the Jerusalem agreement (ii.3–10). It is much more likely that what the James people insisted on was at least formally within the terms of the Jerusalem agreement, and that their demand was for Jewish believers to live lives whose Jewish character was much more clearly demarcated. 'The issue is not circumcision but purity' (Betz 104).

What Peter and the others thought would be the effect of their withdrawal from the communal meals on their Gentile fellows is not clear: as already suggested (see on ii.13), if Peter had given some forethought to the likely consequences of his action, he probably deemed it not unfair to ask the Gentile believers to conform more fully to Jewish scruples. Alternatively, since there would have been many house churches in Antioch, they may even have thought that the different (Jewish and Gentile) churches could be content with separate social life-styles. However, for Gentile believers, who understood that by conversion and baptism they had entered into the blessings of the promise to Abraham, and who wished to maintain fellowship with the heirs of Abraham by physical descent, their conduct would, of course, exert a strong element of 'compulsion to judaize' (whether explicit or implicit). The echo of ii.3 ('not compelled to be circumcised') is probably deliberate: what Paul objected to so vehemently was that an element of compulsion on Gentiles to adopt distinctive Jewish laws and customs as a *necessary* part of the gospel, which Paul thought had been ruled out at Jerusalem, was now once again being reasserted in defiance of the spirit of that agreement – and unilaterally, without the sort of discussion which had made the Jerusalem agreement possible.

Although Paul continues to restate his rebuke to Peter (ii.15ff.), his account of the Antioch incident as such is already effectively concluded. It has to be noted that he does *not* say that Peter accepted his rebuke and resumed his former practice. Paul would almost certainly have noted this further victory for his understanding of the gospel, had he been able to win Peter over, just as he obviously took pains to describe his earlier victory in Jerusalem (ii.1–10). The matter was too crucial to the outcome of the similar crisis confronting the Galatian churches for Paul to pass over such a victory in total silence.[1] His silence, in fact, points in quite the other direction: that Peter did not accept or heed his rebuke, and that Paul received no real backing from the rest of the Antioch Christians – apparently Gentiles as well as Jews ('the absent James was a more powerful influence than the present Paul' – Barrett, *Freedom* 13). This presumably means that the Christian Gentiles accepted the terms for table-fellowship which the Jewish believers were implicitly requiring if fellowship was to be resumed, and 'judaized' accordingly. This in turn must have meant that Antioch ceased, in Paul's eyes, to represent the Gentiles (the agreement of ii.9, as Paul understood it). In consequence, Paul must have concluded that his responsibility towards the Gentiles could now only be executed in independence of Antioch, as is also suggested by the record of Acts where Paul is shown as moving his base further out into the diaspora, first to Corinth, and then to Ephesus (Acts xviii.11; xix.10), with Rom. xv.24 implying that latterly he hoped to use Rome itself as a base for his mission to Spain.

The defeat at Antioch, therefore, in all probability involved a triple breach – with Jerusalem (hence the distancing formula, particularly of ii.6), with Barnabas (cf. Acts xv.36–41), and with Antioch (which, even according to Acts xviii.22, he only visited once more). We need not assume that all these breaches were

---

1 This view is now common; see e.g. my 'Incident' 173 n.126; R. E. Brown & J. P. Meier, *Antioch and Rome: New Testament Cradles of Catholic Christianity* (London: Chapman, 1983) 39; Borse 106; P. J. Achtemeier, *The Quest for Unity in the New Testament Church* (Philadelphia: Fortress, 1987), 59. Typical of the older view is Rendall 162 – 'he refrains from recording Peter's humiliating retreat from a false position'.

equally deep or permanent: Barnabas is subsequently recalled without rancour (1 Cor. ix.6; Col. iv.10); Acts xviii.22 may imply a reconciliation with Antioch (Taylor, *Paul* ch. 7), and Paul himself is regarded highly by Ignatius, bishop of Antioch, sixty or so years later (*Ephesians* xii.2); and Paul's efforts on behalf of 'the poor among the saints at Jerusalem' became an increasingly important concern for him (Rom. xv.26–7; see on ii.10). The other side of the picture, however, is the increasing hostility through this period and beyond towards Paul by conservative Jewish Christians (Acts xxi.21; pseudo-Clementines in Betz 331–3).

8 PAUL'S RESTATEMENT OF HIS CASE ii.15-21

(15) We are Jews by nature and not 'Gentile sinners',[1] (16) knowing[2] that no human being is justified by works of the law but only through faith in Jesus Christ,[3] and we have believed in Christ Jesus,[3] in order that we might be justified by faith in Christ and not by works of the law, because by works of the law shall no flesh be justified. (17) But if in seeking to be justified in Christ we find that we too are 'sinners',[1] is then Christ a servant of sin? Impossible! (18) For if I build again the very things which I demolished, I demonstrate that I myself am a wrong-doer. (19) For I through the law died to the law, in order that I might live for God. I have been crucified with Christ; (20) and it is no longer I that lives, but Christ lives in me. And the life I now live in the flesh, I live by faith which is in the Son of God[4] who loved me and gave himself for me. (21) I do not nullify the grace of God; for if righteousness is through the law, then Christ has died to no purpose.

1 As in ii.14, the words in quotation marks were probably deliberate echoes of statements made by the group from James.

2 Most read the clause as an adversative – 'but we know'. However, the 'but' is not attested by the oldest manuscript (p^{46}) as well as others; and had Paul wished to say 'but we know' he would probably have used the indicative (as in Rom. viii.28) rather than the participle which indicates more of a continuity of thought from the main clause (cf. Rom. vi.9; 2 Cor. iv.14). The 'but' was probably introduced because later scribes assumed that the whole of verse 16 stood in contrast to verse 15 (Borse 112).

3 Manuscripts vary between reading 'Jesus Christ' and 'Christ Jesus'; the order evidently was not considered to be very significant.

4 The reading 'faith in God and Christ' is quite strongly attested, but Paul nowhere else speaks thus of God as the object of Christian faith, and the variant can easily be explained as an attempt to correct scribal error (Metzger 593).

It is generally accepted that Paul here restates the position he argued for at Antioch in the confrontation with Peter. The thought certainly seems to flow directly on: the readers of the letter could hardly understand the 'we' of ii.15 as other than a reference to Peter and Paul; there seem to be clear echoes of the confrontation in the language used in ii.15b and 17; and ii.18 surely refers back to the sort of conduct denounced by Paul on that occasion. At the same time, if, as seems most likely, Paul failed to carry the day at Antioch, and was now confronted by a situation in Galatia which he saw to be equally as serious, if not more so, it would be natural for him to attempt to restate the argument used on that occasion in the hope that it would prove more effective on this occasion. To that extent Betz 114, 121–2 is justified in seeing in ii.15–21 the equivalent of the *propositio*, whose objective in rhetorical practice, according to Quintilian, was to sum up the position so far, including the points of agreement, and to provide a transition to the main stage of the argument following (the *probatio*); though he over-elaborates his case, particularly in finding verses 19–20 to contain 'four theological theses, to be elaborated upon later'. Whatever the rhetorical precedents, however, a little reflection indicates the importance of the section and its function. For as it now reads, the Antioch incident does not end with any clear success for Paul (indeed his failure is implied; see on ii.14). So, to narrate it *after* the success of the Jerusalem agreement left Paul and his interpretation of the Jerusalem agreement very vulnerable. It was essential, therefore, that he counter that impression. Verses ii.15–21 are the beginning of his attempt to do so, and mark a transition and lead into the letter's main argument (chs. iii–iv). This confirms Bligh's suggestion (see Introduction to ii.11–14) that the whole letter is in effect Paul's attempt to undo the damage of what had happened at Antioch. On the passage see also M. Bachmann, *Sünder oder Übertreter. Studien zur Argumentation in Gal. ii. 15ff.* (WUNT 59; Tübingen: Mohr, 1992); E. Kok, *'The Truth of the Gospel', A Study in Galatians 2.15–21* (Durham University PhD, 1993).

15 Paul begins to answer the question he had asked Peter (ii.14) – **We are Jews by nature** (BAGD, *physis* 1) **and not Gentile sinners**. To be noted at once is the characteristic Jewish language, in which once again the world is seen as divided into two distinct groups – Jews and the rest, Jews and 'the nations' (see on ii.13). More striking still is the description of Gentiles as 'sinners'. For 'sinners' in Jewish thought meant pre-eminently those whose lawless conduct marked them out as outside the covenant, destined for destruction and so not to be consorted with (e.g. Pss. i.1, 5; xxxvii.34–6; lviii.10; Prov. xii.12–13; xxiv.20; Sir. vii.16; ix.11; xli.5–11). Thus it could be used, as here, as synonymous with 'Gentiles', those who, by definition were lawless (outside the law) and whose conduct therefore was inevitably in breach of the law (Ps. ix.17; Tobit xiii.6; *Jub.* xxiii.23–4 *Pss. Sol.* ii.1–2; Matt. v.47/Luke vi.33) (cf. *TDNT* i.325–6, 328). Still more striking, however, is the fact that the same epithet was often used in intra-Jewish polemic, by one faction, who claimed to be 'righteous', against another faction, whom they regarded as 'sinners', because the latter failed to conform to their (sectarian) definition of 'righteousness' (e.g 1 Macc. i.34; ii.44, 48; *1 Enoch* v.4–7; 82.4–5; 1QH ii.8–12; 1QpHab v.4–8; *Pss.Sol.* iv.8; xiii.6–12) – a usage which, of course, makes perfect sense of the criticism of Jesus that he 'ate with sinners' (Mark ii.16) (see further my 'Pharisees' 73–7; *Partings* §6.2).

This language rings oddly on the lips of Paul, until we realize what he was doing. Paul was putting himself in the shoes of a typical Jew who looked out at the rest of the world as outside the realm of God's covenant righteousness and sinful (cf. Eph. ii.12). More to the point, he was using the language of typical Jewish factionalism, which was ready to condemn those Jews who disagreed with the sect's interpretation of what the law required as 'sinners' – outside their sectarian understanding of the covenant, which meant, of course, from the sectarian viewpoint, outside the covenant. In fact, Paul was probably echoing the language used by the 'individuals from James' when they spoke against the Jewish Christians' table-fellowship with the Gentile believers: such table-fellowship with 'Gentile sinners' was unacceptable (see also on ii.14 – 'living like a Gentile and not like a Jew').

Ironically, then, the language used by Paul here is the language of conciliation. In character with the *propositio*, Paul was looking for common ground with his fellow Jewish believers. In reaching out to Peter, he took his stand with him, even in the attitude Peter had acted out in Antioch – 'we are all Jews by nature' – that is, Jews born and bred, not proselytes, far less resident aliens or God-fearers. He looked out with them from that perspective at the rest of humankind, echoing the dismissive attitude of the faithful member of the covenant people towards the non-Jews – 'Gentile sinners'. Burton 119 and Mussner 167 obscure all this by inserting a qualifying conjunction – 'We, though by nature Jews . . .'. And Suhl 3099–106 both forces the natural sense of the syntax (where the phrases 'by nature *Jews*', 'from Gentiles *sinners*' form the antithesis) and ignores the historical context completely by attempting to defend the strained paraphrase, 'We, of course, Jews by nature and not stemming from the Gentiles, are nevertheless sinners (as much as them)'.

16 Of course, Paul's objective was to turn Peter away from the attitude which had resulted in the breach in Antioch. But in order to win him over, Paul had to start with what they agreed on. So he continues – **knowing that no human being is justified by works of the law but only through faith in Jesus Christ**. Paul appeals to their common knowledge – that is, their common knowledge as 'Jews by nature' who believed in Christ. Just what that common knowledge and experience consisted in is disputed; and since the passage is obviously crucial to Paul's statement of his position ('This is the text on which all that follows in the Epistle is commentary' – Duncan 64–5) we need to examine it with some care.

The verb 'justify' is predominantly Paul's word in the NT (the Pauline corpus contains 27 of the 35 NT occurrences), and Galatians (8) and Romans (15) dominate Paul's usage, with four of Galatians' eight coming in ii.16–17. It is a metaphor drawn from the law court to describe the judge's responsibility to give a fair verdict and to 'justify', that is, acquit the innocent, as in typically Jewish usage (Exod. xxiii.7; Deut. xxv.1; 2 Sam. xv.4; Pss. li.4; lxxxii.3; Isa. v.23; xliii.26; Mic. vi.11). As used here, therefore, it reflects the axiomatic assumption among Jews (cf. Rom. iii.6) that God exercised and would exercise the role of end-time judge in relation to the world, both Jew and Gentile (see e.g. *TDNT* iii.935). The one thus 'justified' or acquitted was thereby found to be 'righteous'; the ground of a favourable judgement was the 'righteousness' of the one judged (all three words come from the same root in both Hebrew and Greek); to be 'justified' was to be formally recognized as 'righteous'. At this point, however, Hebrew and Greek concepts diverged. For whereas in Greek thought 'righteousness' or 'justice' was an ideal norm by which particular claims or duties could be measured, in Hebrew thought 'righteousness' was more a concept of relation. People were 'righteous' when they met the claims which others had on them by virtue of their relationship (see e.g. *TDNT* ii.195–6; *IDB* iv.80–5). For Israel that meant pre-eminently the relationship with Yahweh, that is the covenant he had made with Israel when he chose Israel to be his people: to be righteous was to live within the covenant and within the terms it laid down (the law); to be acquitted, recognized as righteous, was to be counted as one of God's own people who had proved faithful to the covenant (so most clearly at Qumran – see e.g. Mussner 168–9; and further my *Romans* 40–1 [bibliography 36–7]; *Partings*.§§2.2–3).

Thus far Paul had used language familiar to anyone who was 'a Jew by nature'. But he immediately qualifies it in a way which shows that he was speaking as a Jew who was also a believer in Messiah Jesus. For he denies that acceptance or acquittal by God the judge is 'on the basis of works of the law'. This has traditionally been understood as a denial that human beings, even the most religious of individuals, can achieve salvation by their own 'works';[1] they cannot 'work' their passage to heaven; they cannot earn salvation by their own efforts. Valid as that is as a theological insight of tremendous importance, it is doubtful whether it quite catches Paul's meaning here. Paul was evidently objecting to a current Jewish conviction. But so far as we can tell, the typical and traditional Jewish view of the time was *not* that anyone could earn God's favour. On the contrary, the whole of Israel's religion was founded on the axiom that God had chosen Israel as an act wholly undeserved. Membership of the covenant people already presupposed God's gracious election and sustaining favour; it did not have to be earned (see further particularly Sanders, *Paul*; also my 'New Perspective'). Nor does the phrase itself denote human deeds of meritorious quality. What then was Paul denying? What did he mean by saying that 'works of the law' provide no ground for justification? The point is obviously of central importance to Paul's argument, since he states it no less than three times in this one verse (also iii.2, 5, 10; it is equally central to the summary statement in Rom. iii.20).

The phrase itself ('works of the law') means most naturally 'deeds or actions which the law requires'. It has no immediate parallel in the OT; but in typical Jewish understanding the law had been given as part of God's covenant, to show covenant members how to live within the covenant and to enable them to do so (we need mention only Deuteronomy). So most Jews would, again most naturally, understand the phrase to mean 'the obligations laid upon Israelites by virtue of their membership of

1 It is taken typically in traditional scholarship to denote (human) 'achievements': e.g. 'deeds of obedience to formal statutes done in a legalistic spirit' (Burton 120); 'meritorious works of the Torah' (Betz 117); 'any and all works as works-of-merit' (Fung 114, citing R. Bultmann, *Theology of the New Testament* [London: SCM, 1952–5] i.283); 'merit-amassing observance of Torah' (Longenecker 86); 'social and cultural achievements . . . brought about by law – in principle, by any law' (Georgi, *Theocracy* 38); righteousness merited by performing the law (T. R. Schreiner, '"Works of Law" in Paul', *NovT* 33 [1991] 217–44).

Israel' (more or less, in fact, what Sanders meant when he coined the inelegant phrase 'covenantal nomism' to describe this Jewish attitude). However, as we have already noted, second-Temple Judaism was split into various factions, each claiming to have the proper understanding of the law and of its obligations (see on ii.15 – 'sinners'). 'Works of the law', then, would probably reflect this factionalism and the common concern within second-Temple Judaism to draw the lines of demarcation round covenant righteousness as clearly as possible. This is confirmed by what is a close parallel to the phrase within one of the most prominent of these factions – the Essene community at Qumran. In the DSS it was precisely the covenanter's 'deeds of the law' which had to be tested in order to check whether his membership of the community could be sustained (1QS v.21, 23; vi.18); the implication of 4QFlor. i.7 is that only at Qumran were 'the works of the law' able properly to be performed; the Qumran document known as 'Some of the Deeds of the Law' (whose contents have only recently been made public) contains a series of distinctive Qumran rulings on disputed points of law (4QMMT). In other words, at Qumran 'works of the law' denoted a sectarian understanding of the law, denoted, indeed, the sect's distinctive understanding and practice of the law – that understanding and practice of the law which marked it out from others, including other Jews (see also on iii.10).

'Works of the law' therefore was probably used initially in a polemical context (as with several other of the phrases used here – see on ii.14 and 15), to denote particularly those obligations of the law which were reckoned especially crucial in the maintenance of covenant righteousness, in the maintenance of an individual Jew's status within the covenant. In principle that meant all that the law required. But in practice the faithfulness of the sectarian was determined by his demonstration of loyalty to the sect's distinctive interpretations of the law on disputed points. So too in second-Temple Judaism at large. 'Works of the law' would mean in principle all that the faithful Israelite had to do as a member of the chosen people, that is, as distinct from 'Gentile sinners'. But in practice there were a number of test cases, several specific laws which in the history of earliest Judaism had brought the issue of covenant loyalty to clear decision, boundary issues where the distinctiveness of Jew from Gentile was most at stake. Two have already been mentioned – circumcision and food laws (see on ii.3 and ii.12). Evidently these two in particular had been 'make or break' issues for Jewish identity and covenant faithfulness since the Maccabean crisis. It should occasion no surprise, then, that it had been just these two issues which had dominated the immediately preceding context in Gal. ii (circumcision – ii.1–10; food laws – ii.11–14), for these were precisely the test cases of Jewish distinctiveness over against Gentiles which were in danger of splitting the Jesus movement. In thus introducing the phrase immediately after his report of the two encounters Paul could expect his readers to recognize that 'works of the law' summed up the issue posed by these two test cases in particular; that the two encounters had made 'covenantal nomism' an issue, at least in so far as it required a clearly defined boundary to be maintained between Jew and Gentile. The issue expressed in 'works of the law', in other words, was *not* whether membership of the people of God entailed various obligations (Paul had no doubt that it did), but whether it entailed an in effect sectarian interpretation of these obligations, whether it entailed obligations designed to exclude others, whether it entailed that Jew remain distinct from Gentile (similarly Rom. iii.20 – see my *Romans* 153–5, 210, 213; also 'Works' 219–25, 237–41; also 'Once More, Works').

The point here clearly is Paul's denial that 'works of the law' are a basis of God's favourable judgement. But he also claimed that this was part of the common ground between him and Peter ('in this context the doctrine of justification by faith is part of a Jewish-Christian theology' – Betz 115). This was certainly true in the case of one of the two test cases (circumcision); to that extent Paul was able to appeal to the Jerusalem agreement (ii.3–10). But Peter had taken up a different stand on the second test case (food laws) in the Antioch incident (ii.11–14). An appeal to Peter on this issue, then, was likely to be a double-edged weapon. So, what could Paul mean? The answer presumably lies in the final phrase – 'but only through faith in Jesus Christ'. This phrase clearly functions as some sort of qualification of the main sentence. But what sort of qualification? The linking conjunction is exceptive and not adversative; that is, it is not simply equivalent to 'but', but to 'but only' (see my 'New Perspective' 212). Which means that 'works of the law' and 'faith in Jesus Christ' are not necessarily being posed here as mutually exclusive antitheses. In other words, as in the two earlier cases in Galatians where Paul uses the equivalent linking conjunction (i.7, 19), the relation of the qualifying phrase to the preceding clause is ambiguous: does 'the gospel' wholly exclude the 'other gospel' or allow that it might be called 'gospel' in an exceptional way? do 'the other apostles' exclude James or include him? does 'faith in Jesus Christ' exclude 'works of the law' or is it the one exception to the rule that 'no one is justified by works of the law'?

This ambiguity was nicely calculated precisely with a view to gaining Peter's assent. For its ambiguity reflected precisely the ambiguity of Peter's position – Peter who at Jerusalem had agreed that faith in Jesus Christ made circumcision of Gentiles unnecessary, but who now had acted as though Gentiles should be required to observe the Jewish food laws – Peter who thus on the one hand said works of the law were unnecessary (faith in Christ alone was sufficient), but who on the other hand also said that works of the law should still be obligatory for members of the covenant (cf. James ii.17–26). The logic of the Jewish-Christian position, we may say, was that 'faith in Jesus Christ' was an intra-Jewish possibility – a challenge to those already in the covenant people, who took the necessity of 'works of the law' for granted; it was this 'view from inside' which Paul took up in order to question it. At all events, the bottom line is clear: Peter evidently would have affirmed with Paul, as a matter of common Christian conviction, that 'a person is justified by faith in Jesus Christ'; but his actions in Antioch showed that he also believed that 'works of the law' were consistent with such faith. Paul's purpose in ii.16 was precisely to argue that these two beliefs could no longer be held together: the Antioch incident showed what happened when they were; and the danger confronting the Galatians was that they too would be persuaded to act like Peter and qualify their original faith with 'works of the law' (iii.2–3).

The phrase 'faith in Jesus Christ' is clearly an important one: Paul's gospel can be summed up in terms of 'justification by faith' (ii.16; iii.6, 8, 11, 24; v.5; see also on i.23). However, it is now frequently taken in the sense 'the faithfulness of Jesus Christ'; that is, Christ's faithfulness in going the way of the cross, a covenant faithfulness which made good the unfaithfulness of Israel; or indeed Jesus' own faith in God which is now the basis of Christian living and in which Christians now share (particularly Hays, *Faith*, ch. 4; Hooker, *Adam* 165–86; bibliography in Longenecker 87). Most however continue to take it as 'faith in Christ'. The word itself can, of course, mean either 'faith' or 'faithfulness' (BAGD, *pistis*). And the genitive construction in itself is indecisive either way (cf. Mark xi.22 – 'faith of = in God'; Acts iii.16 – 'faith of = in his name'; Col. ii.12 – 'faith of = in the working of God'; 1 Thess. ii.13 – 'faith of = in the truth'; Phil. iii.8 – 'knowledge of Christ Jesus'). But among the chief considerations in favour of the usual view are the following. (1) 'Faith' = 'belief or trust in', as a religious term was familiar in the Hellenistic world (BAGD, *pistis* 2; *TDNT* vi.179–82). This would be the most natural sense to expect a reader to take, whereas 'the faithfulness of Christ' would require a good deal of unpacking, which Paul never provides. (2) One would expect phrases using the verb to function as equivalent alternatives to phrases using the noun. This is just what we do find here (the next clause) and in iii.6–9, 22 (as still more clearly throughout Rom. iv); whereas we never read in Paul of Christ 'believing'. (3) Both here in Galatians and in Romans the issue addressed by Paul is how someone is 'justified'. His key text is Gen. xv.6 (Gal. iii.6; Rom. iv.3), which he clearly understands to say that Abraham was justified by his faith. Gal. ii.16 is most obviously heard as sounding the first note of that theme. (4) As an antithesis to 'works of the law', 'faith of/in Christ' is most naturally understood as posing alternative human responses to God's initiative of grace (so also in iii.2, 5, 14 and v.5, 6). In short, the phrase is still best taken as expressing faith in Christ, that is, acceptance of the reliability of what was said by and about Christ (acceptance of the gospel message – iii.2, 5) and trust in, reliance upon the Christ of whom the gospel thus spoke (BAGD, *pisteuō* 1 and 2; see further my *'Pistis Christou'* and on ii.20). It is worth noting that Paul says 'through' faith (as in Rom. iii.22, 30; Phil. iii.9): this trust as the medium through which God's acceptance comes to effect. But Paul can equally well say 'from faith' (as in ii.16c); for Paul the difference was largely stylistic (cf. Rom. iii.30).

Paul continues to appeal to the common ground he shared with Peter – **and we** (yes, even we Jews) **in Christ Jesus have believed**. The statement is not tautologous (thus indicating that 'faith in Jesus Christ' should be rendered differently). The repetition is deliberate, for the sake of emphasis: we do not simply know that justification is by faith in Christ as a matter of principle; we have actually so believed; the principle has been tried and proven in our own experience. This, in fact, is where the transition from the shared viewpoint of the preceding clause begins. Paul looks back to his own experience on the Damascus road and recalls Peter to the equivalent experience of a grace reaching out to him which he could only accept and trust himself to; he had 'got to know Cephas' (i.18) well enough to know that Peter would so speak of the commitment of his discipleship (cf. Acts xi.17). The usage ('believing into') is distinctively Christian, though Paul speaks of 'believing into Christ' (= commitment to Christ) in only two other passages (Rom. x.14; Phil. i.29; cf. Col. ii.5).

But in appealing to Peter's earlier experience of belief and commitment Paul was trying to get back behind Peter's subsequent action at Antioch. The point of that initial experience of faith was **in order that we might be justified by faith in**

Christ and not by works of the law. If faith in Christ was sufficient then for discipleship and membership of the Jesus movement, that still remained true, and could not be nullified by disagreement over 'works of the law'. In other words, Paul was trying to move Peter away from the ambiguity of the opening statement (ii.16a), from the ambiguity reflected in his conduct at Antioch, from the ambiguity regarding the acceptability of Gentiles who like him had 'believed in Messiah Jesus'. And that required a resolution to the ambiguity of the opening statement, a resolution of the possible 'both-and' (faith and works) which Peter had practised, into a straight 'either-or' (faith and *not* works) which his earlier experience of faith had indicated (the 'in order that' signifying God's purpose). The fact that according to Acts xi.17 Peter talks of Gentile 'believing' precisely in the same terms as his own may reflect the fact that Paul's appeal included reference to Peter's earlier experience with Cornelius.

As is his wont elsewhere (cf. particularly Rom. i.17), Paul rounds off this crucial statement of his case by citing a scriptural proof text – **because by works of the law shall no flesh be justified**. The echo of Ps. cxliii.2 is clear enough – 'no living person will be justified before you' (it is even clearer in Rom. iii.20). The sentiment was thoroughly Jewish – that no one could claim to be sinless before God, worthy of (final) acquittal by reason of the quality of his life (e.g. Job ix.2; Ps. xiv.1–3; Isa. lix.2ff.; *1 Enoch* lxxxi.5; 1QH ix.14–15). Paul modified the text slightly by omitting 'before you' (it was implicit anyway). More significant was the change of 'no living person' to 'no flesh'. The phrases were synonymous (cf. again *1 Enoch* lxxxi.5), with 'flesh' simply underlining the finitude, weakness and corruptibility of all human existence (cf. e.g. Gen. vi.12; Isa. xxxi.3; Sir. xxxi.1; 1QH xv.21; John iii.6; Rom. viii.3, 8; *TDNT* vii.107, 109, 111–12; see also on v.13). But 'flesh' is also the realm where outward and ethnic distinction is most clearly marked, as Jewish concern over circumcision also showed (Rom. ii.28; see on iii.3 and vi.13; also my 'New Perspective' 199–200). Most significant of all was the introduction of the key phrase in ii.16 – 'works of the law'. This was not a merely arbitrary move, such as might nullify the effect of the scriptural allusion, but a particular application of what would be recognized as a more general principle in Jewish thought. If *no one* could claim to be sinless or just before God, that included members of the covenant people. The theological logic was that 'works of the law', covenant faithfulness over against Gentile sinfulness, was no exception, as 'the righteous' too often assumed (the assumption attacked by Paul in Rom. ii – see my *Romans* 81ff). In other words, Paul was once again endeavouring to expose the ambiguity of Peter's position and to drive him into the either-or of faith and not 'works of the law'.

17 Having gone back to 'first principles' (their common experience of 'believing in Christ Jesus', and the scriptural axiom in Ps. cxliii.2), Paul now moves forward again and applies the theological logic of these first principles to the situation at Antioch – **but if in seeking to be justified in Christ we find that we too are 'sinners'** . . . The verb 'seek' can mean simply 'desire to obtain' (BAGD, *zēteō* 2) and need carry no implication of anxious searching. 'Justification' here is thought of more as a future hope – in the final judgment (cf. v.5). For 'in Christ' see on i.22. But here the phrase encapsulates the core of Paul's gospel: that believers are counted acceptable to God because they are 'in Christ'; he will take up the point in ii.19–20 and develop its significance in iii.13–29, with further echoes in iv.19 and v.4–6, 24 (see also on v.6). The verb 'find' (literally 'we have been found') indicates a result not envisaged by those 'seeking' (BAGD, *heuriskō* 1b). The surprising discovery for Paul (and Peter) was evidently that their eating with Gentiles caused them to be regarded as 'sinners', even by their fellow believers (REB catches the sense nicely – 'we ourselves no less than the Gentiles turn out to be sinners'). Even though they all, Jew and Gentile alike, had 'believed in Christ Jesus in order to be justified by faith in Christ', the James faction still insisted on regarding Gentiles as 'sinners', and those Jews who disregarded or treated lightly the traditional boundary lines by eating with them as equally 'sinners' (see further on ii.15). The echo of ii.15 surely indicates that Paul's thought went back at this point to the Antioch incident, with 'sinner' indicating conduct repugnant to traditionalist Jewish Christians, and not merely justification by faith itself.

But the implication of such an attitude was intolerable: **is then Christ a servant of sin? Impossible!** To regard those accepted by and in Christ as 'sinners' was to make Christ one who waited on and supported sin – 'sin' here in the characteristic Pauline sense of the personified power which exercises a fatal attraction over humankind, turning it in upon itself, forgetful of its creatureliness, and prey to animal appetite and death (as particularly in Rom. v.12–viii.10). The image of Christ as 'servant' will almost certainly be an echo of the context in Antioch, since the word still retained much of its original sense of 'table-waiter' (BAGD, *diakonos*; *TDNT* ii.82). Some allusion to Jesus' own words recalled in Mark x.42–5/Luke xxii.27 is also likely (Paul plays with the same thought in Rom. xv.8). Jesus' remembered readiness to 'wait upon' his disciples would in turn link in naturally to the memory of his own table-fellowship 'with sinners' (Matt. xi.19/Luke vii.34; Mark ii.16). Who could deny that Jesus would have been ready to 'wait upon' the meal tables of Jewish and Gentile disciples at Antioch? If such table-fellowship made Jewish believers 'sinners', it also made Christ 'servant of sin', one who was at sin's beck and call. That was the ludicrous corollary which followed inevitably from the attitude of the James people, the *reductio ad absurdum* of Peter's theology. It is not impossible that Paul was here echoing a further comment of the James people: but where they had seen the corollary to require withdrawal from table-fellowship with sinners, Paul's deduction was that continued categorization of Gentile believers as 'sinners' was wholly inappropriate. The strong response, 'may it not be so, of course not', is a feature of Paul's vigorous style (always after a rhetorical question); here also in iii.21 (cf. vi.14), and regularly in Romans (BAGD, *ginomai* I.3a).

18 Lest his logic be unclear, Paul elaborates − **for if I build again the very things which I demolished** (BAGD, *kataluō* 1.bβ) **I demonstrate that I myself am a wrong-doer** (not 'prove that I was wrong before' NJB). The metaphor of pulling down and re-erecting a construction would be familiar to Paul's Jewish or judaizing audience, particularly from its use in Jeremiah (i.10; xii.16−17; xxiv.6; xxxi.4, 28; xxxiii.7). 'The very things' probably include at least a reference to the food laws which were the occasion of division between Jew and Gentile at Antioch (Wilckens, 'Entwicklung' 170 − 'the observances of the law through which the boundaries between Israel and the goyim were established'); so the imagery is probably that of Israel protected as God's own possession and marked off from the other nations by a wall (Isa. v.2, 5; *Aristeas* 139; Eph. ii.14). Paul, evidently, was still harking back to the Antioch incident, but now in first-person terms, since, presumably, the sharpness of the contrast evoked (destruction/reconstruction) was true of him in a way that was not so true of Peter. Paul in effect divides his life into three possible phases: the time when his life was protected by a wall; the time when he tore that construction down; and the possibility of rebuilding it again. The point is that his tearing down was an essential part of the complete turn-around which his encounter with the risen Christ on the Damascus road entailed, the destruction of what he had previously regarded so highly (cf. Phil. iii.7); that old 'way of life in Judaism' (see on i.13−14) Paul recognized to be wholly at odds with faith in

Christ and the commission to 'preach him among the Gentiles' (see on i.16). For Paul now to rebuild what he had torn down would be to revert to that old attitude, where such table-fellowship as he enjoyed at Antioch would make him not simply an involuntary 'sinner' like the Gentiles, but a conscious lawbreaker (that 'transgressor' meant 'transgressor of the law' would be self-evident – cf. the use of the word elsewhere in the NT, Rom. ii.25, 27 and James ii. 9, 11). For Paul now to be asked to accept that his whole life as a Christian, in its outreach to Gentiles, was one long act of transgression, which put him beyond the pale of God's acceptance, was an impossible contradiction of what the gospel meant.

19 The contrast between Paul's way of life before his conversion-commissioning and his work among Gentiles since, can be expressed even more sharply, not just in terms of demolition and reconstruction, but in terms of death and life – **for I through the law died to the law, that I might live to God**. This is the first note of a characteristic Pauline theme, which sees the transition of believing in Christ as a dying which results in a different kind of living (cf. particularly Rom. vi.2–8; vii.6; Col. ii.20; iii.3). Whether the 'I' is generalized or not (true of all believers), the sentence is certainly a personal statement of Paul himself. For it was true of him more than anyone else that he 'through the law died to the law'. In the flow of thought running through verse 18 this can hardly be other than a reference once again to the contrast already described in i.13–16 (not to the earlier event described in Rom. vii.8–11, as GNB implies). It was in the full heat of his zeal for the law ('through the law') that he had wielded the sword in order to preserve Israel's distinctive identity and prerogatives (see again on i.14); it was in order to maintain the law as marking out Judaism, at the bidding of the law as he then understood it, that he had embarked on the course which brought him face to face with the risen Christ (see also on ii.21). And that encounter so completely turned upside down his understanding of the law and the covenant promises, that the law ceased from that time to exercise the same hold over him; that which had been his constant stimulus to action now failed to find any response in him; he became dead to what had previously been his primary motivating force. The thought is stark, but is not made easier by taking 'through the law' as a reference to 'the law of faith' (Rom. iii.27); nor is the issue here to be translated simply into ritual versus moral law.

The other side of the event of his conversion-commissioning was that he died to the law 'in order to live for God'. As in *4 Macc.* vii.19 and xvi.25, the thought is of life beyond death, not just a different version of this life, but a life which has experienced death and over which death has no more say (Rom. vi.10–11). That meant, for Paul, an irreversible change: to return under the law was for him as inconceivable as for one who enjoys life beyond death to return to life before death, life under death. It also meant a highly negative verdict on his previous way of life: not necessarily that it had not been 'to God', but that his encounter with Christ resulted in the possibility of living to God liberated from the constraints of that old life, that is from the mistaken perspectives which his old covenantal nomism had entailed (cf. Rom. xiv.8); the contrast with his previous attitude, that life was coterminous with doing the law (see on iii.12 and 21), is striking. All this was possible, as Paul is about to make clear, because his dying and new life were a sharing in Christ's death and risen life (cf. Rom. vi.8–11; vii.4). By implication, Christ's death was also a dying through the law and to the law in order that the constraints of the law might be lifted (cf. iii.13–14), so that the encounter with and openness to his risen life meant *ipso facto* an openness to the Gentiles which Paul had previously fought against (i.13–16).

Paul was anxious to make it clear that his about-face regarding the law was no mere idiosyncratic decision on his part; on the contrary it was the inevitable working out of Christ's death; it was part and parcel of Jesus' own death. 'I died to the law' means also **I have been crucified with Christ**. Still more prominent in Paul's theology than the thought of conversion as a 'dying' is his thought of it as a 'dying with Christ' (Rom. vi.4–6; 2 Cor. iv.10; Phil. iii.10), part of a much richer sequence of 'together with' vocabulary very characteristic of Paul (*TDNT* vii.786–7). Here particularly striking is the tense used – not aorist (my crucifixion was an event which was over and done some time in the past), but perfect (I have been nailed to the cross with Christ, and am still hanging there with him); so also in Gal. iii.1, vi.14 and Rom. vi.5.[1] Paul evidently thought of his life as a Christian as one in transition between Christ's death and Christ's resurrection (hence the future tense in Rom. vi.5b), as a process of being conformed to that death (Phil. iii.10) (see further my *Jesus* 330–4). But Christ's death was that of an outcast, the body hanging on the tree a defilement (see on iii.13); so that Paul's identification with him in his death left him in

---

1 Despite particularly Schlier 99–101, the tense makes an allusion to baptism highly improbable – still immersed! (see further my *Romans* 308, 311–17).

the same position. It was precisely as one who by his identification with the crucified Christ numbered himself with the outcast, that Paul found it inconceivable that he should withdraw from table-fellowship with Gentile believers.

20 There was a completely different focus to his life now – **it is no longer I that lives, but Christ lives in me**. The language is startling, and of course exaggerated (NJB, following KJV and RV, attempts unwisely and unjustifiably to weaken it – 'and yet I am alive; yet it is no longer I . . .'). But the exaggeration was obviously to make a point. And the point was to bring out the very radical nature of the personal transformation effected by Paul's encounter with the risen Christ. The old 'I' was dead, and had been replaced by a new focus of personality. That meant, on the one hand, that Paul was no longer the 'I' of i.13–14 – the 'I' which had found its identity 'in Judaism', as one for whom maintenance of the law in order to preserve Jewish distinctiveness was the very reason for existence. That was why reversion to a table-fellowship which excluded Gentiles as Gentiles was impossible for Paul; it simply would not have been him. On the other hand, the new focus of his personality was not simply a transformed 'I'; it was Christ. It was only Christ whose death had been effective to destroy the division between Jew and Gentile – himself the 'seed' of Abraham, whose death had been that of an outlaw (see on iii.16 and again on iii.13). It was this Christ who was now the focus of Paul's life – the Jewish Messiah who was also for the out-law, the non-Jew. The 'I' which had fought to maintain its identity as a Jew in distinction from Gentile, now saw itself only as a vehicle for the expression of Christ's life. These contextual considerations show that the train of thought is different from that in Rom. vii; but as in Rom. vi–viii, an Adam christology lies in the background (cf. Col. iii.4, 9–10), as also a powerful sense that the new age of God's purpose has dawned (the 'Christ in me' is the risen Christ).

The idea of 'Christ indwelling' the believer (Rom. viii.10; 2 Cor. xiii.5; Col. i.27; Eph. iii.17) is much less common in Paul than its reverse, the believer 'in Christ' (see on i.22 and ii.17). More typical of Paul is the thought of the Spirit indwelling or acting in the believer (Rom. v.5; viii.9, 11, 15–16, 23, 26; etc.; see on iii.2). Experientially, it comes to the same thing: the awareness of a new focus of identity expressed in different goals and new inner dynamic, with Christ as the inspiration and Christ-likeness the paradigm ('mystical' if you like, though many are suspicious of the word's connotations). Theologically, it means that for Christians the Spirit of God is also now to be recognized as the Spirit of Christ and the personal existence of the post-resurrection Christ cannot be thought of simply as having an individual bodily focus (see further my *Jesus* 318–26; and *Christology* 136–49). Nor should the continuity with verse 19c be forgotten: 'The Christ who lives in me is the crucified Christ' (Ebeling 149).

That the language of verse 20a was overdrawn for effect is shown by the way Paul continues. In more sober terms what he means is that **the life** (literally 'that which' – cf. Rom. vi.10) **I now live in the flesh, I live by faith which is in the Son of God.** 'In the flesh', as in 2 Cor. x.3 and Phil. i.22, 24 (cf. 2 Cor. iv.11), means basically, in the normal human bodily existence in all its weakness and corruptibility (see on ii.16 and v.13). It is important to grasp the fact that Paul did *not* think that conversion removed a believer from the realm of the 'flesh', or that the believer was no longer 'in the flesh', that is, no longer subject to its weakness and animal appetites (Rom. vii.5 and viii.9 must therefore be understood differently; see also on v.17 and my *Romans* 363–4, 428); to misunderstand Paul on this point forces his theology in a dualistic direction and gives his teaching on the process of salvation an unrealistic character (see further my *Jesus* 308–18). But any conscious polemical thrust at this point is probably aimed in a different direction. For more important here is the fact that Paul's references to the 'flesh' often and characteristically include an allusion to ethnic origin (as in Rom. i.3; iv.1; ix.3, 5, 8; xi.14) and particularly to Jewish trust 'in the flesh' (especially Phil. iii.3–4; see further on iii.3 and vi.13). The point then is that Paul does not deny or renounce his continuing Jewishness in order to live as a Christian. His claim is rather that the life he now lives as a Jew born and bred ('by nature' – ii.15; 'in the flesh') he now lives by a different orientation – no longer by reference primarily to the law, but now by his faith in the Son of God. The latter phrase is more cumbersome than usual ('faith which is in . . .') and again makes better sense as 'faith in the Son of God' than 'by the faith(fulness) which is of the Son of God' (cf. Hays, *Faith* 167–9, 250; see further on ii.16). The reversion to 'Son of God', rather than 'Christ' is determined partly by the formula about to be cited, and partly because the 'inclusiveness' of Jesus' sonship is an important part of his argument (see on i.16). It is no longer the relationship of the flesh which is important for Paul (ethnic identity) but relationship with God's Son.

As elsewhere in Paul (Rom. v.10; viii.32), the thought of Jesus as God's Son is tied in to the thought of Jesus' death – **who loved me and gave himself for me** – but here, as in i.4, expressed in terms of self-sacrifice. The echo of formulaic language (see on i.4) should not be taken to mean that Paul picks up some familiar formula woodenly or merely out of habit. The more familiar formula is here adapted by two modifications. (1) The talk of Jesus' love (cf. Eph. v.2) reflects the familiar Jewish thought of God's love both of Israel as a people (as in Deut. vii.8, 13; 1 Kings x.9; Ps. xlvii.4; Isa. xliii.4; Jer. xxxi.3; Hos. iii.1; *Pss. Sol.* ix.8) and of individuals within Israel (as in Deut. iv.37; 2 Sam. xii.24; Ps. cxlvi.8; Prov. iii.9; Sir. iv.14; Wisd. Sol. iv.10; more sectarian in 1QS iii.26 and CD viii.17); and also the idea of the martyr's willingly giving his life for that which he holds most dear (as in 2 Macc. vii.9; viii.21; *4 Macc.* i.8, 10). However, the main inspiration here will probably have been the recollection of Jesus' own willing self-sacrifice for his own (reflected particularly in Mark x.42–5; John x.11; xv.13). That the love of God and the love of Christ are one and the same for Paul (Christ's loving act the expression of God's love) is clearly implied in Rom. v.7–8 and viii.32–9. (2) The whole phrase is radically personalized – 'loved me and gave himself for me' (contrast i.4). To take the 'me' here as a generalized 'I' retains the sense of an immediate relationship between Christ and the believer; but it loses too much of Paul's own sense of wonder and gratitude so clearly evident. The thought, of course, is not 'only me', but 'even me'. At the same time Lührmann is right to caution that 'the legitimation of his gospel lies for Paul in the content of the preaching not in his own conversion. . . . He reduces his own biography to the gospel and not conversely the gospel to his own experience' (p. 47).

21 Paul had let his thought run on from the protest of verse 17: developing the contrast between his old way of life (reflected in a restricted table-fellowship) and his new life in Christ – destroyed not to be rebuilt, put to death with Christ and living a life differently focused, still in the flesh but determined by faith in God's Son; and foreshadowing themes he would develop in the next two chapters. But now he rounds off this initial restatement of his case – as though conscious that the format of an extended reminiscence of his reply to Peter at Antioch was becoming too strained, and that he must begin to address the challenge of the Galatian situation more directly. So he concludes – **I do not nullify the grace of God**. The verb means 'render ineffective, inoperable' (cf. Mark vii.9; Luke vii.30; 1 Cor. i.19; Gal. iii.15). For 'grace' see on i.3 and 6; here Paul obviously has in mind 'the grace of God' manifested in his calling and in his successful missionary work (i.15; ii.9). It was of the essence of that grace, in

Paul's experience and understanding, that it was to be freely extended to the Gentiles as well. So any retreat back into a Judaism, or Jewish Christianity, which insisted that Jew and Gentile should eat separately was to render invalid the whole gospel – as indeed also Israel's own election (Rom. xi.5–6)! In this case an echo of a charge laid against Paul by the James people is less likely, since 'grace' is so much Paul's own word (in terms of LXX usage 'mercy' would have been the preferred word – 'By so freely accepting Gentiles Paul nullifies the mercy of God, that is, towards Israel').

In concluding the line of argument briefly outlined in these verses Paul can summarize his reasoning in a single sentence: **for if righteousness is through the law, then Christ has died to no purpose**. As implied in ii.16, 'righteousness' draws its significance from the dynamics of relationship, here primarily the covenant relationship between God and his people. God was understood to be 'righteous' when he fulfilled the obligations which he had taken upon himself in entering into covenant with Israel, rescuing Israel and punishing its enemies (e.g. Exod. ix.27; 1 Sam. xii.7; Mic. vi.5), restoring and sustaining Israel despite its sin (e.g. Pss. xxxi.1; xxxv.24; etc.; Isa. xlvi.13; li.5). To be recognized as 'righteous' by God was to be recognized as belonging to his people, members of that covenant, within the sphere of his righteousness/saving action (e.g. Pss. v.12; xi.7; xxxiv.15–22; lv.22; Isa. lx.21). In Jewish theology that also and inevitably meant maintaining one's status within the covenant by doing what the law laid down ('covenantal nomism'). 'Through the law' here has no different meaning from ii.19, both having in mind the understanding over-exemplified in Paul's previous life-style (i.14; see on ii.19). Paul now rejected that understanding as it was traditionally implemented: by over stressing human obligation the prior grace of God was being set aside – God's righteousness was being made too much the corollary to human righteousness, rather than vice versa. And in particular, when Israel's righteousness was understood to require discrimination between Jew and Gentile, and God's righteousness was being made to depend on 'works of the law' like circumcision and food laws ('righteousness through the law' is evidently a summary statement of the point denied repeatedly in ii.16), then the grace of God on which the covenant itself had been based was itself rendered null and void. In view of the positive role Paul can still recognize for the law, even in Galatians (v.14), the fact that his talk of 'righteousness through the law' is a summary of 'being justified by works of the law' (ii.16) and has in mind the attitude which came to expression in

Peter's action at Antioch is important: Paul's object here is not the law *per se*, but the law understood as preventing Gentiles' full and free participation in the grace of God as Gentiles.

What demonstrated conclusively to Paul that 'righteousness through the law' was a false summary of God's grace was once again the inevitable corollary regarding Christ. As in ii.17, it was the logic of the Jewish-Christian view as it affected the Christian understanding of Jesus, which reduced that view to absurdity. But why should the claim that 'righteousness is through the law' render the death of Jesus 'in vain' (BAGD, *dōrea* 3)? The key is to remember that Paul was still reflecting on the disastrous theological corollaries of Peter's action in Antioch, and that it was Peter's retreat once again behind the boundary of the law as marking off Jew from Gentile which cut so sharply at Paul's own understanding of his commission and gospel. For Paul the death of Christ had evidently broken through that boundary and abolished the law in its boundary-defining role. What he meant by this he would explain more fully in iii.13–14. But the implication is already there: that Christ's death had been effective precisely because it undermined the assumption that God was only for 'the righteous', only for those who lived by 'works of the law', and had done so by demonstrating that God's Messiah completed his work in the rejection of the cross, 'numbered among the lawless' (Isa. liii.12; see on iii.13). So far as Paul was concerned, to fail to recognize that significance of the cross was to lose all (see also on v.11 and vi.12).

Alternative explanations of Paul's line of thought here do not give enough weight to the consistent 'Jesus for Gentiles' motif, clearly expressed in such closely related passages as i.15–16 and iii.13–14, and implicit in this paragraph from ii.15 on, and tend to forget that the doctrine of 'justification by faith' so powerfully expressed in this passage first appears in Paul's thought as a key element in that motif (as both Galatians and Romans demonstrate).

With this summary affirmation Paul has now completed his opening statement. The thematic claim of i.11–12 has been defended by documenting his contacts with the Jerusalem leadership since his conversion-commissioning. He received the gospel at that time directly from God through 'the revelation of Jesus Christ': his understanding of it as a commission 'to preach him among the Gentiles' was not given him by any competent human authority, including the Jerusalem leadership (i.15–17); he could not have first received it from Cephas when he first got to know him three years later (i.18) or from the other apostles whom he did not even see, but only James (i.19); and when he did lay his gospel to the Gentiles before the 'pillar apostles' at Jerusalem, fourteen years later, they recognized his commissioning from God, added nothing to his understanding of the gospel, agreed to a division of responsibility as between Jews and Gentiles, and sealed their fellowship with a handshake (ii.1–10). That agreement had come 'unstuck' at Antioch, through Peter's cowardice and hypocrisy (ii.11–14), and Paul had now briefly restated the defence of the position he had maintained on that occasion (ii.14–21) with a view to the similar and pressing crisis among his Galatian congregations. He was now ready to address them directly.

C The main argument – the testimony of experience and of scripture   iii.1–v.12

1 THE APPEAL TO EXPERIENCE: CONTINUE AS YOU BEGAN   iii.1–5

(1) You foolish Galatians! Who has bewitched you[1] – you before whose eyes Jesus Christ was openly portrayed as crucified? (2) This only I want to learn from you: was it by works of the law that you received the Spirit, or by hearing with faith? (3) Are you so foolish? Having begun with the Spirit are you now made complete with the flesh?[2] (4) Have you experienced so much in vain? If it is indeed in vain. (5) So I ask again, he who supplies the Spirit to you and works miracles among you, is it by works of the law or by hearing with faith?

With the background clarified by the recital of the most relevant elements of his *cursus vitae*, Paul could now at last begin to address the Galatian crisis directly, and thus to embark on the main section of his exposition. The implication of the preceding section is that Paul saw the Antioch incident as a first test case of the crucial Jerusalem agreement and the crisis in Galatia as a second test case, in which the issues were the same. Consequently, the stand Paul took there, on the basis of the

1 Some manuscripts and versions add 'from obeying the truth' – presumably a scribal attempt to fill out the sense by drawing in a phrase from v.7.
2 The simple dative here is unusual in Paul and its precise force uncertain. But Paul used it to balance the simple dative of 'Spirit' (more typical of Pauline use), and he was presumably content with the resulting lack of precision of meaning. In such a case it is not the responsibility of exegesis to push the text into a grammatical choice which the author himself refrained from making.

common ground of faith in Jesus Christ and the common gospel of his self-giving on the cross, was equally applicable to the Galatian believers. But much of that implication Paul left his readers to find for themselves. In turning to address the Galatians directly again (for the first time since i.13) Paul immediately plays his other main trump card (the first being the Jerusalem agreement) – viz. their own experience when they first believed. Their own experience of receiving the Spirit simply through faith should have been enough to fix for them the character of the gospel and the life of faith. This is his first point in an argument which uses appeals to experience and personal relationship, exposition of salvation-history, exegesis of scripture and theological logic set out in a sequence in interlocking strips like a well-made page of papyrus (iii.1–iv.31). The emphasis of the opening verses is frequently recalled in what follows (see iii.8, 14, 27; iv.5–7, 29; v.1, 5, 7–8, 16–18, 21–2, 25; vi.8) and establishes 'the central place of the Spirit in Paul's argument throughout his Galatian letter' (Longenecker 101–2). Cosgrove, *Cross* 2, takes iii.1–5 as 'the decisive clue to Paul's view of the "problem at Galatia"'.

1 The impatience and concern which Paul had expressed so sharply in i.8–9 and in the barbed language of ii.12–14, burst forth again – **You foolish Galatians** (cf. 2 Cor. vi.11; Phil. iv.15). The rebuke was not uncommon in contemporary diatribe, a style to which Paul reverted frequently in both Galatians and Romans (see BAGD, *anoētos* 1); and if he was addressing south Galatian churches it would be all the more cutting, and consequently, in Paul's hope, more effective. For Paul, however, its force was not simply rhetorical: he found the Galatians' failure to recognize the character of the gospel baffling (so again in iii.3); the adjective indicates lack of comprehension, not lack of intelligence. On who the 'Galatians' were, see Introduction §3.

Who has bewitched you? The question may again reflect contemporary rhetoric (Betz 131 – 'Its purpose was to characterize opponents and their sophistic strategies'). It certainly cannot be assumed that the other missionaries in Galatia were actually resorting to magic (as Schlier 119 seems to believe), though Paul may indeed be suggesting that the Galatian about-face could only be put down to 'demonic power' (see particularly J. H. Neyrey, 'Bewitched in Galatia: Paul and Cultural Anthropology', *CBQ* 50 [1988] 72–100); only that would have been sufficient to explain how those whose experience of the Spirit had been so rich (iii.2–5) could have left it behind (cf. 2 Cor. iv.3–4). The force of the question is partly to reinforce

Paul's bewilderment at the Galatian about-face (i.6): can such an apostasy be explained without inferring that someone has put the evil eye on them? And partly to characterize the motives of the other missionaries: for the verb (only here in the NT) also has the sense 'begrudge' (LSJ, *baskainō*; so in its four occurrences in LXX — Deut. xxviii.54, 56; Sir. xiv.6, 8); and envy has commonly been understood to be the cause of the 'evil eye' (the power to harm someone by a glance). The implication is that the other missionaries in Galatia must begrudge the Galatians' experience of the Spirit, received without any commitment on their part to observe the works of the law.

Their looking at the cross ought to have had sufficient power to avert or counter any evil spell — **you before whose eyes Jesus Christ was openly portrayed as crucified**. The imagery is very powerful — of the crucified Christ so vividly represented to the Galatians that they could see him on the cross with their own eyes (BAGD, *prographō* 2; the point is well made by Betz 131). The language tells us much about both the style and the content of Paul's preaching. It is important to grasp the fact that Paul could sum up his preaching of the gospel precisely as a preaching of the cross (so also particularly 1 Cor. i.23; ii.2). In each of these contexts the appeal is to the cross as countering other understandings of the gospel and philosophies of salvation and as showing their inadequacy. But, it should be noted, Paul had evidently so proclaimed Christ crucified before these alternatives had been put before his converts. Evidently this had been the impact of the cross on himself, his realization that the crucified Jesus was God's Messiah *precisely as the crucified* — here again, as in ii.19, the perfect tense. It had turned his own values completely upside down (i.13—16; ii.21; iii.13—14; more explicitly in Phil. iii.5—8); so much so that he could not understand how his Galatian converts could not see the same significance (see on iii.13—14). There may also be an implication ('bewitch' in contrast to the open preaching of Paul) that the tactics of his opponents had been underhand and secretive.

2 As a good teacher Paul appeals to his audience's own experience and tries to draw out his point from them — **This only I want to learn from you**. The question he puts is significant — not 'What did you hear or learn from me?', not 'What did you believe?', not 'Who baptized you or with what form of words?', but, **Was it by works of the law that you received the Spirit or by hearing with faith**? He focuses immediately on the Galatians' experience of 'receiving the Spirit'. This formulation was already more or less a technical term to speak of conversion and the beginning of Christian discipleship (Rom. viii.15; 1 Cor. ii.12; 2 Cor. xi.4; Gal. iii.14; elsewhere see e.g. John vii.39; Acts ii.38; x.47; xix.2). It focuses the fact that for Paul and the first Christians this was the decisive and determinative element in the event or process of conversion and initiation; hence the nearest thing to a definition of 'Christian' in the NT, in Rom. viii.9, makes possession of the Spirit the *sine qua non* (see further my *Baptism*). Moreover it cannot really be understood in other than experiential terms (as though 'receiving the Spirit' was a matter of purely rational conviction, or simply a deduction to be drawn from the fact of their having been baptized). The appeal is clearly to an event which Paul could expect them vividly to remember (as he could expect them to remember the character of his preaching – iii.1). Hence a question can be asked (as in Acts xix.2) which assumes that the answer was obvious to all parties.

The coming of the Spirit in these earliest days of Christian mission was evidently something which made an impact on the lives of those who received it, an impact at emotional as well as rational level. This would include, in at least some cases, dramatic and ecstatic experiences (as iii.5 and 1 Cor. i.5–7 imply; also consistently in Acts – ii.4, 33; viii.17–18; x.45–6; xix.6), in other cases deeply moving experiences (cf. Rom. v.5; 1 Thess. i.6; see further on iv.6), and Paul characteristically thought of the impact of the Spirit as an experience of liberation (Rom. viii.2; 2 Cor. iii.17) and as having immediate consequences for daily living (Rom. viii.4ff.; Gal. v.16ff.) (see further my *Jesus* and on iv.6). To see here then a 'recall to baptism' is to run the serious risk of obscuring the powerful experience of personal transformation which was the reason for Christianity's earliest success, and the immediacy of the link between thus 'receiving the Spirit' and 'hearing with faith' (cf. particularly D. J. Lull, *The Spirit in Galatia: Paul's Interpretation of* Pneuma *as Divine Power* [Chico: Scholars, 1980] ch. 3). Such experiences, understood in the context and as the consequence of 'hearing with faith', were evidently adjudged to be proof sufficient that God had given to those concerned his Spirit (see also on v.7); 'this reception of the "Spirit" is the primary datum of the Christian churches in Galatia' (Betz, 'Spirit' 146). That meant in turn that God had accepted them – and accepted them without waiting for them (or therefore requiring them first) to be inducted formally to his people by the appropriate ritual act. Since God had thus united them to his eschatological people, on whom the Spirit had been poured (e.g. Isa. xxxii.15; Ezek. xxxvii.4–14; Joel ii.28–9), nothing more than that common participation in the Spirit was necessary for them formally to be recognized as part of that people (cf. Acts x.47–8). This clearly is the logic of the appeal which Paul here starts to make. We may contrast the DSS and the *Odes of Solomon* which both reflect similar claims to experience of the Spirit (e.g. 1QS iv.21; CD ii.12; 1QH xii.12; xiv.13; xvi.12; *Odes Sol.* vi.2; xi.2; xix.2ff), but which also re-express the more traditional Jewish hostility to the nations (e.g. CD xi.15; 1QSa i.21; 1QM xvi.1; 1QpHab. v.3–4; *Odes Sol.* x.5; xxix.8).

The question Paul poses was whether the Galatians had come into this experience of God's Spirit by observing regulations of the Torah. The regulations he would have in mind in particular would be those being pressed upon the Galatians themselves, which he would know, or could guess, were the very ones which traditionally minded Jews (including Jewish Christians) regarded as essential for Gentiles to undertake if they were to cease being 'sinners' (see on ii.15). It is not yet clear at this point in the argument (see v.2; also iv.10) whether circumcision and food laws were specifically in mind, but that is implied by the way Paul had introduced the phrase initially (see on ii.16 – 'works of the law'). Paul can ask the question in full confidence, of course, because he had been there at the time and knew that 'works of the law' had had no part in the Galatians' initial experience of the Spirit. 'The two contrasted phrases . . . express the leading antithesis of the whole epistle' (Burton 147).

Paul also knew that the Spirit had come to the Galatians simply by their 'hearing with faith'. The word translated 'hearing' can mean either the act of hearing, or that which is heard, with the genitive (literally 'hearing of faith') construed appropriately. It would be possible to take the phrase here in a different sense, therefore: 'as the result of preaching which demanded (only) faith' (BAGD, *akoē* 2); 'by believing the gospel message' (NEB/REB; so NIV, NJB, NRSV and the majority of commentators). But the phrase is more obviously to be taken as describing an action of the Galatians (in antithesis to 'works of the law'): the hearing which stimulated and expressed itself in the faith by which in the event they received the Spirit (GNB; so also iii.14; cf. Acts xi.17; xix.2; Eph. i.13). In the nearest parallel passage (Rom. x.14–17) Paul stresses the importance of 'hearing' in the reception of the gospel (so also x.17; see my *Romans* 623). And note how Paul elsewhere makes use of the Hebrew understanding of obedient or heedful hearing (Rom. i.5; xv.18; 2 Cor. x.5; *hupakoē*, 'obedience', and *akoē* come from the same root – *akouō*, 'hear'; see also on iv.21). Hence S. K. Williams' rendering – '"the hearing of faith", that "hearing" which

Christians call *faith*' ('The Hearing of Faith: *AKOĒ PISTEŌS* in Galatians iii', *NTS* 35 [1989] 82–93, here 90).

3   The answer to Paul's question was so obvious to him: they had received the Spirit without any mention being made of their taking on the traditional practices which marked off Israel from the nations; how could they not see that they had been thus fully accepted by God and did not fall short in any degree in their standing before him? **Are you so foolish? Having begun with the Spirit are you now made complete with the flesh?** That Paul is drawing a sharp double contrast is clear – begun/complete, Spirit/flesh. But its precise force is less clear.

The fact that both verbs were used in cultic contexts (beginning of a sacrifice, performing a religious act – see LSJ and BAGD, *enarchomai, epiteleō*; Lagrange 59–60) is probably a sidetrack. Certainly one could see in the latter some allusion to Jewish ritual (see *PGL*, *epiteleō* 2) – the requirement, in other words, to 'perform' such works of the law as sabbath (cf. iv.10) and circumcision (v.2) (Betz 134 n. 58 cites Epiphanius: 'the sabbath and circumcision and all other things which are performed by Jews . . .'). But (1) the words have a much more general use in the senses 'begin' and 'end, complete' (LSJ; *TDNT* viii.61) – so also in the only other occurrences of the antithesis in the NT (2 Cor. viii.6; Phil. i.6); (2) the thought of 'performing a religious act' is hard to fit into the second half of the antithesis (most naturally taken as personal subject of a passive verb); and (3) the introduction of a ritual reference in the first half would seem to run counter to the contrast between Spirit and flesh. Paul, in other words, was not saying, 'Our ritual (baptism) is more effective than theirs (circumcision)'; the contrast is rather between the immediacy of their reception of the Spirit ('by hearing with faith') and an emphasis which reasserted physical and ethnic distinctions as a matter of primary importance (the flesh). Even so, an allusion to language used by the other missionaries is possible; compare James ii.22(!), though James at least safeguards his talk of 'faith completed by works' by avoiding any linkage between 'works' and 'flesh' (ethnic identity).

The antithesis Spirit/flesh itself has a double significance: (1) between Spirit as divine power and enabling, and flesh as weak, self-centred, self-indulgent humanity (see on ii.16; this contrast is developed powerfully from v.16 on). (2) Jewish emphasis on ethnic identity (see on ii.20), as exemplified in the demand for circumcision (vi.13), came into the picture on the wrong side of the same antithesis (so also in Rom. ii.28–9; Phil. iii.3); the parallelism between verses 2 and 3 clearly links 'Spirit' and 'faith' on the one side and 'flesh' and 'works of the law' on the other. The insistence on circumcision was therefore doubly wrong in Paul's eyes: it re-erected an ethnic barrier which limited the grace of God; and it left those who lived by such emphases caught in all the weaknesses of the flesh (these two aspects explain the Spirit/flesh antithesis, which should therefore not be pushed into a sharper ontological or dualistic antithesis – cf. again ii.20!). How those who had already experienced the eschatological hope of Israel (the Spirit) could revert to that which Paul now saw as a limited and unsatisfactory prelude to the fulfilment of that hope (iii.15–iv.7), the very opposite of completion, was a matter of sore perplexity to him. The answer being, of course, that while the Galatians had shared Paul's experience of the Spirit, they had not shared his earlier experience of 'life within Judaism' (i.13).

In view of a continued emphasis within Christianity on the Spirit as a second experience, subsequent to conversion (so still in classic Pentecostalism), it is important to note that Paul saw reception of the Spirit as essentially the 'beginning' of Christian discipleship (see again my *Baptism*, here 107–8). Moreover, he was concerned about a teaching on completion or perfection which actually ran counter to and nullified the shared experience of the Spirit, as both the common basis of all Christian fellowship (2 Cor. xiii.13) and as characterizing the whole life of discipleship from the beginning. As is also implicit in Paul's talk of the Spirit as 'first-fruits' (Rom. viii.23), the 'end' is already contained in the 'beginning'.

4 The appeal to experience on Paul's part was not peripheral or accidental. It lies at the heart of his attempt to retain the Galatians for the/(his) gospel – **Have you experienced so much in vain? If it is indeed in vain**. The verb elsewhere in the NT has a bad sense, 'suffer', and when used absolutely that would be the normal implication (*TDNT* v.905; so here NIV). But LSJ and BAGD (*paschō*) do attest more neutral usage, and that certainly is the most natural sense here (a sample of seven occurrences in the whole Pauline corpus is too small to allow us any firm conclusions as to how or how not Paul might have used the word). Whether there is an implication of ecstatic experiences which involved some suffering ('violent and beneficial experiences' – *TDNT* v.912) Paul's readers would know; but we do not (BAGD translates, 'have you had such remarkable experiences?'). The point here, however, is to remind the Galatians of a range of experiences which should have been enough to demonstrate that they were indeed recipients of the eschatological Spirit and that the way they had come into these experiences remained the pattern for life in the Spirit (v.25). The 'so much' indicates that the experiences referred to were not simply a 'one-off' ecstatic experience at conversion, but a continuing experience which marked their whole 'beginning' period with which Paul was familiar.

The 'in vain, to no avail', as in iv.11 and the equivalent in ii.2, indicates a real concern on Paul's part that his work in Galatia could still 'come to nothing' (REB). His fear of a falling away from faith is well attested elsewhere (Rom. viii.13; xi.20–2; 1 Cor. ix.27; x.12; xv.1–2; 2 Cor. xiii.5; Col. i.22–3). Here it should be noted that the falling away envisaged is not strictly speaking from 'Christianity'; the other missionaries also believed in Christ (cf. ii.15–16) and would no doubt claim to have received the Spirit (cf. 2 Cor. xi.4; also Qumran – see on iii.2). It was more precisely a falling back from what Paul saw as liberty and maturity in the Spirit (Gal. iv.1ff.; v.1ff.), into a constriction of social and ritual practice and closedness of mind and spirit which Paul could only see in terms of confinement and immaturity – such as to make his whole work and the gospel itself pointless. But Paul has still high hopes of preventing this catastrophe – 'if it really is in vain'.

5 Paul rounds off his appeal to the Galatians' own experience by one last reminder both of how rich it had been and of the way in which God had bestowed on them such blessings – **So then, he who supplies the Spirit to you** . . . The reference is to God: Paul never ascribes the giving of the Spirit to Christ, only to God (1 Cor ii.12; 2 Cor. i.21–2; v.5; Gal. iv.6; 1 Thess. iv.8; also Eph. i.17); this is part of the careful balance he maintains between the exalted Christ, God and the Spirit of God (see my *Christology* 143–8; see also on i.6). The verb is quite often used to indicate the proper discharge of responsibility: of a husband providing for his wife (LSJ, *epichorēgeō*; hence Sir. xxv.22); of the head nourishing the body (Eph. iv.16; Col. ii.19; cf. 2 Cor. ix.10). The implication being that the giving of the Spirit is fully in accord with God's nature as God. The present tense could reinforce this sense – this is what God does (cf. again 1 Thess. iv.8). But here, in conjunction with the same tense in the following verb the implication is probably that the 'supplying of the Spirit' was a sustained and continuing action of God for the Galatians. In which case the thought is not so much of repeated givings of the Spirit as of a steady supply (cf. again Eph. iv.16; Col. ii.19). The point, which the Galatians seem to have

forgotten, is that their reception of the Spirit was not simply a single event in the past, but had been the beginning of a continuing relationship with God sustained by him through the Spirit (cf. 1 Cor. vi.17). It is the immediacy and directness of that relationship with God (as Gentiles) which had been put at risk by their being caught up in questions of ethnic identity (flesh) and 'works of the law'. Paul's dispute with the Galatians turns on this question (Cosgrove, *Cross* 85).

Their experience of God was of one who not only supplies the Spirit but who also **works miracles among you.** For the verb see on ii.8. Here the thought was particularly of divine energy manifested in powerful actions (as in Mark vi.2/Matt. xiv.2 and 1 Cor. xii.10; cf. Col. i.29; 2 Thess. ii.9). The plural (literally 'powers') was regularly used in the sense 'miracles' (BAGD, *dunamis* 1, 4), since it obviously had in view actions with the character of power, that is, as explainable only in terms of divine power, or as actions with visible and often striking effects. The implication is that the miracles were understood as manifestations or charisms of the Spirit (as in 1 Cor. xii.10, 28–9), but it evidently came to the same thing to ascribe the source of such power to God or the Spirit (cf. Acts x.38; Rom. xv.19; 1 Cor. xii.6, 11; 1 Thess. i.5; 2 Tim. i.7; Heb. ii.4; vi.4–5). It is not unimportant to note that with such reports from Paul we have firsthand (not just second- or thirdhand) testimony to 'miracles' in earliest Christianity (so also Rom. xv.19; 2 Cor. xii.12), though what was included under that label we cannot now tell (see further my *Jesus* 209–10). That such otherwise inexplicable (in terms at least of the understanding of nature then current) events took place should not be doubted; so much so that Paul could cite the Galatians' own experience of such events in their midst (though perhaps performed by only one or two) as further proof that God continued to be active among them. See also on iv.6 and v.7.

Paul equally had no hesitation in repeating the key question – **Is it by works of the law or hearing with faith?** The tense is not given, but in keeping with the present tenses of the two preceding verses in the sentence, a present tense ('is it') would most naturally be understood. Paul evidently could refer the Galatians not only to their beginning experience of the Spirit, but also to what had been their characteristic experience since then – as an experience of engracing and empowering which had been independent of any works of the law and had come to them solely as they heard and responded with faith to the message preached. For the phrases see further on iii.2.

2 THE APPEAL TO SCRIPTURE (1): THE BLESSING OF ABRAHAM – TO FAITH iii.6–9

(6) Just as 'Abraham believed God, and it was reckoned to him for righteousness'. (7) Know then that those of faith, they are Abraham's sons. (8) And scripture, foreseeing that God would justify the Gentiles[1] from faith, preached the gospel beforehand to Abraham, 'In you shall all the nations[1] be blessed'. (9) Consequently, those of faith are blessed with faithful Abraham.

Paul now embarks on an elaborate exposition of scripture which stretches to the end of chapter iv. This in effect is Paul's third line of argument to counter the threat to his gospel and converts in Galatia: first, the agreement on the gospel reached at Jerusalem (ii.1–10); second, their own experience of the Spirit (iii.1–5); and now, third, the proof from scripture (iii.6–iv.31). Verses 6–9 serve as the initial expression of Paul's case – citing first the crucial text Gen. xv.6, which gives rise to the thematic statement of verse 7, then the second crucial text Gen. xii.3, with the equivalent summary conclusion drawn immediately. The first scripture linked promise, seed, and faith; the second linked promise, blessing, and Gentiles. When put together, as was quite legitimate, since they referred to the same promise made to Abraham, the result was to tie the whole into a single package, so that faith and blessing, seed and Gentiles could be seen to belong to one another. This is the package which Paul proceeds to unpack in the following verses, in what can be regarded as a midrash on the two texts cited: iii.10–14 – a blessing to Gentiles which the curse of the law could no longer prevent; iii.15–18 – a promised seed whose extent could not be determined by the law; iii.19–29 – a faith restricted for a time by the law, but now with the coming of Christ, the means by which all who believe may be counted seed, in Christ, heirs of the promised blessing. It is very arguable that Paul was responding to arguments he knew had been put by the other missionaries, or were likely to be put by them, and that it was they who introduced the theme of sonship of Abraham (see Introduction §6.3). For a possible reconstruction of their arguments see e.g. Barrett, *Freedom* 22–4.

6 Since the Jews in general held as a foundational belief that God had revealed his will in the holy scriptures, it was of central

1 'Gentiles' and 'nations' translate the same word. The different translation (as in NJB and NIV) helps to bring out the different nuances intended by Paul: 'all the nations' include, of course, 'the Gentiles' (see on i.16).

importance for Paul to be able to demonstrate the validity of his gospel from these same scriptures. Those among the Galatian churches attracted by the appeal of traditional Judaism would put no less weight on the scriptures, and would be likely to find unconvincing any argument which could not cite scriptural support. Paul indicates his awareness of this importance of scriptural proof by his opening conjunction – **Just as** – which is more or less an abbreviation for the fuller formula, 'as it is written' (as in Rom. i.17; ii.24; iii.10; etc.). He does not say explicitly that he is citing scripture (contrast Rom. iv.3), but the introductory formula was sufficient indication and the following words are a precise quotation from Gen. xv.6 (Longenecker 112, however, prefers the translation, 'Take Abraham as the example', following JB). In accordance with his normal practice, the scriptural proof or precedent is appended to the principal claim: for Paul the mutual confirmation of experience and scripture was fundamental. The implicit equation of 'receiving the Spirit' and 'being reckoned righteous' (different ways of describing the opening up of a positive relationship with God) is confirmed in iii.14. The exposition proceeds in typical Jewish fashion by interweaving scriptural passages (iii.6–14) and by use of recognized exegetical rules (iii.16).

The theme of Paul's exposition is the sons, or as we would say today, the offspring of Abraham. Who are the heirs of the blessing and promise given to Abraham? There was nothing artificial or surprisingly abrupt in this appeal to **Abraham**. He was naturally regarded as the father of the Jewish people, the founder of the Jewish race (Gen. xii–xxiv; Isa. li.2; Matt. iii.9; *TDNT* v.976). Israel naturally thought of itself as 'the seed of Abraham' (as in Ps. cv.6; Isa. xli.8) and counted descent from him a matter of pride (as in *Pss. Sol.* ix.17; *3 Macc.* vi.3). When Philo, the Alexandrian philosopher and Paul's older contemporary, came to Gen. xv.1–3 in his exposition of the Pentateuch he too found it natural to begin with the question, 'Who is the heir' (*Heres*)? Moreover, Abraham at this time was regularly understood within Jewish circles as the model of the devout Jew: 'Abraham was perfect in all of his actions with the Lord' (*Jub.* xxiii.10); he 'was accounted a friend of God because he kept the commandments of God' (CD iii.2). And not least of importance here, as one who had himself abandoned idols at the call of God, he was remembered as in effect the first proselyte and type of true conversion (*Jub.* xii; *Apoc. Ab.* i–viii; Philo, *Abr.* 60–88; Josephus, *Ant.* i.155). Abraham, therefore was the classic test case for what acceptance by God involved (see further Hansen 179–88, 194–9). Whether or not the other missionaries in Galatia had cited Abraham as the decisive precedent on their side, as is likely (see Introduction §6.3), Paul could hardly avoid taking up the challenge; if he could not defend his position here his case was already lost.

The test-case scripture was also obvious – Gen xv.6, which Paul quotes more or less verbatim from the LXX, itself a close enough rendering of the Hebrew: Abraham **believed God and it was reckoned to him for righteousness**. From Paul's side it was obvious since in the scriptures dealing with Abraham this was the only passage which spoke of Abraham's faith and of the righteousness attributed to him by God. But it was also obvious from the side of the more traditionalist Jewish view maintained by his opponents. For, as 1 Macc. ii.52 and James ii.23 show, it was customary in Jewish understanding of Abraham to link Gen. xv.6 with the other promise-to-Abraham passages in Genesis, particularly Gen. xxii, climaxing as it does in xxii.17–18. That is to say, it was customary to interpret 'Abraham believed God' in the light of Abraham's subsequent faithfulness under trial, so that it was by virtue of Abraham's faith, that is faithfulness, that 'he was reckoned righteous' and given the promise (Sir. xliv.19–21; 1 Macc. ii.52; *Jub.* xvii.15–18; *m. Abot* v.3); to rephrase such language in terms of 'meritorious achievement' (Fung 135), however, is to transform it into a later issue (cf. Philo, *Heres* 94; *Abr.* 262; and Lightfoot's 159–63 still valuable comparison of Philo and Paul at this point). Not least of interest is the fact that the same formula, 'it was reckoned to him for righteousness', was used within the tradition of the faithful zealot, like Phinehas, and Simeon and Levi (Ps. cvi.31; *Jub.* xxx.17–19), since Paul had previously counted himself as belonging to that tradition (see on i.14).

It was this understanding of Gen. xv.6 which Paul had to counter. Not by attempting to argue that the traditional Jewish exposition was wrong; in an exegetical tradition which looked for the maximum meaning which might be drawn from a text (rather than an either-or exegesis) such a ploy would have been ineffective anyway. But rather by arguing from what seemed to him the obvious meaning of the text. He was probably safe in assuming that this meaning would also be recognized by his readers. For 'reckoned for righteousness' by God was common currency between them (ii.16) – that is, as denoting a relationship of acceptance by God, that status or character of a life which God regarded as acceptable (for 'righteousness' see on ii.21; thus to understand 'righteousness' in relational terms short-circuits the old Reformation debate as to whether Paul had in mind merely 'imputed' or actually 'infused' righteousness).

What it was that was 'reckoned' (the metaphor is drawn from the business world of commerce – 'reckon or put to someone's account' – BAGD, *logizomai* 1) as righteousness was likely to be more controversial. Was it faith, or faithfulness which God thus counted as acceptable? In a subsequent letter Paul found it necessary to argue for the former with some care (Rom. iv); perhaps because his failure to do so here left his exposition of Gen. xv.6 open to easy counter. But here he evidently felt able to take for granted that 'Abraham believed God' would be taken in the sense of 'faith/believe' as used in ii.16. Presumably because this was part of the common ground won and sustained at the Jerusalem consultation. It was not the need to believe, in Jesus Christ or in God, which was at issue; that was agreed on all sides. It was what followed from that faith, the ongoing demands of the covenant law on the covenant member which were at issue. At this point, however, Paul was content to stand on the common ground and build his case on that. That he could so assume that 'faith in Jesus Christ' was of a piece with 'believe in God' is clear proof that the opposition in Galatia was Jewish *Christian* and not a *Jewish* mission as such.

7 On the basis of this common ground Paul can make his central assertion: **Know then** (probably intended as imperative and so as drawing attention to the importance of the claim being made – Betz 141) **that those of faith, they are Abraham's sons**. That Abraham is a paradigm of right relationship with God is taken for granted (see on iii.6). The scripture (Gen. xv.6) shows that it was Abraham's believing that was 'reckoned for righteousness'. The inference which Paul draws is that those who believe like Abraham are equally acceptable to God. The crucial claim, however, is that such faith constitutes the believer as a child of Abraham. It is a thematic statement, of course, and will have to be unpacked – a task to which Paul devotes the next two chapters. But the outline and issues are already clear enough.

(1) Paul assumes an awareness of the immediate context of Gen. xv.6 – that what Abraham believed was the promise that he would have a son and seed/descendants innumerable (Gen. xv.4–6). The immediacy of this link between promise, children of Abraham and faith provides the central dynamic for his argument. Since the promise became effective in Abraham through faith, it is faith which characterizes the promise and its fulfilment. It is 'those of faith' who participate in such a promise; the scope is deliberately unrestricted. The semitic usage, 'son of', to denote share in a particular quality or characteristic (a son of strength = a strong man; sons of injustice = unjust men; BDB, *ben*

8; Bligh 243 cites Matt. v.44–5 and John viii.44) would make the transition in thought from 'like Abraham' to 'sons of Abraham' all the easier for Paul; and Greek readers would no doubt be familiar with similar usage (BAGD, *huios* 1c). Presumably Paul also avoided the alternative terminology, 'seed of Abraham', because he wished to build a different argument on it (iii.16).

(2) In the wake of ii.16 and the antitheses of iii.2 and 5, it is clear that 'those of faith' presupposes by way of contrast 'those of the circumcision' (ii.12), 'those of works of the law' (iii.10; cf. Rom. iv.14). The 'they' is emphatic, even exclusive: they and not others (Paul may be responding to the teaching of the other missionaries at this point); faith is the decisive factor in determining and characterizing this sonship. The implication, then, is that 'those of faith' are those whose identity is grounded in faith, and whose relationship with God grows out of faith, is characterized and determined by believing and trusting (the promise of God, the gospel of Jesus Christ), without reference to any 'works of the law'. Paul thus drives a wedge between the two senses of *pistis* (faith, faithfulness) and in effect questions the assumption that Abraham's faith and faithfulness could not be distinguished. Already implicit is the interpretation of Gen. xv.6 which Paul only later elaborated in Rom. iv. It is misleading to describe the contrast as 'anti-Jewish' (Betz 142) or even 'unJewish' (Mussner 218); rather Paul seeks to shift the focus of Jewish covenant identity away from its preoccupation with the law and back to its original focus in the grace of God (cf. Rom. ix.7–12). The fact that 'those of faith' is clearly a generalization from 'Abraham believed God' rules out any suggestion that 'those of faith' means 'those whose relationship with God derives from the faithfulness of Jesus Christ' (see on ii.16).

8 If the link between promise to Abraham, seed of Abraham and Abraham's faith is central to Paul's argument, equally important for Paul was the fact that the promise to Abraham had in view the Gentiles from the first. So, a further part of the proof from scripture (iii.6) is a second text drawn from the same section of the Torah, this time making the link – promise, blessing, Gentiles. **And the scripture, foreseeing that God would justify the Gentiles from faith . . .** To be noted is the fact that Paul does not introduce the sentence with a 'For', which would have indicated that the sentence functioned as the beginning of the elaboration of the claim made in verse 7 (cf. iii.10). Instead the simple 'And' indicates that the following scripture is to be taken as conjoint with the first, providing the basic scriptural proof which can then be elaborated in the following verses (iii.10ff). Typical of the high view then common of the divine inspiration and authority of the sacred text is the personification of scripture (cf. iii.22; iv.30; Rom. ix.17; SB iii.538). The formulation is partly stylistic: he hardly conceives 'scripture' here as an entity independent of God; rather as the immediate expression of the divine will (Lagrange 65; *TDNT* i.754). At all events, it is clear what Paul means: the wording of God's promise to Abraham indicates that it was always God's intention from the first to accept Gentiles on the basis simply of their believing. Once again Paul takes it as a given and indisputable fact, that Gentiles have experienced God's acceptance in the gift of the Spirit simply through their believing the gospel proclaimed to them and trusting in the one thus proclaimed (iii.2–5). This integration of experience and scripture is what clinches the matter for him. The verb 'would justify' (present tense) could, of course, refer also to the final judgement (cf. ii.16d). Paul's formulation embraces the ambiguity (probably deliberately): God's acceptance of the Gentiles is on the basis of faith from start to finish (cf. iii.3; v.5). To take 'from faith' here as a reference to God's faithfulness expressed in the faith act of Christ (Howard, *Crisis* 57–8) ignores the clear parallelism between verses 6 and 7.

The scripture **preached the gospel beforehand** (only here in the NT) **to Abraham, 'In you shall all the nations be blessed'.** Strictly speaking the passage is a mixed quotation from Gen. xii.3 ('In you shall be blessed all the tribes of the earth') and Gen. xviii.18 ('in him shall be blessed all the nations of the earth'). But the promise was repeated several times within the patriarchal narratives (also Gen. xxii.17–18; xxvi.4; xxviii.14), and such variation of detail was inconsequential. At the same time it may be significant that Paul cites the first two expressions of the promise, with the implication that the promise had a universal aspect from the first. And it may not be accidental that he avoids the later forms of the promise. For though Gen. xxii.18 and xxvi.4 vary it in terms that invite the subsequent exposition (Gal. iii.16) – 'in your seed shall be blessed all the nations of the earth' (cf. Acts iii.25) – they also link this reaffirmation of the promise to Abraham's obedient faithfulness subsequent to the initial fulfilment of the promise in the birth of Isaac, rather than to his response of trust when he was still childless (Gen. xxvi.4–5 – 'in you [Isaac] shall be blessed all the nations of the earth, because Abraham your father obeyed my voice and kept my ordinances, my commands, my statutes and my laws'). The different forms of the promise thus marked out the range of debate between Paul and the competing Jewish-Christian missionaries. Both agreed that the Gentiles could share in Abraham's blessing. Paul's concern was to insist on the basis of Abraham's own experience that God's acceptance could be complete prior to and without reference to such obedience to specific laws, the 'special laws' of the Jews.

Paul was not concerned here to make anything of the idea of being 'in' Abraham, since he can equally formulate the same point in terms of 'with' Abraham (iii.9). Betz 143 n. 41 is right to reject Mussner's 222 use of the problematic category 'corporate personality'. The only 'incorporation' Paul had in mind in this context was the 'in Christ' (iii.28) which made it possible for him to number Gentiles within the seed of Abraham, heirs of the promise (iii.16, 29).

The idea of 'blessing' is very Jewish. In Greek the verb meant simply 'to speak well of, praise' someone. In Greek-speaking Judaism, however, this verb was used to translate the Hebrew *barak*, where the sense is much stronger – 'bless' in the sense of bestow grace and peace, sustain and prosper (cf. Num. vi.24–6). The promise, then, was that the nations would share in the benefits, the well-being and wholeness, individually and socially, which was the consequence of Abraham's positive relationship with God. It is important to appreciate that for *both* sides of the debate this blessing was to come in and through Abraham; it was simply the *means* by which this was to come about which were in dispute. Since Paul is citing the LXX the greater ambiguity of the underlying Hebrew (see e.g. Bruce 156) is irrelevant.

The significance of Paul's saying that 'scripture preached the gospel beforehand to Abraham' in the words of this promised blessing should also not be lost sight of. (1) For one thing it underlines the fact that Paul saw the gospel of Jesus Christ simply as the working out of that first promise. The promise which constituted Israel as heirs of the promise, seed of Abraham, also placed the blessing of the Gentiles to the forefront. Paul takes the '*all* the nations' seriously – Gentiles as well as Jews, not Gentiles distinct from Jews. The promise to Abraham's seed was incomplete without the Gentiles' sharing in the *same* blessing. Consequently, Paul did not see himself as doing anything which was contrary to the spirit and character of his ancestral faith. On the contrary, *his mission to the Gentiles was nothing other than the fulfilment of Israel's mission.* This claim of Paul needs to be given more prominence in Jewish-Christian dialogue, and in response to the still continuing sense within traditional Judaism that Paul was a traitor and apostate. The continuity which Paul saw and claimed for the gospel with

God's saving purpose through Abraham and in continuation of Israel's hope and calling was the reason why Marcion excised this passage from his text of the epistle. In his rejection of the paragraph Marcion saw its significance more clearly than those modern commentators who play down this continuity in favour of the sharp discontinuities of an apocalyptic schema.[1]

(2) And for another, Paul could describe the promise to Abraham as 'gospel'; not as a prefiguring of the gospel, not as an incomplete forerunner, but as the good news itself preached beforehand (cf. 'saw beforehand' – iii.8; 'promised beforehand' – Rom. i.2; 'written beforehand – Rom. xv.4). This is a further reminder of how inextricably at the heart of the gospel for Paul was the openness of that good news to the Gentiles (cf. i.16; Howard, *Crisis* 55 – 'the chapter as a whole is an elaboration on the implications of the promise of iii.8'). But it also means that for Paul the gospel had to do from start to finish with the initiative of God in blessing his human creation, and in human openness to that blessing. Of course for Paul that divine initiative has taken definitive form in the cross of Christ (ii.21; iii.1, 13–14), but he would no doubt have recognized that wherever divine blessing is received in simple trust, there is the gospel at work; we should not be in a hurry to restrict the scope of 'those of faith' (iii.7; cf. Heb. xi). Is this a 'problem' for Paul's theology (Betz 143 n. 41) or simply for those who wish to systematize Paul's thought into a narrower consistency than he himself saw as either necessary or desirable?

9 Consequently (cf. iii.24; iv.7) – the force of the two scriptures taken together was compelling for Paul – **those of faith are blessed with faithful Abraham**. The link provided by the first scripture (promise, seed, faith), when added to the link provided by the second (promise, blessing, Gentiles), pointed clearly to the conclusion that the blessing of Abraham came to the faith of Abraham, and thus to those who shared that faith ('with Abraham' is a proper rendering of the Hebrew *b^e*, usually rendered 'in'; 'in Abraham', 'with Abraham', 'sons of Abraham' are all overlapping categories in Hebrew). The present tense is

1 J. L. Martyn, 'Events in Galatia', *Pauline Theology. Vol. I*, ed. J. M. Bassler (Minneapolis: Fortress, 1991) particularly 174 and 176, fails to integrate the emphasis of such verses as i.4 and vi.14 with the equally clear promise/fulfilment theme in Galatians, or to take adequate account of the continuity Paul sees in 'sonship of Abraham' (iii.6–29) between Israel, as heir and minor under the protection of the law (see on iii.23–4), and the fuller inheritance of sonship (iv.1–7; vi.16). B. R. Gaventa, 'The Singularity of the Gospel: A Reading of Galatians' in the same volume (pp. 147–59) achieves a better balance. See further my *Theology*.

deliberate: it is not simply that the way had now become open for Gentiles of faith to share the promised blessing in the future; it is rather that they were *already* sharing that blessing. Once again Paul allows his experience to inform his theology: he could not deny that the Gentiles who had responded to his preaching of the gospel were being as richly blessed as any devout Jew; the manifest testimony of his missionary success confirmed what now appeared to him the obvious exegesis of these passages.

Particularly striking here is Paul's boldness in speaking of 'faithful Abraham' (the natural translation). For that could easily have been understood as a concession to the more traditional view which he was in process of contesting – that the promised blessing was conditional on Abraham's faithfulness when tested in the offering of Isaac (see on iii.6). Paul was certainly aware of the danger in his subsequent treatment of the same theme, when he went to great lengths to demonstrate that Abraham's 'faith' was nothing other than naked trust in the promise of God (Rom. iv.16–22). But here for some reason he saw no danger in speaking of Abraham's faithfulness. Possibly because the other missionaries in Galatia had not used that argument on their own part. But perhaps because he was so convinced that faith in Jesus Christ was such an invulnerable common ground between himself and those Jewish Christians who disagreed with him, that he could extend the thought of Abraham's faith to cover that of his faithfulness. Where contemporary Judaism read Abraham's initial faith (Gen. xv.6) in the light of his subsequent faithfulness, Paul makes bold to reverse the process: Abraham's faithfulness has to be understood in the light of his initial faith, 'believing Abraham' (see also on v.22). To that extent the modern translations are justified – 'Abraham who had faith/believed' (RSV/NRSV), 'Abraham, the man of faith' (NJB/NIV), 'Abraham the believer' (Betz 137) – but none the less they obscure the risk which Paul was taking.

3 DESPITE THE CURSE OF THE LAW iii.10–14

(10) For all who rely on works of the law[1] are under a curse; for it is written, 'Cursed is everyone who does not abide by all that has been written in the book of the law to do it'. (11) And that by the law no one is justified before God is plain, because 'The righteous from faith shall live'.[2] (12) But the law is not from faith, rather 'The one[3] who does them will live by them'. (13) Christ has redeemed us from the curse of the law having become a curse on our behalf – because it is written, 'Cursed is everyone who has been hanged on a tree' – (14) in order that to the Gentiles the blessing of Abraham might come in Christ Jesus, in order that we might receive the promise[4] of the Spirit through faith.

Paul has now set out the basic parameters of his case from scripture:

Abraham's righteousness—> faith—> Abraham's children (iii.6–7)
Abraham's blessing—> faith—> all the nations (iii.8–9).

The problem for his exegesis lay in bringing the last two elements together (Abraham's children/all the nations). Why so? Because in traditional Jewish thinking the two were clearly distinct categories – Jews/Gentiles. Paul had so far offered a plausible interpretation of the two Genesis texts, but his position was completely vulnerable, as he must have been aware, to a speedy reply: that when these same texts were set in the context of the fuller portrayal of Abraham in Genesis, a rather different emphasis emerged. An Abraham who was required by God to be circumcised as an integral part of the covenant God had given him (Gen. xvii.9–14). A promise whose repetition presupposed Abraham's faithfulness to God's commands (Gen. xxii.16; xxvi.4–5). The logic of the other missionaries' demands on the

1 NEB and REB lose the important phrase 'the works of the law' by translating 'those who rely on obedience to the law' (cf. NIV, which at least retained consistency with its translation of the earlier occurrences of the phrase in ii.16).
2 The phrasing should be left ambiguous, in preference to either RSV ('He through faith is righteous shall live'; so NEB/REB) or NRSV ('The one who is righteous will live by faith'; so NJB, NIV).
3 Some scribes and versions filled out the quotation by adding 'human being', as in Lev. xviii.5 and Rom. x.5.
4 Some witnesses, chiefly Western, but including p[46], read 'blessing' instead of 'promise' – either a slip or a deliberate attempt to clarify the connection of the thought from iii.2 to iii.14.

Galatians was clear enough, therefore, and they would have had no difficulty in calling on scriptural authority in turn, and very likely already had done so: in order to share in the blessing promised to Abraham's seed you must not only believe as he believed but do as he did.

The factor which made the difference, in other words, was the law, the commandments of God. Paul therefore turns at once to deal with it. Having expressed the position as set out in the initial statements of the promise to Abraham, he now turns immediately to the position as it is. The jump in thought between verses 9 and 10 simply indicates that he was taking for granted two presuppositions which shaped the traditional Jewish attitude to the other nations.

(1) The law was central to God's covenant with Israel; it was law-keeping which marked out the Jew from the (by definition) law-less Gentile. The antithesis was fundamental to Jewish identity, as the Antioch incident had already confirmed (see on ii.14–15). It was the law, then, which prevented the blessing of Abraham reaching out to the Gentiles, by functioning as a mark which distinguished Jew from Gentile, as a barrier between Jew and Gentile. The mind-set is clearly reflected in Rom. ii.17–20 and Eph. ii.11–16.

(2) Talk of God's blessing inevitably called to mind its antithesis – God's curse. Anyone familiar with Jewish covenant theology would naturally recall the principal statement of that theology within the Torah, Deuteronomy, with its repeated exposition of the two ways which Moses set before the people of Israel – blessing or curse, life or death (Deut. xi.26–9; xxvii–xxviii; xxx). Blessing, yes, if they kept the commandments (xxviii.1); but curse if they failed to do so (xxviii.15). And the curse meant the loss of covenant privileges/blessing, the loss of the land of promise (xxix.27–8). Which is to say, the loss of that which distinguished them from the other nations – a curse which could only be reversed if they returned to the Lord and once again obeyed his commandments (xxx.1–14). Once again the point would have been the same for traditional Jewish covenantalism: to overcome the division between Jew and Gentile, between being inside the covenant and being outside the covenant, it was necessary to keep the law.

The key to interpreting what has always proved a difficult passage, therefore, is given, first, by the recognition that Paul's talk of blessing provides a bracket for the paragraph (verses 8–9, 14), and second, by the recognition that talk of blessing would at once invite the corollary of blessing on law-keeper and curse on law-breaker. The question Paul addresses, without stating it

169

explicitly, is how can the blessing of Abraham come to the Gentiles in view of the curse which separated Gentiles from the people and covenant of promise (cf. particularly Howard, *Crisis* ch. 3; T. L. Donaldson, 'The "Curse of the Law" and the Inclusion of the Gentiles: Galatians iii.13–14', *NTS* 32 [1986] 94–112).

10 The **For** indicates clearly enough that Paul intended what follows as an explanation and exposition of the theme just announced (iii.8–9). **All who rely on works of the law are under a curse; for it is written, 'Cursed is everyone who does not abide by all that has been written in the book of the law to do it'.** The words would be shocking to most of Paul's auditors in the Galatian churches. Not because of the sudden talk of a curse. That would have been a natural corollary to talk of blessing (iii.8–9), the 'curse' in question being defined precisely as the opposite of the blessing – God experienced in judgement rather than in well-being (cf. Deut. xxviii.15–68). Nor because of the quotation from Deut. xxvii.26. This is where talk of blessing and curse would direct anyone well versed in Jewish scripture; the conscious or unconscious elaboration of the LXX text by incorporating the thoroughly Deuteronomic phrase, 'written in the book of the law' (Deut. xxviii.58, 61; xxix.20–1, 27; xxx.10), simply underlines the extent to which Paul was recalling the whole of that concluding section of Deuteronomy, indeed 'the book of the law' itself and the whole mind-set of nomistic covenantalism which Deuteronomy established for Jewish thought. It was of the essence of that position that continuance of divine blessing, continuance within the covenant, depended on 'remaining within' and 'doing' everything laid down in the book of the law; failure so to do brought God's curse on the offender, that is, effective exclusion from the covenant and its blessings. The point is well made by Bruce: 'By their "Amen" the people as a whole dissociate themselves from such evil actions and those who practise them; the curse thus involves exclusion from the covenant community' (p. 158); 'The curse of Deut. xxvii.26 was pronounced at the end of a covenant-renewal ceremony and had special reference therefore to the covenant-breaker' (p. 164).

What would have been surprising and shocking for most of the addressees would have been the boldness of the opening words, and the brazenness of the attempt to link them to the Deuteronomy text. For in typical Jewish thinking, 'all who rely on works of the law' were one and the same as 'everyone who remains within . . . the law to do it'. *They* were precisely the ones who were *not* under the curse, but could expect God's blessing. Paul's opening claim was exactly the opposite from what it should have been; the text from Deuteronomy simply contradicted the claim it was supposed to support. What could Paul be thinking of? Clearly the logic of the train of thought in verse 10 is that 'reliance on works of the law' amounts to *failure* to do all that the law requires. But how could he hope to sustain such an idiosyncratic reading of Deut. xxvii.26 in face of the traditional reading of it?

Most attempt to resolve the riddle by reading in a further assumption of Paul: that 'those who rely on works of the law' means those who seek to achieve their own righteousness before God; and that in quoting Deut. xxvii.26 Paul presupposed that it is impossible to fulfil *all* that the law requires (the 'all' is found only in LXX, not in the Hebrew). The hidden presumption is that complete or perfect obedience to the law is beyond human capacity: however zealous any might be, they fail to abide by everything written in the law, and so fall under its curse. The problem for this reading is twofold. (1) We have already seen that Paul's talk of 'works of the law' should not be taken as an attack on self-achievement (see on ii.16). (2) There is no hint in Deut. xxvii.26 or in Paul's use of it that the obedience called for is impossible. Deuteronomy certainly did not think so (Deut. xxx.11–14); and neither did Paul (Rom. viii.4; see on v.14). The mistake, once again, has been to read into the argument the idea that at this time the law would be satisfied with nothing less than sinlessness, unblemished obedience, that the law was understood as a means to achieving righteousness from scratch. But in Jewish thought to 'abide within all that was written in the law and do it' meant living within the provisions of the law, including all its provisions for sin, through repentance and atonement (see particularly Sanders, *Paul*). That was why Paul was able to describe himself as 'blameless' before his conversion (Phil. iii.6; see also on i.14); *not* because he committed no sin, *not* because he fulfilled every law without exception, but because the righteousness of the law included use of the sacrificial cult and benefit of the Day of Atonement. That the Judaism, against which Paul here reacts, called for an impossible perfection is not part of the context of the argument at this point and should not be read into it (see also on v.3 and vi.10).

Recently Wright 141–2 has argued that in iii.10 Paul is in fact echoing a widespread belief among his fellow Jews that Israel *was* under the curse of Deut. xxix, the curse of exile, including those living within a promised land ruled by Herod and Pilate. But the passage he cites (CD i.5–8) assumes that the events it refers to mark the *end* of the exile; and the key descriptive phrase here, 'all who rely on works of the law', presumably reflects a similar confidence of a re-established and sustained covenant.[1] Certainly the attitude within Judaism attested by Paul from his own experience in such passages as Rom. ii.17–20, x.2–3, Gal. i.13–14 and Phil. iii.6 evinces no sense of being still under the curse of exile. And no doubt it is this self-understanding of 'Judaism' (i.13–14) against which Paul directs his exposition here. Similar considerations tell against the argument of Thielman 68–9, that it was 'common knowledge' that Israel had been disobedient and therefore was experiencing the curses spoken of in Deuteronomy.

The answer is more likely to be found in a closer analysis of the main subject of the statement – 'all who rely on the works of the law'. Literally Paul says, 'as many as are from works of the law', admitting no exception. The phrase is clearly framed in contrast to the repeated phrase of the preceding paragraph – 'those who are from faith' (iii.7, 9). It thus denotes those whose identity was grounded on works of the law, whose relationship with God was characterized and determined by works of the law, in contrast to those characterized by faith. And 'works of the law', as we have seen, is Paul's code for those requirements of the law in particular which brought to sharpest focus Israel's claim to be distinctive from others as God's covenant people, as also at Qumran (see on ii.16). By the phrase 'those who rely on the works of the law', therefore, Paul meant those who, in his judgement, were putting too much weight on the distinctiveness of Jews from Gentiles, and on the special laws which formed the boundary markers between them, those who rested their confidence in Israel's 'favoured nation' status, those who invested their identity too far in the presumption that Israel was set apart from 'the nations' – including, of course, the Jewish Christians in view in i.6–8 and ii.4, 12.[2]

It is this attitude which Paul now makes bold to claim as a failure to do all that the law requires, and thus as falling under God's curse. The reason, which could be deduced from the

1 The most remarkable parallel here is 4QMMT which also talks of the blessings and curses written in the book of Moses in relation to 'works of the law', but where it is precisely the doing of these works (the Qumran halakah) which ensures the blessings and which 'will be reckoned to you (the covenanters) for righteousness'.

2 In questioning 'whether Paul had the Jews in mind at all in the present passage', C. D. Stanley, '"Under a Curse": a Fresh Reading of Galatians iii.10–14', *NTS* 36 (1990) 481–511, here 498–50, ignores the social role of the law precisely as defining who Jews are – 'those whose identity is given by works of the law', those 'within the law', those 'under the law', 'the circumcision', etc.

contrast with 'those of faith', is confirmed in the following two verses (iii.11–12). To focus the law's requirements in this way, that is, on the restrictiveness of covenant grace, on the exclusion of the Gentiles, is itself an abuse of what God demands of those in relationship with him, since that relationship is always constituted by and dependent on faith. What the covenant law demanded, in Paul's view, is the obedience which expresses such faith (Rom. i.5), the love which is the outworking of such faith (Gal. v.6), *not* requirements of the law understood and practised in such a way as to deny the sufficiency of the very faith on which the covenant was based. Where his opponents argued from the working out of the covenant:

covenant—>works of law—>exclusion of Gentiles

Paul argued from the foundational character of the covenant.

covenant—>faith—>blessing open to all nations.

Since the 'works of the law' attitude thus prevented the fulfilment of a central feature of the covenant promise it was in fact being false to the covenant, it put itself outside the terms of the covenant, and consequently under a curse (see also on v.14). If we add in the more thoroughgoing argument of Rom. ii.1–iii.20, the point seems to be that over-confidence in possession of the law, as marking Israel's distinctiveness from and advantage over those outside the law, blinds 'the Jew' to the seriousness of his sin. His assumption that he is safe 'under the law' puts him all the more firmly 'under sin', together with sinners of the nations at large (see further my 'Once More, Works' 106–9).

Such seems to be Paul's reasoning; apart from anything else, it explains how Paul could think of a curse on *Jews* (iii.10) whose removal was necessary for *Gentiles* to experience Abraham's blessing (iii.13–14). We can hardly assume that such reasoning would have cut much ice with the other missionaries, since works of the law like circumcision were also so clearly among those requirements written in the law to be obeyed. But those who recognized that the covenant with Israel was founded first on grace and promise might well be persuaded that thus was established the primary and governing principle of the covenant to which all other features of the covenant had to be conformed. And as for the Gentile converts at Galatia, their own experience of receiving the Spirit through faith should have been sufficient to confirm the basic position; all that was necessary beyond that was a sufficiently coherent defence to enable them to counter the

173

propaganda of the other missionaries and to maintain their own self-understanding.

11 At the heart of Paul's argument, then, is the conviction that relationship with God begins from faith (on the human side) and is maintained on the basis of faith throughout. Anything which diminished or denied that axiom was *ipso facto* self-condemned. The principle was so luminously clear to Paul that he could assume, realistically or rhetorically, that it was equally self-evident to his readers. **And that by** (or, in) **the law no one is justified** (see on ii.16) **before God is plain.** Here 'by or in the law' is evidently shorthand for 'by/from works of the law' (as the parallel with ii.16 makes clear): 'no one in the law' = 'as many as are from works of the law' (iii.10). The law, particularly its distinctive works, was not the *basis* of the covenant; not the means by which the right relationship with God was established for archetypal Abraham. That should be 'evident' (LSJ, *dēlos*; BAGD, *dēlos*; Oepke 105–6) to anyone. Not least in the light of the other passage in the scriptures which linked righteousness and faith (Hab. ii.4) – **because 'The righteous person from faith will live'.**

The continuing argument as to whether 'from faith' should be taken with the subject ('the righteous one') or the verb ('shall live') (see e.g. p. 168 n. 2 above) is beside the point. Paul's point is precisely that the identity of 'the righteous person' *per se* derives from and is determined by faith. And that includes his 'living' as 'one who is righteous'; 'from faith' characterizes and constitutes his relationship with God from beginning to end. The same is true with Paul's other citation of the same text (Rom. i.17), where the same fruitless argument persists (see my *Romans* 45–6). This is presumably why Paul omitted the personal adjectives which feature in both the Hebrew ('by his [i.e. his own] faith') and the LXX ('by my [i.e. God's] faith'). He wished to characterize the relationship as constituted by 'faith' through and through. The point would be all the more weighty in the circumstances since 'the righteous' was such a familiar self-identification in Jewish factionalism and in demarcating the righteous Jew from the Gentile sinner (see on ii.15; cf. use by Qumran of the same text – 1QpHab viii.1–3). Even those Jews most conscious of and concerned with their distinctiveness over against 'sinners' must recognize on the basis of Hab. ii.4 that their righteousness and their life as the righteous were 'from faith'. The attempt to give 'the righteous' reference exclusively to Christ (so that, once again, the faith is Christ's faith) (Hays, *Faith* 150–7) is misguided, since 'the righteous one' of verse 11b answers to the 'no one' of verse

11a; Hab. ii.4 only demonstrates the claim of iii.11a if it refers to *everyone* who considers himself 'righteous'. And had Paul wanted 'from faith' to be understood in iii.7–12 as God's 'faith-act/faithfulness' (Howard, *Crisis* 57, 63–4) he would have had every reason to retain the LXX's 'my (= God's) faith(fulness)'; but Howard is nevertheless right to insist that 'the key to Paul's thought in Galatians is his doctrine of the inclusion of uncircumcised Gentiles' (*Crisis* 82).

12 The law then is not the basis of the covenant relationship with God – **But the law is not 'from faith'.** The dogged repetition of the same phrase ('from faith'), for the fifth time in six verses (iii.7, 8, 9, 11, 12), makes Paul's point: the law is not identical with the basic faith relationship; the law is not a substitute for or alternative to the 'from faith'; the law does not dispense with or render redundant the 'from faith'. Rather the law is other than the 'from faith'; it is additional to the 'from faith'; it is built upon the more fundamental relationship based on and sustained through faith (this is a point he will develop in iii.17ff). **Rather, 'The one who does them will live by** (or in) **them'.** The text is from Lev. xviii.5, which Paul also quotes in Rom. x.5. Paul evidently took the Leviticus passage in the sense of the same, more regularly occurring motif in Deuteronomy (iv.1; v.32–3; viii.1; etc.; and not least xxx.15–20); that is, as referring to life within the covenant (as also subsequently, e.g. Bar. iv.1; 1QS iv.6–8; *Aristeas* 127; Philo, *Cong.* 86–7), and not just to life after death (see further on iii.21 and my *Romans* 601). The law, in other words, was the means of regulating life within the covenant, not the basis of the covenant itself. The difference between Hab. ii.4 and Lev. xviii.5 is that the former talks of a relationship lived out on the basis of faith, whereas the latter has the more limited purview of doing the law and of living within its terms. If Paul's opponents would deny that there is a difference (Hab. ii.4 and Lev. xviii.5 refer alike to life within the covenant) Paul at least has grounds (from the history of Abraham at least) for the claim that 'the righteous one from faith' is a prior and more fundamental statement of the covenant than 'the one who does them'.

It needs to be stressed that this is essentially a *positive* view of the role of the law; the idea that the Torah was given to be broken and in order to generate sin (Betz 145) is not found in Galatians (see on iii.19); and Beker's 54 talk of a '"gnosticizing" opposition of gospel and law' here (similarly Drane) is at best unwise and misleading (not least in view of v.14). Paul recognized the important role the law had in the period when the covenant was effective for only Israel, as a means of directing life within the covenant people; the mistake was to confuse that role with the more basic role of faith. So too we should again simply note that the thought is badly skewed if the emphasis is placed upon 'doing' the law (Schlier 134–5; Wilckens, 'Entwicklung' 167–8; Georgi, *Theocracy* 40 – 'it is this constraint to act, to achieve, that is the curse of the law'), as though that for Paul was a negative shorthand for the objectionable idea of achieving righteousness (contrast Rom. ii.13); in contrast, the curse clearly falls on *not* doing, not on *doing*. To dismiss Lev. xviii.5 as 'legalism' (as Burton 167) also mistakes its character of covenant paraenesis (see also on vi.10). Nor is the thought of the unfulfillability of the law anywhere in sight here (despite Mussner 229–31). And to attempt to take 'he who does them' as a reference to Christ (Bring 120–6) completely distorts the train of thought here, where Lev. xviii.5 is clearly understood as a description of the limited role of the law. See also on v.14. On the other hand, it is highly pertinent to note that in context Lev. xviii.2–5 emphasizes the distinctiveness of Israel's way of life from that of the surrounding nations.

13 Thus far Paul has attempted to show how clearly distinct from each other are the 'from works of the law' attitude, and the 'from faith' understanding of the covenant relationship with God. 'From works of the law' is a too restricted understanding of 'doing all that the law requires', which in turn is a step beyond the 'from faith' and in no sense a substitute for it. Now Paul turns to the other part of his claim in verse 10: the 'from works of the law' attitude entails a curse, the curse of the covenant God on the covenant-breaker, which reinforces the distinction between those who are 'in' (blessing) and those who are 'out' (curse). **Christ has redeemed us from the curse of the law, having become a curse on our behalf**. The metaphor is of buying from or back, and so of redemption by payment of a price (not necessarily as a technical term for purchasing the freedom of a slave – cf. v.1). The image is of a seriously disadvantaged status or condition (under the curse) having been rectified by a decisive act by another (the cross) on behalf of those disadvantaged (cf. the Levites' redemption of the first-born in Num. iii.44–51). Here the cursed status or condition is that of the covenant-breaker, put out of the covenant people, a status and condition like that of those who are outside the covenant to start with (outside the realm of covenant blessing = in the realm where the curse operates). Hence Paul can say 'us', meaning both Jew and Gentile, not just Jewish Christians or Jews (for the different opinions see Betz 148, n.101; Fung 148–9; also *JPL* 235–6 n. 58). For the 'from works of the law' attitude was typically Jewish (iii.10), and had been Paul's before he came to share in Christ's redemption (i.13–14). And the curse functioned to reinforce the 'outsideness' of the other nations: it was the same 'works of the law' attitude which underlined the Jew/Gentile antithesis, and prevented both from participating in the blessing of Abraham. It was precisely this 'us' and 'them' dichotomy of grace which Paul sought to combat: Christ died to benefit all whose misunderstanding or ignorance of the grace of God through faith put them effectively outside its full sweep (see also *JPL* 237).

'Become a curse' is, of course, simply a more vivid way of saying 'become accursed' (Mussner 233 compares Jer. xxiv.9; xlii.18; Zech. viii.13). Despite Burton's 164–5, 168–72 repeated insistence, no distinction between the curse of the law and the curse of God is intended (*TDNT* i. 450). The curse is not rebuked but remedied. 'Having become a curse for us' is a combination of martyr theology (itself using the imagery of the sacrificial cult) and Adam christology. That is to say, the thought is not just of an action by one which had benefit for others (a man laying down his life for his friends or country). Much more the thought is of Jesus as acting in a representative capacity, so that his death and its consequences were an enactment of human destiny with effects on humanity; the law printing its curse on Jesus, as it were, so that in his death the force of the curse was exhausted, and those held under its power were liberated. Cf. particularly 2 Cor. v.21 (*TDNT* viii.509–10); M. D. Hooker, 'Interchange in Christ', in *Adam* 13–25, here 14–16; and see further my 'Paul's Understanding'; also on iv.5, with which (despite Betz 144 n. 57) there is no discrepancy. If Paul does indeed regard the law in Galatians as a kind of angelic power (see on iii.20 and 23), then the possibility of integrating this passage with the imagery of Col. ii.14–15 also becomes clearer.

Paul may be modelling his language here on the conciseness of other already traditional formulae (as in i.4 and ii.20); but it is less likely that he is drawing on a pre-Pauline formula as such (as suggested by Betz 150 and Longenecker 121–2), since the terminology is so tightly tied into the context and integral to Paul's distinctive argument at this point, with proof text following in characteristic Pauline style. The words of Deuteronomy again provide the justification and explanation of the train of thought – **because it is written, 'Cursed is everyone who has been hanged on a tree'**. The verse is from Deut. xxi.23 (probably modified in wording to incorporate an allusion also to Deut. xxvii.26 and to ensure that the curses of verses 10 and 13 were seen to be identical) and refers to the exposure of a criminal after capital punishment had been inflicted on him. But we know from the DSS that by the first century the language was being referred to the act of crucifixion itself (4QpNah i.7–8; 11QTemple lxiv.6–13; cf. Acts v.30 and x.39), and it is a very plausible, if unprovable, guess that the passage had been used in early Jewish sectarian polemic against the Nazarenes' claim that the crucified Jesus was Messiah (cf. particularly J. A. Fitzmyer, 'Crucifixion in Ancient Palestine, Qumran Literature and the New Testament', *CBQ* 40 [1978] 493–513). If so, the ingenuity of Paul is shown by the fact that he does not dispute the charge (a crucified Jesus was accursed by God), but turns it to his own ends. For him the crucial factor was that the curse denoted a status outside the covenant, 'expelled from the people of God': the cursed criminal was a defilement of the land of inheritance (Deut. xxi.23); the curses of Deut. xxvii and xxviii not only involve the withdrawal of covenant blessing, but climax in being put outside the promised land to live among the Gentiles. So too in 11QTemple the punishment of crucifixion was for those who were guilty of breaking the covenant bond. To affirm that the crucified Jesus was cursed by God, therefore, was tantamount to saying that he had been put outside the covenant, outside the people of God. Which also meant (this is the implicit corollary) that God's resurrection of Jesus signified God's acceptance of the 'outsider', the cursed law-breaker, the Gentile sinner.

14 This is why Paul can immediately go on – Christ redeemed us from the curse of the law, having become a curse for us, **in order that to the Gentiles the blessing of Abraham might come in Christ Jesus**. Here Paul confirms that all this talk of 'curse' had to do with what prevented the blessing of Abraham coming to the Gentiles (iii.10–14 as explaining the 'mechanism' by which the blessing of iii.8–9 came to effect). So long as the 'outsider' was under a curse, the Gentiles could not participate in the blessing reserved for the 'insider'. But the effect of the 'from works of the law' attitude was to put those who held to it equally under the curse, outside the covenant (iii.10), because it was a fatal misunderstanding of the fact that covenant status is 'from faith', first, foremost and all the time (iii.11–12). The death of Christ restored the position, because when God declared himself 'for' this crucified and cursed Jesus (by resurrection), he also declared himself 'for' those affected by the curse (iii.13), particularly the Gentile 'sinner'. The barrier between blessing and curse had been broken down; now 'in Christ' (see on i.22 and ii.17) the blessing could come to Gentiles too (in effect an echo of Gen. xxii.18 more than of Gen. xii.3, but in anticipation of Gal. iii.16). *This* is the conclusion Paul draws from his understanding of Christ's death as bearing the curse of the law, that the effects of the *curse* have been abolished for Gentiles, that the restrictiveness of a law which marked off Jew from Gentile as such had been overcome, not that the *law* has been abolished, rendered null and void, or without further relevence to Christians (see also on i.16 and ii.21; also v.11 and vi.12).

Another way of stating the same objective is in **order that we might receive the promise of the Spirit through faith** (cf. the double 'in order that' formulation of iv.4–5). This second formulation has several added advantages. (1) 'The promised Spirit' (cf. Acts ii.33) ties the thought back to the beginning of the chapter, reinforcing the complementary nature of the Galatians' own experience and the argument from scripture. In so doing Paul confirms that the reception of the Spirit (see on iii.2) was equivalent in his thought to being reckoned righteous – two ways of describing the same positive relationship with God through which his blessing flows. Paul does not allow his theology of conversion or the Christian life to fall into an unbalanced emphasis on either formal relationship or spiritual experience; the two go together as two parts of the one whole. 'The experience of the Spirit and the status of justification are, for the apostle, inconceivable apart from each other' (Williams, 'Justification', here 97; see also on iii.21).

(2) The first-person plural ('we') confirms that Paul takes the 'all the nations' of verse 8 seriously – not just Jews, not just Gentiles, but all who have actually received the Spirit, Jews and Gentiles. The curse which shut Gentiles out also prevented the Jews who lived 'from works of the law' from entering the full blessing of Abraham. The curse-bearing death of Jesus thus broke open that too restricted view of covenant righteousness for both Jew and Gentile to share in its eschatological fullness.

(3) 'Through faith', given the climactic place of emphasis, reasserts once again the fundamental character of faith for the proper understanding of and participation in the covenant blessing. Just as the Gentile reception of the Spirit confirmed that God's full acceptance came to effect through faith alone (iii.2–5), so the failure of the Pharisaic Judaism which Paul knew so well to receive the same experience of the Spirit confirmed that its focus on (works of) the law rather than on faith was a mistaken perception of God's covenant promise.

(4) Not least, the reformulation of 'the blessing of Abraham' in terms of 'the promise (of the Spirit)' provides the transition into the next section (see further on iii.18). Here it is important that he can portray the coming of the Spirit as eschatological fulfilment of long-established Jewish hopes for the age to come (Isa. xxxii.15; xliv.3; lix.21; Ezek. xi.19; xxxvi.26–7; xxxvii.1–14; xxxix.29). Since this hope included also 'all flesh' (Joel ii.28–9), the implication is that the coming of the Spirit to the Galatians (Gal. iii.2–5) should be taken as an indication that the new age had come, and therefore also as the fulfilment of the Abrahamic blessing promised to the Gentiles (iii.8).

In short, iii.10–14 could well be taken as a midrash on Deuteronomy's three-stage schema of salvation–history,

covenant with Israel—> Israel's failure (curse of exile)

—> Israel's restoration (Deut. xxviii.63ff.; xxx.1ff.)

– with the final stage understood in terms which broke through the traditional covenantal mind-set of Deuteronomy (cf. Jer. xxxi.31–4) – that is, in terms of the gospel of Christ (hence the interpretation of Deut. xxx.11–14 in Rom. x.5–10) and of the promise of the Spirit (Gal. iii.14).

4 BECAUSE GIVEN BY PROMISE   iii.15–18

(15) Brothers, I speak in human terms.[1] Even a human will[2] once ratified, no one sets aside or adds to. (16) But the promises were spoken to Abraham and to his 'seed'. It does not say, and to his 'seeds', as to many, but as to one: 'and to your seed' – who[3] is, Christ. (17) My point is this: a covenant[2] ratified beforehand by God[4], the law which came four

1 Some modern translations tend in effect to run the first clause and the opening of the second clause together: as e.g. NRSV – 'I give an example from daily life . . .'.

2 Schlier 146, n.4, supported by Betz 157 n. 42, maintains that the same word should be used to translate the Greek *diathēkē* in verses 15 ('will') and 17 ('covenant'). The weakness of this suggestion is that no single word, including 'testament', far less 'covenant' (Burton 179, 501–5; Duncan 105–6), contains the full scope of the word play used by Paul.

3 Some scribes evidently thought it proper to polish the grammar by changing the masculine to neuter (to agree with 'seed').

4 The addition of 'to (or in) Christ' became established in the later MSS tradition.

hundred and thirty years later does not make void so as to render the promise ineffective. (18) For if the inheritance is from[1] law, it is no longer from promise; but to Abraham God gave it freely through promise.

Paul's central claim is that the blessing of Abraham operates 'from faith', and so comes to Gentiles on the same terms (iii.8–9). He has now met the first unexpressed response to that claim: the curse which is the correlative of the blessing in covenantal logic is no obstacle. It applies primarily to the covenant-breaker (iii.10), 'those of the works of the law'(!), who have quite misunderstood the 'from faith' character of righteousness (iii.11–12); and it has been rendered ineffective by its application to Jesus, the crucified Christ (iii.13). Consequently the blessing of Abraham can come without more ado in Christ Jesus to the Gentiles, as it already has in their reception of the promised Spirit (iii.14).

But he has still to meet the other most obvious response from the side of traditional Jewish covenantalism: that his exposition of scripture has blatantly ignored the fact that Abraham also obeyed the commands of God, including circumcision. The issue was the same as that thrown up by the Antioch incident. How could Paul treat the law of the covenant so lightly, the law which the covenant laid upon its members? How could Paul distinguish so casually between faith and faithfulness, between what seemed so obviously the two sides of the same coin? Paul's polemic against 'works of the law' had already been a partial answer: that understanding of the law too quickly degenerated into one which undermined the primacy of 'from faith'. But 'works of the law' were not the law; what about the law itself? Paul had already given a hint of his answer in verse 12. Now he seeks to elaborate it.

15 Brothers – the word denotes both frustrated affection and gentle coercion (see on i.2, 11) – **I speak in human terms**. The phrase indicates an awareness that the illustration to be cited (a will) was a weak and inadequate parallel to the covenant God made with Abraham (cf. Rom. iii.5; BAGD, *anthrōpos* 1c; C. H. Cosgrove, 'Arguing like a Mere Human Being: Galatians iii.15–18 in Rhetorical Perspective', *NTS* 34 [1988] 543–5); and perhaps also a recognition that the argument to be based on it was a case of special pleading. **Even** (RSV, NEB, NJB; cf. 1 Cor. xiv.7, Paul's only other usage): the sense of the word is disputed, and would

1 p[46] reads 'through' – presumably an alteration to parallel the 'through promise' of the second half of the verse.

normally be taken to mean 'nevertheless' (LSJ, *homōs*), although 'likewise, equally', a sense which the word formation would allow, is possible (BDF §450(2); BAGD, *homōs*; NIV). The parallel is with **a human will,** (which) **once ratified, no one sets aside or adds to** (the verbs are all legal technical terms; see Schlier 143, n. 8 and Betz 156). It gains its force from the fact that the same word (*diathēkē*) was used both in Hellenistic Greek in the sense 'will, testament' (LSJ, *diathēkē*) and in the LXX to translate *bᵉrit*, meaning 'agreement, covenant', particularly that made by God between him and his people, including both the patriarchs and Israel at Sinai (BDB, *bᵉrit* II; BAGD, *diathēkē* 2). Here the passages Paul would have in mind were no doubt Gen xv.18 and xvii.2–8, including the 'covenant' that Abraham would be 'the father of a multitude of nations' (Gen. xvii.4; cf. Rom. iv.17).

The fact that, unlike a testator, God does not die, hardly weakens the word play.[1] The point of the parallel is that a human *diathēkē*, once signed and witnessed, could not be set aside in favour of some other document claiming to represent the mind of the testator but lacking ratification, and could not be added to by some other and subsequent authority ('no one' = no one else'). The parallel is hardly a strong one, since in Roman law at least one will could be set aside in favour of a later will drawn up by the same testator, who could, alternatively, add a codicil to the first will (cf. the dispute between Archelaus and Antipas over the will of Herod the Great – Josephus, *War* ii.20–1, 35); in Greek law wills were only necessary when there was no son (*OCD*, 'Inheritance, Law of'). The parallel is all the weaker when it is recalled that *diathēkē* was also used for the covenant given at Sinai, that is, the law (Exod. xix.5; xxiv.7–8; etc. including also Deut. iv.13 and xxix.1, 21). Paul's argument, therefore, was open to the immediate rejoinder that God *had*, in terms of the illustration, either supplemented or replaced the first covenant with Abraham by the subsequent one at Sinai. Equally weakening of his claim was the observation that the first covenant (with Abraham) had explicitly included circumcision (Gen. xvii.9–14) – circumcision 'a sign of the covenant', a covenant in Abraham's flesh (xvii.11, 13).

The force of Paul's argument depended therefore partly on the narrow point of the precise terminology used in the actual words to Abraham (iii.16); partly on the effect of recognizing a time

---

1 E. Bammel's suggestion that what is in view is a '*mattenat bari*', a transfer of property which is not conditional on the donor's death but takes place at once, has attracted much support – 'Gottes DIATHEKE (Gal. iii.15–17) und das jüdische Rechtsdenken', *NTS* 6 (1959–60) 313–9; see discussion in Betz 155, Bruce 170–1 and Longenecker 128–30.

gap between Abraham and Moses (iii.17), with the implication that the covenant with Abraham had a primacy which whatever followed could not weaken; and partly on the distinction between promise and law (iii.18), which in fact moves away from the *diathēkē* = testament parallel. The fact that Paul recast the 'before and after' argument in Rom. iv.9–12 suggests that he recognized the unsatisfactory character of the Galatians' version. Note also the danger of confusion introduced by his later discussion of *two* covenants (iv.21–31; see on iv.24).

16 The point of the parallel focuses on the precise wording used in the Genesis accounts. **But the promises** – the key word of the section is introduced surreptitiously (see on iii.18), but here can quite properly serve for the various matters already touched on or implied (offspring – iii.6–7; blessing to the nations – iii.8; to be their God – Gen. xvii.7) as central provisions of the covenant with Abraham (cf. Rom. ix.4; 1 Clem. x.2) – **were spoken to Abraham and to his 'seed'**. The thought of iii.7 is now picked up ('sons of Abraham'), to become with 'promise' the central motif of the rest of the main argument (to iv.31). **It does not say** (cf. iii.8), **and to his 'seeds', as to many, but as to one: 'and to your seed'**. The text which Paul had in mind was the repeated promise that God would give the land of Canaan to Abraham 'and to your seed' (Gen. xiii.15, 17 LXX; xv.18; xvii.8; xxiv.7). The fact that the promise always had the land specifically in view was a complicating factor in the case, since it would seem to weigh in favour of Paul's opponents by linking the promise more to national Israel. Hence probably Paul's reworking of the argument in Rom. iv.13–17 – 'the promise to Abraham and his descendants that they should inherit the world', 'father of many nations' (see my *Romans* 212ff). But it is not critical here, since the argument at this point turns on the two key words: 'promise', which, of course, is not used in the Genesis passages (see on iii.18), but which could quite properly summarize the various passages where God says 'I will give', that is, both the land (as above) and a son (xv.2–3; xvii.16); and 'seed', which was not necessarily dependent on the promise of the land.[1]

Much more artificial to modern sensibilities is the argument based on the fact that 'seed' is singular. For, of course, it was a collective singular: the promise, after all, was for 'seed' as numberless as the dust of the earth, or the stars of heaven, or the

---

1 Hays, *Echoes* 111, notes that *Jub.* xvi.17 can be translated, 'All the seed of (Abraham's) sons should be Gentiles . . .'.

grains of sand on the sea shore (Gen. xiii.16; xv.5; xvi.10; xxii.17); hence the quite proper translation of the Genesis references as 'descendants'. The Targums usually render the Hebrew 'seed' by the Aramaic 'sons' (Wilcox, 'Promise' 3). And Paul was in no doubt himself as to that collective force of the singular (cf. Gal. iii.29; Rom. iv.16, 18 − 'all the seed', 'many nations'). The very fact that Paul could argue thus elsewhere, however, shows that such criticism of his exegesis here (as artificial) is not to the point. For to find significance in a particular feature of a text (which might be irrelevant on other occasions) lay well within the proprieties of Pharisaic exegesis of the time, at least so far as we can gain an insight into the pre-70 period from rabbinic traditions available to us. For many rabbis certainly, the significance of a letter in a word in the sacred text, or lack of it, could be the basis of a whole argument in favour of some ruling. In the generation after Paul, rabbi Akiba was to become well known, if not notorious for such exegetical reasoning. Here, however, it would be unjust to speak of extravagant exegesis. For 'seed' is in fact an ambiguous word, referring initially to the individual Isaac, as well as beyond, so that a rhetorical play on the ambiguity is invited (see also D. Daube, 'The Interpretation of a Generic Singular', *The New Testament and Rabbinic Judaism* [London: Athlone, 1956] 438–44; Bruce 172–3). It was an exegetical device, of course, but in its own terms and in its own day it would be recognized as a legitimate device to bring the promise of Abraham to focus in a single, or, we may say, singular seed − **who is Christ.**

In fact Paul's interpretation is thoroughly rabbinical in character. It is true that we have no parallel in rabbinic literature where Abraham's seed is identified with the Messiah (SB iii.553). But the obvious link between seed of Abraham and seed of David (suggested in Ps. lxxxix.3–4) naturally invited a messianic interpretation for more Jewish teachers than Paul (Wilcox, 'Promise'; Bruce 173). Since the Messiah was to be of David's seed ('seed' taken as singular in 2 Sam. vii.12–14!), and since for many Jews the Messiah was a prominent expression of their hopes for an eschatological fulfilment of all the promises to Abraham, the focusing of the particular promise of 'seed' on the Messiah was entirely proper and would have appealed to many devout Jews (Mussner 239 gives some examples of 'motif transposition'; Duncan 108 notes that in Isa. vi.13 'the holy seed' is the remnant). We may compare particularly *Jub.* xvi.17–18, where in the expansion of Gen. xx–xxi Levi seems to be singled out for special prominence among the rest of Abraham's seed (note *Jub.* xxx–xxxii). Paul's point is somewhat analogous, in that the intention is not to deny that Abraham's seed is multitudinous in number, but to affirm that Christ's preeminence as that 'seed' carries with it the implication that all 'in Christ' are equally Abraham's seed (iii.26–9). Nor should it be forgotten that fundamental to Jewish thought was the claim that of Abraham's several offspring (not forgetting Gen. xxv.2) only one was counted 'seed' (cf. Rom. ix.7). This, however, does not imply that Paul thought of Isaac as a type of Christ in terms of Gen. xxii, which would have diverted the train of thought once again on to Abraham's faithfulness under trial, and so away from Paul's principal promise–faith thrust.

17 My point is this (literally, But this I say). The force of the analogy from a human testament is now pressed home: a **covenant** (using the fact that 'testament' and 'covenant' are the same word in Greek) **ratified beforehand by God** (probably thinking again particularly of Gen. xv.18 and xvii.2–8; the contrast with the too human parallel in iii.15 is deliberate), **the law which came four hundred and thirty years later** (presumably based, as Josephus, *Ant.* ii.318, on the figure given in Exod. xii.40 for the length of time the people of Israel dwelt in Egypt – 'and in Canaan', adds LXX; contrast Gen. xv.13 = Acts vii.6 = Josephus, *Ant.* ii.204; but precise totals are irrelevant to the case at this point) **does not make void** (as in verse 15, the language draws on legal terminology – BAGD, *akuroō*) **so as to render the promise ineffective** (using a verb which is almost wholly Pauline in the NT – 'nullify, make invalid, set aside' – BAGD, *katargeō*; Schlier 148 n. 2). Since the argument is based solely on the wording of the promise ('to your seed', singular), Paul could just about hope to get away with it. For neither the law (covenant!) at Sinai, nor the specific command to Abraham concerning circumcision as the necessary sign of the covenant, changed or set aside the wording of the original promise.

But Paul had another line of argument in mind at the same time – the argument which has underlain the whole epistle so far: that what begins with grace/Spirit must continue so; that what comes after the gospel of faith must be consistent with it (i.6–9; ii.6, 14–21; iii.3–4); so here, that what comes after promise must be consistent with promise. In effect then, Paul's argument depends not only on the actual wording of the promise, but on the fact that it was given (and effectively received) as *promise.* The law cannot set aside the wording of the prior promise, but neither can it change its character as promise. That argument, of course, was more easily countered by pointing to Gen. xvii.9–14, not to mention Gen. xxii.16 and xxvi.4–5, as indicating that the promise did have conditions attached to it; Abraham himself could be said to have kept the law (see also on iii.6). Nevertheless, as an appeal to the divine initiative and priority of grace, whether in the promise given to Abraham, in the election of Israel, or in the experience of the first apostles or of the Galatians themselves, it carried weight independent of the particular promise/law distinction being pressed here.

18 That verse 17 did not rely simply on the more dubious argument that priority means superiority is confirmed by the explicatory **For** which begins verse 18. **If the inheritance is from law, it is no longer from promise; but to Abraham** (in the position of emphasis) **God gave it freely through promise.** Paul stakes his case on the theological axiom that salvation is always, first to last, a matter of divine initiative and grace. The point is strengthened by the idea of inheritance (a further key theme in this whole section – iii.29; iv.1, 7, 30), since the disposition of an inheritance is wholly in the hands of the testator. The word 'inheritance' is particularly appropriate here since it not only keeps the thought tied into the illustration of iii.15, but it also strongly recalls the language of Genesis and Deuteronomy. It is true that there the thought is primarily, once again, of inheriting the land (Gen. xv.7–8; xxviii.4; Deut. i.39; ii.12; etc.; as consistently in Jewish usage – *TDNT* iii.769–80), but the crucial Genesis passages include the thought of being Abraham's heir, which ties in to the central strand of Paul's argument (Gen. xv.2–4; xxi.10, quoted by Paul at iv.30). Moreover, the imagery lent itself to eschatological reference (as in Ps. xxxvii.9; Isa. liv.17), and it was also being spiritualized in talk of 'inheriting eternal life' (*Pss. Sol.* xiv.10; *1 Enoch* xl.9; *Sib. Frag.* iii.47; *Test. Job* xviii.6–7). These trends had already been extended in early Christian circles by referring to the Spirit as the beginning of Christian inheritance (see on iv.7 and v.21), so that by drawing in the imagery here Paul could integrate into his argument both an established Christian theme and, once again, the experience of his readers (Gal. iii.2–5, 14). Compare the way in which Hebrews spiritualizes the promise of the land (Heb. iii–iv; vi.12; xi.8–16).

The alternative which Paul rejects is that this inheritance of Abraham is 'from law' (similarly Rom. iv.14). Paul is still in danger of building too much on the fact that the first recorded word of God to Abraham on the theme of inheritance was of promise and not of command or condition (see on iii.15–17 above). But the 'from law' was probably intended to have the same overtones as 'from works of the law' (iii.10) in contrast to

the repeated 'from faith' (cf. particularly Rom. iv.14 and xi.6) –
that is, as denoting a mind-set too narrowly focused on the law
and an identity too much understood in terms of the law (see on
iii.7 and 12 'from faith'). However justified was the response that
divine commands (including circumcision) were bound up with
the promise more or less from the first, Paul's insistence on the
priority of divine grace (cf. again Rom. xi.6) effectively
relativizes everything else, including not least a rules and
regulations (what we today would call a 'bureaucratic') mind-set.

The key word, of course, is 'promise' which is used eight times
in chapter iii (plus the verb in iii.19). Somewhat surprisingly the
Greek word has no immediate equivalent in Hebrew (hence its
almost complete absence from the LXX); and in fact the sense
'promise' seems only to have emerged in wider Greek usage in
the second century BC (cf. LSJ and BAGD, *epaggelia*). But, of
course, it was quite legitimate to describe the undertakings freely
made by God to Abraham as 'promise'; no one would have
considered that Paul was introducing a later concept unfairly.
What is more interesting is the fact that when the word
'promise' does begin to feature in Jewish vocabulary it is much
more integrated with the law (2 Macc. 2.17–18 – 'God has
returned the inheritance . . . as he promised through the law';
the promise, in effect, to those who keep the law – *Pss. Sol.* xii.6;
Sib. Or. iii.768–9; *2 Bar.* xiv.12–13; lvii.2). It is this same taken-
for-granted of Jewish piety that Paul here questions, in the light
of ii.7–9, 11ff. The correct understanding of the promise/law
relationship is that the promise has precedence and determines
how obligations of the law apply (see also on iv.23).

The point is underlined in the final clause by use of the
verbal equivalent to 'grace' (cf. Rom. viii.32; 1 Cor. ii.12): 'God
gave it (the inheritance) as a free gift (NEB/REB), or as a
favour' (BAGD, *charizomai*; Schlier 149, n.3); whereas the LXX
accounts in Genesis all simply use the more regular 'give'. The
perfect tense underscores the sense of a gift once given and of
continuing validity for the heirs. Paul's case is built entirely on
the interlocking character of the three concepts, grace–promise–faith.
For Paul they established the character of Abraham's inheritance
so firmly that nothing else could alter it.

5 WHEREAS THE LAW'S ROLE WAS INTERIM iii.19–22

(19) Why then the law?[1] It was added for the sake of transgressions, until the coming of the seed to whom the promise was made, having been ordered through angels by the hand of an intermediary. (20) Now an intermediary means that there is not just one party; but God is one. (21) Is then the law against the promises (of God)?[2] Not at all! For if the law had been given which could make alive, then righteousness certainly would be from[3] the law.[4] (22) But the scripture confined everything under the power of sin, in order that the promise might be given from faith in Jesus Christ to those who believe.

Paul's triple argument in iii.15–18 – the inheritance of sonship was given (1) by promise (2) to the seed = Christ, (3) a promise whose character and effectiveness cannot be modified or nullified by the law given subsequently – has been entirely in line with his attempt throughout the letter to dispute the other missionaries' right to modify or nullify the character of the gospel which first converted the Galatians (i.6–9; ii.6, 11ff.; iii.3). But it inevitably raises the question: What then is the point of the law? To this question, so crucial in his debate with the Galatians and through them the missionaries, Paul now turns.

19 Why then the law? Paul's argument thus far seems to have rendered the law redundant, since promise and inheritance were, on his reckoning, completely independent of it. But no, Paul does see a role for it. **It was added for the sake of transgressions.** The verb occurs only here in Paul, but its meaning is clear; the note of subsequence (iii.17) echoes the near synonym used in ii.6. 'Transgression' is a legal term – 'overstepping, contravention' (*TDNT* v.739; BAGD, *parabasis*). The sentence is almost always taken in a negative sense: added in order to produce, or increase transgressions (e.g. Betz 165–7 – 'wholly negative . . . due to a

1 The various alternate readings (see Aland[26]) simply indicate attempts to make better sense of a difficult text.
2 'Of God' is omitted by two major witnesses (p[46] and B), so that a firm decision as to whether it was added or omitted in transmission is difficult to achieve (Metzger 594–5).
3 p[46] reads 'in/by the law'. Both are Pauline (cf. iii.11 and 18), but the parallel with 'from faith' and the weight of manuscript evidence favours 'from the law'.
4 'Would be from the law': differing word order in various manuscripts attests attempts to improve the syntax.

later state of depravation in the Jewish religion'), or, more cautiously, 'to make wrong-doing a legal offence' (NEB/REB). The reason is twofold: the parallel drawn between this sentence and Rom. iv.15 and particularly v.20 – 'the law came in to increase the trespass'; and the link with the negative function of the law implied in verses 22–3. On this exegetical foundation is built the strong evangelistic doctrine that the role of the law is to shut up in sin, in order to leave the individual no choice other than faith (cf. iii.23–4). This is a sharper expression of the older view that what Paul has in mind here is the thought of Rom. iii.20 – the purpose of the law was to make sin a conscious act.

Attractive as such a reading is, it is probably a mistaken exegesis at this point. (1) It is a mistake to read Galatians as though it had been written in the light of the later Romans. We have already noted several points in iii.15–18 at which Paul seems to have revised his argument in the later letter (see on iii.15 and 16); so that we can hardly rule out the likelihood that he developed or even changed the Galatians' argument at this point too. (2) This possibility is strengthened by a comparison of Gal. iii.19 with Rom. v.20. In the former, the word rendered 'for the sake of', or 'on account of', has, if anything, a positive ring (LSJ, charis VI.1); so it would hardly invite the Galatian audience to interpret it as 'in order to provoke'. In the latter, the negative ring is given not only by the 'in order that' clause, but already in the personifying of 'the law' (to associate it with the evil powers, sin and death), and by the verb, 'sneaked in' (as in Gal. ii.4 – the only two occurrences of the verb in the NT); the Roman readership could hardly be in doubt as to Paul's meaning. (3) The reading of the sentence as a negative is too much dependent on the assumption that Paul's attitude to the law was wholly negative, in this letter if not so much in Romans (particularly Hübner 29–32, 36). But this assumption is rendered suspect as soon as we realize that Paul's critique is directed against a 'works of the law' attitude, against an identity determined 'from (works of) the law' (see on iii.10 and 18); that his statement in iii.12 is descriptive of the function of the law for life within the law, and more neutral (or positive) than negative (see on iii.12); and that Gal. v.14 shows Paul still to retain a highly positive view of the law for Christians as well.

The more likely reading of iii.19a in its own terms, and within the context of Galatians, therefore, is as a positive description of the role of the law in the period prior to the coming of Christ – 'added', that is, by God. 'For the sake of, on account of trangressions' means probably not 'in order to provoke (or prevent) transgressions', but 'in order to provide a way of dealing with, in order to provide some sort of remedy for transgressions' (cf. the value placed on law in Hellenistic society, as cited by Betz 164). What was in view, in other words, would be that whole dimension of the law so largely lost to sight in modern Christian treatments of Paul – viz. the sacrificial system, whereby transgressions could be dealt with, whereby atonement was provided (alluded to by Paul in his use of sacrificial terminology to interpret the death of Christ – particularly Rom. iii.25, with its talk of God's 'passing over sins committed in former times'). This would make better sense of the divine rationale implied in the subordinate clause – **until the coming of the seed to whom the promise was made**, already identified as Christ (iii.16). For an interim measure which went on provoking transgressions for more than a millenium, without providing remedy for all that time, would imply a remarkably heartless picture of the God who so failed to provide. The more natural sense is that the law was provided as an interim measure precisely to deal with the problem of transgression, until it could be dealt with definitively and finally in the cross of Christ (cf. the formula, 'until there should come', in Ezra ii.63; Neh. vii.65; 1 Macc. iv.46; xiv.41); see further iv.4–5. Paul's formulation is, of course, a substantial modification of the more typically Jewish assumption of the eternal validity of the law (see e.g. Bar. iv.1; *1 Enoch* xcix.2; Schlier 155 n. 1; Betz 168 n. 48); but this is not a straight Christian-versus-Jewish debate, as Matt. v.17–19 and James i.25 remind us.

The misunderstanding of iii.19a is compounded by further confusion over the final clause of iii.19 – the law **ordered through angels by the hand of an intermediary**. The talk of an 'intermediary' is straightforward enough – presumably a reference to Moses (as most agree; see particularly Longenecker 140–3): the phrase 'by the hand of' is a semitic idiom = 'through' (*TDNT* ix.430–1), and probably echoes consciously or unconsciously its use in Lev. xxvi.46 (cf. Deut. v.5; Philo, *Mos.* ii.166; *Test. Mos.* i.14; *TDNT* iv.615, 852–3; Schlier 158–60); Betz 170 also notes that 'by the hand of Moses' became almost a formula in the LXX. That amounts simply to an elaboration of the contrast between the law and the promise already clearly stated in iii.18. However, the reference to angels, taken in conjunction with the typically negative understanding of the previous clauses, has made it possible to read this final clause in even more negative terms: e.g. 'a categorical denial of the divine origin of the Torah' (Drane 34, 113); the law 'is the product of demonic angelic powers' (Hübner 24–36); 'on the way to a Gnostic understanding of the law' (Schlier 158). It is true that such an interpretation goes back as far as Barn. ix.4 ('they erred because an evil angel was misleading them'). Nevertheless the interpretation effectively ignores the fact that the association of angels in the giving of the law was a quite familiar and unthreatening motif in Jewish thought of the time (Deut. xxxiii.2 LXX; *Jub.* i.29–ii.1; Philo, *Som.* i.143; Josephus, *Ant.* xv.136; *Apoc. Mos.*, preface), including Acts vii.38, 53 and Heb. ii.2 (see also SB iii.554–6 and T. Callan, 'Pauline Midrash: The Exegetical Background of Gal. iii.19b', *JBL* 99 [1980] 549–67). Nor does Paul's language amount to a denial that the law originated with God: the role of the angels is mediatory ('through'); and the one who so 'ordered' things was certainly God, not least since a continued echo of testamentary terminology (iii.15–18) may be audible – 'bequeathed' (LSJ, *diatassō* II). What then is Paul's point? The answer becomes clearer with verse 20.

20   Now an intermediary means that there is not just one party (literally, 'is not of one'); **but God is one.** The thought is very compressed and filling it out has occasioned much discussion (Lightfoot 146 already knew of 250 or 300 interpretations; see e.g. the brief review in Oepke 117–18, and the tortuousness of the discussion reviewed by Bruce 178–9). But the point seems to be clear enough. Paul was probably attempting a not very successful (as subsequent confusion has shown) epigrammatic play-off between the thought of God's oneness and the fact that mediation implies more than one (between whom to mediate). As NEB/REB boldly paraphrase: 'an intermediary is not needed for one party acting alone, and God is one'. The appeal at first, then, seems to be directed to the basic Jewish axiom of monotheism (Deut. vi.4–5; in Paul, Rom. iii.20 and 1 Cor. viii.6; further data in Betz 172 n. 87); but in the context the real point is that God does not need an intermediary. In other words, there is here a further contrast between the law, given through intermediaries (angels and Moses), and, once again, the covenant, given *directly* to Abraham 'by God' (iii.17) himself (iii.18).[1]

---

1 The plurality of the angelic mediation is less to the point (despite e.g. Lietzmann 23), since Paul does not dispute that God is the ultimate giver of the law (iii.19). Bring's suggestion (pp.148–54) that the 'of one' refers to *Israel*, and that the emphasis on God as one has the same force as in Rom. iii.29–30 (God is one = God of Gentiles and Jews alike) contains good insights, but deviates too far from the flow of the argument at this point. As does Wright's rather tortuous argument that the 'of one' refers to the one seed = family (pp. 163–70).

But in that case why the emphasis on the double intermediary role — not just 'through/by the hand of Moses', but 'through angels'? The answer is probably that Paul is playing on an equally well-established motif in Jewish theology, whereby they could integrate the particularism of election with the universalism of monotheism: viz. that whereas God has appointed angels to direct other nations, he has chosen Israel for himself (Deut. xxxii.8–9; Sir. xvii.17; *Jub.* xv.31–2; *1 Enoch* xx.5; *Targ. Ps. Jon.* on Gen. xi.7–8; cf. Isa. lxiii.9; 1QS iii.20–6; *Clem. Recog.* ii.42). Paul's point then is probably that the Jewish motif of the law given through angels was tantamount to abandonment of the claim that Israel was different from the other nations; or, more precisely, that for Israel thus to have accepted the law 'through angels', and so its position as 'under the law' (iii.23; iv.4–5), was tantamount to identifying the law itself with the angels, tantamount to making the law itself a kind of guardian angel, equivalent to the 'elemental forces' (iv.3) which ruled over the (other) nations. Hence the lament of iv.9–10: to submit to the law's demands was a form of slavery to the elemental forces. Such at least seems to make best sense of the line of argument which runs through iii.23–5 and iv.1–5 to iv.10 (see further on iii.23 and Howard, *Crisis* ch. 4).

21 That the basic contrast is still between the law (given through intermediaries) and the promise (given directly to Abraham) is confirmed by the way Paul takes up and rephrases the question of verse 19 — **Is then the law against the promises (of God)?** — a fair question if the law does indeed interpose between Israel and God and thus, ironically, indicate a lack of immediacy in relationship, in contrast to that between God and Abraham and promised for his seed (Gen. xvii.7). But Paul replies with his usual indignant rebuttal of his own rhetorical questions (see ii.17) — **Not at all!** The response indicates clearly that Paul would deny the very antithesis between law and promise which so many infer from verse 20. On the contrary, the role of the law is consistent with, integrated into that of the promise.

For if the law had been given which could make alive. This line of argument has caused commentators difficulty, since it seems to deny the established Jewish association between the Torah and life, to which Paul has already referred (iii.12; e.g. Lev. xviii.5; Deut. vi.24; Prov. iii.1–2; vi.23; Sir. xvii.11 — 'the law of life'; Bar. iii.9; iv.1; *Pss. Sol.* xiv.2). The solution almost certainly lies in the different verbs used. The verb 'make alive' in its usage, mostly biblical, almost always describes a work exclusive to God (2 Kings v.7; Neh. ix.6; Job xxxvi.6; Ps. lxxi.20; *Joseph and Asenath* viii.3, 9; xii.1; xx.7; *Aristeas* 16; John v.21; Rom. iv.17; 1 Cor. xv.22) or to his Spirit, a particularly NT emphasis (John vi.63; Rom. viii.11; 1 Cor. xv.45; 2 Cor. iii.6; 1 Pet. iii.18). Whereas the 'life' of which Lev. xviii.5 etc. speak is life lived within the covenant, 'the way of life' (Prov. vi.23; see on iii.12; and for Rom. vii.10, see my *Romans* 384). The point is, then, that it was not the law's function to 'make alive'; that is a power which only God can exercise. The implication is clear: to exalt the law, in effect, to the status of an angelic power, as though it could fulfil the divine role of making alive, is a mistake. That is not the role intended for the law by God – the passive of 'give' indicating God as the giver.

To be noted is the important corollary: that this is *not* a negative assessment of the law ('keeping the law becomes a sinful effort' – Fung 163 n. 62); simply an assertion that the role of the law is different from that of God or his Spirit. The law's proper role was already indicated clearly enough in iii.12 – a role of directing life within the covenant, not the making alive by which God begins a new relationship (cf. Rom. iv.17) or completes it (cf. Rom. viii.11). The fact that Paul thought of 'making alive' as particularly a work of the Spirit also reinforces his earlier contrast between the Spirit and the law (iii.2–5; also iv.4–6; v.18–23). The function of the law is not the same as and not as important as that of the Spirit. The mistake of the other missionaries in Galatia was to confuse the two and to give the law a pre-eminence which in effect rivalled that of God's Spirit; since angels were also thought of as heavenly spirits (e.g. *1 Enoch* xv.7; *Jub.* ii.2; Heb. i.7,14), any loose thinking at this point would easily slide into such confusion (law—>angelic power—>heavenly spirit—>life-giver).

If God had so intended the role of the law, **then righteousness certainly would be from the law**. Here again the implication is clear. In the two balanced lines of Paul's reply, 'righteousness' (see on ii.21) is equivalent to 'make alive'. That is to say, 'righteousness' describes the status before God of one who has been 'made alive' by his Spirit; 'to reckon righteous' and 'to make alive' are two sides of the one coin (see also on iii.14). That also means that 'righteousness' is more fundamental than the law, the starting-point rather than the objective of the law's function (it would be truer to say that the law is 'from righteousness', rather than the reverse); it may regulate the life of righteousness (iii.12), but it is not the basis or source of that righteousness. The mistake of Paul's Jewish-Christian opponents was to assume in effect that righteousness, acceptance by God and sustaining within the relationship with God, came 'from the law' rather than from the life-giving Spirit ('from the law' has the same force as in iii.18; NEB/REB's 'from keeping the law' is too restrictive). The parallel with ii.21 is also noteworthy: righteousness through/from the law = nullifying the grace of God/rendering the death of Christ pointless/attributing to the law the power to make alive = (in Paul's reasoning) treating the law as though it was as fundamental as God's grace/limiting the gracious, life-giving power of God to ethnic Israel.

22 But the scripture confined everything under the power of sin. Here (unlike iii.19) the thought does come very close to Paul's later formulations in Romans: particularly Rom. xi.32 – 'God confined, or imprisoned (he uses the verb only here, iii.22–3, and Rom. xi.32; see BAGD, *sunkleiō*) all in disobedience, in order that he might have mercy on all'; but also Rom. iii.9 – '. . . both Jews and Greeks, all alike under sin' ('under sin' only in Rom. iii.9, vii.14 and here). This suggests that the underlying theology was the same in both cases and helps us to fill out what is a tightly compressed train of thought. Paul was evidently able to assume that his audience also followed the apocalyptic schema of two ages in regarding the present age as 'evil' (see on i.4). Here he rephrases it by describing the present human condition ('everything', not just 'every one') as 'under (the power of) sin' (as in Rom. iii.9; for sin as a personified power see on ii.17).

The singular 'scripture' could refer to a single text, or, more probably stands for the collectivity of scriptures (as in *Aristeas* 155, 168 and Philo, *Mos.* ii.84; for the personification of 'scripture' see iii.8). In which case the scriptures Paul had in mind probably at least included those cited in Rom. iii.10–18 in proof ('as it is written') of the claim that 'all are under (the power of) sin' (Rom. iii.9). Indeed, the fact that he could assume his readers' awareness of pertinent scriptures suggests that Rom. iii.10–18 might have been a catena of scripture which Paul had used for a long time in his preaching, including his preaching in Galatia.

In this case also, the thrust of the sentence focuses on the 'everything' (as also in Rom. iii.9 and xi.32 – 'all, everyone'). The point, in other words, is that everything, 'the whole world' (NEB/REB, NIV), Jew as well as Greek, Israel as well as the nations, is 'under the power of sin'. This was the reality of 'the present evil age'. Israel was *not* in a privileged position, as though protected under the guardianship of the law given 'through angels'. 'Under the law' they were indeed (iii.23), but that did not exempt them from being 'under sin' (NJB's 'sin is master everywhere' destroys the parallel with iii.23). Here again it is the limited power of the law which is in view: it was not so ultimate or important a factor in the divine purpose as grace and Spirit, as promise and inheritance received through faith; nor so ultimate and powerful as sin (hence the defence of the law possible in Rom. vii.7–25). Hence, of itself, the law provided no real answer to the power of sin, and the 'from the law', 'from the works of the law' mentality simply gave the effective power of sin a new twist (cf. Rom. ii.1–iii.20). Only the grace of divine promise was able to break the power of sin and free those trapped in the present evil age.

This indeed was the divine rationale: to confine everything under the power of sin **in order that the promise might be given from faith in Jesus Christ to those who believe**. 'The promise', of course, is still that given to Abraham (see on iii.18), but with the fulfilment in Isaac as the prototype of its larger fulfilment in and through Christ also in mind. Bound up in Paul's theology of promise there are several strands: that promise by its character, and as attested by the paradigm of Abraham, has precedence over law; that it was maintained throughout the subsequent period, all of it 'under sin', as the embodiment of the divine power which alone could defeat the rule of sin; that it always had the Gentiles in view as well from the first; and that its eschatological fulfilment would be marked by the overthrow of the universal rule of sin in the extension of the promise to all. The law was not the vehicle of this promise of God, so that a 'from the law' identity for Jews constituted a limitation of that promise, and of the power of the promise. Paul can even say that God confined a whole epoch of universal history 'under the power of sin' simply to bring out the fact that the power of the promise only comes to effect within the human condition 'from faith'.

Here again the issue arises as to whether 'the faith of Jesus Christ' could refer to Jesus' faith(fulness) (Howard, *Crisis* 58, 65; Hays, *Faith* 124, 157–67; Hooker, *Adam* 170–5): it would make theological sense – a reference to Christ's self-giving in death, equivalent to i.4; and it would remove the apparent tautology of 'from faith to those who believe'. But even here the suggestion is unlikely. The whole argument of iii.6–29 is an exposition of iii.6 – 'Abraham believed God and it was reckoned to him for righteousness'; the repetition of 'from faith' in iii.7–12 is most obviously understood as a characterization of those who share Abraham's faith (iii.7, 9); and it is this characterization ('from faith') which is resumed here – now with the fuller specification as 'faith in Jesus Christ' (as in ii.16). So too 'promise' had become the key word from iii.14 to sum up what Abraham had believed, as expressing the unconditional character of the divine covenant, which could only be accepted in unconditional trust (= faith). Thus 'faith in Jesus Christ' is the eschatological equivalent of Abraham's faith (cf. Rom. iv.17–24), since the gospel of Jesus Christ is now (for Paul) the place where God's unconditional promise of grace comes to clearest expression. Hence the phrasing may be more accurately translated as 'in order that the promise-from-faith-in-Jesus-Christ might be given to those who believe'. And 'to those who believe' is best seen as emphasizing the point, equivalent to the 'to all who believe' of Rom. iii.22, but here with the force 'might be given precisely (or indeed, only) to those who believe', or 'might be given to those who believe without works of the law' (Lightfoot 148; cf. the progression of thought in ii.16). So NEB – 'so that faith in Jesus Christ may be the ground on which the promised blessing is given, and given to those who have such faith'. See further my '*Pistis Christou*'

6 UNTIL THE COMING OF FAITH   iii.23–5

(23) However, before the coming of this faith we were held in custody under the law, confined till the faith which was to come should be revealed, (24) so that the law became our custodian[1] to Christ, in order that we might be justified from faith. (25) But with faith having come, we are no longer under the custodian.[1]

Paul's answer to the question, Why then the law? (iii.19), has thus far made four points: (1) it was added to deal with transgressions until the Christ came (iii.19); (2) in this role it was inferior to the promise, since it had been mediated through angels and Moses (iii.20); (3) it was not the source of the living relationship with God, though it regulated life within the covenant for the people of Israel (iii.21); (4) so it did not deal with the problem of a whole epoch under the power of sin, which only the more immediate action of God through faith could resolve (iii.22). It is this last point which he now

---

1 Choosing a suitable translation of *paidagōgos* is problematic: 'custodian' (RSV) mirrors the full sweep of the metaphor, though its modern image of 'museum keeper' is against it; 'disciplinarian' (NRSV) is too one-sided; others resolve the problem by using a phrase (NJB – 'a slave to look after us'; NIV – 'under the supervision of'; REB – 'put in charge of ').

elaborates. In so doing he takes up the earlier allusions to a periodization of history (iii.8, 13–14, 17, 19) and provides a further explanation of the law's role within that schema:

PROMISE GIVEN (Abraham)—>LAW (Moses)
        —>PROMISE FULFILLED (Christ)

23 **However** (the *de* indicating some element of contrast), the picture of the period **before the coming of this faith** was not wholly black. 'This faith' seems to be the best way to take the definite article with 'faith' – that is, 'the faith' just referred to; not 'the faith' = the body of belief, Christianity (BAGD, *pistis* 3); nor 'the pattern of faithfulness revealed in Jesus' (Hays, *Faith* 231–2). Paul does not necessarily deny that others believed as Abraham believed prior to the coming of Christ, but affirms that God's purpose and promise have been realized in Christ (cf. iii.19), so that he is now the natural and proper focus for the promise-releasing-and-fulfilling faith. Prior to that **we were held in custody under the law**. Very strikingly, Paul speaks of the law as a spiritual power, like sin(!) in verse 22. This confirms that Paul in this section (iii.19–iv.11) was playing with the thought of the law as a kind of angelic being (see on iii.20). Paul accepted the implication of the traditional Jewish view of the law, as treating it in effect as equivalent to Israel's guardian angel, but did so only to limit that role to the period before the coming of Christ. Note the repetition of the phrase 'under the law' in iv.4–5, 21 and v.18 (also iii.25 – 'under the custodian').

Here again it is important to realize that this role attributed to the law is essentially positive. In itself, the verb 'held in custody' could have a negative sense, 'hold in subjection' (as Polybius xviii.4.6; LSJ, *phroureō* IIb); in which case, here, it would parallel the 'under sin' of verse 22 (cf. NIV – 'held prisoners by the law, locked up'). But its principal sense is 'guard, watch over' (LSJ, *phroureō*; as a city garrison – so 2 Cor. xi.32), 'protect, keep' (as clearly in the only two other NT uses – Phil. iv.7 and 1 Pet. i.5). So what Paul had in mind was almost certainly a *protective* custody – very similar, in other words, to the role of the law as 'custodian' (see on iii.24; so iii.25 – 'under the custodian'). That is to say, he saw the law's role not as equivalent to that of sin (iii.22), but as a counter to it (hence the contrasting *de*; also the positive sense of 'for the sake of transgressions' in iii.19), as providing some protection for Israel during the time when sin ruled supreme in 'the present evil age' (i.4), before the coming of Christ – Israel like a city garrisoned by the law within a larger territory ruled by sin. This also means that the 'we' here will, unusually, mean 'we Jews': Paul was thinking so much in Jewish terms (the law as a heavenly power protecting Israel) that he naturally spoke as from a Jewish standpoint (one of the people who had been so protected); hence the 'all/you' emphasis of iii.26–9 in contrast to the 'we' of iii.23–5.

But this was an interim role which the law fulfilled. And it also had a negative side, since it did mean a period of restriction – **confined** (the same verb as in iii.22) **till the faith which was to come should be revealed**. The contrast between promise and law, which so far had been posed in terms of the promise preceding the law (iii.15ff.), is now looked at from the other end – the law's role as protective custodian lasting till faith such as Abraham had exercised could be expressed with reference to the fulfilled promise. The contrasting epochs can be summed up simply by their most characteristic features – law (for Israel) and faith. Faith (the faith of Abraham, and faith in Christ) brackets the interim epoch of the law. That Paul was again deliberately drawing on the apocalyptic conception of two ages (as in i.4) is confirmed by his use of the two verbs, 'coming, which was to come' (eschatological in implication, as in Rom. v.14, viii.18 and Col. ii.17), and particularly 'to be revealed', with its force of a heavenly revelation breaking into the epoch confined 'under sin' and 'under the law' (see on i.12 and 16; 'a prison in the ancient world was always dark' – Lagrange 90). The restrictive character of that epoch, and so of the function of the law as a remedy for sin, is underlined by every phrase: 'confined'; limited in scope and provisional in comparison with faith; faith 'revealed' with immediacy (cf. i.12, 16) and with eschatological finality, in contrast to the law given through intermediaries. This limited, provisional role of the law is reinforced by the imagery of the next two verses, as carried over also into iv.1–10.

24 Paul draws the consequence from the metaphors used in verse 23 and reinforces it by use of a further, complementary metaphor – **so that the law became our custodian to Christ**. The image is that of the slave who conducted a boy to and from school (LSJ, *paidagōgos* – literally, 'boy-leader'); he was not properly speaking a teacher (BAGD, *paidagōgos*), a misunderstanding still encouraged by NEB's 'a kind of tutor'. Although the ancient world was fully conscious of the danger of a slave's abusing such responsibility, by his greed or intemperance (*TDNT* v.599; Oepke 121–2), the role was essentially a positive one – to protect and guard his charge, though that included responsibility to instruct in good manners, and to discipline and correct the youth when necessary.[1] The reinforcement of the previous portrayal of the law, in all its aspects, is obvious. Israel was like a child growing up in an evil world (i.4): the law gave it the protection it needed from idolatry and the lower moral standards prevalent in the Gentile world; the law thus involved a degree of restriction for Israel and separation from the rest of the world; but it was a temporary role, since the child would grow up, and when that happened there would be no need of the custodial slave and the restrictive rules which separated the growing youth from the rest of the world could be removed (see also on iv.2). Suggested also may be the contrast between 'custodian' and 'father' (as in 1 Cor. iv.15, the only other use of the imagery in the NT), since it would correspond to the contrast between the law given through intermediaries and the promise given directly to Abraham. 'To Christ' can be understood either spatially – 'to Christ', as the proper teacher, to whom the slave leads his charge (so Chrysostom and Luther, but now generally rejected, since in that case the more suitable preposition would have been *pros*, rather than *eis*); or, more likely, temporally – up until the time of Christ, when the custodial role of the law *vis-à-vis* Israel would have ended with the arrival of the time of maturity (iii.23; iv.1–7).

This desired objective can again be expressed in terms of the chief theological motif – **in order that we might be justified from faith**. As in iii.21, the recall of the thematic text (see on iii.6) serves to link both ends of the epoch of the law together (see also on ii.16). The law could not achieve this end of itself (iii.21); it was only a holding operation until the conditions typified in the case of Abraham (promise before law) could be realized in eschatological fulness with the coming of Christ. But now that Christ had come, and this faith in Christ was now possible, the law should be seen as a stepping stone *to* faith, not as something of equal importance with faith – with the 'from faith' life-orientation of Abraham (see on iii.7 and 12) seen now as the experience of liberating maturity after the more restricted scope and immature perspective of 'from the law'. By 'we' Paul still thinks as a Jew (see on iii.23) who recalls his own coming to

1 See particularly D. J. Lull, '"The Law was our Pedagogue": A Study in Galatians iii.19–25', *JBL* 105 [1986] 481–98; N. H. Young, '*Paidagōgos*: The Social Setting of a Pauline Metaphor', *NovT* 29 [1987] 150–76; Longenecker 146–8. Most commentators, however, take the image as primarily negative in force – e.g. Schlier 168–70; Betz 177–8, 'the pedagogue . . . an ugly figure', 'the radical devaluation of the Law'.

faith in Christ, after his earlier experience which he would now have understood as 'under the law' (i.13–14).

25 Verse 25 simply makes explicit the corollary which was already implicit – **But with faith having come we** (that is, we Jews – see on iii.23) **are no longer under the custodian**. Here we can certainly say that Paul envisages the role of the law as at an end. But this is not a blanket dismissal of the law (on Rom. x.4 see my *Romans* 586–91). What has come to an end, clearly, is the law's role precisely as 'custodian' of Israel – that is, of protecting Israel from the evil of the world by separating Israel from the world, and restricting the liberty of faith (see on iii.24). And it has ended only for those for whom 'faith has come', that is, faith in Christ (see on iii.23); unlike their compatriots, in Paul's view, Jewish believers have 'come of age' (so iv.1–6). The two-fold corollary is also obvious: for the Gentile Galatians now to seek to emulate the traditionalist Jews would mean a return to immature, restricted childhood (Paul will develop the point in iv.1–11; cf. particularly iv.21 – 'you who wish to be under the law'); at the same time, apart from its custodial function, the law still has a positive role, so long as it does not conflict with the 'from faith, by the Spirit' life-orientation which had characterized the Galatians' response to the gospel in the first place (Paul will develop this aspect in v.13–26; cf. particularly v.18 – 'if you are led by the Spirit, you are no longer under the law').

7 CONCLUSION: ALL SONS IN CHRIST THROUGH FAITH iii.26–9

(26) For all of you are sons of God, through this faith, in Christ Jesus.[1] (27) For as many of you as were baptized into Christ have put on Christ. (28) There is neither Jew nor Greek, there is neither slave nor free, there is no male and female; for you all are one in Christ Jesus.[2] (29) And if you are Christ's, then are you Abraham's seed, heirs according to the promise.

Paul has thus given a full (though not complete) exposition of the role of the law in relation to the promise (iii.15–25), an issue

---

1 '. . . through this faith, in Christ Jesus': the awkwardness of the phrasing resulted in some textual amendments – e.g. p[46] reads simply 'through Christ Jesus'.
2 'One in Christ Jesus': again p[46] represents attempts to polish – 'you are all Christ's (with a view to verse 29).

left hanging by his claim that the blessing promised to Abraham always had the Gentiles in view from the first (iii.6–14). To the typically Jewish understanding of the law as a special privilege, marking out Israel in covenant distinctiveness from the other nations, Paul has in effect responded: the law was given to Israel indeed, but as marking a less direct relation with God, an interim measure to provide temporary protection for Israel until the more direct relation expressed in the promise to Abraham could be realized in its final form as and through faith in Messiah Jesus. With that point clarified, Paul could now return to the earlier claim – that the blessing of Abraham was to Gentiles as well as Jews.

Popular today is the suggestion that Paul has lifted iii.26–8, in whole or part, from a pre-Pauline baptismal liturgy (see particularly Betz 181–5 and MacDonald, *Male* 4–9 with bibliography). That such a liturgy fitted his argument so neatly is by no means impossible, though the existence of such elaborate liturgies at this early stage is questionable (see my *Unity* 141–7); and when the key evidence is from the Pauline letters themselves, it becomes methodologically difficult to distinguish more widespread patterns from characteristic Pauline themes and forms.

26 For all of you are sons of God. The 'For' indicates that the following assertion is as much the basis of the argument just completed (iii.23–5) as its conclusion. It was Paul's realization that the gospel was for Gentiles as much as for Jews which had prompted him to recognize that the law which distinguished Jew from Gentile was a restrictive more than a beneficial factor. But as the argument has developed here, the sudden switch from 'we' to 'all you' ('all' in the place of emphasis) denotes the conclusion towards which Paul has been driving: that the coming of faith is *not* simply for the (Jewish) 'we' who experienced the law as 'custodian', but for all *Gentiles* who believe also; to argue that the 'we' = the 'you' (Bruce 183) obscures the point. Paul poses an 'us'/'you' antithesis (iii.23–5/26–7), in order precisely to affirm that it is no longer relevant: no more 'Jew or Greek' (iii.28); for Gentile believers are 'in Christ' and as such, Abraham's seed and heirs of the promise given to Abraham (iii.28–9).

'Sons of God' would be a familiar idiom by which to indicate likeness or relatedness to God or the gods. Stoicism, for example, talked of Zeus as father of all, since all shared the same divine reason (cf. Acts xvii.28). Kings and those who displayed eminent wisdom could be regarded as 'sons of God/the gods' because they exercised divinely bestowed authority or showed themselves to have been specially favoured by the gods (see e.g. *TDNT* viii.336–7; my *Christology* 14–15). But Paul here no doubt was speaking from a monotheistic Jewish standpoint – 'sons of (the one) God' (cf. iii.20). And no doubt too he had in mind the more specifically Jewish claim to divine sonship: that Israel was God's son (Exod. iv.22–3; Jer. xxxi.9; Hos. xi.1) or God's sons (e.g. Deut. xiv.1; Isa. xliii.6; Hos. i.10; *Jub.* i.24–5; *Pss. Sol.* xvii.30), or the righteous within Israel in particular (Sir. iv.10; li.10; Wisd. Sol. ii.13–18; v.5; 2 Macc. vii.34; *Pss. Sol.* xiii.8) (*TDNT* viii.351–5, 359–60). The point of the emphasis, 'all of you', thus becomes clearer. Paul says in effect: 'all you Gentiles are already sons of God' (elsewhere in Paul particularly Rom. viii.14, 19). That is to say, they already shared fully in the closeness of relationship with God which Israel, or 'the righteous' among the Jewish people, usually saw as confined to themselves, as indeed their heritage from Abraham (cf. Gen. xvii.7; Hos i.10; and the catena of verses cited in 2 Cor. vi.16–18) – and did so in contrast to most Jews still living 'under the law' (iv.1–7).

This had been made possible by the two factors which Paul proceeds to itemize, without attempting to relate them to each other – **through this faith** (the climax to the train of thought running from ii.16 through iii.14; after which 'faith' disappears till v.5–6), **in Christ Jesus** (not 'faith in Christ Jesus'; see Schlier 171). It was because they shared in Abraham's faith that they could share the immediacy of relationship with God which he had enjoyed: 'those from faith are sons of Abraham' (iii.7), and, as enjoying such favour from God, 'sons of God' in the idiom of the time. But this was possible in turn because their faith was in fact faith in Christ, which brought them into a living relationship with Christ, wherein they shared in *his* sonship of Abraham, as also in *his* sonship of God. As 'faith' has replaced the law as the distinctive mark of the 'sons of God', so 'Christ Jesus' has replaced ethnic Israel as the social context of this sonship. Such is the implication of the phrase 'in Christ Jesus' (already used in i.22, ii.4, 17 and iii.14; see on i.22 and ii.17); but Paul obviously felt the need to unpack it at least a little because of its importance at this point in the argument (iii.27–9, and through to iv.7).

27 In elaboration of the 'in Christ Jesus' formula, **For**, Paul reminds his readers, **as many of you as** (assuming this as the Christian norm, but allowing that visitors might well be present in the Galatian congregations) **were baptized into Christ**. The phrase is more or less exactly the same as in Rom. vi.3 and, as there, Paul's way of introducing it implies that the phrase itself (Christians as those who 'have been baptized into Christ') would be familiar to those to whom his letter would be read. Although it is attested only in Paul, we may assume nevertheless, therefore, that it was a regular part of Christian catechesis (Paul could assume that the home churches in Rome, which he had never visited, would be equally familiar with it). Its force is also clear from the context here: the 'into Christ' explains the 'in Christ' of verse 26; it was by being 'baptized into Christ' that they had become 'in Christ'. This suggests that the 'into Christ' is more than simply an abbreviation of 'into the name of' used in baptism (as implied in 1 Cor. i.13), although it probably included the significance of the latter. 'Into the name of' was probably a transfer formula drawn from commerce (*TDNT* v.245) = 'to the account of'; baptism thus being understood as the formal act of transfer from one lordship (of sin? – cf. iii.22 with Rom. vi.16-23; of the law? – cf. iii.23-5 with Rom. vi.15) to the lordship of Christ (cf. iii.29, 'you are Christ's', with 1 Cor. i.12, 'I am Christ's'). But 'into Christ' has more the sense of 'into' so as to become 'in', as describing the moment in which and action by means of which their lives and destinies and very identities became bound up with Christ (see further on i.22).

It is generally assumed that this moment and action, indicated by the fuller phrase, 'baptized into Christ', refer to the act of baptism as such. The present author seems to be very much in a minority in asking whether the phrase was not primarily metaphorical, modelled originally on the Baptist's metaphor of the Coming One's action of baptizing in Spirit and fire (Mark i.8 pars), as adapted by Jesus himself in referring it to his death (Mark 10.38-9 pars), and taken up again more in its original form by the first Christians including Paul (Acts i.5; xi.16; 1 Cor. xii.13) (see my *Baptism* and 'The Birth of a Metaphor – Baptized in Spirit', *ExpT* 89 [1977-8] 134-8, 173-5); the parallel in thought between 1 Cor. xii.13 and Gal. iii.26-7 is obviously close. By that I mean a metaphor drawn from the ritual act, but not identical with it. We may assume that the two moments (ritual act and metaphor) were regularly experienced as one – hence the vitality of the metaphor, and the force of the subsequent theology of sacrament (a spiritual reality in, with and under the physical action). But we cannot assume that this was always the case (cf. Acts ii.4; viii.12-16; x.44-8). Moreover, in Galatians this is the only reference to baptism (if it is so); whereas Paul speaks regularly of the conversion experience of grace or justification or dying/living or Spirit (i.15-16; ii.16-21; iii.2-4; etc.). Evidently Paul could assume that that experiential reality was so vivid in

THE EPISTLE TO THE GALATIANS

his own and his converts' memory that he could refer to it
directly (see on iii.2); whether through a reference to baptism as
metaphor or ritual act is a matter of less moment; it was their
experience of the Spirit as such to which his primary appeal was
addressed. It is also worth noting that the Paul who was so
adamant that his converts should not be circumcised (even
though circumcision provided a powerful metaphor of similar
force) would probably have been conscious of the danger of
giving baptism the same exclusive force as his opponents gave
circumcision (cf. Burton 205 – 'if, in denying all spiritual value
to such a physical rite as circumcision, he ascribed effective force
to baptism, his arguments should have turned, as they nowhere
do, on the superiority of baptism to circumcision'). For the issue
of whether Paul's understanding of baptism was influenced by
the mystery cults see A. J. M. Wedderburn, *Baptism and
Resurrection. Studies in Pauline Theology against its Graeco-
Roman Background* (Tübingen: Mohr, 1987) and my *Romans*
308–11.

That Paul was thinking in metaphors is further suggested by
the next phrase – all who were baptized into Christ **have put on
Christ**. Paul rings the changes in his attempts to express the
reality which he and the first Christians experienced – a reality
which we can describe most simply as a profound sense of
identification with Jesus. Hence the talk of 'in Christ' and 'into
Christ' (i.22 etc. and above), of crucifixion with Christ and of
Christ living within (ii.19–20), and now of 'putting on Christ'.
The imagery is obviously of putting on clothes. It could be a
further allusion to a ceremony of initiation, if indeed baptisands
did put on a fresh robe or tunic after baptism (but such is not
attested for Christian baptism for some time – Lightfoot 149–50;
see further my *Romans* 790–1). But the imagery of donning new
clothes, as a metaphor for taking on certain characteristics or
virtues, was widely used (BAGD, *enduō* 2b), and in Jewish
thought not least for spiritual renewal (e.g. Isa. lxi.10; Zech.
iii.3–5; *TDNT* ii.319); an older line of thought (as in Rendall
174) ties it into the line of thought from iii.24 to iv.5 by
recalling the change of robe which marked the transition from
boyhood to manhood. Moreover, the imagery was also used in an
intensive way with a personal subject in acting = 'to play the
part of' (BAGD, *enduō* 2b; Burton 204). And in view of the
prominence Paul gives to the Spirit in Galatians, he may also
have been influenced by the idea of the Spirit's 'putting on'
Gideon etc. (Judg. vi.34; 1 Chron. xii.18; 2 Chron. xxiv.20; Luke
xxiv.49). Elsewhere in the Pauline letters the metaphor appears
as an exhortation to Christians: 'put on Christ', as the epitome of

ethical paraenesis (Rom. xiii.14; cf. Col. iii.10–12; Eph. iv.24) with a view to eschatological completion (Rom. xiii.11–14; cf. 1 Cor. xv.49–54; 2 Cor. v.3). So Paul could have had in mind the thoroughgoing transformation of personality which a good actor could achieve by immersing himself in a character, by 'living a part' (not to be parodied as 'mere play-acting'), or may specifically have recalled the personality transformations which the coming of the Spirit had wrought among the Galatians during his ministry (iii.2–5; cf. 1 Cor. vi.9–11; 2 Cor. iv.16–v.5). That was what the act of believing into Christ (ii.16), of being baptized (in the Spirit?) into Christ (iii.27) involved; 'it affects something within me so deeply that Christ himself becomes my own self (ii.20)' (Ebeling 212). By such variation of metaphor Paul was thus able to bring out further aspects of what identification with Christ should mean for these first Christians.

28 Paul reminds his Gentile readers of what their conversion-initiation meant. The 'into Christ' and 'in Christ' were not an end in themselves, at least so far as the present argument was concerned. It was Paul's way of breaking down the boundary which had hitherto divided Jew from Gentile. So he continues, with the unqualified abruptness of an axiom that brooks no qualification – **there is neither Jew nor Greek**. This was how the Jew saw the world, as divided into two categories – the Jews and everyone else (the Jewish equivalent to the Greek view of the world as divided between 'Greeks and barbarians'). The 'everyone else' here are characterized as 'Greeks', rather than 'Gentiles' – reflecting the all-pervasiveness of Hellenistic culture in the Mediterranean world, but also the Jewish sense of distinctiveness within an intellectual culture of which they were a part (cf. 2 Macc. iv.36; xi.2). This is normally the way Paul expresses the contrast (Rom. i.16; ii.9–10; iii.9; x.12; 1 Cor. i.22, 24; x.32; xii.13; Col. iii.11), rather than 'Jews and Gentiles' (Rom. iii.29; ix.24; Gal. ii.14–15; 1 Thess. ii.14–16); but it amounts to the same thing. Paul's point, of course, is that this 'us/you', 'Jew/Greek' attitude which marked the epoch of the law (hence the 'us/you' of iii.23–6) has been rendered redundant by the fulfilling of the Abrahamic promise 'in Christ'. 'Neither Jew nor Greek' means a oneness of Jew and Gentile in faith, without the law's interposing between them to mark them off as distinct from each other. That this was a fundamental axiom of Paul's mission is indicated by the repetition of the formula, not just in the other letter most concerned with the Jew/Gentile question

(Rom. x.12), but also in its formulaic character as here in 1 Cor. xii.13 and Col. iii.11 (cf. Acts xv.9 and the fuller treatment in Eph. ii.11–22).

The other two parallel phrases (the first precisely parallel) are probably intended as elaborations of the first, the primary point (as in Col. iii.11): there is neither Jew nor Greek, just as **there is neither slave nor free, there is no male and female** (the first also in 1 Cor. xii.13 and in the fuller formula of Col. iii.11). These were the two other most profound and obvious differences in the ancient world. Slavery at this stage was not thought of as immoral or as socially degrading, but it did provide for the lower end of the economic spectrum, and, more important, it was completely antithetical to the Greek idealization of freedom = not to belong to someone else (*TDNT* ii.261–4; *OCD* 994–6). Paul would also, no doubt, be mindful of the fact that he was about to make extensive use of the metaphor of slavery as an analogy for the condition of Israel 'under the law' (ch. iv). As an elaboration of the principal 'neither Jew nor Greek' assertion, therefore, 'neither slave nor free' is a further way of saying that 'in Christ' the profound barrier of the law can be, and has been ended (for the wider contemporary critique of slavery see Betz 193–5).

The words for 'male' and 'female' emphasize gender, particularly sexual differentiation; in the NT the latter is always used in conjunction with the former (Matt. xix.4 = Mark x.6 = Gen. i.27; Rom. i.26–7). There is some indication that in Asia Minor women were able to hold more positions in public life (Ramsay, *Church* 67–8, 161–2; P. R. Trebilco, *Jewish Communities in Asia Minor* [SNTSMS 69, Cambridge University, 1991], ch. 5), to a degree which would have been unusual in Jewish society (cf. 1 Cor. xi.2–16; Josephus, *Apion* ii.201 – 'the woman, says the law, is in all things inferior to the man'); in which case the emphasis of the 'neither Jew nor Greek' may carry over to this last member of the trio as well (see also B. Witherington, 'Rite and Rights for Women – Galatians iii.28', *NTS* 27 [1980–1] 593–604). Some have heard an echo of the Jewish prayer in which the male Jew thanks God that he was not created, *inter alia,* a Gentile, a slave or a woman, though there is no firm evidence of the prayer's being as early as the first century (but see Bruce 187; cf. *m. Ber.* iii.3; vii.2; SB iii.559–62). The suggestion, however, that Paul assumes here a doctrine of an androgynous Christ-redeemer (Betz 197–200; MacDonald, particularly 113–26) diverts the thought much too far from Paul's line of argument; as so often with the hypothesis of Gnostic influence on Paul, the influence most obviously ran the other way, with a passage like Gal. iii.28 providing one of the points round which the Gnostics wove the detail of their systems (see also my *Romans* 277–9).

Paul's choice of contrasts covers the full range of the most profound distinctions within human society – racial/cultural, social/economic, sexual/gender. The language implies a radically reshaped social world as viewed from a Christian perspective (cf. particularly W. A. Meeks, 'The Image of the Androgyne: Some Uses of a Symbol in Earliest Christianity', *HR* 13 [1974] 165–208), equivalent to the 'kingdom-perspective' which informed Jesus' ministry – a powerful integrating force for the different social groups in the earliest diaspora churches (Lührmann 66–8). Paul's point, of course, was not that all of these distinctions had been removed: Jews in Christ were still Jews (ii.15); Christian slaves did not cease to be slaves (1 Cor. vii.21; Col. iii.22). Rather that these distinctions had been relativized (cf. Gal. v.6; 1 Cor. vii.22; Phm. 16). As distinctions, marking racial, social and gender differentiation, which were thought to indicate or imply relative worth or value or privileged status before God, they no longer have that significance. In particular, in the context it is the Jewish assumption that being 'under the law' showed Jews to be more highly regarded by God than Greeks which governs the force of the sequence. So, by implication, what Paul attacks in this version of a common theological affirmation in Hellenistic Christianity, is the assumption that the slave or the woman is disadvantaged before God or, still more, is an inferior species in the eyes of God (cf. i.10). How Paul saw the application of this principle, for example, in the ministry of slaves and women in the churches he established, depends on further exegesis of such passages as 1 Cor. xi.2–16, xiv.33–6 and Rom. xvi.1–12. But it is highly unlikely that he would have allowed gender or social status as such, any more than race, to constitute a barrier against any service of the gospel. See further E. S. Fiorenza, *In Memory of Her. A Feminist Theological Reconstruction of Christian Origins* (London: SCM, 1983), ch. 6.

Paul sums up the thrust and point of such a sweeping assertion – **for you all** (with some emphasis) **are one in Christ Jesus.** The phrasing is similar to that of verse 26, with the main emphasis on 'all', but with 'one' replacing 'sons of God through faith'. Elsewhere Paul never expresses himself in just this way, but he regularly spoke of many believers as 'one', using the imagery of a single body consisting of many members (Rom. xii.4–5; 1 Cor. vi. 15–17; x.17; xii.12–20; Col. iii.15; also Eph. iv.4–16), and this is probably what he had in mind here, as the parallel between the trains of thought in 1 Cor. xii.13–14 and verses 27–8 suggests (for origin of the imagery see my *Romans* 722–4). In which case the character of the 'oneness' becomes clearer: not as a levelling and abolishing of all racial, social or gender differences, but as an integration of just such differences into a common participation 'in Christ', wherein they enhance (rather than detract from) the unity of the body, and enrich the mutual interdependence and service of its members. In other words, it is a oneness, because such differences cease to be a barrier and cause of pride or regret or embarrassment, and become rather a means to display the diverse richness of God's creation and grace, both in the acceptance of the 'all' and in the gifting of each. Since the 'all' and 'you' are both given emphasis, Paul may have intended to link the thought with iii.13–14: 'all you' Gentiles could be 'in Christ', because Christ in his death had been put outside the law, where they were – 'in Christ' outside the covenant, understood as it was to limit God's blessings to Israel (for 'in Christ' see also on i.22).

29 All that is required is to round off the argument (iii.6–29) by bringing home the force of the larger claim (verse 28) in its application to the particular case Paul has been intent to make – **And if you** (again with some emphasis) **are Christ's** (clearly taking up the preceding clause – to be 'in Christ' means also to be part of Christ, or to belong to Christ – cf. Rom. viii.9; xiv.8; 1 Cor. i.12; iii.23; xv.23; 2 Cor. x.7; Gal. v.24), **then are you Abraham's seed** (the point of iii.16), **heirs** (picking up the theme of iii.18, to become the springboard into the next section) **according to the promise** (the key word in iii.14–22). The claim of iii.7, 'Know then that those from faith, they are Abraham's sons', had been startling. Now Paul has completed his attempt to justify it, with an argument outrageous in its bold simplicity. To believe 'into Christ Jesus' (ii.16), to be 'baptized into Christ' (iii.27), was to become so identified with Christ as to share in his status, not only before God ('sons of God' – iii.26), but also in relation to Abraham, as Abraham's seed and therefore participant in the promise given to Abraham and his seed (iii.16). Thus the 'mechanism' is explained whereby the eschatological blessing promised also to the Gentiles was realized, in accordance with the character of its first giving and receiving ('from faith'). And those believers in Galatia who had been told that they could not share in the blessing of Abraham without sharing in Abraham's seed by means of circumcision could be reassured that their share in that inheritance was already secure.

8   THE COROLLARY – THE DANGER OF REVERTING TO THE OLD STATUS   iv.1–11

No longer children and slaves, but sons and heirs

iv.1–7

(1) I tell you: as long as the heir is a child, he[1] is no different from a slave, even though he owns everything. (2) But he is under guardians and stewards, until the time set by the father. (3) Thus also we, when we were children, were enslaved under the elemental forces of the world. (4) But when the fullness of the time came, God sent his son, born of woman, born under the law, (5) in order that he might redeem those under the law, in order that we might receive the adoption. (6) And in that you are sons, God sent the Spirit of his Son[2] into our[3] hearts crying, 'Abba![4] Father!' (7) Consequently you are no longer a slave, but a son. And if a son, then also an heir through God.[5]

Verse 29 had the ring of an argument from scripture (iii.6–29) successfully concluded, tying together the key elements of its major premise: his Gentile readers as offspring of Abraham (iii.7,16) in Christ (iii.14, 16, 19, 22, 24, 26–8), and so heirs (iii.18) of the promise given to Abraham (iii.8–9, 14–22). Since the minor premise had dealt with the function of the law within the larger scheme of promise – its rule over Israel as a temporary restrictive measure until the coming of Christ (iii.19–25) – Paul was thus able to draw out the obvious and powerful corollary: to submit now to the rule of the law was to turn the clock back to a previous stage of God's purpose, and so to return to a more limited and unnecessarily restricted status before God (iv.1–11).

1 NRSV avoids gender-specific language by translating the masculine singular as a plural. However desirable this may be on other grounds, it fails to represent the historical position to which Paul appeals, which has to be appreciated anyway, otherwise Paul's likening of a son under age to a slave will also be misunderstood.
2 'Of his Son' is omitted by p[46] (to give 'God sent his Spirit') – an attempt, perhaps, to achieve what the scribe perceived to be greater theological consistency.
3 Some later witnesses read 'your' (Metzger 595) – an understandable correction in view of the second person in the rest of verses 6–7.
4 Clearly vocative, despite the *ho patēr* (Mark 14.36; BAGD, *abba*; Sokoloff, *'ab*).
5 '. . . through God': the awkwardness of these final two words led to a range of improvements – including 'on account of God', 'through Christ', 'through Jesus Christ', 'of God' (cf. Rom. viii.17) (see Metzger 595–6) – a reminder that the early scribes did not think of the text they were copying as 'set in stone'.

In effect iv.1–7 constitutes a recapitulation of the final section of the preceding argument (iii.23–29):

iii.23–9	iv.1–7
(23) Before the coming of faith we were held in custody under the law confined until the coming faith . . .	(1) As long as the heir is a child . . . (2) he is under guardians and stewards until the time set by the father.
(24) the law is our custodian until Christ . . .	(3) As children we were enslaved under the elemental forces . . .
(25) But when faith came we were no longer under a custodian.	(4) But when the fullness of time came . . .
(26) we are all of you are sons of God . . .	(5) in order to redeem those under the law.
(27) You all were baptized into Christ . . .	(5) God sent the Spirit of his Son . . .
(29) So then you are Abraham's seed, heirs in accordance with promise.	(7) So that you are no longer slave but son, and if a son, then an heir through God.

1 Having given his quick sketch of salvation history Paul hastens to draw the appropriate lessons in face of the crisis presented to him in Galatia. **I tell you** – literally, 'But I say', but with greater force in the Greek idiom, as drawing attention to what follows as a declaration of personal conviction, but also of great moment to his readers (cf. BAGD, *legō* II.1e); we might equally translate, 'And I tell you this', or, 'My point is this' (cf. iii.17; v.16). The point he wishes thus to press upon his readers is a simple elaboration of the metaphor of heir and inheritance – **for as long as** (cf. Mark ii.19; Rom. vii.1; 1 Cor. vii.39) **the heir is a child** (in the legal sense, 'a minor, not yet of age'), **he is no different from** (or superior to – BAGD, *diapherō* 2) **a slave, even though he owns everything** (literally, 'being lord of all', that is of the whole estate to which he is heir). The contrast may seem to modern ears overdrawn, but Paul was no doubt thinking of the *patria potestas* in Roman law, the absolute power which the head of the family exercised over his household (in its widest sense *familia* included all persons and property in the control of the *paterfamilias*). '*Patria potestas* was essentially proprietary in character and in early law differed little from the ownership of slaves . . . Thus the formalities for *emancipatio* and for *adoptio* of another's (son) were essentially the same as those for the conveyance and claiming of property. . . . Persons *in patria potestate* could (like slaves) own nothing . . .' (*OCD*, 'Patria Potestas'). This equivalency of status between child and slave (equally unable to enjoy the inheritance) is one which Paul will draw out in the succeeding verses (iv.3, 5, 7, 8–9). The situation envisaged, of course, is an ironic reversal of the claim made in iii.28: 'in Christ' means an equality of *liberty* for slave and free; 'under the law' means an equality of *restriction* for slave and heir under age.

The idea of the (Jewish) child as 'lord of all' may well reflect and affirm the tradition already well established which interpreted the land promised to Abraham as the whole earth (e.g. Sir. xliv.21; *Jub.* xxii.14; xxxii.19; *1 Enoch* v.7; Philo, *Mos.* i.155). Scott ch. 3, argues that verses 1–2 refer to Israel's redemption from Egypt (under Egyptian taskmasters) as a type of the eschatological redemption effected by Christ, the second Moses (iv.3–7).

2 But (he) **is under guardians and stewards.** The distinction between the two terms is not clear (Paul was striving for comprehensiveness rather than distinction). Both denote one to whom something has been entrusted. And in the spirit of the analogy both could be translated 'steward or administrator (of the estate)' (LSJ, *epitropos, oikonomos*). But the first was also quite common in the sense 'guardian (of a minor)' (MM, *epitropos;* BAGD, *epitropos* 3), and so was probably intended in the more specific sense of legal responsibility for the child as such, as appointed by the father, to see to the child's support and education, and to administer the inheritance in his interest (*TDNT* v.150; Betz 202–3). More to the point here, in the Roman Empire as a whole at this time the *oikonomoi* were usually of servile origin (slave or freed) (Martin 15–17), so that the situation of the child 'under the *oikonomos*' is closely parallel to the situation of Israel 'under the *paidagōgos*' (see on iii.24), 'under the law' (iii.23, 25). The choice of preposition was no doubt deliberate – 'under': being 'under the law' was just like being a child under age or a slave (so explicitly, verse 3). This also confirms the 'mixed' character of the previous description: held in protective custody under the law (iii.23) = under the oversight of a custodian (*paidagōgos;* iii.24–5) = under a guardian (iv.2); 'confined under the law' (iii.23) = 'under a slave custodian' – the more negative aspects of the *paidagōgos* (iii.24–5) = 'no different from a slave' (iv.1). The positiveness of the status of the child should not be lost sight of, nor therefore of the situation 'under the law'; under age he may be, but he is still a son of the father (*filiusfamilias*) with all the prospective rights and privileges which make his status very different from that of the slave (see also on iii.24).

The child's inferior status lasts only **until the time set by the father.** *Prothesmia,* literally the '(day) set beforehand', was a legal term for the fixed time or day before which money was to be paid, claims made, etc., after which no proceedings were allowed (LSJ, *prothesmia*). The date in question here, obviously, is that on which the child reached his majority. Whether Paul implies that the father had the right to fix the date of his son's coming of age, or was simply continuing the emphasis on the *patriapotestas*, or indeed was already anticipating the application of the analogy about to be made ('the father' reflecting the still greater power of, God – hence iv.4) is unclear.

3 **Thus also** (Paul draws the analogy – cf. Matt. xviii.35; Mark xiii.29; Luke xvii.10) **we, when we were children, were enslaved** – literally, 'we were in a state of having been enslaved'. The analogy is in effect an extension of the slave-custodian (*paidagōgos*) analogy in iii.24–5, the period when the son is 'under the custodian' (usually from the age of about six to sixteen) being equivalent to the period of minority – a period, in other words, of sonship unfulfilled, relatively disadvantaged. The contrast, of course, is between the status of 'child' (iv.1, 3) and that of 'son' (iv.6–7). To be noted is the fact that Paul does not use this analogy as a definitive mark of distinction between 'before Christ' and 'after Christ', or between committed believer and non-believer; for elsewhere he uses 'child' of his Christian addressees, in the sense of 'immature' (1 Cor. iii.1; cf. Eph. iv.14; Heb. v.12–13). Here however he may well have had in mind the attitude of the typical 'Jew' whom he characterizes in Rom. ii.20 as confident that he is 'a teacher of children, having the embodiment of knowledge and of truth in the law'. The assumption of maturity by virtue of having the law Paul now sees rather as a mark of immaturity under the law.

This suggests that the 'we', as in the parallel iii.23–5, refers primarily to Paul's fellow Jews or, more precisely, Christian Jews. At the same time, there seems to be a transition in thought, equivalent to that in iii.14, in which the 'we' also has in view the 'we' who have received the adoption and Spirit of sonship (iv.5–6; that is, including Gentiles; thus also the 'you' of iv.6 and 7, equivalent to the 'you' of iii.26–8). This was possible because Paul had already made the link, child·= slave (iv.1), so that he could move from the thought of 'childhood' (most appropriate for his fellow Jews) to the thought of enslavement (most appropriate for Gentiles – iv.8).

The enslavement of this period of childhood was **under the elemental forces of the world**. The long-running dispute over the precise meaning of the phrase (*ta stoicheia tou kosmou*) here (iv.3, 8) and in Col. ii.8, 20, is another example of either-or exegesis (see bibliography in *TDNT* vii.670 and Betz 204–5 n. 30; review in Mussner 293–7). Does it denote 'the elemental substances' of which the cosmos is composed, earth, water, air and fire (cf. 2 Pet. iii.10, 12); or 'the elementary forms' of

religion (cf. Heb. v.12), now superseded by the coming of faith
in Christ; or 'the heavenly bodies, the stars' understood as divine
powers which influence or determine human destiny (for the
range of alternatives see especially Burton 510–18; BAGD,
stoicheion 2–4; *TDNT* vii.671–85)? The answer is probably 'All
three!' Or more precisely, that Paul did not have such
distinctions in mind (cf. particularly Wisd. Sol. xiii.1–2, Philo,
Decal. 52–6 and Rom. viii.38–9). Rather we would do better to
suppose that this phrase was his way of referring to the common
understanding of the time that human beings lived their lives
under the influence or sway of primal and cosmic forces,
however they were conceptualized. As Betz 205 indicates, it
would be a mistake to attempt resolution of the issue in terms of
a distinction between personal and impersonal forces (as does
Oepke 131), since 'fate' could be personified ('the Fates') or
attributed to a personal *daimōn* (OCD, 'Fate; LSJ, *daimōn*), and
since the 'elemental substances' could be given the names of
deities (Philo, *Vit. Cont.* 3). Such a cosmic perspective was not
unfamiliar within Judaism (e.g. Deut. iv.19; *Jub.* ii.2; *1 Enoch*
lxxv.1; lxxx.6–7); and it may not be irrelevant that Josephus
could describe the Pharisees and particularly the Essenes as
believers in Fate: 'The sect of Essenes declares that Fate is the
mistress of all things, and that nothing befalls men unless it be
in accordance with her decree' (*Ant.* xiii.172).

It is important for the flow of Paul's thought from iii.19 on to
appreciate the fact that he clearly understood the law to be
functioning in effect as one of these forces (as most recognize).
This in fact was his great criticism of contemporary Judaism:
that by treating the law as ruling over and marking out Israel
exclusively, his fellow Jews were doing the very opposite of what
they thought they were doing; instead of demonstrating God's
special preference for Israel, the law had become like (in the
language of *Jubilees*) one of the spirits which God caused to rule
over the other nations 'so that they might lead them astray' (*Jub.*
xv.31; hence also the rejoinder of verse 3a in effect to the Jewish
assumption characterized in Rom. ii.20). This is precisely why
the reference of the 'we' in verse 3 has such ambiguity, and why
in iv.8–10 the idea of the Galatians' putting themselves under
the law is equivalent to the idea of their reverting to their
previous pagan religions.

4 But when the fullness of the time came. This is obviously
equivalent to the child's coming of age in the analogy of iv.2 and
to the 'coming of faith' in the parallel of iii.23–5. The imagery is
of a container being steadily filled (the passage of time) until it

is full (for range of meaning see BAGD, *plērōma*). The implication is of a set purpose of God having been brought to fruition over a period and its eschatological climax enacted at the time appointed by him (cf. iv.2; 1 QpHab. vii.2; Eph. i.10; Mark i.15; Heb. i.2; *TDNT* vi.305). This conviction that the eschatological climax had *already* arrived set up the 'eschatological tension' between the already and the not-yet which was so characteristic of earliest Christian theology (O. Cullmann, *Christ and Time* [London: SCM, 3rd edition 1962]; see also my *Jesus* 308–18).

This clause together with the following read very rhythmically, with balanced and answering clauses, whose effect is best seen if set out as follows:

> But when the fullness of the time came,
> God sent his Son,
>> born of woman,
>>> born under the law,
>>>> in order that he might redeem those under the law,
>>> in order that we might receive the adoption.
> And to show that you are sons, God sent the Spirit of his Son . . .

The parallel with Rom. viii.3–4 is noteworthy:

> What the law was unable to do . . .
> God sent his own Son
>> in the very likeness of sinful flesh
>>> and as a sin-offering,
>>> and condemned sin in the flesh,
>> in order that the requirement of the law might be fulfilled in us
>> who walk not in accordance with the flesh
> but in accordance with the Spirit.

God sent his Son. The reason for speaking of Jesus as 'Son' (see on i.16) here is obvious. The connecting thread of thought since iii.6 consists of the interwoven strands of 'seed', 'heirs', 'children' and 'sons', including the interplay between 'sons of Abraham' and 'sons of God' (iii.7, 26). Paul's point is precisely that the Galatian believers by sharing in Christ's sonship (iv.6–7) share also in the sonship of Abraham (iii.29); or rather, that they share not only in the lesser sonship of Abraham but even in sonship of the Christ. So, by implication, how could they think to treat their sonship of God so lightly by coveting an inferior sonship of Abraham (through circumcision)? The ordering of the lines and balance of the clauses also indicate that the talk of Christ's divine sonship was intended to find its answering emphasis in the talk of receiving adoption. This strongly suggests that the main thrust of the reference is forward looking, and is primarily soteriological, as emphasizing the means by which the Son achieved this end – that is, by his death (see below), a characteristic emphasis in Paul's thought of Jesus as God's Son (Rom. v.10; viii.3, 32; Gal. ii.20; *TDNT* viii.384).

Whether Paul also thought of Jesus as God's Son 'sent forth' from heaven is less clear, though usually assumed (cf. the probably later formulations of John iii.16–17 and 1 John iv.9). Such language ('send forth') is used in Jewish and Christian tradition equally of the sending of a heavenly messenger (an angel – e.g. Gen. xxiv.40; God's Spirit – Zech. vii.12 and Gal. iv.6; divine wisdom – Wisd. Sol. ix.10), and of the sending of a human messenger, particularly the prophets (e.g. Judg. vi.8; Jer. vii.25; Ezek. ii.3; Hag. i.12; also Paul himself – Acts xxii.21). However, it is as likely that Paul was influenced by the tradition of Jesus' sayings which expressed his own sense of commissioning (Mark ix.37 pars; Matt. xv.24; Luke iv.18; x.16) – Mark xii.6 pars providing probably the closest parallel, with its thought of Jesus as 'beloved son' being sent as the eschatological climax of God's dealings with Israel and being killed for his inheritance as a consequence of his mission (see further my *Christology* 38–44; Scott 165–9). At this stage the language was neither 'unJewish' nor as much of a stumbling block to Jewish monotheism as Mussner 273–4 seems to think (see further my *Partings*, ch. 10).

Born (BAGD, *ginomai* I.1) **of woman**. In connection with the preceding discussion it needs to be remembered that 'born of woman' was a typical Jewish circumlocution for the human person (Job xiv.1; xv.14; xxv.4; 1QS xi.21; 1QH xiii.14; xviii.12–13, 16; Matt. xi.11; SB iii.570). So it refers not to the process by which God's Son became a man (his birth), nor does it contain any reference to a virgin-birth tradition (as is now generally recognized), but simply describes his human condition – one 'born of woman'. Here again it is important to bear in mind the sequence of thought and balance of clauses in verses 4–5, since the line 'born of woman' finds its answering echo in the second purpose clause of verse 5 – 'in order that we might receive adoption'. What is set in contrast, in other words, is the ordinary humanness of God's Son in his mission, and the adoption of ordinary human beings to divine sonship. This suggests in turn that the sequence of six lines was determined in part at least by Paul's Adam christology – Christ as the man who retraced the course of Adam through his fallenness to death (cf. Rom. viii.3), in order by his exaltation to complete the divine purpose in creating humankind, that is, to put all things under his feet (Ps. viii.6), in order that those in him might share in this completion of the divine purpose for creation (cf. 1 Cor. xv.25–7, 45–9; Phil. ii.6–11; Heb. ii.6–9; see further my *Christology* 107–23; also *Partings* 191–5).

Fundamental to Paul's point, however, is that Christ in his mission of redemption represented not only humankind as a whole, but also the Jewish people in particular (cf. Rom. xv.8). Hence the parallel clause – **born under the law**. It is the addition of this clause (and its echo in verse 5a) which marks off this version of the formulation most clearly from its parallel in Rom. viii.3 – a further reminder of the extent to which the argument from iii.19 has been driven by the thought of being 'under the law'. The additional thought is precisely that of the law's functioning in effect as one of those elemental forces to enslave – like the guardian angels appointed over nations who kept the nations from the knowledge of God (iv.8–9) and truth of the gospel (cf. 2 Cor. iii.12–iv.4) (see on iii.20 and 23, and iv.3). Here, of course, the Jewishness of Jesus, and indeed his practice as a devout Jew, is emphasized: it was by his sharing in Israel's subjection to the law during his life, as by his sharing in the status of the outcast from the law in his death (iii.13), that his death and resurrection were able to effect redemption for both Jew and Gentile (the train of thought is similar to that in the climax to Romans – xv.8–13). Paul does not achieve universality of effect by abandoning historical particularity.

5   Answering to the clause depicting the status of Jews as such (Jesus included) as 'under the law', comes the first purpose clause – **in order that he might redeem those under the law**, that is Jews. The verb is the same as that in iii.13, but this time with the thought much more to the fore of purchasing a slave in order to free him (see on iii.13) – the slavery in question being that to 'the elemental forces of the universe' (iv.3), including the law ('under the law' – see on iv.4). The fact that Paul uses this verb in only these two verses in his undisputed writings strengthens the parallel in thought between them:

iii.13–14	iv.4–6
having become a curse for us,	born under the law,
Christ redeemed us from	in order that he might redeem
the curse of the law	those under the law
. . . .	. . . .
in order that we might receive	in order that we might receive
the promise of the Spirit	the (Spirit of) adoption

The parallel indicates that the redemption was achieved not by incarnation, but by death (cf. Rom. viii.3), and strengthens the recognition that Paul saw Jesus' ministry in almost exclusively soteriological terms: the purpose of his coming, not as a teacher of Torah or of wisdom, but in order that, by his identification with the human condition (here, of Jews), his death might be the price necessary to free them from the slavery endemic to that human condition – a good example of what has appropriately been called 'interchange in Christ' (Hooker, *Adam* 59–60). Betz's 207 n. 51, assumption that iii.13 and iv.4–5 cannot be harmonized ignores the fact that each is an abbreviated reference to a larger story (Hays, *Faith* 118–21) and betrays his failure to appreciate the scope of 'under the law' for Paul.

The second purpose clause extends the effect of Christ's redemptive action to the Gentiles – **in order that we might receive the adoption**. As in iii.14 the 'we' is best understood as referring to all who had received the Spirit – Gentiles as well as Jews (see on iv.3) – thus answering to the generic condition of humankind ('enslaved under the elemental forces' – iv.3; 'born of woman' – iv.4). The parallel with iii.14, and between iv.5–7 and Rom. viii.15–17 (see below), also indicates that by 'adoption' Paul has in mind the reception of the gift of the Spirit (see on iii.2).

In the NT the metaphor of 'adoption' is distinctive to the Pauline corpus (Rom. viii.15, 23; ix.4; Eph. i.5). It was no doubt drawn from Paul's experience of Roman law and custom, since it was not a Jewish practice as such (though see Bruce 197), and thus extends the analogy which dominates this paragraph (iv.1–7). Almost certainly Paul had in mind the legal act of *adoptio*, by which a Roman citizen entered another family and came under the *patria potestas* of its head (see on iv.1). Paul also had embraced the thought of the similarity of the status of son to that of slave (see again on iv.1). So here his thought may have included the legal possibility of a father's releasing his son from his *potestas* by formally selling him (*emancipatio*). According to early Roman law, if this was done three times the son was finally free of his father's *potestas*. After the first two sales, however, the son could be manumitted (like a slave) back to his father, who would receive him back by a fresh act of *adoptio* (see *OCD*, 'Adoptio', 'Emancipatio'). This helps explain how Paul's thought could move so easily from the thought of redemption (from slavery) to that of adoption to sonship. Presumably also included in Paul's use of the analogy was the fact that the adopted person was for all legal purposes in the same position as the natural son, with the same rights of succession – so that 'adoption' is fully equivalent to 'sonship'.

The same context of thought (the laws governing sons and slaves) probably also explains Paul's use of the compound verb for 'receive' (*apolambanein*, rather than *lambanein*, as in Rom. viii.15), since it was usually by a similar compound that 'freedmen' were known – *apeleutheros* (rather than simply *eleutheros*; LSJ, *apeleutheros*). The son 'emancipated' and then manumitted back, literally 'receives back' (the compound form of the verb can have the force 'receive back, recover') by 'adoption' the status of son. In which case Paul presumably integrated the thought into his Adam christology: the purpose of Christ's death was to recover for the 'sons of Adam' the status of 'sons of God' (cf. Luke iii.38).

At all events, the terms of the analogy should not be allowed to become fixed terms or means of differentiation (Jews as 'sons', Gentiles as 'adopted sons'; conversion-initiation as the single decisive action of 'adoption'), since Paul can use the same metaphor (adoption) both of Israel's status (Rom. ix.4) and of the final redemption of the body (Rom. viii.23). If such a distinction is in mind it would be between Christ's (natural!) sonship and Christians' (adopted) sonship; though it is worth noting that whereas John's Gospel distinguishes Christ as 'Son' (*huios*) from Christians as 'children' (*tekna*), Paul does not hesitate to use the same term (*huios*) for both.

The parallel between verses 5–7 and Rom. viii.15–17 is strong:

Rom. viii.15–17	Gal. iv.5–7
(15) You received not the spirit of slavery . . .	(5) In order that he might redeem (from slavery) those under the law,
but you received the Spirit of adoption,	in order that we might receive the adoption,
by whom we cry 'Abba! Father!'.	(6) God sent the Spirit of his Son into our hearts crying 'Abba! Father!',
(16) The Spirit itself bears witness . . . that we are children of God.	to prove that you are sons. . . .
(17) And if children, then heirs . . . of God.	(7) And if son, then also an heir through God.

The extent of the parallel, with variations, strongly suggests that Paul was rehearsing a familiar line of argument rather than echoing a formulation more widespread in the earliest diaspora churches.

6 The opening words of verse 6 would quite naturally be translated 'because you are sons' (so RSV/NRSV and NIV; so the majority, e.g. Schlier 197, with bibliography in n.3). Yet it is most unlikely that Paul wished to suggest that the Spirit was a gift consequent and subsequent upon their being made sons. Such an inference would have been quite counter to his basic argument: that the Galatians' receipt of the Spirit was the *beginning* of their experience as Christians (iii.2–3) and amply demonstrated their full acceptance by God, that is, as sons of Abraham and sons of God (iii.7, 26). It would also run counter to the parallel thought expressed in Rom. viii (see on iv.5), where it is clear that possession of the Spirit is coterminous with sonship (Rom. viii.14) (see further my *Baptism* 113–15). Possibly, then, Paul used the conjunction here in a more explanatory sense – 'that' = '(to show or prove) that' (NEB/REB, GNB; Zahn 202–3; Lagrange 103–4; Lietzmann 27; C. F. D. Moule, *An Idiom-Book of New Testament Greek* [Cambridge University, 1959] 147; Rohde 173). This would fit best with the witness-bearing function of the Spirit in the parallel Rom. viii.16, which in turn may suggest that Paul still had in mind the Roman form of adoption, with the Spirit sent to act as witness in the formal act of *adoptio* (J. D. Hester, *Paul's Concept of Inheritance* [Edinburgh: Oliver & Boyd, 1968] 60–2). The problem probably arose because Paul has attempted to express himself in a too compressed way, in the confident assumption, no doubt, that the Galatians' appreciation of the legal analogy running through these verses, as well as their vivid memory of their own experience (iii.2–5), would fill out the ellipse for them. Hence the translation – **and in that you are sons.**

God sent the Spirit of his Son. The use of the same verb as in iv.4 (the only occurrences of this form in Paul) increases the parallelism of the two missions. The parallel may be in terms of origin (from heaven), with a possible echo of Wisd. Sol. ix.10, 17 –

> Send her (Wisdom) forth from the holy heavens
>
> . . . .
>
> Who has learned your counsel, unless you have given wisdom
> and sent your holy spirit from on high?

Or it may be in terms of the twin effects of the two missions: both with a view to effecting sonship – that is, not only in (legal) fact (iv.4–5), but also in the reality of subjective experience. Hence **into our hearts.** For in Paul's anthropology the 'heart' denoted the seat of the inner life, the inner experiencing 'I', both as a rational, decision-making being, and as a being with emotions and desires (BAGD, *kardia*; R. Jewett, *Paul's Anthropological Terms* [Leiden: Brill, 1971] 305–33). And it is precisely Paul's point, that the reality of God's adoption/acceptance reaches to the motivating and emotive centre of the person (Rom. ii.29; v.5; vi.17; x.8–10; 2 Cor. i.22; iii.2–3; iv.6; Phil. iv.7; 1 Thess. iii.13). This is why Paul could begin by appealing so confidently to his readers' experience of the Spirit when he launched into the main section of his argument (iii.2–5); though here he switches back, unconsciously or unavoidably, from the 'you' of personal address (iv.6a, 7) to the 'we' of shared experience (iv.5b, 6b). Thus it would be more appropriate here to speak of 'the language of experience' or even 'Spirit language' than of 'baptismal language'.

The soteriological lynchpin of Paul's argument at this point is the theological claim that the Spirit is 'the Spirit of God's Son'. It is this which ties the Galatians' experience of the Spirit (iii.2–5) into the crucial assertion that they are 'sons' (sons of Abraham, sons of God – iii.7, 26). Their reception of the Spirit proved that they were sons, because the Spirit is the Spirit of the Son, that is, of him who is both son (seed) of Abraham and Son of God (see on i.16). The redefinition of the Spirit thus implied ('the Spirit of his Son') was not Paul's alone (also Rom. viii.9 – 'the Spirit of Christ'; Phil. i.19 – 'the Spirit of Jesus Christ'), but part of a wider reassessment of previous categories, occasioned by the Christ event for those who believed in him and who wished not only to believe but to make theological sense of their faith (so also Acts xvi.7 – 'the Spirit of Jesus'; 1 Pet. i.11 – 'the Spirit of Christ').

The full theological significance of this claim is immeasurable. For at a stroke it linked the whole sense of transcendent power – in the experience of awesome natural phenomena (e.g. Exod. xiv.21; 1 Kings xix.11), of the mystery of life (e.g. Gen. vi.17; Ps. civ.29–30; Ezek. xxxvii.9), or of special inspiration (e.g. Judg. vi.34; 1 Sam. x.6, 10), of which 'enslavement to the elemental forces' was the negative counterpart (see on iv.3) – to the historical figure of Jesus the Christ. And not only linked it to, but defined it by reference to this Jesus. Within the range of such experiences, including the impersonal and amoral (e.g. Judg. xiv.19; 1 Sam. xvi.14–16; 1 Kings xxii.19–23), those attributable to the divine Spirit could now be recognized by the fact that this was the Spirit of the Son, the Spirit whose character was attested by the character of Jesus as known to them from the Jesus tradition. That is to say, the character of Jesus' sonship provided the parameters for the experiences which could be attributed to the Spirit.

It is important to appreciate the clear implication: that in iii.2–5 Paul was not making an uncritical appeal to the Galatians' experience of the Spirit (as though any and all emotional reactions to the preaching of the gospel were *ipso facto* experiences of the Spirit); the experience of the Spirit is the experience of sonship and bears the mark of Christ's own sonship (see also on v.7 and 22–4). To that extent at least Beker 294 is unjustified in arguing that the 'inherently triumphant manner' of Paul's talk of the Spirit 'prevents its integral relation with the weakness and suffering of the crucified Christ'. Moreover, this reinterpretation of the Spirit set in train a dynamic redefinition of God which was to become the principal reason why Christianity separated from Judaism – foreshadowed already in the seven words of this clause: '*God* sent the *Spirit* of his *Son*'. Jesus the Christ was not only to be understood as God's Son, but the Spirit of God was to be understood as the Spirit of Jesus the Son – the Son as attesting the character of God, the Spirit as expressing the character of God's Son (but the text gives no ground for the insertion of the *Filioque* clause into the Nicene Creed). The redefinition of God thus involved took centuries to work through and is still only provisional, but it grew directly out of these first attempts to integrate the experience of the first Christians, Gentile converts not least, into the larger scheme of salvation history drawn from the Jewish scriptures and already being reinterpreted in the light of Jesus' life, death and resurrection.

The experiential character of the subject is also indicated by the particular activity attributed to the Spirit – **crying, 'Abba! Father!'** The verb used, as also in Rom. viii.15, indicates a cry of some intensity, whether of feeling or of volume (cf. BAGD, *krazō*), inspired and possibly ecstatic, at all events 'from the heart', with the overtones of emotional depth and sincerity which that implies. This suggests in turn that the prayer thus envisaged was more in the nature of a brief, spontaneous ejaculation, than that the words recorded here refer to a more elaborate prayer like the Lord's prayer. In fact Paul probably saw the prayer as an echo of Jesus' own prayer style, and thus as proof that those who so prayed thereby attested that they shared his sonship. The point can be stated briefly. The retention of the Aramaic ('Abba'), even when the Greek equivalent is attached, clearly indicates a prayer form well established prior to its transposition into Greek (hence the almost formulaic ring of iv.6 = Rom. viii.15). And since that transposition happened at a very early stage ('Hellenists' = Greek speakers already a significant body in Acts vi.1), the reason for the cherishing of the Aramaic form most probably reaches back behind the earliest Aramaic-speaking community (if there ever was an only-Aramaic-speaking community in the first place). That ties in to the tradition that 'Abba' was a characteristic prayer form of Jesus himself (explicitly, Mark xiv.36; see further my *Jesus*, ch. 2, and *Christology* 26–33; Bruce 199–200). But this is precisely the implication here: that the Spirit of the Son prays the prayer of the Son and so attests the sonship of those who thus pray; hence also the further thought of Rom. viii.17 – not only heirs, but 'heirs together with Christ'. At all events, quite clearly it is because the Spirit, who in their hearts cried 'Abba, Father', thus attested their sonship, that Paul refers once again to this common experience of Jew and Gentile convert ('our'): the theological argument of iii.6–29 is underpinned at both ends (iii.1–5 and iv.1–7) by the appeal to the reality and vitality of their shared experience.

7 The conclusion can be drawn with beautiful simplicity: **consequently you** (singular) **are no longer a slave, but a son** (because of the centrality of the slave/son comparison in his argument, iv.1–7, Paul elaborates the formulation which he also used in Rom. viii.15–17 at this point). As Paul had brought his self-defence to a close with the personal testimony of his own experience of Christ's sonship (ii.20), so now he addresses himself to each person listening to his letter's being read in the Galatian churches. For all that a son (under age) and a slave were little different in legal status in relation to the father (iv.1), the status of a son was not to be compared to that of a slave – the difference lying in potential for inheritance. And this was equally true of the adopted son: whatever his status before, by adoption he became the full heir of the father. So with the Gentile Galatians: their status had been transformed from a slavery (iv.8) outside God's family (Israel) to that of son within the seed of Abraham, by adoption, through receiving the Spirit of the one who was Abraham's seed pre-eminently.

And if a son, then also an heir (as in Rom. viii.17), that is, of the inheritance promised to Abraham (see on iii.18). This had been the point of the argument: if Paul was correct, the Gentile Galatian believers need do or receive nothing more in order to be sure of belonging to God's family; they were sons already, and so their share in the inheritance of Abraham was secure, even if they were only adopted sons. For it had all been done **through God**, that is, presumably (Paul again being unnecessarily elliptical), by the action of God (so NEB/REB and NJB – 'by God's own act'; cf. i.1 and 1 Cor. i.9), that is, in terms of the analogy, the one who as father had adopted into his family those who had been born outside it, and who had done so by bestowing on them not only the status of sons but also the spirit

of his own Son's sonship; less satisfactory is NIV – 'since you are
a son, God has made you also an heir'. For the further thought
of the 'kingdom of God' as the 'inheritance' see on v.21.

So why return to the old status?   iv.8–11

**(8) Formerly, however, when you did not know God, you
were in slavery to beings that by nature are no gods. (9) But
now that you have come to know God, or rather to be known
by God, how is it that you are turning back again to the weak
and beggarly elemental forces? Do you want to be in slavery[1]
to them once again? (10) You are observing days and months
and special times and years. (11) I am afraid that perhaps I
have laboured[1] for you to no avail.**

In his exhortation to the Galatians Paul had now come back
again to the same point which his argument from scripture had
reached in iii.29, both by drawing out the analogy of a son and
heir (iv.1–5), and by tying it in to their own experience of the
Spirit (iv.6–7). But iv.1–5 had also provided a valuable before-
and-after analogy – the transition from minority to majority,
from slave-like childhood to adult sonship. An analogy which
could refer equally to the before and after of the Christian
Gentile as of the Christian Jew. It is this aspect of the analogy
which he now takes up, as the rebuke of i.6–9 and iii.2–5
becomes a passionate appeal.

8   Formerly, however (literally, 'But then'), **when you did not
know God you were in slavery to beings that by nature are
no gods** (literally, 'to gods which by nature are not'). This is the
clearest indication in the letter that Paul's audiences in Galatia
were Gentiles, or at least that those to whom the appeal of the
letter was addressed were the Gentile converts tempted to
judaize. In their former state (that is, before they heard and
responded to the gospel) they had not 'known God'. This status
of Gentile former slavery is clearly different from that of Jewish
minority sonship. Even in likening Israel's minority status to that
of Gentile slavery, Paul maintains an awareness of Israel's
privileged position.

1 Some important early manuscripts indicate at these points scribal alterations
to the verbal tenses which the scribes would probably have expected.

'Knowledge of God' was a characteristically Jewish theme. It included the idea of acquaintance with (Israel's own experience of God's dealings) and acknowledgment of (hence of obedience due to God). This was Israel's privilege (Deut. iv.39; 1 Sam. iii.7; Pss. ix.10; xlvi.10; Isa. xliii.10; Hos. viii.2; Mic. vi.5; Wisd. Sol. ii.13) – that which they should cherish and to which they should aspire (Prov. ii.5; ix.10; Jer. xxxi.34; Dan. xi.32), that for failure in regard to which they were rebuked (Judg. ii.10; Isa. i.3; Jer. xxii.16; Hos. iv.6; v.4; vi.6). The converse was the equally characteristic Jewish claim that the other nations did *not* 'know God' (Ps. lxxix.6; Jer. x.25; Judith ix.7; 2 Macc. i.27): that is, the Gentiles had had no experience of his covenantal grace, and did not realize that he was the only God – hence the gods they actually worshipped were 'no gods' (2 Chron. xiii.9; Isa. xxxvii.19; Jer. ii.11; v.7; xvi.20; Wisd. Sol. xii.27; the repeated theme of the Epistle of Jeremiah – 23, 29, 51–2, 64–5, 69, 72). It is significant, then, that Paul speaks from a thoroughly Jewish perspective and as a Jew (as in 1 Cor. i.21; viii.4; 1 Thess. iv.5 and 2 Thess. i.8). Eph. ii.12 filled out the corollary: Gentiles were 'alienated from the commonwealth of Israel, and strangers to the covenants of promise, having no hope and without God in the world'.

By adding 'by nature', however, Paul was evoking a whole sweep of Greek philosophical (particularly Stoic) thought in its attempt to speak about the nature of reality, the true nature of things (LSJ, *physis* III–IV; *TDNT* ix.252–66; 'nature' is not a Hebrew concept), which thus was not unrelated to the idea of elemental forces of the cosmos (iv.9; see on iv.3); hence the quite proper translation 'in reality', 'not really gods at all' (NJB). The phrase indeed may also indicate Paul's awareness of the distinction sometimes made within Greek thought (Euhemerism) between 'gods in reality' and 'gods by human convention' (see Betz 214–15). Whether Paul thought of these other gods as literally 'non-existent', or as demonic powers (cf. LXX of Ps. xcvi.5; 1 Cor. x.20–1), is less than clear (1 Cor. viii.4–6), especially since the chief powers of which he speaks in his principal theological treatise (Romans) are 'sin' and 'death'. Thoroughly Greek are the implicit desirability and wisdom of living in accordance with the truth of reality. All this enabled Paul to tie his analogy of under-age sonship equivalent to slavery (iv.1) to the condition of the Galatian Christians prior to their conversion. For a Hellenized Jew or judaizing Gentile would readily acknowledge that, whereas knowledge of God is liberty (the liberty that knowledge of the truth brings), the worship of idols is a form of slavery (to the consequences of ignorance or a false perception of reality). Paul shows himself here to be a citizen of two cultures, able to integrate two world-views and to angle his argument in a way which would be likely to have most impact on his readers. It is this amalgam which enables Betz 215–16 to speak tendentiously here of 'gnostic' ideas.

9 But now (the antithesis is structured in the classic Greek idiom) **that you have come to know** (the tense pointing back to their conversion) **God** (Paul continues to speak as a Jew – conversion of Gentiles meant entering into that relation with God which was characteristic of Israel's covenant identity), **or rather to be known** (again the same tense) **by God** (cf. 1 Cor. viii.3; xiii.12). This was the other side of the 'knowledge of God' – that God had chosen to acknowledge Israel, despite knowing the reality of Israel, to take them into a personal relationship with himself, with the obligations which that entailed (Gen. xviii.19; Hos. v.3; xiii.5; Amos iii.2). Paul's correction here is important: it underscores his recognition that any relation of acceptance by God is of divine initiative. It is a two-way relationship, of acknowledgment and obligation; but the personal knowing of God is made possible only by God's knowing the person. The point is that the Galatians had already begun to experience that personal knowing and being known which were at the heart of Israel's covenant relationship with God, prior to and apart from the law, even though the law had provided the guidelines for Israel for life within that relationship.

How is it (then) **that you are turning back again to the weak and beggarly elemental forces?** Again the idiom is very Jewish. 'Turn back' was the characteristic Jewish call for repentance – to turn back to God, to turn back from evil (BDB, *šūb* 6c, d). But the same word was also used of turning back *from* God, that is, of apostasy (e.g. Num. xiv.43; 1 Sam. xv.11; 1 Kings ix.6; Ps. lxxviii.41; Jer. iii.19; but LXX usually uses a different compound of the verb – *TDNT* vii.724). The assessment was not merely ironic: in turning *to* the traditional Jewish understanding of the covenant as defined by the law, they were actually turning *away from* the God of Israel's covenant. Paul was convinced that Gentiles who believed in the gospel of Christ and received the Spirit of God's Son had thereby come to experience and share in what the choice of Abraham and of Israel had been all about. In seeking to grasp Israel's privilege more firmly the judaizing Gentiles were in danger of losing that very promise and blessing in which they already shared. The present tense (in contrast to the two preceding verbs) indicates Paul's understanding that the apostasy was still in process (conative present = 'trying to turn back'), and so could still be averted.

The situation and status to which they were in danger of reverting were those of enslavement 'under the elemental forces of the world' (iv.3). Here the inference continues to be clear that Paul counted the law as one of these 'elemental forces'. That is to say, the law regarded in the way it typically was within contemporary Judaism, the law being treated as it was by the other missionaries and the judaizing Gentile converts, was functioning in effect as one of those cosmic forces which were then popularly thought to control and dominate life (see on iii.20 and iv.3). Life under such a power was a life dominated by fear of infringing its taboos and boundaries (cf. Rom. viii.15; Col. ii.20–2; see also on iv.10). Since they had already experienced freedom from precisely such slavery Paul found it hard to credit the reports that they wished to exchange their slavery to things which were in reality no gods for a slavery to the law misrepresented to function just like another false god.

Paul calls the elemental forces 'weak' partly in contrast to the strength of the truth of divine reality. But probably also because to live life by reference to a false god, to a power which only gains its power by human misunderstanding and presumption, superstition and fear (cf. 1 Cor. viii.4–6), is a form of weakness, not of strength (of principle or conviction or whatever); the elemental forces are weak because they weaken those who rely on them (hence Rom. xiv.1–2; 1 Cor viii.7, 9–12; ix.22); Lagrange 107 notes the description of the law as weak in Rom. viii.3 and Heb. vii.18. Similarly Paul calls the elemental forces 'poor' partly in contrast to the richness of divine reality (Rom. ii.4; ix.23; xi.33; Phil. iv.19; Col. i.27; the antithesis of poverty/wealth was quite often evoked by Paul – Rom. xv.26–7; 2 Cor. vi.10; viii.2, 9). But probably also because life under such a power, life under the law, was an impoverishment in comparison with the riches of grace which Paul had experienced through Christ (Rom. x.12; 1 Cor. i.5; 2 Cor. ix.14–15; cf. Eph. ii.4).

Do you want to be in slavery to them once again? (Literally, 'to which you want to be in slavery again'). Paul was evidently aware of just how attractive the teaching of the other missionaries was for the Gentile Galatians (cf. i.7; iv.21). That which continued to attract proselytes and God-fearers to Judaism would have made very logical and spiritual sense for many of them; Judaism continued to exert a powerful attraction for many Christians for a long time thereafter (e.g. Ignatius, *Magn.* viii.1 and x.3; Barn. iii.6; Justin, *Dial.* xlvii.4). The implication here may be that the experience of God's acceptance and of the Spirit which still gripped Paul so powerfully was already fading for many of his converts; or that the well-developed system of centuries-old Judaism made the still undeveloped ritual and liturgy of the churches seem bare and less satisfying.

10 Be that as it may, it certainly seems to have been the ritual of the liturgical calendar which had exerted most attraction on the Galatians. **You are observing** (conative present?) **days and months and special times and years.** By 'days' Paul would no doubt mean particularly the Sabbath, but also other special days like the Day of Atonement. The Sabbath was another of the Jewish laws which was seen to mark out Israel as distinctive and to function as a boundary between Jew and Gentile (e.g. Exod. xxxi.16–17; Deut. v.15; Isa. lvi.6) – one of the main 'works of the law' which Paul presumably had had in mind earlier (see on ii.16). Already before the Maccabean crisis 'violating the sabbath' ranked with 'eating unclean food' as the two chief marks of covenant disloyalty according to Josephus (*Ant.* xi.346). The increasingly elaborate halakah attested in *Jubilees* (ii.17–33; l.6–13), in the Damascus document of Qumran (CD x.14–xi.18) and in the Gospels (Mark ii.23–iii.5 pars), indicates the importance of the Sabbath as a test of covenant righteousness within the factionalism of late second-Temple Judaism. Within the diaspora the unusual religious practice of having one day in seven as a day of rest was no doubt one of the factors which attracted sympathetic Gentiles to Judaism (Philo, *Mos.* ii.21; Josephus, *Ap.* ii.282; Juvenal, *Satires* xiv.96; see further my *Romans* 805–6).

'Months' almost certainly refers to the new-moon festival which was part of the Jewish cult (Num. x.10; xxviii.11; 2 Kings iv.23; Ps. lxxxi.3; Ezek. xlvi.3, 6–7; *TDNT* iv.639–41), as the parallel with Col. ii.16 certainly confirms. Since the moon was one of the 'elemental forces' (understood to include the planets – see on iv.3), a parallel between pagan religious practice (*TDNT* iv.638–9) at this point and nomistic covenantalism could readily be drawn (see also Bruce 204).

The 'special times' were probably the 'appointed feasts' (regularly linked with 'sabbaths and new moons' in 1 Chron. xxiii.31; 2 Chron ii.4; xxxi.3; Neh. x.33; Isa. i.13–14; Hos. ii.11), that is, the three pilgrim festivals in particular, presumably called '(special) times', or 'festal seasons' from the regular usage in the Pentateuch (Exod. xiii.10; xxiii.14, 17; xxxiv.23–4; Lev. xxiii.4; Num. ix.3). Since the degree to which diaspora Judaism

THE EPISTLE TO THE GALATIANS

observed such feasts is still disputed (almost no one could have made the three-times pilgrimage to Jerusalem), this text provides a valuable indication that some sort of observance was maintained in the diaspora (cf. Col. ii.16).

More puzzling is the reference of the final item on the list – 'years'. The sabbatical year of Lev. xxv.1–7 is unlikely: it would hardly seem to be relevant outside Palestine; though it could possibly have had relevance as part of sectarian dispute (cf. 1QS x.6–8 and below). But the analogy of 'months' for new-moon festivals suggests that annual festivals were in mind, presumably (on the analogy of 'month' denoting 'first of the month') the disputed New Year festival (cf. 1QS x.6; see further *IDB*, 'New Year'; Schürer, index 'New Year').

It should be noted that, as with the Sabbath, the issue of the right observance of these feasts was a matter of sectarian dispute within the Judaism of the period. This was principally because the calendar by which the dates of these feasts were reckoned (solar or lunar) was not agreed by all parties. Hence the dispute: to observe a feast on the wrong date was *not* to observe the feast, but to 'forget the feasts of the covenant and walk in the feasts of the gentiles, after their errors and after their ignorance' (*Jub.* vi.32–5), to commit 'sin like the sinners' (*1 Enoch* lxxxii.4–7; see also 1QS i.14–15; CD iii.14–15). That such disagreement lies behind the present passage is suggested by such parallels as *Jub.* ii.9 – 'The Lord set the sun [solar calendar] as a great sign upon the earth for days, sabbaths, months, feast (days), years . . . and for all the (appointed) times of the years'; and *1 Enoch* lxxxii.7, 9 – 'True is the matter of the exact computation of that which has been recorded . . . concerning the luminaries, the months, the festivals, the years and the days. . . . These are the orders of the stars which set in their places seasons, festivals and months' (see further Schlier 204–5; Mussner 298–301). In view of the *1 Enoch* passage, it is probably also significant that the verb used ('observe') would usually have the force of 'watch closely, observe carefully, scrupulously observe' (Lightfoot 172; BAGD, *paratēreō*; Schlier 203 n. 3; cf. on i.14), so that Paul may very well have chosen it in order to evoke the careful calculations of feast dates ('calendar piety' – Mussner) which such disputes entailed (though Josephus also uses it for observance of sabbath and festival days – *Ant.* iii.91; xi.294; xiv.264).

Of particular relevance for us here is the evident integration of 'Torah piety' and 'calendar piety' achieved within such Jewish groups, and the importance of the heavenly bodies in determining the right dates for such Torah observances (Josephus could even claim that the Essenes prayed to the sun – *War* ii.128).[1] Against such a background Paul's association of the Torah with 'the elemental forces of the world' becomes a natural rejoinder on his part: 'under the law' = too dependent on the movements of the heavenly bodies. Here too, then, as in ii.14–15, we probably have to allow for an element of Jewish factionalism to have been in play in the Galatian crisis. In particular, the proper observance in the diaspora of a festival whose correct timing depended on the actual sighting of the new moon, was likely to add a further twist to the disputes reflected in *1 Enoch* and *Jubilees* (above), even though tradition has it that the responsibility for fixing such dates during the final decades of the second Temple rested with the Sanhedrin (*m. Roš Haš*, ii.5–iii.1). In short, Paul was not necessarily confronting a uniform Jewish position on such matters. His was a further alternative (observance not necessary) *within* the spectrum of Jewish opinion, itself part of the factionalism which marred the latter decades of second-Temple Judaism.

Betz fails to recognize the importance of this background, how closely Paul's talk of 'days, and months, and times' echoes Gen. i.14 and such passages as 1 Chron. xxiii.31 and *Jub.* ii.9, cited above, and how Paul's language would thus be heard to characterize the attraction of such traditional or sectarian Jewish practices as presented by the other missionaries. But to reduce the issue between Paul and his opponents to one simply of ritualism (so also Lightfoot 173) or 'cultic observances in a general sense' (Betz 217–18) is inadequate; what was at stake in all this was the character of the covenant and the identity of the people of God as the children and heirs of Abraham. So too Betz's 217 assumption that the present tense of the verb should not have its natural force, as describing an activity on which Paul's readers were already embarked, is unnecessary: the attractiveness of Jewish feasts to non-Jews, as already noted, was something of which Josephus could make apologetic use (*Ap.* ii.282); and it was precisely the transition from a God-fearing observance of Jewish customs to full proselyte status which the other missionaries would naturally encourage (cf. Josephus, *Ant.* xx.41–6; Juvenal, *Satires* xiv.96–9).

---

1 Note also *Kerygma Petrou* (*NTA* ii.100), a passage with several echoes of Gal. iv.8–10: 'Neither worship him in the manner of the Jews; for they also, who think that they alone know God, do not understand, worshipping angels and archangels, the months and the moon. And when the moon does not shine, they do not celebrate the so-called first Sabbath, also they do not celebrate the new moon or the feast of unleavened bread or the feast (of Tabernacles) or the great day (of atonement)'.

11 Paul ends with a heavy sigh – **I am afraid that perhaps I have laboured** (one of his favourite words for the hard work of service of the gospel – Rom. xvi.6, 12; 1 Cor. iv.12; xv.10; xvi.16; Phil. ii.16; Col. i.29; 1 Thess. v.12) **for you to no avail** (the same word as in iii.4). Paul did not hesitate to face the possibility that the fruit of his labours would not last (the force of the perfect tense) (cf. ii.2). Very similar is the anxiety expressed in 1 Thess. iii.5. But the tentative expression of it both indicates Paul's hope that it would not be so and encouragement to his addressees to prove his fear misplaced. That Paul's attitude could be so much more relaxed in Rom. xiv.5–6 is in large part explained by the probable fact that traditionalist Jewish Christians were very much in the minority in Rome at that time (see my *Romans* 812).

9   A PERSONAL APPEAL   iv.12–20

(12) Become as I am, brothers,[1] I beg you, because I also became[2] as you are. You have done me no wrong; (13) for you know that it was on account of the weakness of the flesh that I preached the good news to you earlier; (14) and you did not despise or spit at what was a provocation to you[3] in my flesh, but welcomed me as an angel of God, as Christ Jesus. (15) Where[3] then is[3] your blessing?[4] I testify on your behalf that if it had been possible you would have torn out your eyes and given them to me. (16) So now I have become your enemy by telling you the truth?[5] (17) They are zealous

1 See above p. 23 n. 3.

2 The epigrammatic form is best filled out by reading 'as I became', to complete the parallel with the first half, but not 'as I was', since the change in sense could hardly have been left out, had that been the meaning intended (Burton 236–7).

3 At these points (see examples on p. 231) various scribes attempted to smooth off or round out Paul's rather compressed language and cryptic allusions. In the first case (iv.14), Borse 151 prefers the reading of p[46] and some other witnesses – 'my temptation/provocation'.

4 The variety of translations shows how difficult it is to produce a satisfactory rendering: 'What has become of the satisfaction/good will you felt?' (RSV/NRSV); 'Have you forgotten how happy you thought yourselves in having me with you?' (NEB); 'What has become of the happiness you felt then?' (REB); 'What has happened to the utter contentment you had then?' (NJB); 'What has happened to all your joy?' (NIV); 'You counted yourselves happy then' (Bruce 207).

5 The sentence could be punctuated, perhaps more appropriately, with an exclamation mark (Burton 244–5; Longenecker 193).

over you[1] for no good purpose, but wish to shut you out, in
order that you might be zealous[2] over them. (18) It is always
good when zeal is displayed[2] in something good, and not only
when I am present with you. (19) My children,[3] over whom I
am again in the pain of childbirth until Christ is formed in
you; (20) I was wishing I could be present with you now and
could change my tone, for I am at a loss in your case.

Although Paul had still another argument from scripture to
bring in to play (iv.21–31), it evidently seemed appropriate at
this point to make a personal appeal to his readers on the basis
of his own experience with them when he first brought them the
gospel. The emotional bond formed then, in part by their
concern over his physical condition, and in part by their own
experience of blessing (iv.13–15), was already a strong strand
into which Paul could weave his own concern for them now
(iv.19). The mutual sincerity of that bond could also be appealed
to, in some contrast to the relationship which the other
missionaries were attempting to bring about (iv.16–18). The style
is very elliptical, 'betraying the inner agitation of the author'
(Bonnard 91), and the train of thought is somewhat erratic,
particularly at verses 12c/12d, 16/17, 18/19 and 19/20. But the
effect is to heighten the emotional impact of the whole (Betz's
221 description of the section as 'a string of topoi belonging to
the theme of "friendship"' does not bring out clearly enough the
emotional intensity of the passage). In all this it would be
ungenerous to suggest that Paul was being calculatingly
manipulative. There is no reason to assume that the feelings
which Paul expresses here were anything other than sincere ('an
argument of the heart' – Schlier 208), even if he shows himself
well skilled in the art of persuasion.

It is also worth noting that Paul could thus appeal, apparently,
to all his addressees: not only were they all his brothers (iv.12),
but they were all involved in his previous visit (iv.13–15, 18), all

1 Note again the variety of translations: 'they make much of you' (RSV/NRSV);
'The persons I have referred to are envious of you, but not with an honest
envy: what they really want is to bar the door to you so that you may come to
envy them' (NEB); 'Others are lavishing attention on you, but without sincerity:
what they really want is to isolate you so that you may lavish attention on
them' (REB); 'Their devotion to you has no praiseworthy motive; they simply
want to cut you off from me, so that you may centre your devotion on them'
(NJB); 'These people are zealous to win you over, but for no good. What they
want is to alienate you [from us], so that you may be zealous for them' (NIV).
2 See footnote 3, p. 230.
3 'Little children' (teknia) is not so strongly supported as 'children' (tekna). The
former fits the context (birth) better (Longenecker 195); but that consideration
tells equally for a scribal alteration to teknia as for its originality.

Paul's own converts (iv.19). This suggests either that Paul was attempting to speak only to those who were his own converts within churches which had continued to grow since his visit, or that after the first spurt of growth the intervening period had been one of consolidation. In the latter case it would also mean that the other missionaries had concentrated their attention on converting more fully Paul's converts (encouraging them to become full proselytes), rather than on winning fresh converts directly from Gentile paganism.

Longenecker 184–7, followed by Hansen 16 and 59, maintains that 'rhetorically, a major shift in Paul's argument occurs at iv.12' (p. 184), as Paul switches from forensic rhetoric to the exhortation more characteristic of deliberative rhetoric. See further Introduction §7.

12 The way in which Paul launches his personal appeal is significant – **Become as I am, brothers, I beg you, because I also became as you are**. The appeal is not simply for imitation of his priorities and life style (as in 1 Cor. iv.16; xi.1; Phil. iii.17; 2 Thess. iii.7–9) (NEB/REB's 'Put yourselves in my place' is too bland). As most recognize, it is more a reminder that Paul, though himself a Jew, had become as one who was (like the Galatians) 'without the law', 'outside the law', in order to bring the gospel to them as 'lawless' Gentiles (cf. 1 Cor. ix.21). The appeal then is that if the Gentile converts in Galatia *were* already putting themselves 'under the law', by judaizing in the matter of the Jewish feast days (iv.10), they should take the further step of 'dying to the law' (ii.19). Or, in terms of principle, that they should follow Paul in recognizing that the promise of Abraham and participation in his blessing were not dependent on Torah observances ('works of the law') like the feast days which so distinguished Jews from the other nations. By calling them 'brothers' (see on i.2 and 11) at this point Paul effectively reminded them that it was precisely as uncircumcised Gentiles that they already were part of God's family, brothers to a man whose mission in life was based on the recognition that God no longer made a distinction between Jew and Gentile in his purposes of salvation. The 'I beg you' also underlines the intensity of Paul's desire (cf. 2 Cor. v.20; viii.4; x.2).

As elsewhere in Paul's letters, the appeal is based on the memory that in his time with his converts no one had tried to take unfair advantage of the other (2 Cor. vii.2; xii.13; 1 Thess. ii.3–12; cf. Acts xx.33–4); though here the thought is of the Galatians' not taking unfair advantage of Paul – **You have done me no wrong** – whereas elsewhere Paul evidently found it necessary to defend himself against the equivalent charge. In an age when wandering preachers and miracle workers included not a few charlatans and cheats (see e.g. warnings against false prophets and apostles in Did. xi–xiii, and Lucian's account of Alexander of Abonoteichus in *Alexander the False Prophet*), a firm foundation of mutual respect and trust was essential if a mutually beneficial relationship was to be built up. The transition is rather abrupt, but probably Paul's mind moved rapidly in memory from their initial reception of his law-free message to the warmth of their welcome.

13 What Paul particularly had in mind were the circumstances of his first visit – **for you know that it was on account of the weakness of the flesh that I preached the good news to you earlier**. The reference is obviously to some illness or ailment or physical condition (see on iv.14 and 15). 'On account of' implies that his coming to them was occasioned by it: the condition prevented his going elsewhere (cf. Acts xvi.6), or made the alternative of a trip into the (south) Galatian highlands more attractive or even essential. Whatever the reason for his coming to Galatia, Paul had used the opportunity to 'preach the gospel' (see on i.8). His ailment could not suppress or disable his primary passion (cf. 2 Cor. v.11–21). Although 'weakness of the flesh' was no positive factor (cf. Rom. vi. 19; viii.3), Paul found it could be a means to more effective reliance on God's grace (2 Cor. xii.7–10). It is certainly very possible that 'the weakness of the flesh' was the same as 'the thorn in the flesh' of 2 Cor. xii.7, and even that it was the necessity of his visit to Galatia and the success of that trip which taught Paul the lesson he learned in 2 Cor. xii.9 (we do not know how long after the great vision of 2 Cor. xii.2–4 came the reply of xii.9).

The phrase translated 'before' could be rendered either 'the first time', implying the first of two visits, or 'once', as not necessarily implying more than one previous visit (BAGD, *proteros* 1bβ). Strictly speaking, the former is the more natural sense. It thus can provide support for the view that Paul initially visited Galatia during his (first) missionary journey, when he was a missionary of the church in Antioch – Acts xiii.14 (the 'south Galatian hypothesis'); the implied second visit would then presumably be that referred to in Acts xvi.1–5 (would Acts xiv.21 be regarded as a separate visit?). Alternatively the first visit could be Acts xvi.6 and the second Acts xviii.23. However, since the latter sense ('once') is also quite possible, not very much weight can be placed on the usage here in any attempt to resolve what Paul meant by 'Galatia' (as is generally recognized; see particularly Burton 239–41; Introduction §§3 and 6.3); for the view that Paul had visited the Galatians only once see particularly Borse 150–1, 160–2.

14 What Paul's physical condition was during that (first) visit remains a mystery. Since his addressees knew to what it was he was referring, of course, there was no need for him to be more explicit. But the allusions he now makes give us some further clues – **and you did not despise or spit at what was a provocation to you in my flesh**. The latter part of this sentence is very compressed (literally, 'your temptation in my flesh'), but presumbly indicates that Paul's condition had been a 'trial' to them (RSV, NJB, NIV), or had put them to the test (NRSV; NEB/[REB] – 'you resisted the temptation to show scorn or disgust at the state of my poor body'). The meaning, then, is clear enough to the extent that Paul's physical condition had been such as would normally occasion contempt or scorn or revulsion in those with whom he came in contact (see BAGD, *exoutheneō* 1, 2). The second verb, however, raises a further possibility. It can mean simply 'spit out' in disdain, but here it may well contain a further allusion to the ancient practice of spitting out as a defence against sickness or other demonic threats: 'the Galatians resisted the temptation to see in Paul someone demonically possessed because of his sickness' (Schlier, *TDNT* ii.448–9). Here we should recall iii.1, with its likely evocation of the evil eye (see on iii.1), since according to Theocritus vi.39 (3rd century BC) one could ward off the evil eye by spitting three times (BAGD, *baskainō* 1). All this does not help us much in identifying Paul's ailment, but when added to Paul's talk of the 'elemental forces of the cosmos' (see on iv.3), the picture of the Galatians' world-view and superstitions becomes clearer.

But whatever precisely it was that might have provoked such a response from the Galatians, in the event they had **welcomed me as an angel** (or messenger) **of God**. The contrast is the apposite one: instead of regarding Paul as a tool or victim of demonic powers, they had realized that he came with God's message, that is, as one sent from God (*TDNT* i.74–6). Perhaps Paul means also that they recognized that the manifest workings out of the spiritual realm in and through Paul attested the power of God (in weakness) rather than a pitiful victim of sorcery (see above). 'Welcome' is the normal word for 'receive as a guest' (BAGD, *dechomai* 1; for the obligation and importance of hospitality in the ancient world see e.g. *TDNT* v.17–25). Since Hermes was thought of as the messenger of the gods, an ironic allusion to Acts xiv.12 is not out of the question. To be noted here is the thoroughly positive status and function which Paul naturally attaches to the word 'angel' (see also on iii.19).

And not only as an angel of God, but even **as Christ Jesus** himself. Paul echoes here the then typical understanding of commissioning: that the one sent is as the one sending; that is, the properly commissioned messenger can speak with the authority, or even in the person of the sender (cf. *TDNT* i.399–402, 407–14). He may even have echoed, consciously or unconsciously, the words recalled as part of Jesus' own commissioning of his disciples for mission (particularly Matt. x.40; John xiii.20; also Mark ix.37). At all events, Paul's language indicates the strength of his conviction that he had been commissioned by the risen Christ directly and with full authority to speak for him (see also on i.1), the degree to which his message focused on Christ Jesus (see on i.16), and the speed with which the Galatians came to appreciate the significance of the message of Christ Jesus for them and to welcome it.

15 As Paul recalled the rather surprising warmth of the Galatians' welcome, he could recall also the benefits they had received as a result of their responding so positively to his message – **Where then is your blessing?** The language is again compressed, but again clear enough in broad terms (see above p. 230 n. 4). The word 'blessing' is strictly a verbal noun (= a noun expressing action – BDF §109(1)), so that it could properly be translated 'pronouncing happy, blessing' (LSJ, *makarismos*) and denote 'the frame of mind in which you blessed yourselves' (BAGD, *makarismos*; hence NEB and Bruce on p. 230 n. 4 above). But in the only other occurrences in the NT, Paul uses it to describe the state of the one who has been blessed by God, in being counted righteous by God and in having his sins not counted (Rom. iv.6, 9, referring to Ps. xxxii.1–2). Since Rom. iv moves in the same train of thought as Gal. iii (both expositions of Gen. xv.6), it is likely that Paul had in mind the blessing (different word) of Abraham which they had received (Gal. iii.9, 14). At the same time, the train of thought ('angel' from heaven) suggests Paul's awareness that in Greek thought 'blessed, happy' was classically used to describe the happy state of the gods above earthly sufferings and labours (*TDNT* iv.362). The language suggests the typical euphoria which converts often feel and which buoys them up for some time thereafter. It may also imply that, as again so often in converts, the fading of the initial flush of enthusiasm resulted in an increasing dissatisfaction which may have been a factor in their responding so positively to the other missionaries – in the hope that a further act of commitment would have brought again that 'first fine careless rapture'.

Particularly poignant is Paul's recollection of the depth of the Galatians' concern for him on that first visit – **I testify on your behalf** (dative of advantage, as in Rom. x.2 and Col. iv.13) **that if it had been possible you would have torn out your eyes and given them to me**. The further reference to eyes is striking, coming as it does after the probable allusion to the 'evil eye' in iii.1 and iv.14 (see *TDNT* v.376). However, the meaning cannot be that they would willingly have torn out their eyes to prevent their looking at Paul in his afflicted state. An action of supreme friendship is certainly in view, the eyes being reckoned as the most precious of human organs (LSJ, *ophthalmos* IV; Schlier 211 and n. 5). But the purpose of such tearing out (an understandable hyperbole) would evidently have been to give the eyes thus removed to Paul, and presumably not merely as a gruesome gift or act of homage. Despite the majority, therefore, and given the train of thought (iv.13–15), the most obvious implication is that Paul's ailment affected his eyes most of all, presumably leaving him with greatly restricted vision and in a painful(?) condition which excited the pity of the Galatians (see also on vi.11). Beyond that it is all guesswork. Suggestions of what the ailment was include malaria, epilepsy and ophthalmia (Bruce 208–9; see further Borse 153–6; and for older discussion Lightfoot 186–91).

16 Paul knows how to press his appeal with greatest effect. The greater the depth of concern they had displayed to him originally, the more striking the contrast with their present attitude. **So now** (the wholly unlooked for consequence gives Paul's query a note of not altogether gentle irony) **I have become your enemy by telling you the truth** (see above p. 230 n. 5)? The overstatement ('enemy') indicates an element of bitterness at the betrayal of his Galatian converts in going over to those who were apparently so resolutely opposed to Paul and to his presentation of the gospel. But it may be that the antagonism was not his, or at least not initially. On the contrary, it is likely that Christian Jews who belonged to the traditionalist faction would regard Paul as an apostate and traitor. Those who could condemn Peter for 'living like a Gentile' and continue to think of Gentiles dismissively as 'gentile sinners' (see on ii.14 and 15) would be likely to regard Paul's more thoroughgoing removal of the Torah barriers between Jew and Gentile with more virulent hostility. Certainly this was how Paul was perceived subsequently within the continuing Jewish Christianity of the second and third centuries; much cited is *Epistula Petri* ii.3, where Peter calls Paul (under the guise of Simon Magus) 'the man who is my enemy'. Consequently, what had initially been received with joy seems, as a result of the subsequent propaganda, to have become an occasion for hostility (see also on v.20). By 'telling you the truth' Paul presumably means 'the truth of the gospel' (ii.5, 14) and refers to what for Paul was its fundamental feature: that God's blessing was open to the Gentile as Gentile. It was precisely this dismissal of Israel's 'most favoured nation' status, and of the Torah praxis which protected it, which brought down such wrath upon Paul's head from his fellow Jews, Christian Jews not least.

17 That Paul's thought had already switched to the other missionaries is evident from the way in which he suddenly reintroduces them without further specification and reminder simply as **They** – the Galatians knew well enough whom he meant! His complaint is that they **are zealous over you for no good purpose**. The verb could be rendered differently: 'strive, desire, exert oneself earnestly', and with a personal object, 'be deeply concerned about, court someone's favour', or negatively, 'be filled with jealousy or envy towards someone' (BAGD, *zēloō*; hence the various translations on p. 231 n. 1 above). But the threefold use of the same verb in verses 17 and 18, and the use of the corresponding noun ('zealot') in i.14 to characterize the attitude which Paul now contested, strongly suggest that Paul had in mind the same attitude here, if not, indeed, that the language had been used by the other missionaries themselves (in Acts xxi.20 'zealot' is used by James in effect in self-definition; note also Rom. x.2 with similar qualification – 'they have a zeal for God but not in accordance with knowledge'). That is to say, even if using the more common language of 'flattery' (particularly Betz 229–30), Paul may very well also be evoking here characteristic Jewish 'zeal' to maintain and defend Jewish covenant prerogatives (see on i.14). The claim made for and by Galatian Gentiles to full participation in the covenant of Israel, without regard for the distinctive 'works of the law', would be precisely the challenge which would arouse a Phinehas-like zeal – a challenge met, in the case of the other missionaries, by the attempt to eliminate such a breach of covenant boundaries by fully incorporating the Gentile converts in question. Needless to say, Paul regarded the attempt as objectionable – something done 'not well' (literally); the dismissal is broad and imprecise enough to cover a range of dissatisfaction – from the vague 'inappropriately' to the stronger 'morally unacceptable'.

A still clearer insight into the tactics of the other missionaries is given by the next clause – **but they wish to shut you out**. At first the objective seems surprising: was the aim of the other missionaries not precisely the reverse? – to draw the Galatians more fully *into* the people of Israel through circumcision? The key however is the stated objective: 'to shut out'. The metaphor is clearly of being shut out or excluded, as from a city or an alliance (LSJ, *ekkleiō* 2; so RSV/NRSV, NEB); to take it in the sense 'exclude you (from Paul and other Gentile Christians)', as NJB and NIV (see above p. 231 n. 1), or 'that you should exclude Paul', would involve a less natural use of the metaphor or a more forced sense for the Greek (as Burton 246 notes). The metaphor in fact is complementary to that used in iii.23: the law which 'watched over, guarded the city' was the law which shut out the aliens. It is thus very well suited to describe the typical attitude of the Jewish zealot – that is, to draw the boundary line sharply and clearly between the people of the covenant so as to exclude those not belonging to Israel (see again i.14); or, in particular, of the Jewish-Christian zealot – to exclude all Gentiles other than proselytes from Christ, the Jewish Messiah, and from the eschatological community of his people. It was another way of describing the consequence of the action of Peter and the others at Antioch: by withdrawing from table-fellowship they effectively excluded the Christian Gentiles from the one covenant community (ii.11–14). In the Galatian churches, then, the tactic of the other missionaries had clearly been to draw again these firm boundaries as laid down by the Torah, and to point out the (to them) inevitable corollary: that the Gentile converts were still outside them.

Their hope however was not so negative, as in the classic models of 'zeal'; they were missionaries! Their intention was to raise the barriers between Jew and Gentile **in order that you might be zealous over them** (for the syntax cf. BDF §148). That is to say, by demonstrating what membership of the covenant people actually involved ('the works of the law'), they hoped to incite a godly desire for that membership in those whose Godfearing had already shown the seriousness of their wish to be numbered among Abraham's heirs. They hoped to convert the Galatians not simply to Judaism but to Judaism as they understood it. By showing 'zeal for the covenant' themselves, they hoped to spark off an equivalent zeal among the Galatians. Or, more precisely, by showing such zeal with regard to the Galatians, their hope was that the Galatians would come to show a similar zeal with regard to them – so that, apart from anything else, each could share fully in the others' table-fellowship without compromising the others and in a mutually sustaining way. This reading gives more weight to Paul's language and recognizes greater point in his charges than most of the current translations (above p. 231 n. 6).

18 Paul was well aware that 'zeal' was a two-edged virtue – highly desirable, but easily prone to excess. So he goes on to qualify the more thoroughgoing negative tone of verse 17 – **It is always good when zeal is displayed in something good, and not only when I am present with you.** In the NT, references to 'zeal' are almost equally divided between good and bad (BAGD, *zēlos* 1, 2); for the verb we may compare Acts xvii.5 and 1 Cor. xiii.4 (bad) with 1 Cor. xii.31 and 2 Cor. xi.2 (good). Paul had no objection to zeal in itself: to the onlooker, indeed, Paul was still something of a 'zealot', who had simply redirected the zeal with which he had persecuted the church into zeal for mission (cf. particularly 2 Cor. xi.2 – 'I am zealous over you with the zeal of God'; zealots like Phinehas would also no doubt have seen their zeal as an expression of 'the zeal of God' – note particularly Deut. iv.24 and vi.15). However, the zeal Paul had previously displayed (i.14), and which the other missionaries in Galatia now displayed and sought to inculcate in the Galatians, he no longer regarded as praiseworthy (the Greek word has a range like the German *schön*, 'beautiful, fine, good, splendid'). He already knew from his own time with them (verses 13–15) how keen his Galatian converts had been to engage his friendship and to share the fullness of the gospel (cf. iii.2–5). In warning them against the zeal of the other missionaries (verse 17), therefore, he did not wish to demotivate them in their faith and practice.

19 But word games could not express or match the depth of Paul's concern. The appeal to positive memories of his time with them gives way abruptly to the deeper claim of parenthood. **My children, over whom I am again in the pain of childbirth until Christ is formed in you.** Paul uses the image of parent and child for his relationship with his converts on several occasions (1 Cor. iv.14, 17; 2 Cor. vi.13; xii.14; Phil. ii.22; 1 Thess. ii.11). But the address here is more direct and simple – the earlier sharpness of his language (i.6–9; iii.1; iv.16) matched now by the depth of personal concern. The same imagery (spiritual generation) was used in hellenistic religion (*TDNT* v.953–4; Oepke 145) and for the relationship between teacher and pupil (*TDNT* i.665–6; cf. Philo, *Legat.* 58). Paul however heightens the emotional impact by likening the anguish and worry which he was feeling for the Galatians to the pain of childbirth; the use of the imagery of labour-pains for a male is striking, but talk of someone as 'born/begotten' from a male as from a woman was not uncommon (BAGD, *gennaō* 1; note also 1QH iii.7ff.), so there is no need to postulate Paul's dependence here on hellenistic mysticism or Gnosticism. The implication may be that Paul had previously thought that all the 'labour' exerted during his first visit would have been enough to ensure their 'safe delivery', and was now surprised to be going through the same agonies all over again. Or it may rather be that he had not realized the process of spiritual formation of his converts would be so long drawn out and involve such further pain and anxiety on his part.

It is probably significant that Paul thus extends the imagery of childbirth, rather than recalling the complementary imagery of youth and maturity (iv.1–3) which might have seemed more appropriate – brought to birth by Paul on his first visit, but still evidently in a state of immaturity like under-age Israel. He chooses rather to portray the very process of spiritual birth as a long-drawn-out affair. In fact the imagery thus stretched fits well with his understanding of the process of salvation as expressed elsewhere. Three features are particularly noteworthy.

(1) 'Being saved' (e.g. 1 Cor. i.18) is a life-long process of 'transformation' (note the present tenses in Rom. xii.2 and 2 Cor. iii.18; the motif is related to the verb used only here in the NT in the same way as in English – 'trans-form'), elsewhere expressed in terms of 'putting off' and 'putting on' (see on iii.27), of inward renewal and outward decay (particularly 2 Cor. iv.16), or of sharing in Christ's death as well as in his risen life (see on ii.19 and vi.14). The long-drawn-out nature of this (re)birth process makes an allusion to baptism unlikely.

(2) That is also to say the process is eschatological in character – as a process already involving the Spirit of God's end-time purpose, but only as a beginning (hence the sequence, 2 Cor. iv.16–v.5; cf. Rom. viii.23 and 2 Cor. i.22; see on iii.3), and looking for final completion in the renewal of the whole person in the climax of God's purpose ('redemption of the body'; e.g. Rom. viii.11, 23). Hence the appropriateness of the metaphor of birth-pains, since it was already used, as Mark xiii.8 implies, for the birth-pains of the new age (*TDNT* ix.670–1; see also B. R. Gaventa, 'The Maternity of Paul: An Exegetical Study of Galatians iv.19', *Studies in Paul and John*, J. L. Martyn Festschrift, ed. R. T. Fortna & B. R. Gaventa [Nashville: Abingdon, 1990] 191–4).

(3) Not least of significance is that the end-point of the whole process was conforming the character of the one thus being saved to the character of Christ, that is, the restoration of the image of

God in humankind (particularly Rom. viii.29; 2 Cor. iii.18–iv.4;
Col. iii.10), including the resurrection body like his (1 Cor.
xv.45–9; Phil. iii.10–11, 21) (see further my *Jesus* 308–18,
326–38). The merging of the imagery of childbirth with that of
'Christ in you' (see on i.16 and ii.20; cf. particularly Col. i.27;
iii.4; Eph. iii.17) has a somewhat grotesque aspect (not really
helped by NEB's 'until you take the shape of Christ'). But the
point is clear enough: Paul's concern was that the Spirit of Christ
might have such full sway in their lives, and they should become
so like Christ in character, that they would be able to share in
the fullness and freedom of life 'in the flesh' (ii.20) which Christ
himself had enjoyed – not least in regard to the law. The
complementary corporate sense of 'Christ in you or among you
(as the body of Christ)' is not excluded.

20 The personal appeal ends on a note of pathos – perhaps as
much by unconscious artifice as by careful design. **I was wishing
I could** (conative imperfect – BDF §326) **be present with you
now and could change my tone** (BAGD, *allassō* 1), **for I am at
a loss in your case.** Paul knew all too well how his teachings
and opinions and counsels could be so easily misrepresented and
misunderstood when he was not present personally to explain
and defend himself. The tone of reprimand was one he would
rather not have had to use, in view of the difficulty of gauging
the right weight to bring to bear (Lagrange 118 and Schlier 215
n. 1, list an extensive range of overtones heard by commentators
in the phrase), and particularly at such a distance (the
characterization of his relationship to them had swung from
enemy to father – verses 16, 19); NJB is effective – 'and find the
right way of talking to you'. The thought could easily merge into
'(ex)change my voice', that is, for this letter, by a personal visit.
The final confession of perplexity and uncertainty (cf. Acts
xxv.20; 2 Cor. iv.8) is as much an apology, both for his inability
to speak more effectively to their situation and in case what he
has already said had missed the mark and caused needless
offence.

10 THE APPEAL TO SCRIPTURE (2)
THE TWO COVENANTS   iv.21–31

(21) Tell me, you who want to be under the law, do you not listen[1] to the law? (22) For it is written that Abraham had two sons, one by a slave girl, the other by a free woman. (23) But the son of the slave girl was born in accordance with the flesh, whereas the son of the free woman was born through promise[2]. (24) Such things are to be interpreted allegorically. For these women are two covenants; one from Mount Sinai gives birth into slavery – such is Hagar. (25) This Hagar-Sinai[3] is a mountain in Arabia; she belongs to the same column as the present Jerusalem, for she is in slavery with her children. (26) But the Jerusalem above is free; such is our[4] mother. (27) For it is written:

Rejoice, you barren one who bears no children,
Break forth and cry aloud, you who experience no labour pains;[5]
Because many are the children of the deserted wife,
More than of her who has her husband.

(28) And you[6], brothers,[7] like Isaac, are children of promise. (29) But just as then, the one born in accordance with the flesh used to persecute the one born in accordance with the Spirit, so also now. (30) But what says the scripture? 'Throw

1 Some scribes, perhaps forgetting that most people 'heard' rather than 'read' the law, altered the text to correspond to their own experience by replacing 'listen to' with 'read'.

2 An early improvement was the addition of the definite article before 'promise'.

3 'Hagar' is omitted by many witnesses (so NEB/REB – 'Sinai is a mountain in Arabia'; also NJB; Mussner 322–4) – probably because of the difficulty of the sentence; most of these also read *gar* for the conjunction (instead of *de*), which may well have been a contributing factor – the *gar Hagar* allowing for some natural confusion in copying (Metzger 596).

4 A later 'improvement' was the addition of 'all' ('mother of us all'). The theological and pastoral motives are understandable, but the exposition here depends entirely on there being a clear sequence of contrasting pairs. See also Metzger 596.

5 NEB's 'you who never knew a mother's pangs' was inadequate and misleading; REB has properly revised to 'you who have never been in labour'.

6 A number of important witnesses read 'we' (accepted by Borse 174); but that was probably inserted under the influence of the first-person plural in verse 26 (Metzger 597). It is to be noted again that scribes did not hesitate to amend the text before them if they thought a slip had been made by earlier copyists.

7 See above p. 23 n. 3. (Further example on p. 243.)

out the slave girl and her son; for the son of the slave girl will never inherit with ⁸the son of the free woman'.¹ (31) Wherefore, brothers,⁷ we are children not of the slave girl but of the free woman.

Having made his personal appeal, Paul returns again to scripture. The argument he had already mounted on the basis of the promises to Abraham was already well enough established (iii.6–29) and its corollaries pressed home (iv.1–20). What follows then could be regarded not so much as a further or independent argument, but as an illustration or additional documentation of the point already made, in which Paul demonstrates how well the actual history of the initial fulfilment of these promises exemplifies or foreshadows the eschatological fulfilment now happening through his ministry, and by means of which he can reintroduce the key theme of freedom (iv.22–3, 26, 30–1). It also gives Paul the opportunity, in the more relaxed mood which may be detected in the first part of this paragraph (cf. Oepke 147 – 'perhaps after a pause in dictation'), to demonstrate his skills as an exegete and the elegance with which he can document his case from scripture. And the imagery of birth in iv.19 provides quite an effective transition to talk of two child-bearing covenants.

Most however think that Paul was forced to take up this particular scriptural material because it had been used by the other missionaries to prove *their* case: to be a son of Abraham like Isaac it was necessary to be circumcised, like Isaac (see particularly C. K. Barrett, 'The Allegory of Abraham, Sarah, and Hagar in the Argument of Galatians', *Essays* 118–31; Longenecker 200–6 provides a lengthy excursus on the use made of the Isaac/Ishmael contrast particularly in rabbinic Judaism). That would certainly help explain why Paul has left his own handling of the scriptural texts till this point: without the preceding appeals to experience and scripture his exegesis here might seem to his readers rather forced; his concern, in other words, was not to convince his audience, but to give those already convinced a way of handling and thus countering a key scriptural argument of the other missionaries. That would also help explain why the presentation is not more argumentative in character. A further factor would probably have been the possibility given by the scriptural material of climaxing the exposition with the forcible command of Gen. xxi.10 in verse 30.

1 '. . . with the son of the free woman': some manuscripts revert to the LXX and read 'my son Isaac'.

The passage as a whole is clearly constructed in a sequence of contrasts:

	Abraham had two sons
one by a slave	and one by a free woman
born according to the flesh	born through promise

	Allegorically the women correspond to two covenants
Mount Sinai for slavery	Free
= Hagar	(= Sarah)
= the present Jerusalem	= the Jerusalem above
bearing children in slavery	bearing children of promise (Isaac)
according to the flesh	born according to the Spirit.

Martyn, 'Antinomies 418–19, in particular, has drawn attention to the way Paul has set his exposition as a sequence of antithetical correspondences (antinomies), though this applies primarily to the comparison of the two women in the first part (verses 22–7). The 'oppositional columns' may be set out thus:

	two covenants
(first covenant)	(second covenant)
slave girl	free woman
gives birth according to the flesh	gives birth through promise
Mount Sinai	(promise)
bears children into slavery	mother (of the free)
Hagar	(Sarah)
present Jerusalem	the Jerusalem above
in slavery	free
wife with few children	abandoned, barren wife with many children.

In the second part (verses 28–30) the allegorical sequence gives way more to a typological comparison between the two children:

	two sons
born according to the flesh	born according to the Spirit
persecutes	child of promise
to be driven out – no inheritance	alone inherits
born of slave girl	born of free woman.

Although Paul does not fill out the second column quite so fully as the first, that does not necessarily mean that 'the weight of Paul's allegorical interpretation falls on the Hagar side' (Cosgrove, *Cross* 82). The other best examples of Paul's skill as an interpreter of scripture are Rom. iv, 1 Cor. x.1–13 and 2 Cor. iii.7–iv.6.

21 From the confession of uncertainty and perplexity Paul picks himself up and in a more upbeat, even bantering tone, he challenges his Galatian audiences – **Tell me, you who want to be under the law, do you not listen to the law?** Those addressed are evidently Gentiles (not the other missionaries), since the implication is that they wished for a relationship ('under the law' – see on iii.23) which they had not previously enjoyed (cf. iv.9). The terms of the challenge show more clearly than anything so far what Paul perceived the threat to be: that Gentiles who had already believed in Christ, and already enjoyed the gift of the Spirit, wished now to enter formally into the Jewish people, to come under the authority, and protection, of the law, and thus, presumably, to ensure and secure their status as heirs of Abraham's promise. The bantering tone enters, because Paul knew very well that they had been listening to the law; they would get to know it by 'hearing' it read; in Greek the verb 'obey' is a compound of the verb 'hear', which thus can also carry something of the overtone of the Hebrew equivalent, 'hear with attention, obey' (see also on iii.2). It was no doubt precisely Gen. 17 in particular which the other missionaries had used to press their case home. The double reference to 'law' shows that Paul was well aware of the breadth of meaning of 'Torah' (including narrative as well as laws); the fact that one reference has the article and the other not has no significance for the meaning here (or elsewhere).

Here it needs to be recalled that the Jewish scriptures were still the only scriptures for these earliest congregations. The passage also reminds us of how well the LXX would be known to Gentiles who came into Christianity through the synagogue. As God-fearers, who had already been attracted by the character of Judaism, and who had learned from Paul that they could receive all the benefits held out in these scriptures without undergoing the painful rite of circumcision, they now were being told otherwise by authoritative teachers. Paul could therefore assume a keen and well-informed audience for the *tour de force* on which he was about to embark.

22 **For it is written** (using the normal formula for introducing a scriptural reference, as in iii.10 and 13, but not here as a direct quotation) **that Abraham had two sons, one by a slave girl** (*paidiskē* = diminutive of *pais*, 'girl', but an indication of status more than of age), **the other by a free woman** ('his free-born wife' – NEB). The reference is to Gen. xvi.15 and xxi.2 (the record that Abraham had had further children [Gen. xxv.1–4] would not be seen as weakening the point). In the former (Gen.

xvi.15), Sarah, Abraham's wife, having despaired of bearing him a child, had given him her Egyptian maid, Hagar, as concubine. This was evidently in line with the custom of the time (as attested also in Gen. xxx.3, 9 and the Nuzi texts), according to which the wife was entitled to treat the concubine's children as her own (*ABD* iv.1156–62 iii.574). In the latter (Gen. xxi.2), Sarah herself conceived and bore Abraham a son, though she was long past the normal age of child-bearing. The common denominator, of course, is that both were children of Abraham. Thus the theme which was the main feature of the first exposition of scripture (Who are the seed/children of Abraham? – iii.6–29) is resumed, but with new possibilities for important distinctions. Not least of which is the possibility of reworking the slave/son distinction (iv.1–7) into one between child of a slave girl and child of a free-born woman. The topic of freedom (see on ii.4), initially alluded to as a given of the gospel in ii.4, and implicit in the earlier exposition (iv.7), was evidently held back for the climax of the main argument, but can now be appropriately reintroduced (by means of the contrast between Hagar the slave girl and Sarah) as part of the sequence of antithetical correspondences, to become the main thread running through this paragraph and linking into the next section.

23 Corresponding to the status of the slave girl is the character of her child-bearing – **but the son of the slave girl was born** (the perfect tense as usual indicating the continuing effect of a past action) **in accordance with the flesh** ('born in the [ordinary REB] course of nature' – NEB/REB, so NIV). The initial reference, on the surface of the story, is, of course, to the circumstances related in Gen. xvi. As usual in Paul, the phrase 'in accordance with the flesh' has a negative ring (see on my *Romans* 13), particularly when set in contrast to 'in accordance with the Spirit' (see on iv.29), or in contrast to 'through promise', as here. Even on the surface, then, the implication is clear that Abraham's resort to Hagar was an act of weakness (see above on ii.16; also v.13, 16–17, 19 etc.) – the weakness of human sexual appetite (perhaps) and longing for an heir, but particularly the attempt to bring about the fulfilment of God's extraordinary promise (Gen. xv.5–6) by ordinary human capacity. But 'flesh' was also the ground on which the other missionaries in Galatia were in effect relying – their physical ('according to the flesh') descent from Abraham (cf. Rom. iv.1; ix.3, 5), and a covenant which had to be sealed in the flesh (circumcision) if it was to be valid (see also on vi.13; cf. Rom. ii.28). Underlying the surface account, therefore, is the deeper message – that as Abraham was wrong to turn to Hagar, relying on the flesh for the fulfilment of the divine promise, so those who likewise rely on the flesh (ethnic descent from Abraham, signified by circumcision) were in the wrong.

Whereas in contrast (Paul uses the classic formula of contrast), **the son of the free woman was born through promise.** Again the initial reference is clear: to the fact that Isaac's birth from Sarah was wholly extraordinary – when Sarah was long past child-bearing (Gen. xvii.15–19; xviii.11–13), and as a conception divinely contrived (Gen. xvii.16; xviii.10, 14; xxi.1–2; cf. Philo, *Cher.* 45–7). This was the point Paul was to develop with greater effect in Rom. iv.17–21 and again in Rom. ix.7–9 (citing Gen. xviii.10). Abraham's initial weakness (Gen. xvi) in response to the earlier form of the promise (Gen. xv.4–5) was a potential complication for Paul's argument, since the strong faith which he exercised was not in the promise of Gen. xv.4–5 (despite Gen. xv.6!), but in the promise as repeated in Gen. xvii (and linked with circumcision!). Moreover, other promises were attached to Ishmael (Gen. xvi.10; xvii.20; xxi.13). Even so the primary 'according to flesh'/'through promise' contrast holds good none the less. Somewhat surprisingly Paul refrains from using the complete contrasting phrase – '*in accordance with* the promise'. That cannot be because he thought the preposition inappropriate (cf. iii.29). But it may be that, as in iii.18, he wished to emphasize the instrumentality of the promise (*through* promise) – that God's word effected what it promised (cf. e.g. Gen. i.3; Isa. lv.11). The thought, of course, is of an extraordinarily late but otherwise ordinary birth.

24 Having reminded his audiences of the basic data of the account of Abraham's two sons, Paul proceeds to dig below the surface. **Such things** (that is, presumably, 'Such details or facts') **are to be interpreted allegorically** (only here in biblical Greek, but quite frequent in Philo). The basic assumption of allegorical exposition is that the text has a deeper meaning or reference than appears on the surface. Such interpretation goes back to the fifth century BC (BAGD and LSJ, *allēgoreō*), and probably entered Jewish hermeneutical practice through Alexandrian Judaism (*TDNT* i.260–3). The classic exponent of the technique within Judaism was Paul's older contemporary, the Alexandrian philosopher Philo. Thus e.g. in discussing the city built by Cain in *Post.* 51, Philo notes 'that it is better to take the words allegorically, as meaning that Cain resolves to set up his own creed, just as one might set up a city'. So too Deut. xiii.4 ('thou shalt go in the steps of the Lord thy God') can hardly refer to the use of our legs, 'but is evidently speaking allegorically of the way the soul should comply with the divine ordinances' (*Migr.* 131). And on *Jos.* 28 he comments, 'After this literal account of the story, it will be well to explain the underlying meaning, for, broadly speaking, all or most of the law-book is to be taken allegorically'. In his own comments on *Abr.* 99 he notes that some 'natural philosophers' interpreted the name Sarah allegorically as denoting 'virtue' (see further Bruce 215). And in writing on *Vit. Cont.* 28–9 he notes that the sect of the Therapeutae also sought a hidden meaning underlying the literal text of the scriptures.

Paul is clearly moving in a similar circle. One can certainly say that his allegorical meaning here is a good deal less arbitrary than most of Philo's: the 'according to the flesh/through promise' antithesis is both given in the context of the story of Abraham and Sarah, and fundamental to the theological distinction Paul seeks to draw. But the contrast with Philo cannot be pressed very hard: the link Paul proceeds to draw between Hagar and Sinai (iv.25) seems arbitrary enough; whereas Philo's exposition, for example, of Abraham's faith would have found sympathetic echoes in Paul (see *Philo*, Loeb edition vol. X, Index, p. 274). Again, it could be argued that Paul was thinking of sonship to Abraham in more typological than allegorical terms; that is, the historical facts, as given in the narrative of Genesis, foreshadowed and were finding an eschatological correlate in the events of the Gentile mission (see e.g. *TDNT* viii.251; discussion in Mussner 319–20 and Longenecker 209–10). And certainly the eschatological dimension to Paul's handling of the scriptures marks his exposition off quite clearly from Philo's. But the basic point of similarity between Philo and Paul remains: that each was willing to look below the surface of the literal sense of the text to find a deeper meaning. And the subsequent irresponsibility (as it may seem to us now) of the method of allegorical interpretation, as we find it particularly in Alexandrian Christianity and thereafter, should not prevent us from recognizing something of the technique in Paul.

The crucial theological point for Paul is the one already argued theologically in the first exposition of scripture (iii.6–29) and now further illustrated by another mode of interpretation: that the understanding of God's purpose in terms of promise brings us closer to the heart and character of that purpose than an understanding in terms of the Torah.

For (now comes the deeper meaning) **these women are** (= signify – cf. 1 Cor. x.4 and 2 Cor. iii.17) **two covenants.** The fact that Paul makes the primary identification in terms of two *covenants* is striking. For the earlier exposition (iii.15ff.) suggested that Paul would wish to reserve the category of 'covenant' for the promise to Abraham; by implication, the law given through Moses was a different category, or at best/(worst) an unauthorized codicil or later document misunderstood as a superseding document (see on iii.15). And talk of a second covenant might seem unwelcome, since it could be taken to undermine the initial thrust of that earlier exposition, by suggesting the possibility that God had after all replaced or elaborated the earlier covenant with the later. The reason why Paul uses the category now must be that it was such a fundamental category in Jewish self-understanding – Israel as the elect people of God, the nation with whom among all the nations he had chosen to make his covenant, and to whom he had given his law. This is the repeated assumption in such writings as ben Sira, *Jubilees*, the Damascus document of Qumran (CD), and *Pseudo-Philo* (see e.g. my *Romans* lxviii–lxix and *Partings*, ch. 2). The point which Paul chose to ignore in iii.15ff. (see again on iii.15), he now readily acknowledges: that Israel's relationship with Yahweh was also a covenant. What thus at first seemed to be the opposition of covenant promise and law is now redefined as a contrast between covenant promise and covenant law. The point is important: for not only does it constitute Paul's acknowledgment of this fundamental category of Jewish self-definition; but it also moves the dispute beyond the question of whether Israel stood in covenant relationship with God.

It is tempting to understand the two covenants as old covenant and new covenant (cf. 1 Cor. xi.25, 2 Cor. iii.6 and particularly Heb. viii.6–13). But in fact only one covenant is at issue here – the covenant with Abraham and his seed promising blessing to the nations; strictly speaking there was no covenant with Ishmael (Gen. xvii.18–21). It is the single issue of relationship to and descent from Abraham which is refracted into two contrasting sequences (see on iv.25). What Paul describes as two covenants for the purposes of his exegesis are in effect two ways of understanding the one covenant purpose of God through Abraham and for his seed. What Paul is about to argue is that the Abraham covenant seen in terms of freedom and promise is a fuller expression of God's electing grace and a fuller embodiment of the ongoing divine will than the Abraham covenant seen in terms of law and flesh. The danger of confusion here is perhaps the reason why the category 'covenant' is not much used by Paul; despite 1 Cor. xi.25 and 2 Cor. iii.6, when Paul returns to the theme in Romans it is once again 'promise' which he prefers to set over against 'law' to make clear the distinction he is striving for (Rom. iv.13–22; ix.7–9; xv.8; contrast the use of 'covenant' in ix.4 and xi.27).

One of these covenants is **from Mount Sinai** and **gives birth into slavery.** In terms of the allegorical exposition **such is Hagar;** that is, in the story told in Genesis xvi and xxi, Hagar represents the covenant as understood in terms of Sinai. 'Sinai' refers of course to the mountain on which Moses was given the Torah (e.g. Lev. vii.38; xxvi.46; BAGD, *Sina; TDNT* vii.282–4). It thus represents – and no one would have missed the point – the covenant with Israel understood as embodied in the Torah. Paul defines the relationship to which Sinai gave birth as one of slavery (the children of slaves being themselves slaves). This is not a new claim: it had been implicit in the talk of the Jewish people as 'under the law' (see on iii.23); and explicit in the likening of Jewish minority (under the law) to the condition of slavery (iv.1, 3; also iv.8–10). What is new is the description of this relationship in terms of 'covenant'. What Paul seemed to give back by his acknowledgment of Israel's covenant relationship with God, he at once qualifies by recalling the earlier analogy and argument.

In a further analysis of the passage Martyn draws attention to the present tense used by Paul here – 'gives birth', not 'gave birth'. From this he deduces that what is in view is not ethnic Israel or Judaism as such, but precisely, once again, the other missionaries ('giving birth' not to individuals but to churches), with 'the present Jerusalem' of verse 25 referring to the Jerusalem church ('Covenants' 177–84). But it is questionable whether the aim of the other missionaries was to make fresh converts ('give birth') or to make Paul's converts full proselytes (see Introduction §6 and introduction to iv.12–20); in either case it is also very doubtful whether their proselytizing of Galatians could be described as 'persecution' (see on iv.29); and anyway the present tense here ('gives birth') can be understood simply as referring to those continuing to be born within 'Judaism' (but for 'Judaism' see on i.13). On the other hand, Martyn's exposition gives particular focus to the command of iv.30, as directed against the other missionaries; and he is certainly correct to warn against reading the passage as a polemic against Jews as a whole or Israel as such (see on iv.30).

25 The next sentence is something of a puzzle, and the textual variations indicate that it was so more or less from the beginning. If we assume that we have the earliest form of the text (see above p. 242 n. 3), it would be possible to translate as with RSV/NRSV – 'Now Hagar is Mount Sinai in Arabia' (so also NIV). The difficulty here is that the identification between Hagar and the covenant from Mount Sinai has already been made in the immediately preceding clause. A repeated identification, albeit with Mount Sinai itself, seems tautologous. Also the word order suggests that 'mount' is not adjectival (as in verse 24) but either the predicate, or the subject 'the Hagar Sinai mountain'; and the textual variations confirm that the RSV/NRSV solution did not appear obvious to the copyists.

The better alternative is take 'Hagar' and 'Sinai' in apposition (Hagar as adjectival), and the clause as a clarificatory explanation regarding the identification (Hagar = covenant from Sinai) just made. Thus, either 'The Hagar Sinai mountain is in Arabia', or **This Hagar-Sinai** (Sinai taken as neuter in agreement with 'mountain') **is a mountain in Arabia.** The difficulty in this case is imagining why Paul should think it necessary to add such a geographical note, when he could assume as much knowledge of the Pentateuch on the part of his readers as he does. Attempts to alleviate the difficulty based on the facts that 'hajar' in Arabic means 'stone' and that names compounded with it are found on the Sinai peninsula (BAGD, *Hagar;* details also in Betz, *Galatians* 245 and Bruce 219–20; but see Lietzmann 30–1), or on the possibility of identifying Mount Sinai with the Nabatean centre of El-Hegra in the north-west part of the Arabian peninsula (but see G. I. Davies, 'Hagar, El-Hegra and the Location of Mount Sinai', *VT* 22 [1972] 152–63), or on the targumic rendering of Gen. xvi.7 as 'the angel found her (Hagar) . . . by the spring on the road to Hagra' (M. G. Steinhauser, 'Gal. iv.25a: Evidence of Targumic Tradition in Gal. iv.21–31', *Biblica* 70 [1989] 234–40), or on the belief that the Arab peoples look back to Hagar's son Ishmael as their progenitor, seem too remote from the movement of thought here (Oepke 149–50). The suggestion of a later gloss (Burton 259–60) raises the same question: why was such an explanation thought necessary? And if a later copyist thought it necessary, so might Paul himself. Borse's 171 suggestion, that it is the feminine 'Arabia' which makes the link between Sinai and the earthly (feminine) Jerusalem, is far-fetched. A more plausible suggestion is that of Ridderbos 177 and Mussner 322–4, who resolve the problem by giving the *de* of verse 25 adversative force: to be sure, Mount Sinai (in geographical terms) is in Arabia, but (allegorically understood) can be linked with the present Jerusalem; this could be adapted to the rendering given above. Perhaps, however, and for all the difference it makes, it is best to regard the clause as something of an afterthought by Paul in case any of his audiences did not know where Mount Sinai was; since the name 'Sinai' as such does not appear very frequently in the OT he might have thought such a fuller identification could be helpful for some. At all events, it cannot be denied that 'the exact meaning . . . remains obscure' (Schlier 220; Rohde 199–200).

The main line of exposition resumes: she (Hagar, or Hagar-Sinai) **belongs to the same column as the present Jerusalem** (on the form of the name see Bruce 220). The verb (only here in biblical Greek) is drawn from the military metaphor of soldiers 'standing in the same line or rank'. It had already become a technical term in grammatical and logical discussion when talking of a series of related concepts, particularly in the Pythagorean tables of categories (LSJ and BAGD, *sustoicheō*). This is clearly what Paul had in mind here – two parallel columns set up to bring out a sequence of parallel antitheses (see especially Lightfoot 181; Lietzmann 31; Martyn, 'Antinomies' 419–20). In the two columns which he has clearly been constructing (see Introduction to this section) Hagar-Sinai belongs in the *same* column as Jerusalem; (despite Gaston 91, the Greek cannot mean 'is in the opposite column', which would require *antistoichein*). The alternative, but usual translation 'corresponds to' (RSV/NRSV, NIV; BAGD; Burton 261–2; Schlier 221; Longenecker 212–13) likewise confuses the metaphor, since it implies correspondence between items in the *opposite* columns (*TDNT* vii.669). The further alternative, 'represents' (NEB/REB, NJB), abandons the metaphor altogether.

The description of this item in the column as 'the now Jerusalem' (literally) indicates that Paul's columns are determined partly by salvation-history contrasts (along the lines of the exposition in iii.15–iv.7), and partly by apocalyptic contrasts. The power of 'Jerusalem' as symbol for Israel, the chosen people, is here clearly evident (see further *TDNT* vii.305–27), a power exerted not only on traditionalist Christian Jews, as the next verse shows. Unusually, however, the 'now' stands on the negative side of the contrast, whereas elsewhere in Paul 'now' usually breathes a note of eschatological expectation or fulfilment (cf. especially Rom. iii.26; xiii.11; 2 Cor. vi.2). Here 'the now Jerusalem' in effect stands in the same column as 'the present evil age' (i.4), under the power of the elemental forces (iv.3, 9). **For she is in slavery with her children.** The switch from Hagar, mother of the Arabs, to Jerusalem, mother of the Jews, is only awkward when we forget that, in terms of the technique Paul is using, the items in the columns need have no closer relation than the fact that they belong to the same column. Paul has already made the point that the Jewish people's subordination 'under the law' is, in effect, no different from the slavery of the other nations to the elemental forces (iv.1–10). So he is simply transposing that conclusion into its appropriate place in the appropriate column. But the abruptness of the reversal of categories and its hurtfulness to typical Jewish self-understanding are indicated by John viii.33 – 'We are Abraham's seed and have never been enslaved to anyone' (see further Mussner 324–5).

26 But in the opposite column stands **the Jerusalem above.** Here Paul clearly had in mind the strand of Jewish apocalyptic thought which presumed that there was a heavenly Jerusalem, that is, an ideal form of Jerusalem in the purpose of God, waiting, as it were, in heaven to be revealed at the end time, when God's purpose would be completely fulfilled. This was obviously based on Exod. xxv.9, 40 (cf. Wisd. Sol. ix.8), where Moses was told to construct the tabernacle in accordance with the pattern shown him on the mountain. Hence subsequently the explicit denial of *2 Baruch* that Isa. xlix.16 refers to the earthly Jerusalem:

> *2 Bar.* iv.2–6 – Or do you think that this is the city of which I said: 'On the palms of my hands I have carved you?' (Isa. xlix.16). It is not this building that is in your midst now; it is that which will be revealed, with me, that was already prepared from the moment that I decided to create Paradise. And I showed it to Adam before he sinned . . . After these things I showed it to my servant Abraham in the night between the portions of the victims. And again I showed it also to Moses on Mount Sinai when I showed him the likeness of the tabernacle and all its vessels. Behold, now it is preserved with me – as also Paradise (Charlesworth).

Likewise *4 Ezra* promises that 'the city which now is not seen shall appear' (vii.26); 'and Zion will come and be made manifest to all people, prepared and built, as you saw the mountain carved out without hands' (xiii.36; cf. viii. 52; x.25–59). And Enoch speaks of his going 'up to the highest heaven, into the highest Jerusalem' (*2 Enoch* lv.2 – longer recension) (see further SB iii.573, 796; *TDNT* vii.325–7; Schlier 222–3; Longenecker 214). The same apocalyptic schema is presupposed elsewhere in the NT, particularly in Hebrews (Heb. viii–x – viii.5 explicitly citing Exod. xxv.40; xi.10, 16; xii.22–3; xiii.10–14; cf. Philo, *Som.* ii.250) and Revelation (Rev. iii.12 [see on ii.9]; xxi.1–3, 10–11, 22–7).

The corollary of such a schema, particularly in apocalyptic thought, is that the present equivalent is an inadequate copy, provisional, awaiting eschatological transfiguration into or replacement by the intended ideal. Hebrews draws out that corollary at considerable length, and Paul does so here too in his own way. Reference to later Gnostic development of the same contrast (Schlier 224–5) is unnecessary.

The Jerusalem above, standing in the same column as Sarah, the free-born wife, **is free**. This, of course, is the corollary of the allegorical parallel. But Paul would not think of the freedom merely as an allegorical category. The slave/free contrast corresponds to the contrast between the present Jerusalem, in slavery to the elemental forces, and the freedom from all merely physical and fleshly constraint which is the divine reality as purposed by God. More to the point, that freedom is something already experienced by the Christians, who have learned that they need be under neither elemental forces nor the law. **Such** (the same allegorical identifying formula as in verse 24) **is our mother** (the emphasis falls more on 'our' than on 'mother'). The imagery is well rooted in Jewish thought (cf. the LXX of Ps. lxxxvii.5 where 'Mother Zion' is addressed; also Isa. l.1; li.18; Jer. l.12; Hos. iv.5; *4 Ezra* x.7; *2 Bar.* iii.1; SB iii.574); once again the normal sequence of related themes has been completely transposed. In the matching column Sarah stands with and allegorically for a heavenly reality, that is, without such physical or fleshly constraint, which is therefore not limited to a single ethnic or national group, and which therefore can be shared by all races and nations in freedom from such merely ethnic and fleshly considerations (hence the 'our'). Here again emerges the characteristic tension in earliest Christian theology between the 'not yet' of a heavenly purpose still to be fully realized, and the 'already' of the experience of renewal and liberation enjoyed by the first Christians; though it would be a mistake to make anything like a straight identification of 'the heavenly Jerusalem' with the church (too incautiously by Schlier 223–4 and Guthrie 125).

27 In accord with his usual technique in constructing a theological argument, Paul draws in a scriptural text which confirms or illustrates his claim – **For it is written** (as in iii.10 and iv.22). The quotation is a verbatim reproduction of the LXX of Isa. liv.1, itself a close translation of the Hebrew –

Rejoice, you barren one who bears no children,
Break forth (that is, in joyous shout, as the Hebrew makes
clear)

> **and cry aloud, you who experience no labour pains;**
> **Because many are the children of the deserted** (BAGD,
>   *erēmos* 1b) **wife** (understood),
> **More than of her who has her husband.**

The quotation is highly appropriate, for it comes at the
beginning of a passage where, in the words of second Isaiah,
Yahweh comforts the exiled Judeans, by reassuring Israel that
Yahweh would take her again to wife (liv.4–8), and that a new
beginning was in prospect like that following the flood (liv.9–10)
– a powerful image of the hoped-for new age. The echoes of the
covenant promise (liv.3, 10) would confirm the correspondence;
and the idealized description of Jerusalem as to be built with
precious stones (liv.11–12) would naturally suggest a vision of
the new, heavenly Jerusalem (cf. Rev. xxi.10–11, 18–21). In
particular, the image of a barren woman would link in
immediately to that of Sarah. And her promised fertility would
point back at once to the promise that Sarah would be the
mother of nations and that the nations would be blessed in her
offspring. Paul's claim, therefore, is that Isaiah's hoped for
restoration of Judea/Zion was best understood as fulfilled
eschatologically in the amazing fruitfulness of the Christian,
including the Gentile mission.

As might be expected, the passage was made much of in
Jewish theology (already at Qumran, 4Q164 – Bruce 222; cf. Bar.
iv.12 – left desolate because her children had turned away from
the law of God), with the link to Sarah also perceived, and the
Targum of Isaiah identifying the deserted wife with 'desolate
Jerusalem', and the wife of the last line with 'inhabited Rome'
(SB iii.574–5; Betz 248 n. 102). Paul's use of Isa. liv.1 here may
indicate that such a line of interpretation was already current (cf.
particularly *4 Ezra* x.45–6; *2 Bar.* x.14). Be that as it may, it is
important to appreciate that Paul once again felt able to apply a
prophecy regarding Judea and Jerusalem to this wider mission
(as in Rom. ix.25–6; x.20; but not dissimilar to *2 Baruch's*
reinterpretation of Isa. xlix.16, as cited in verse 26 above). Paul
genuinely believed that his apostleship to the Gentiles was in
continuity with and fulfilment of God's covenant promise to and
through Israel. The text is also prominent in later Christian
literature – for example, 2 Clem. ii.1–3 offers a more elaborate,
line-by-line exposition of Isa. liv.1.

28 What started as an allegorical exposition regarding
Abraham's two sons (iv.22) had become somewhat sidetracked
into an exposition of the deeper significance of the two women.

But Paul now returns to his principal subject – **And you, brothers** (see on i.2), **like Isaac** (literally, 'according to Isaac' – the only time Isaac is expressly named, anywhere in Paul), **are children of promise**. What had been implicit Paul now makes explicit. As in iii.26–9 and iv.6–7, he switches to second-person address (see above p. 242 n. 6) to bring home the point – that is, not 'you' Gentiles over against or excluding Jews in whole or part, but 'you' Gentile believers in particular, 'you too'. Like Isaac they were a fulfilment of the promise made to Abraham (see on iii.8, 16; for 'promise' on iii.18); like Isaac, their birth into freedom was the effect of divine grace; like Isaac, they belong to the column of the covenant of promise. The claim is again a bold one: Jewish tradition took for granted that the line of covenant promise ran through Sarah rather than Hagar, and through Isaac rather than Ishmael; but by focusing on Isaac's character as child of promise, in contrast to his ethnic identity, Paul was able to turn this assumption against his Jewish-Christian opponents (as in Rom. ix.7–9 – using the same phrase, 'children of promise'). This in fact completes the second column and the primary purpose of the allegory; verse 28 effectively rounds off and concludes the exposition.

29 But the Genesis narratives pointed towards a further line of exposition: **just as then, the one born in accordance with the flesh used to persecute the one born in accordance with the Spirit, so also now**. The 'just as then/so also now' indicates that the mode of interpretation has moved from a listing of (somewhat arbitrary) parallels in contrasting columns, to a typological understanding of an event from the earliest days of Israel's history as expressing the character of the events of the end-time. The reference is to Gen. xxi.9 – 'Sarah saw the son of Hagar . . . playing with her son Isaac' (LXX). In the idiom, the reference is to innocent play (so also *Jub.* xvii.4). But the verb 'play' can easily gather to itself darker overtones – play, in the sense of sport with, make fun of, scorn (LSJ, *paizō*; *TDNT* v.625–9); and Sarah's reaction (xxi.10) could easily be taken to imply as much – the older boy (by about fourteen years) making sport of the younger. Certainly there was a later Jewish exposition to this effect (SB iii.410, 575–6; Mussner 329–30; Bruce 223–4; Longenecker 217; perhaps stimulated by the memory of hostility from the Hagrites – Ps. lxxxiii.6; cf. 1 Chron. v.10, 19), which presumably was already current for Paul to develop here. He does so in a quite radical way, reading the original story in the light of its contemporary parallel:

Ishmael's treatment of Isaac foreshadowing the persecution which the sons of the present Jerusalem were visiting on the sons of the Jerusalem above. That there was such persecution of the Nazarenes, with at least some official backing from Jewish authorities, is attested in i.13 (Paul's own role as persecutor; see on i.13), 1 Thess. ii.14–15 (not to be treated as a later interpolation; see e.g. my *Partings* 146–7 and n. 32), and 2 Cor. xi.24. As e.g. Schlier 226–7 notes, this was different from the internal disputes within the Christian movement, though the anti–Paul polemic of the traditionalist Christian Jews would have been similarly motivated (see also on v.11 with vi.12).

Again Paul does not hesitate to make the typological identification. The child of Hagar is the child 'born according to the flesh'; but that corresponds, *not* to the descendants of Ishmael, but to the Jews, or at least those of them who relied on their physical ('according to the flesh') descent from Abraham (cf. again Rom. iv.1 and ix.3, 5). As will become clear in the final section of the letter (v.13ff.), Paul does not draw a distinction between 'flesh' as a moral category and 'flesh' as denoting ethnic identity, at least when that ethnic identity is seen to have determinative significance for participation in covenant blessings. In contrast, the son 'born according to the Spirit' (the closest parallel in Paul to John iii.6, 8) corresponds *not* to the descendants of Isaac, but to those who have received the Spirit (iii.2–5, 14; iv.6). Isaac, in other words, represents a different kind or line of descent, one which stands in contrast to merely physical descent. Isaac represents those born through the power of the divine promise (see on iv.23), which is another way of saying, through the power of God's Spirit (so NIV; the point is obscured by NEB/REB's translation, 'natural-born son . . . spiritual son'). Those, therefore, who show themselves to be wrought upon by the Spirit of God (see on iii.2), that is by the Spirit of his Son (see on iv.6), show themselves to be as much the children of promise as Isaac (iv.28). This is the only time outside Romans that Paul uses the 'according to the flesh/according to the Spirit' in explicit antithesis (Rom. i.3–4; viii.4, 5, 12–13), the antithesis strengthening the negative overtones which generally gather round Paul's understanding of 'flesh' (see again on ii.16).

30 Having made the allusion to Gen. xxi.9 Paul can go on to cite the sequel: **But what says the scripture** (cf. Rom. iv.3)? In the original, the word is Sarah's, but it also speaks as scripture (see also iii.8 and 22). **'Throw out** (Get rid of – NIV) **the slave**

THE EPISTLE TO THE GALATIANS

girl and her son; for the son of the slave girl will never inherit (the key concept in iii.18–iv.7) **with the son of the free woman'**. The quotation is from the very next sentence, Gen. xxi.10. It follows the text of both Hebrew and LXX closely, with a slight change of emphasis: the single negative is strengthened by doubling it, giving it the force of 'never, certainly not' (BAGD, *mē* D; missed by translations except NIV); and the final phrase 'son of the free-woman' replaces the OT's 'my son Isaac' (see also p. 243 n. 1). The latter modification underscores Paul's concern finally to round off the exposition with the focus firmly on Christian freedom (see on iv.31), and thus to lead into the next phase of the argument (v.1). Given the reversal of categories in iv.29, the harsh word of Sarah (spiteful, if Ishmael was only playing with Isaac) becomes a word of powerful application to the present situation – whose power depends not on the propriety of its use here so much as on its emotional impact at the end of the typological allegory. Hansen 145–6, indeed, maintains that 'the focal point in the Hagar-Sarah allegory is the imperative to expel the bondswoman and her son'. Certainly for any who had allowed themselves to be caught up in Paul's exposition, even as an illustration, this final scripture would speak with tremendous force. Here again Paul shows his rhetorical skill.

The degree of overstatement ('never') would also allow Paul both to underscore the importance of the contrast between a sonship of slavery and one of freedom, and to imply his own relative softness: the transition from slave sonship to free sonship is precisely what he sought for all who could hear the gospel (iv.7). Betz 250–1 is justified in pointing to the contrast between the commanded 'Throw out' here and the criticized 'shut out' of iv.17 ('Paul does the same with the Jews as his Jewish-Christian opponents want to do with him'; cf. Lightfoot 184 – Paul 'confidently sounds the death-knell of Judaism'!). Nevertheless, it would be a mistake to read a text cited for rhetorical effect as though it were a dogmatic statement. That Paul has the other missionaries particularly in view is certainly likely (particularly Mussner 332, Longenecker 217 and Martyn, 'Covenants'), but it is doubtful whether the rhetorical flourish can be so restricted.[1] After all, Gen. xxi.12 is cited in Rom. ix.7; and the clear inference that unbelieving Jews are 'vessels of wrath' in Rom ix.13–22, and the use of Isa. xxix.10 and Ps. lxix.22–3 in Rom. xi.7–10, are quite as fierce. It remains a question, therefore, as to

1 Borse 176 ignores the rhetorical effect in maintaining that 'the scripture speaks not to the Galatians, but to Abraham'; and Barrett, *Essays* 165, takes it as a command of God to his [angelic] agents.

whether Rom. xi.25–32 means that Paul revised his ideas (Oepke 152) subsequent to Galatians (and Rom. ix and xi!) or simply his tone.

31 Wherefore, brothers, we are children not of the slave girl but of the free woman. With the same warmth of personal address as in the preliminary conclusion of iv.28 (also to mark the contrast with the harshness of verse 30), Paul sums up the exposition in the terms with which it began (iv.22). The 'wherefore' has the force of Q.E.D., as in Paul's other most thoroughgoing exposition (Rom. iv.22). He has also brought the overall argument back to where it had reached at the end of the first scriptural exposition (iii.29), but reworded in the slave-free antithesis which has dominated chapter iv. As in iii.14 and iv.5–6, however, Paul slips from the second person to the first-person plural – 'we' – that is, all who can count themselves sons of the promise, free-born sons, by virtue of their having been born in accordance with the Spirit (iv.29), Jew as well as Gentile, Gentile as well as Jew, whereas those who were still 'under the elemental forces', including 'under the law', were still in a condition of slavery. The 'of the free' echoes the modified end of the quotation from Gen. xxi.10 (iv.30), and brings the exposition to a triumphant close with the climactic emphasis on the word 'freedom'. That Paul takes Isaac as a type of Christians, rather than of Christ, indicates the 'ecclesiocentric' (rather than christocentric) character of his hermeneutic at this point (Hays, *Echoes* 86–7).

11 CONCLUSION: DO NOT ABANDON YOUR FREEDOM v.1–12

Submission to circumcision is contrary to freedom in Christ v.1–6

(1) For freedom[1] Christ has set us free. Stand firm, therefore, and do not be subject again to a yoke of slavery. (2) Look! I, Paul, say to you that if you are circumcised, Christ will benefit you not at all. (3) I testify again to everyone[2] who is being circumcised that he is obligated to do[3] the whole law. (4) You have been estranged from Christ, you who are seeking to be justified by the law; you have fallen away from grace. (5) For we by the Spirit, from faith, are awaiting eagerly the hope of righteousness. (6) For in Christ Jesus neither circumcision counts for anything, nor uncircumcision, but faith operating effectively through love.

Freedom is the leitmotiv of the letter. Having brought the discussion back round to that theme in iv.22–31, Paul reaches the climax of his exposition and appeal. The whole reason for his writing to the Galatians is summed up in the passionate cry of v.1. And the depth of feeling which so strongly motivated the writing, and which moves disturbingly beneath the surface throughout, bursts through once again in the forcefulness of the appeal. Paul must have felt that this was it! Like a lawyer pleading for a client in danger of being found guilty of a capital crime, he must have seen this as the critical moment. If he could not convince his Galatian audiences now he might never have another chance; his work with them, and their freedom in Christ might be lost irretrievably. Caught up in the movement of his argument and the depth of his concern for the Galatians, his dictation at this point must have assumed new tones of intensity and vehemence. The consequence is a passage almost unique within Paul's letters in its passionate forcefulness, in its polarization of choice, and in its dismissal of those opposing him (with only i.6–9, Rom. ix.1–3, 2 Cor. xi.12–20, and Phil. iii.2 coming close).

1 The manuscript tradition indicates various scribal attempts to soften the abruptness of the transition from iv.31 to v.1 – 'for which freedom Christ has set us free'; 'for freedom, therefore, Christ has set us free'.
2 We could translate 'every man', since only males were circumcised. But it is proper to avoid a gender-specific word when the Greek is less specific.
3 A few witnesses thought *plērōsai* ('to fulfil') made better sense than *poiēsai* ('to do').

Most English commentators see v.1–12 (or v.2–12) as the beginning of the final main section ('exhortation'; see particularly Betz 253–4); but it is better seen as the conclusion to the main argument (the normal division in German commentaries), with the more general exhortation beginning at v.13 (see particularly O. Merk, 'Der Beginn der Paränese im Galaterbrief', *ZNW* 60 [1969] 83–104). But since the exposition leads into the conclusion and the conclusion has the character of exhortation, the disagreement does not amount to much. Bligh 414–16 thinks that iv.31–v.13 is a revised version of the closing section of the discourse at Antioch and notes a sequence of correspondences with ii.14–iii.4. F. J. Matera, 'The Culmination of Paul's Argument to the Galatians: Gal. v.1–vi.17', *JSNT* 32 [1988] 79–91, sees the whole of v.1–vi.17 as the culmination of Paul's argument without noting that the parallels between v.1–12 and the very personal final appeal of vi.11–17 serve more to underline the climactic character of v.1–12.

1 For freedom Christ has set us free. The abruptness of the exclamation, without syntactical link to the preceding theme (see p. 260 n. 1), suggests that Paul wanted the verse to stand on its own, not simply serve as a conclusion to the exposition of iv.22–31 (as in NEB, REB, NRSV). Since the eye of the reader would not run smoothly over a grammatical bridge between iv.31 and v.1, the reader would be forced to pause, and thus to signal to his Galatian audiences a statement of importance to follow. The predominance of long vowels in the Greek and repetition of the theme of freedom (noun and verb) would also serve to give the exclamation the resonance and forcefulness of a slogan or epigrammatical summary which brought to focus the burden of the whole letter.

'Freedom' had been the word which encapsulated the gospel for Paul in ii.4 (see on ii.4). There he had spoken of 'our freedom in Christ'. Here he speaks of the freedom which Christ had achieved – the redundancy of expression ('for freedom . . . set free') underlining its character as *freedom* – freedom given the place of emphasis ('for *freedom*'), freedom as characterizing the gospel from beginning to end, freedom as the goal of the divine act of liberation; 'the freedom is meant to be lived' (Ebeling 241). It is a striking fact that Paul can thus sum up the goal of God's saving act and call (v.13) in the one word 'freedom' (cf. particularly 2 Cor. iii.17; John viii.32, 36), though he will take care to spell out what that freedom involves – both freedom from (v.1–12) and freedom for (v.13ff). Some argue that the first phrase is instrumental – 'by means of, with freedom . . .' (e.g.

Burton 270–1); but at best that is not very meaningful, if not merely tautologous, and takes too little account of the flexibility of the dative in Greek. The verb will refer to the cross, but the metaphor is not more closely specified, whether an act of manumission (particularly Lietzmann 37), or liberation of occupied territories, or release of prisoners (see on i.4 and iii.13).

In these words Paul sums up the whole argument of iii.1–iv.11 – both the recognition (now) that the life he had previously lived 'within Judaism' (i.13–14) was an immature and unnecessarily restricted one (iii.23–4), and the sense of liberation which he personally had experienced through his conversion and which he wanted his converts to experience for themselves in full measure, in contrast to their previous slavery (iv.8–9). It is most unlikely, in contrast, that Paul was citing here a slogan of his opponents in Galatia (so Schmithals, *Gnostics* 51): he would hardly have been so unguarded in his statement at this point, were that the case; and, anyway, the context here is quite clearly that of Jewish proselytizing.

As is often the way with those whose religious commitment is born of and sustained by a vivid experience which authenticates the faith expressed, Paul found it difficult to comprehend how those who had not shared his own experiential pilgrimage could fail to see what was so clear to him. His Galatian converts had shared so much of the experience which Paul had found so liberating (iii.2–5), how could they fail to see that the (to them) new ideas which they were now thinking to embrace ran contrary to and completely undermined that freedom. **Stand therefore**, he cried, almost like a military commander rallying wavering troops. The image was a favourite of Paul – that of taking a firm stand and holding strongly to it. That it could be a firm stand was a consequence of the certainty of the ground on which the stand was taken – 'in the Lord' (Rom. xiv.4; Phil. iv.1; 1 Thess. iii.8), 'in faith' (1 Cor. xvi.13), 'in one Spirit' (Phil. i.27) (*TDNT* vii.637–8). What Paul calls for is a corresponding firmness of resolve on the part of his readers; their firmness of purpose should reflect the assured character of the divine grace in which they already stood (cf. Rom. v.2; xiv.4).

The alternative – **and do not be subject again to a yoke of slavery** – is the acceptance of an inferior and much less favourable condition, already indicated in the slavery metaphor of iv.1–3, 8–9, 22–31. The 'again' echoes the 'again' of iv.9. The verb occurs only here in the NT (2 Thess. i.4 *v.l.*) and could mean 'be caught or entangled in' (LSJ, *enechō* II.1; cf. 2 Macc. v.18), but the sense 'be subject to, loaded down with' is common (BAGD, *enechō* 2). It could also be rendered as a middle – 'do not subject yourselves'; or with conative force – 'do not begin to be subject' (J. H. Moulton, *A Grammar of New Testament Greek*, Vol. 1 [Edinburgh: T. & T. Clark, 1906] 125).

Elsewhere the linked metaphor of the yoke often has a positive sense, as indicating the submission of the pupil to the good teacher (Sir. li.26; Matt. xi.29–30; 1 Clem. xvi.17; Did. vi.2). 'The yoke of the law' was probably already current within Judaism as denoting the obligations and privileges of the religious Jew (cf. *m. Abot* iii.5; Bruce 226). But the link with slavery echoes the equally, or more familiar metaphor of an army or city or people defeated and reduced to the status of slaves – defeat in war being the earliest and still major source of slaves in the ancient world (see e.g. Lev. xxvi.13; Isa. xiv.25; Jer. xxvii.8; xxviii.14; 1 Macc. viii.18; BAGD, *zugos* 1). Both these last two uses of the metaphor will probably have been in mind here: Paul thinks of submission to the law as the enslavement of one people to another; ironically, Judaism's struggle to free itself from 'the yoke of the Gentiles' (1 Macc. xiii.41) was now resulting in the reverse situation, where Jews were trying to bring Gentiles into subserviency to them. Here again, implicit in the play on the metaphor, is confirmation that it was the nationalistic overtones of Judaism's insistence on the law and circumcision to which Paul now took exception (cf. Acts xv.10–11 with xv.12–21). The gospel of Messiah Jesus was not about Gentiles' having to submit to Jewish customs which obliterated their distinctiveness as Gentiles (and so also the oneness of God as God of Gentiles as well as Jews – Rom. iii.29–30), but about freedom from such distinctions for both Jew and Gentile. Contrast Betz 257, who thinks that Paul's concept of freedom means total abolition of or disregard for the law – 'for the Apostle there is no longer any Law, and therefore there are no trangressions'! (but see below on v.6); he is right, however, to note that Paul wants his readers to protect their Christian freedom by exercising it (p. 258).

2 Look! – perhaps a variation of the more normal 'behold' (i.20), reflecting the characteristic Hebrew *hinneh*, 'lo! behold!', which makes the typical Hebrew narrative so graphic (BDB, *hinneh*). Unusual for Paul (the variation appears only here in the NT outside the Gospels), it would, however, be quite understandable if in the emotion of the moment, Paul lapsed into an idiom familiar to him from his youth. It is a way of drawing attention to what is about to be said, less heavy than the affirmation of Rom. ix.1, but still formal in character – **I, Paul, say to you** – having the form of a solemn affidavit (cf.

2 Cor. x.1; Eph. iii.1). What is about to follow is something he wants his Galatian audiences to pay special attention to, something of particular importance to them; perhaps also a clarification of his own teaching on the subject, made necessary by insinuations that his teaching was different (see on v.11). The fact that he was the founder of the Galatian churches and knew the life of the circumcised 'from inside' (Schlier 231) would give his warning all the greater weight.

The solemn affirmation is **that if you are circumcised** (or middle, get yourselves circumcised), **Christ will benefit you not at all** (in the final reckoning – cf. v.5). For the first time in the letter Paul makes explicit what is the challenge confronting him in the Galatian churches: the other missionaries want the Galatians circumcised (cf. ii.3). The reasons why it was that such a demand could now have been made, despite the agreement at Jerusalem (ii.1–10), and why Paul does not now refer back to that agreement, may be linked. That is to say, the agreement may have become a dead letter, perhaps by diminution of Peter's influence in Jerusalem, or perhaps because nationalistic pressures in Judea made it inevitable that the Christian Jews should thus feel the need to express their Jewishness more unequivocally and to insist that Gentile converts to the Nazarenes should likewise identify themselves unequivocally with the Jewish people whose heritage they wanted to enter into (no doubt with reference to Gen. xvii.9–14).

The implication, once again (as in i.6–7 and iv.9–10), is that the deed had not yet been done (Burton 273); Paul's information, presumably, was that the Galatians were considering it. He knew that they were being enticed in that direction (i.6; ii.3; iv.9–10), but no doubt hoped that, even in the interval between the news leaving Galatia and Paul's letter returning there, they would not have taken the final step. This sequence of progressive 'judaizing' = observing the distinctively Jewish customs, with circumcision as the last step, is well enough known to us from elsewhere (Josephus, *War* ii.454; *Ant.* xx.41–5; Juvenal, *Sat.* xiv.96–104). Since it was circumcision which was the final great stumbling block which prevented so many Gentile sympathizers (God-fearers) from going the whole way to become proselytes, Paul could have good hope on this score, even if his information was not up to date. The observance of sabbaths and festivals (iv.10) was a large enough encroachment on their liberty in Christ; but the issue of circumcision was the decisive one. Until they had been circumcised their identity as Gentiles was still distinct. If Paul could stop them before they reached that point, he could still save the day for the freedom of the gospel (cf. ii.4; for the significance of circumcision for the Judaism of that period see further on ii.3).

That Paul could put the point in such a sharp antithesis – 'Christ will be of no benefit to you whatsoever' (for the verb cf. Rom. ii.25; 1 Cor. xiii.3; xiv.6) – indicates clearly how polarized the issue had become in Paul's mind. 'Circumcision' so much embodied and expressed Jewish identity, distinctively Jewish identity (Jews could be identified simply as 'the circumcision' – ii.7–9, 12; 'circumcision in statu confessionis' – Oepke 156), that it had become a mark of Jew as *distinct from* Gentile, not the mark of covenant with the one God of Jew *and* Gentile. A different locus for the identity of the people of God was therefore necessary. And where else than in God's Christ, the Messiah of God's people? Had it been possible to hold the two together, without the Jewishness of circumcision's being its predominant feature, the story of earliest Christianity might have been different. But, regrettably, in the Gentile mission, in Paul's view at least, circumcision became, in effect, a means of Jewish ideological and nationalistic imperialism. Whereas an identity firmly located in Christ (in belief in him and in reception of his Spirit) was independent of circumcision (v.6). Consequently, to make circumcision necessary in addition, was so to shift the focus from Christ as to abandon that solid foundation, so to modify the unconditional character of the grace expressed in the gospel, as to nullify the benefit of Christ completely.

3 The point is so important that Paul reaches instinctively for even more formal legal terminology (quite lost in NEB's 'you can take it from me'), and repeats his plea – **I testify** (by implication, on his own behalf; cf. Acts xx.26 and xxvi.22; Eph. iv.17; different voice from Gal. iv.15) **again** (repeating verse 2, not a warning given during his time in Galatia) **to everyone who is being circumcised** (Paul evidently feared a large-scale falling away, perhaps more or less all of his converts, and perhaps already happening), **that he is obligated to do the whole law.** The play on words between verses 2 and 3 should be noted: Christ will not benefit them (*ōphēlesei*), but, instead, they will be in debt (*opheiletēs*) to the law.

The force of Paul's argument here is often confused. Very unlikely is the suggestion that the 'agitators' in Galatia contented themselves merely with requiring circumcision (Lagrange 136), or played down its consequences (Schlier 232), or said nothing of other law-keeping (e.g. Burton 274; Mussner 347–8) – a policy which would have been hardly thinkable for a covenantal nomistic mind-set (contrast Lietzmann 37 – 'a few ritual observances'), and quite at odds with the typical Jewish understanding of circumcision as the first act of full covenant membership and obligation. For most Jews the proselyte's act of circumcision naturally entailed also commitment to 'judaize', to adopt the Jewish way of life as a whole (as in Esther viii.17 LXX; Eusebius, *Praep.Evang.* ix.22.5; Josephus, *Ant.* xiii.257; see also on ii.3 and vi.13). For most too, a policy of 'gradualism' (Sanders, *Law* 29) would usually have worked up to circumcision as the most challenging demand (for a Greek) rather than taking it as a starting point (see on ii.14 and v.2 third paragraph).

Nor is it likely that Paul reasoned as follows: (1) to accept circumcision, is (2) to accept the need to do the whole law, is (3) to assume that the whole law can be kept, is (4) to make acceptance by God dependent on keeping the whole law = legalism (see particularly Hübner 18–9, 36–9; 'the bookkeeping God of legalism' – Burton 277). The reasoning starts well (cf. after all Rom. ii.25), but begins to veer off course at (3). No more than in iii.10 is there any implication here that the logic under attack assumed the possibility (or necessity) of keeping the law in a complete, that is, perfect sense (so rightly Sanders, *Law* 27–9; see on iii.10). The mistake, once again, has been to individualize the teaching, as though Paul had in mind simply a sequence of individuals confronting each other, Jews and Gentiles, without any sense of the corporate dimension of a tradition which saw salvation in terms of membership of a people.

What is in view, rather, was the typical Jewish mind-set which understood 'doing the law' as the obligation of those within the covenant people, as that which marked out the covenant people, as the way to live within the covenant (iii.12 – Lev. xviii.5). 'To do the whole law' was 'to abide by everything which has been written in the book of the law to do them' (iii.10 – Deut. xxvii.26); that is, (in Paul's perspective not least) to adopt a Jewish way of life through and through. In other words, 'the Jewish way of life' was a complete package (this is the force also of passages like Matt. v.18–19, James ii.10 and *m. Abot* iv.2); though its integrated wholeness ('works of the law', covenantal nomism) could, as we have seen, be focused in a single issue like food laws (as in ii.11–14 and *4 Macc.* v.20–1). To confuse this with the striving of an individual for (in effect) an attainable sinless perfection is the very denigration of Judaism which has caused so much pain in Jewish and Christian attempts to understand each other (see e.g. those cited by Sanders, *Paul* 5–6 and Longenecker 227). No Jew that we know of thought of the Jewish way of life as a *perfect* life, that is, without any sin or failure. Rather, it was a *total* way of life which, through the cult, its sacrifices and atonement, provided a means of dealing with sin and failure. That, no doubt, is what Paul meant in Phil. iii.6 when he described his previous way of life 'within Judaism' as 'without blemish' – without blemish, because all blemishes were covered by the offering of unblemished animals in sacrifice (see again on iii.10).

It is this total way of life to which Paul refers here. He reminds his would-be Gentile judaizers that what was being demanded of them was not simply a matter of a single act of circumcision, but a whole way of life, a complete assimilation and absorption of any distinctively Gentile identity into the status of Jewish proselyte. He must have been aware that it was just this completeness of identification with God's people Israel which no doubt was attractive to many of the Gentiles involved. But presumably he wanted them to be in no doubt that such a degree of assimilation allowed of no continuing residual Gentile identity, and that it made their previous commitment to Christ (in baptism) a pointless rite (v.4). He will also shortly make the point that once the focus of God's promise is seen to have shifted from law to Christ, it will also be seen that 'the whole law is fulfilled' by loving one's neighbour (see on v.14), not by living as a Jew.

4 To drive home the point Paul repeats what he had said in verse 2. **You have been estranged from Christ, you who are seeking to be justified by the law.** The second clause describes an attitude already repudiated in iii.11. As commonly in Greek (and in this letter), the present tense of the verb ('you who are being justified') can indicate an attempted but incomplete action – 'you want/are seeking to be justified' (BDF §319). The contrast between the tenses of the two clauses is striking: even the beginning of such an attempt (present tense) marks a decisive breach with Christ (aorist tense); to go down that road is to have turned one's back on Christ.

The final phrase could be translated 'in/within the law', as denoting an attempt to get within the area of safety marked out by the law, 'in the sphere of the law' (Burton 276), within the boundary of the law, that is, membership of the Jewish people (cf. Rom. ii.12; iii.19 = 'under the law'; see on iii.23). The assumption being criticized would then be that justification/ acquittal in the final judgement was a consequence of membership of the people to whom God had shown his special favour and with whom he had made his covenant. Only by complete identification with the Jewish people (by circumcision) could there be sure hope of participating in the final salvation promised to Israel. Alternatively, if the echo of iii.11 is deliberate, the phrase 'justified in/by the law' would have been intended as a shorthand for the fuller phrase, 'justified by/out of works of the law' (see on iii.11). But since the latter expresses the conviction that living in accordance with Jewish custom, including the distinctive Jewish rituals, is what maintains status within the covenant people, and thus ensures a favourable verdict in the final judgement, the meaning is not so very different.

The precise force of the metaphor in the first clause is hard to tie down, but it certainly denotes the ending of a relationship (the closest parallels are Rom. vii.2, 6) – thus 'released from, removed from, taken from the sphere of influence of' ('your relation with Christ is completely severed', NEB). Paul's point is that to insist on formal identification (through circumcision) with the Jewish people is so to diminish the significance of the Gentile converts' earlier relationship with Christ as to be equivalent to ending that relationship. The irony is that Paul saw the relationship with Christ as inclusive – of Gentile as well as Jew. But by thus making light of it, his Gentile judaizing converts were preventing it from having that universal significance. They, no doubt, did not see the two (relationship with Christ and full proselyte status) as in contradiction (cf. ii.15–16). But by insisting on assuming complete Jewish identity they forced Jesus back into the role of a purely Jewish messiah rather than that of last Adam and Lord of all.

The tragedy is that Paul's insistence on this universal significance of Christ has the sound of an intolerance equivalent to that which he contested and opens the door to the greater intolerance which has so marred Christian relations with the Jews over the centuries. All we can say is that polemic inevitably results in such intolerant-sounding statements: in order to counter the strong insistence that circumcision was essential to salvation (cf. Acts xv.1), Paul's repudiation had to be equally strong. It would be unwise, however, to give such polemical statements born of extreme provocation the central place in any rounded doctrinal statement.

To reinforce the warning Paul expresses it in an alternative metaphor: that of 'falling away' – **you have fallen away from grace** – like a withered flower falling off from its stem to the ground (James i.11; 1 Pet. i.24), or like a ship failing to hold the course which leads to safety and falling away into disaster (cf. Acts xxvii.26, 29). God's grace in Christ (see on i.6) is like the stem which supports the flower and through which the life-sustaining sustenance flows. Or like the channel which leads to

safety between the rocks of disaster, a course from which they
were in danger of being driven by dangerous currents and cross
winds. Once again the tense is aorist, indicating that the initial
succumbing to the urging of the other missionaries would
already be decisive – the means of sustenance already severed,
the channel to safety already lost. So decisive would be even the
initial decision that Christ alone and faith in Christ alone was
*in*sufficient for salvation. REB's 'you have put yourselves outside
God's grace' modifies the metaphor but reinforces the contrast of
two domains, one of law, one of grace. Since the latter enshrines
as its fundamental principle, unconditional grace, any attempt to
add a further fundamental principle (law) was equivalent in
Paul's eyes to abandoning the domain of grace altogether. When
such a fundamental principle was at stake the tolerance of a
both-and policy had to be resisted.

5 For (by contrast) **we** (the word is given the place of
emphasis) **by the Spirit, from faith,** precisely the 'we' who have
experienced the Spirit solely by faith, that is, Paul's audience and
Paul himself (the impact of the word order is often lost in
modern translations), **are awaiting eagerly the hope of
righteousness.** Paul does not dispute the common goal shared by
his readers, himself and the other missionaries in Galatia, as by
the people of Israel generally – 'the hope of righteousness'. The
difference is that the primary and sufficient basis of their hope
was their shared experience of the Spirit received by faith (see
on iii.2; note again the immediacy of the conjunction of Spirit
and faith – baptism is not mentioned), a basis which stress on
physical membership of the covenant people undermined rather
than enhanced. The difference was that 'by the Spirit, from faith'
continued to be the basis, primary and sufficient, so long as that
hope lay before them yet to be fully realized; to think that this
hope could be realized or made more certain in terms of the
flesh (see on iii.3) was to destroy that whole basis. Despite the
lack of the definite article with 'spirit', and the hesitations of
older commentators, it is clear enough that Paul had in mind the
divine Spirit (cf. iii.2 and 3; v.16, 17 and 18; v.22 and 25).

As before, 'righteousness' denotes the state of acceptability
before God, the status of acceptance by God – what is right in
his eyes (see on ii.21; also iii.6, 21). That was their shared hope:
to be thus accepted by God in the end, that is, in the final
judgement, to be the kind of person who will be at home in
God's kingdom. Clearly expressed here is the 'future tense' of
justification – to be justified/counted acceptable to God, not
simply as an initial act (conversion), but as a sustained

relationship with God culminating in the favourable verdict of the final judgement (see also ii.16d); talk of 'double justification' (see Betz 262 n.87), or 'two distinct justifications' (Cosgrove, *Cross* 150) is too static.

'Hope' (only here in Galatians, but quite common in Romans – e.g. v.2–5 and viii.20–5) will have its Jewish rather than Greek sense; that is, a confident expectation of good, rather than an uncertain anticipation of evil (cf. e.g. Sir. xlix.10; and see further *TDNT* ii.519–23); here used in the derived sense 'fulfilled hope' ('the righteousness for which we hope' – NIV; 'hoped-for righteousness' – Burton 279; cf. Tit. ii.13). Those who trust in God's grace alone can have firm confidence in the outcome of God's purpose.

That is no doubt why they can 'await it eagerly' (a thought Paul cherishes – Rom. viii.19, 23, 25; 1 Cor. i.7; Phil. iii.20). The word expresses the character of Christian existence as one of suppressed excitement, as of an adolescent awaiting her/his coming-of-age birthday, or of a family awaiting the home-coming of a dearly loved but long absent member. It thus underlines the 'already/not yet' character of Christian existence for Paul. Once again the implication is that this tension (confident but yet unfulfilled expectation) cannot be resolved or reduced by seeking to make the hope more certain (through circumcision). For the mode of waiting is the same unconditional openness to and reliance on God (faith) to which God gave the Spirit in the first place – the Spirit thus received being precisely the basis of that hope and guarantee of its fulfilment (Rom. viii.23; 2 Cor. i.22).

6 That Paul has been pushing a polemical point and not indulging in a theological aside (verse 5) is confirmed by verse 6. This Spirit-receiving, Spirit-reliant faith is alone the basis of confident hope of God's acceptance, **for** (the logical complement to what has just been said) **in Christ Jesus** – the key phrase summarizing Paul's preceding exposition (see on i.22 and ii.17), so not simply equivalent to 'in Christianity' (as Burton 279) – **neither circumcision** (see on ii.3 and v.2) **counts for anything** (usually intransitive, in the sense 'be strong, powerful, competent', or in the more closely parallel legal usage 'have force, be valid', or accounting usage 'be worth' – LSJ and MM, *ischuō*), **nor uncircumcision, but faith** (active trust, not 'the faith') **operating effectively** (we might translate 'energizing'; cf. ii.8 and iii.5) **through love**. Once again the point is that relationship to Christ means a radical reappraisal of what constitutes acceptability to God. In particular, it wholly

relativizes the traditional circumcision/non-circumcision distinction between Jews and Gentiles (see again on ii.3; cf. Col.
iii.11). Nor does he replace one ritual act (circumcision) by
another (baptism). For Paul, it was the fact that Gentiles were
being given the Spirit through faith which provided proof
sufficient that 'by Spirit, from faith' was the one necessary and
sufficient means of God's acceptance (iii. 1–5), a situation long
ago envisaged in scripture (iii.6–14), the mark of sharing in
Christ's sonship, heirs of the promise (iv.6–7). To be thus related
to God through his Son inevitably meant that other distinctions
became relatively unimportant, even those previously given
divine warrant (posed more radically still in vi.15).

The use of 'power' language ('counts for anything, operating
effectively') is noteworthy (the words are more closely juxtaposed
in James v.16). What are set in contrast are two conflicting
sources of power – rite and status, which are not merely rite and
status, but which give significance to everything else, which
provide a basis for the whole life before God, which determine
and characterize mind-set and community. On the one hand a
community and mind-set determined by a rite which divided
humanity into two thus sharply distinct classes ('the circumcision'
and 'the uncircumcision'; see on ii.3). On the other a mind-set
and community characterized by the openness of faith and the
spontaneity of love. Paul affirms that the coming of Christ and
of being 'in Christ' has radically reduced the power of the first
and has shown that effective power to change life and
community to the righteousness for which God looks lies in the
latter.

The contrast should not be reduced to the simple one of law
vs. love (or law vs. Spirit, or law vs. faith), for Paul is about to
maintain that love of neighbour is a fulfilling of the law (v.14),
thus reminding us that it was the particular understanding and
practice of the law which came to focus in Jewish insistence on
circumcision to which Paul took exception. At the same time it is
striking that Paul should sum up the contrast in the word 'love'
(*agapē* – bibliography in Betz 263 n. 98). For this had been a
little-used word previously (exceptional in non-biblical Greek
before the second or third century AD, and relatively rare in the
LXX, usually in reference to conjugal love). But the first
Christians seized it and made it their own (116 times in the NT),
particularly Paul (75 times in the Pauline corpus). This must be
because for them it expressed with exceptional fitness their sense
of the wholly generous, sacrificial and actively outreaching
concern on their behalf shown by God in Christ (ii.20). The love
which was the basis of their acceptance by God should also be its

271

expression (see also Mussner 353–4; and on v.22). Many commentators observe the close association of the Christian triad in verses 5–6 – faith, hope and love (cf. Rom. v.1–5; 1 Cor. xiii.13; 1 Thess. i.3; v.8).

Equally noteworthy is the dynamic character of the being 'in Christ'. Paul's conception of it could hardly be called static, a mere status. 'In Christ' is rather a source of energy, an energizing relationship which expresses itself in love. This verse provides a basis for response to any criticism of Paul's view of justification by faith – that it encouraged a passive quietism, an inactivism, or even antinomianism (Rom. iii.8; vi.1). On the contrary, Paul understood 'in Christ' as a new and living relationship active in well doing (see also vi.15). He understood justification as a sustained relationship with God through Christ (faith), which produced the righteousness looked for and acknowledged by God (love). The phrase is almost a single concept, faith-through-love, love-energized-faith. *This* is the faith he was talking about; not faith as a beginning and love as an outcome, as though the two were separate (far less faith as theory and love as practice – see Betz 264), but faith coming to expression in and through love. Such an understanding should not be seen as a threat to the *sola fide*; for it is precisely that complete reliance on and openness to God's grace which comes to expression in love; love not as a requirement of faith, but as its natural expression (Oepke 159). But we should do Paul the justice of taking him seriously when he claimed that only through this dynamic relationship could the law be fulfilled as God wanted it fulfilled (v.14; hence the closeness of the parallel with 1 Cor. vii.19, and Paul's talk of 'the obedience of faith' in Rom. i.5); 'the *sola-fide* principle is indeed an exclusive but not a restricted principle' (Mussner 353). Here Paul comes as close as he ever does to James (James ii.18), and 1 Tim. i.5 shows that the point was well taken in the school of Paul's disciples.

Those who advocate it are only trouble-makers v.7–12

(7) You were running well. Who hindered you in[1] not being persuaded regarding the truth? (8) That persuasion is not

---

1 The difficulty of relating the first three words ('Who hindered you?') to what follows evidently prompted some scribes to read these words as forming the question by themselves and to add a clarificatory phrase: 'Who hindered you? Obey no one in such a way as to disobey the truth. That obedience is not from him who calls you' (BDF §488 1b).

from him who calls you. (9) 'A little leaven leavens[1] the whole lump of dough'. (10) I am persuaded with regard to you in the Lord that you will not think otherwise; but he who troubles you will bear his judgement, whoever he is. (11) And I, brothers,[2] if I still[3] preach circumcision, why am I still persecuted? In that case the stumbling block of the cross has been removed. (12) Would that those who are upsetting you might also get themselves castrated.

Paul continues what he evidently saw as the make or break appeal to his Galatian converts. After this paragraph the tension will begin to slacken as he moves on to more general paraenesis, apart from the final anxious personal note of vi.11–16. But here the tension is at its sharpest and most nerve-racking – marked by a series of brief sentences, without elaborate syntax, or connectives (prior to verse 10b) – a series of abrupt expostulations, like snorts of indignation, betraying Paul's extreme anxiety that (as at Antioch, ii.11–14), he might lose out in Galatia also.

7 **You were running well** – one of Paul's favourite metaphors from the athletic race (see on ii.2), and consistent with the use of walking/running metaphors to indicate life-style and conduct (cf. e.g. Ps. cxix.32; see also on v.16). To be noted is the fact that Paul can use such a metaphor even when insisting so strongly as he does in this letter that the Christian way of life is a matter of faith from start to finish. 'Faith working through love' (v.6) requires more than walking – the concentration and self-discipline of the athlete.

The metaphor implies that some time had passed between the Galatians' conversion and the coming of the other missionaries – a time during which Paul was sufficiently in contact with them to know of their progress. This would fit with the hypothesis that Paul had been able to make a second visit to Galatia (see also iv.13; also Introduction §§4 and 6.1). That Paul could be referring to what he had observed during his (initial) visit is less

1 The most significant of a number of minor variations in this section attested by western texts is the reading here of *doloi* ('adulterates') instead of *zumoi* ('leavens'). As in the use of the same proverb in 1 Cor. v.6, the correction was presumably made in order to bring out the clearly negative sense of the metaphor (in contrast to Matt. xiii.33/Luke xiii.21, the only other occurrences of the verb in the NT).
2 See above p. 23 n. 3.
3 The first 'still' is omitted by a similar group of Western authorities, presumably on stylistic grounds, to avoid the inelegance of the immediate repetition three words later (Bruce 236).

likely; on neither of the main hypotheses was he able to spend much time in individual centres in Galatia. Nor are we made aware of regular lines of communication between Galatia and Paul (as later between Paul and Corinth). It is not impossible, of course, that Paul was simply making a charitable assumption regarding their performance prior to the intrusion of the 'agitators'.

Who hindered you? (cf. iii.1). Elsewhere Paul uses the verb to indicate his experience of finding himself prevented from making a desired journey (Rom. xv.22; 1 Thess. ii.18). But here a very literal translation of the verb ('cut in') fits well with the metaphor of a race, perhaps even suggesting that the more modern-sounding usage (to 'cut in' in front of someone else) was already current; so NIV – 'Who cut in on you and kept you from obeying the truth?' (see Bruce 234; Longenecker 230). The answer presumably is the other missionaries: by pushing in front of the Galatians they have caused the latter to stumble (cf. v.11). But Paul may imply more sinister forces at work behind his opponents; in 1 Thess. ii.18 the hindering is attributed to Satan; and here the singular stands in opposition to 'him who called you' (verse 8) = God (*TDNT* iii.856–7). That the question indicates genuine ignorance on Paul's part, and that there were no opponents from outside the Galatian churches, only some of the Galatians themselves becoming drawn to traditional Judaism (Munck) is less likely: the implication of the imagery here, as of i.6–9, is of some intervention from outside the Galatian congregations themselves; and the question itself is a rhetorical strategy to force the auditors to answer it for themselves.

The intensity of Paul's feeling at this point is probably sufficient explanation of the difficult grammatical transition to the next phrase – **in not being persuaded** (whether by design or consequence) **regarding the truth** (see p. 272 n. 1). The verb means basically 'persuade' (see also on i.10); in the passive, as here, 'be persuaded', and so 'obey' (thus NIV, NJB – 'obey'; NEB/REB 'follow' is unnecessarily remote from the Greek and throws the metaphor of a race into some confusion). The language was evidently quite important for Paul since he repeats it in verse 8 ('That persuasion') and in verse 10 ('I am persuaded') – a linkage in thought which is usually lost in modern translation (e.g. NIV – 'obey . . . persuasion . . . I am confident'). 'The truth' is, of course, 'the truth of the gospel' (see on ii.5), here expressed in absolute terms ('the truth').

It should not be ignored that Paul thought of accepting the gospel thus in terms of an intellectual process of being persuaded or convinced as to its veracity, as distinct from some irrational experience from which the mind could be disengaged (cf. iii.2, 5 and see also on iv.6). The dispute between Paul and the other missionaries was a matter of attempting to demonstrate the most persuasive interpretation of the scriptures relating to Abraham's heirs. Paul's surprise was occasioned by the fact that the force of his exposition, wedded to their own experience of the Spirit (iii.2–5; cf. v.10 – 'in the Lord'), had not been enough to convince his readers and to prevent them from being thrown out of their stride by the intervention of the 'agitators'.

8 **That** (literally, the) **persuasion** (a word not attested in Greek before this – see Betz 265 – but clearly referring to the other missionaries' explanation of what participation in the inheritance of Abraham requires; cf. Ignatius, *Rom.* iii.3) **is** (the verb has to be supplied) **not from him who calls you** (that is, as always in Paul, God himself – see on i.6). The present participle indicates not so much a constant invitation by God to the Galatians, as a description of God: God is one who calls, who invites, summons (as in Rom. iv.17; ix.11; 1 Thess. ii.12; v.24). Since the verb as used by Paul often has the sense of an effectual summons (again Rom. iv.17; ix.11; see again on i.6), its use here highlights a tension in Paul's theology of grace; how is it that those who have so experienced God's grace, drawing them to himself in the way it did (iii.2–5), can now disregard that call and succumb to teaching which, however persuasive on one level, was so much at odds with that experience? The impossibility of reconciling divine initiative and human *respons*ibility in an abstract formula, outside the particularity of infinitely diverse specific situations, is as clear here as anywhere.

As earlier (i.6–9; ii.3–6, 11–14; iv.8–11, 16–17), Paul was so convinced of the rightness of his gospel that anything which put in jeopardy its central emphasis (God's grace through faith in Christ) simply could not be from God.

9 With an abrupt change of metaphor Paul indicates a further facet of his concern – '**A little leaven leavens the whole lump of dough**'. It is clear that he is citing a proverbial saying (quite properly put in quotation marks by NEB, REB and NIV): it is not attested elsewhere as such, but Paul uses precisely the same words in 1 Cor. v.6; and the fact that the process of fermentation in bread-making required only a small piece of yeast (leaven) was so well known as to lend itself to such proverbial usage (so also Matt. xiii.33/Luke xiii.21; *Gos. Thom.* 96). That leaven was also a symbol of something unacceptable to God, fermentation as a process of corruption, was also a widespread perception in the ancient world – attested in Plutarch, *Quaest. Rom.* 289F and Philo, *Cong.* 169, *Spec.Leg.* i.291, 293 (Philo reflecting on the prohibition of leaven from offerings at the altar – Lev. ii.11; contrast *Spec. Leg.* ii.182–5); so also in Mark viii.15 pars, Ignatius, *Magn.* x.2; and the whole significance of leaven for the Passover celebration – Exod. xii.14–20; Deut. xvi.1–8; 1 Cor. v.7–8 (see further *TDNT* ii.902–6). The 'little leaven' is best understood in reference to the teaching of the 'agitators': Paul's fear clearly was that the teaching once accepted would corrupt the whole gospel (cf. ii.14–16); or that once some of his converts had been persuaded to accept the teaching of the other missionaries, the rest would be less able to resist (cf. ii.13); or, alternatively, that the acceptance of this teaching by even a few in the Galatian churches would be sufficient to destroy the harmony of the Galatian churches and to undermine the persuasiveness of the gospel for others in Galatia. The point of the proverb is clear enough, however, and Paul makes no attempt to indicate a specific reference for it. So we need not assume that he intended his audience in Galatia to make only one application of the proverb. Where the cap fitted . . . Since it is a proverbial saying and not a description of events in Galatia, it cannot serve as evidence of how far the teaching of the other missionaries had spread, but it at least supports the view that the process was not long under way.

10 Hence Paul's concern to indicate how completely persuaded on the matter he himself was – in the hope that his readers might share his own conviction and confidence in the face of the 'agitators'. **I am persuaded**, a favourite expression in Paul, reflecting his confidence in God (Rom. viii.38; Phil. i.6), in the gospel (Rom. xiv.14), in his relationship with his readers (Phil. i.25; ii.24), or, as here, in his readers themselves (Rom. xv.14; 2 Cor. ii.3; 2 Thess. iii.4; Phm. 21), in each case the perfect passive indicating a firm and fixed assurance (*TDNT* vi.6), **with regard to you** (an unusual formulation, probably, once again, reflecting something of the agitation in Paul's mind) **in the Lord** (that is, as usual, Christ). The last phrase goes with the verb (not with 'you', as NEB, NJB), part of Paul's characteristic expression (Rom. xiv.14; Phil. ii.24; 2 Thess. iii.4). Presumably this is why Paul prefers 'in the Lord' to his more regular 'in Christ', since his confidence was rooted precisely in the Lordship of Christ Jesus (see on i.3): he could be *so* confident since his confidence was derived directly from his own relationship with Christ as Lord, from his commission from the Lord Christ, and from his conviction that Christ as Lord was directing his affairs and overseeing his relationships. In other words, it was the confidence of submission to what he perceived as God's will in and through Christ, rather than the confidence of arrogance in his own status or opinion (even though the line between the two will ever be wafer-thin). Otherwise 'in the Lord' had most of the overtones of 'in Christ' (see on i.22).

His confidence was **that you will not think otherwise**, that is, hold a view different from Paul's (cf. Rom. xii.16; xv.5; 2 Cor. xiii.11; Phil. ii.2; iii.15; iv.2; 2 Clem. xvii.3); 'wrong view' (NEB/REB) goes beyond the Greek, though no doubt so far as Paul was concerned, to 'think otherwise' on this critical issue was wrong. The expression of confidence is, of course, rhetorical: by thus expressing his confidence in his auditors he both strengthens the impression that they were on the same side and thus reinforces the persuasiveness of his appeal; at all events, the issue is not yet settled. That the appeal is not merely rhetorical (Paul in reality fearful of the outcome of his letter) is probably indicated by the verb, which indicates a more settled way of thinking – 'form or hold an opinion, set one's mind on'. Paul's confidence, sustained by his own sense of commission from the exalted Lord Jesus and continuing submission to Jesus as his Lord, was that, however much the Galatians swithered back and forth on this issue, their final and lasting decision would be to side with Paul and to stand firm with the gospel which first brought them to faith in Christ. The fact that his letter was preserved and valued, that is, by (at least some of) the Galatians, indicates that his confidence was not (entirely) misplaced.

The corollary (**but**) of his own firm conviction as to the rightness of his understanding of the gospel was that **he who troubles you**, the trouble-maker (see on i.7), **will bear his judgement**. The latter verb is slightly unusual, though talk of judgement/condemnation seems to have allowed a fairly wide range of associated verbs (BAGD, *krima* 4b), and cf. 2 Kings xviii.14 LXX. The sense is of bearing, or enduring distress or trouble; the verb becomes prominent in ch. vi (vi.2, 5, 17). The idea of divine judgement was common in the ancient world (see e.g. *TDNT* iii.933–5); but as with Paul's other references to the theme, we need not think simply of the final judgement (cf. Rom. ii.2–3; iii.8; xiii.2; 1 Cor. xi.29, 34). Paul's conviction was that opposition to his gospel on this point would incur divine retribution of some sort (cf. i.8–9; 2 Cor. xi. 15; 1 Thess. ii.16).

It is unclear why Paul speaks in the singular – he who troubles you, **whoever he is**. It cannot be that there was only one opponent (as i.7 and v.12 confirm). But it could be that there was one prominent leader of the other missionaries (as Paul was the leader of his mission team). If so, it is idle to speculate who he might have been (see Mussner 358 n. 104), even though 'whoever he is' suggests someone of prominence, and several think that the Jerusalem leadership, or James in particular, must stand in the background (e.g. Oepke 160 and Barrett, *Freedom* 68; cf. the allusive and equally diminishing 'those of repute' in ii.2, 6). It is equally possible, however, that Paul's intention was simply to particularize his warning to each and every one of the other missionaries (cf. i.8–9). We have to imagine a number of small house churches in Galatia, at whose meetings Paul's letter would be read, and in whose midst on that very occasion might be one of the other missionaries.

11 Paul's disjointed prose, indicative of his irritation at the tactics of his opponents and of his anxiety and determination to provide a decisive counter to their arguments, turns abruptly to a different point. **And I** (as in the preceding verse, given the place of emphasis, distancing him from 'the trouble-maker'), **brothers** (see on i.2 and 11), **if I still preach circumcision** (see also on ii.3 and v.2), **why am I still persecuted?** To what it is Paul is referring has been a matter of lengthy and continued debate. There is general agreement that he must be alluding to some claim made by the other missionaries (the news of which, presumably, reached Paul along with the news of the likely disaffection of the Galatian churches). What it was they said about Paul is less clear.

(1) That he had originally 'preached circumcision' during his time 'in Judaism' (i.13–14) (e.g. Burton 286; Bornkamm, *Paul* 12; Longenecker 233)? But we have no indication that Paul was engaged in any evangelistic work prior to his conversion, and the suggestion runs counter to the evidence that second-Temple Judaism was not missionary minded (McKnight). The hypothesis would hardly explain the language anyway ('still preach circumcision').

(2) That Paul's circumcision-free gospel among the Gentiles was not widely known among the more traditionally minded Christian Jews (Howard's principal thesis in *Crisis*), so that the claim that Paul 'still preached circumcision' was simply mistaken? But it is difficult to believe that the terms of Paul's gospel to the Gentiles were not better known among those who counted circumcision important. The task of the other missionaries seems precisely to have been directed to remedying a mission strategy and situation which was only too well known among Christian-Jewish traditionalists (see further Introduction §§6.2–3).

(3) That Paul envisages the possibility of his adopting the policy of circumcising Gentiles – 'If I am yet to preach circumcision . . .'; which possibility should cause his opponents to refrain from persecuting him in the hope of winning him to their cause – 'why am I still or yet (=despite this) persecuted' (so Mussner 359)? But this is a less natural reading, since it requires different senses for the two uses of *eti* ('yet'), which otherwise are nicely balanced in sense and give the question its force. The suggestion that Paul envisaged a purely hypothetical case (Ridderbos 193–4), while technically possible (BDF §372(3)), likewise runs aground on the repeated *eti.*

(4) That Paul turns here to other opponents, the enthusiasts, who accused Paul of not being free enough from his Jewishness (particularly Lütgert and Ropes)? But this disrupts the sequence of thought entirely (on the 'two-front' hypothesis see also Introduction §5; Oepke 161–2, 164).

(5) That Paul's opponents were referring to Paul's warnings against the desires of the flesh, understood by them as expressing 'the ethical meaning of circumcision', and so as 'preaching circumcision' (P. Borgen, 'Paul Preaches Circumcision and Pleases Men', *Paul and Paulinism,* C. K. Barrett Festschrift, ed. M. D. Hooker & S. G. Wilson [London: SPCK, 1982] 37–46, here 41)? But this throws the thought into confusion (the thought is of literal circumcision throughout this section), and were it the case, Paul could hardly have proceeded at once to precisely such a warning against the flesh (v.13ff.) without at least some further clarification.

(6) That Paul was accused by the other missionaries of being inconsistent: that although he preached a circumcision-free gospel to the Galatians, he continued to 'preach circumcision' among Jews? This is the most common explanation and is still the most plausible. Writing probably within two or three years of Galatians, Paul spoke quite openly of his principle of accommodation: 'to those under the law I became as one under the law . . . to those outside the law I became as one outside the law' (1 Cor. ix.20–1; cf. also vii.18–19). To those who measured truth by uniformity of teaching and righteousness by uniformity of practice, such a principle must have appeared unprincipled and inconsistent, and therefore as self-condemned and indefensible (such is always the attitude of the fundamentalist who cannot recognize the relativeness of all expressions of truth and the context-conditionedness of all conduct). There is also a tradition of Paul's actually practising circumcision, in accordance with that principle, even in the midst of his Gentile mission – the circumcision of Timothy 'because of the Jews' in Acts xvi.3.

This is precisely the sort of report, perhaps even this very report, that his Galatian opponents would seize on – all the more so since the incident happened in Lystra (south Galatia) immediately prior to Paul's excursion through (north) Galatia (Acts xvi.6). The argument would be obvious: Paul is inconsistent; he says circumcision does not matter, and yet he had Timothy circumcised; so his own actions belie his words; despite what he has taught you (the Galatians) he *does* regard circumcision as important (the formulation '*preach* circumcision' may be their elaboration of Paul's position, to highlight his inconsistency; or Paul's own formulation, in parallel to 'preach Christ', as in 1 Cor. i.23, xv.12 and 2 Cor. iv.5). It does not take much imagination to see how such an argument could sow doubts in the minds of Paul's converts and generally cause confusion in the Galatian churches, leaving them open in their new uncertainty to the persuasiveness of the 'other gospel'. The verse provides no real support for the view that Paul agreed to the circumcision of Titus (see on ii.3).

Paul, we should note, does not actually deny the claim (a fact which may be taken to reinforce the historical value of Acts xvi.3), but simply goes on to show its inconsistency with continued hostility to himself. The logic is clear: if he did indeed 'preach circumcision', then he should not be persecuted, that is, presumably, by 'those of the circumcision' (see on ii.12). The response is not very strong: the key fact remained, that he did *not* preach circumcision to the Gentiles. But since the claim against him itself was so lacking in cogency and force, Paul presumably thought that a dismissive *ad hominem* response was sufficient.

To be noted again is the talk of persecution as a continuing feature of relationships between Jews (Christian Jews?) and the new outreach of the Nazarene sect to the Gentiles (see also on iv.29 and vi.12; cf. Rom. viii.35; 1 Cor. iv.12; 2 Cor. iv.9; xi.24; xii.10; 1 Thess. ii.14–16; 2 Thess. i.4).

Paul, however, does not leave it there. Although he does not stop to discuss or explain his policy regarding circumcision (of Jews like Timothy), or his larger principle of accommodation (1 Cor. ix.20–1), he cannot refrain from reminding his readers of what was at stake in the controversy in Galatia. **In that case** (were I actually continuing to regard circumcision as essential to the gospel and participation in the inheritance of Abraham) **the stumbling block of the cross has been removed**. The image of 'stumbling block' (BAGD, *skandalon* – 'that which gives offence or causes revulsion, that which arouses opposition, an object of anger or disapproval') was almost exclusively biblical in origin

(*TDNT* vii.339–43) and featured regularly in earliest Christian self-understanding and apologetic (e.g. Matt. xvi.23; xviii.7; Rom. xvi.17; 1 John ii.10; Rev. ii.14; Barn. iv.9). In reference to the cross (that is, self-evidently, Jesus' death on a cross; see iii.1; vi.12, 14), the basic stumbling block, presumably, was the claim that the Messiah had been crucified (so explicitly 1 Cor. i.23; see also on iii.13; cf. Ignatius, *Eph.* xviii.1), this being seen by Christian Jews as the fulfilment of Isa. viii.14 (Rom. ix.33; 1 Peter ii.8) (K. Müller, *Anstoss und Gericht: Eine Studie zum jüdischen Hintergrund des paulinischen Skandalon-Begriffs* [Munich: Kösel, 1969] 115–20; Mussner 360–1). A crucified Messiah was presumably the most offensive point of the earliest Christian reworking of the more traditional messianic expectation of a royal, triumphant figure (as in *Pss. Sol.* xvii). But here Paul probably had in mind also the particular significance of the cross which he has been drawing out in this letter – the cross as marking the end of a clear dividing line between covenant Jew and outlaw Gentile (see on ii.21, iii.13–14 and vi.12), rather than as directed against legal achievement and self-righteousness (as e.g. Schlier 240). Whether this is what constituted the cross as a stumbling block to non-Christian Jews in 1 Cor. i.23 is less clear (1 Cor. i.24), but it was the chief factor in Paul's own career as a persecutor (see on i.13–14); the phrase itself ('offence of the cross') may indeed have originated with Paul himself at that time (Longenecker 233). More to the point here, the cross so understood would seem to have been a stumbling block to Christian Jews (the other missionaries) as well: they could accept the redefinition of Messiah which Jesus' death and resurrection made necessary; but they could not accept that a further redefinition of relationships between Jew and Gentile was also necessary (cf. ii.12 and on ii.15–17; see also my 'How Controversial was Paul's Christology?', *From Jesus to John. New Testament Christologies in Current Perspective*, M. de Jonge Festschrift, ed. M. C. de Boer [Sheffield Academic Press, 1993] 146–65). On such an understanding, the logic of Paul's argument becomes clear: if he indeed preached circumcision, he would after all be reinforcing the distinction and barrier between covenant Jew and outlaw Gentile, and thus removing or abolishing (see on iii.17 and v.4) the offence which his gospel of the cross caused for the more traditional Jewish understanding of God's covenant promise and purpose. 'The persecuted apostle' (we may add 'to the Gentiles') 'is to a certain extent the epiphany of the crucified Christ' (Mussner 362).

We should not fail to note that for Paul, and the first Christians generally, it was essential that the cross should be perceived as an offence; otherwise scripture would not be fulfilled (they would all have agreed on that), human pride in ethnicity and 'works of the law' would remain undisturbed (Paul's main point here), and confidence in human wisdom would remain unchallenged (1 Cor. i.18–25). It is precisely the fact that the cross is an offence that makes 'the theology of the cross' such a powerful critical principle in Christian theology and such a weighty counterbalance to all pride of position, nationhood or life-style. Paul's most thoroughgoing application of this principle is in 2 Corinthians.

It is possible that Paul is harking back to the earlier image of the athletic race (v.7) and making a complex play on the idea of stumbling block, an obstacle in the Galatians' track over which they could not help but stumble. It was his opponents' advocacy of circumcision (and assumption that Paul still regarded it as essential) which constituted such a stumbling block – thus echoing the OT usage as reflected in the LXX occurrences of the same word (*TDNT* vii.342 – 'cause of ruin'), more closely than elsewhere in the NT (though cf. Rom. ix.33; xiv.13; 1 Peter ii.8). To remove the indispensable stumbling block of the cross (by maintaining the barrier between Jew and Gentile which it had abolished) was to replace it with a stumbling block which was wholly destructive.

12 With a final sarcastic and dismissive snort Paul turns his back on the 'agitators'. **Would that** (the form suggesting part irritation, part humour; *ophelon* with future indicative indicating an attainable wish – BDF §384) **those who are upsetting you** (a term not used in classical literature, but known in papyri – MM, *anastatoō*; also Dan. vii.23 LXX, Acts xvii.6 and xxi.38, where it indicates considerable disturbance) **might also get themselves castrated** (the force of the middle – BAGD, *apokoptō* 2). The imagery in mind, of course, is the rite of circumcision: since they are so concerned with cutting off foreskins, they should go the whole way and cut off the whole organ! Implicit is the recognition of the sexual significance of the act of circumcision – still evident in the practice of circumcision around the time of puberty or before marriage (among some Muslims). The original significance of the rite is lost, but the implication is of a dedication of the male sexual organ and means of reproduction to God; on the analogy of Lev. xix.23–4 (*TDNT* vi.75), the removal of the foreskin (the first three years' fruit of newly planted trees) allows subsequent fruitfulness (production of semen, procreation) to be counted as holy. More to the point here is the ruling of Deut. xxiii.1 that no eunuch could participate in Israel's assembly for worship ('he whose testicles are crushed or whose male member is cut off shall not enter the assembly of the Lord'; cf. Lev. xxi.20; xxii.24). The wish then is a savage one: would that the knife might slip in the hand of those who count circumcision indispensable to participation in the assembly of the Lord, so that they might find the same rules excluding themselves. Paul expresses the wish that a rite understood as one of dedication and commitment to Yahweh might become one which excluded from the presence of Yahweh (in the worshipping assembly).

There is something shocking about the vehemence of Paul's language and of the wish itself — 'one of the bitterest and coarsest expressions to be found in all his letters' (Duncan 161). For eunuchs were among the most despised groups of men in the ancient world (Josephus, *Ant.* iv.290–1; Lucian, *Eunuch* 6). And self-castration was a feature of the cult of Cybele which had its home in Galatia; so that Paul's wish in effect was for the other missionaries to lapse into a form of paganism which could not but be thoroughly despised by Jews. Paul may even be playing on the abhorrence Greeks and Romans had for circumcision itself; Hadrian was to compare it with castration (*TDNT* vi.78). Recognition of the horrific nature of what Paul was saying has resulted in various attempts to take the words in a figurative sense — 'cut themselves off = separate themselves from the Christian community' (Ramsay 437–40). But the use of the term in the sense of castration/emasculation is too well known; and in the context (where circumcision is the issue) that sense is unavoidable here (see particularly *TDNT* iii.853–5).

We should, however, (1) remember that such violent metaphors would be much more in character in days when similar and far worse acts of violence were common occurrences; Paul in the heat of the moment lapses into an earthiness which he elsewhere normally avoids. (2) Moreover, such coarse humour related to the sexual organs and reproductive processes is universal; it is the sort of joking remark which might be tossed off lightly, without serious intent (he could hardly have expected it to happen or to be taken seriously), perhaps even to lighten the seriousness of the appeal in this most crucial section of the letter. 'Paul is conforming here to the practice of diatribe preachers, when he salts his arguments with a joke. The ridiculing of eunuchs was a standby of the diatribe preacher' (Betz 270, with documentation). (3) An allusion to Jesus' words recalled in Mark ix.43, 45, about cutting off an offending member (using the same two concepts of 'cause, offence/stumbling block' and 'cut off') is not impossible. In which case Paul would be saying that even such mutilation is preferable to replacing the offence of the cross with the offence of circumcision. (4) Not least, we should also allow the possibility that Paul's intention was actually to undermine the significance, attributed by Judaism especially, to both circumcision and castration. The remark has in view precisely those who made so much of both circumcision and the state of castration (cf. Phil. iii.2). It has the force of a *reductio ad absurdum* argument: one slice with the knife = acceptability to God; another slice with the knife = total unacceptability to God. The ridiculousness of such distinctions makes the requirement of the one (circumcision) as much as the prohibition of the other (the castrated) equally ridiculous in God's sight.

D   The responsibilities of the Spirit's freedom   v.13–vi.10

1   FREEDOM MEANS FREEDOM TO SERVE ONE ANOTHER IN LOVE   v.13–15

(13) For you were called to freedom, brothers;[1] only not the freedom for opportunity to the flesh, but through love[2] serve one another. (14) For the whole law is fulfilled in one word,[3] in the well-known, 'You shall love your neighbour as yourself'. (15) But if you bite[4] and tear at one another, look out lest you are consumed by one another.

The main thrust of Paul's appeal to the Galatians is now complete. But all passion was not spent. For Paul was well aware that freedom is a heady mixture. The removal of old constraints can easily lead to a wider breakdown of discipline. The forces marshalled to break through the earlier servitude may lose direction and cohesion, once that purpose has been attained.

1 See above p. 23, n. 3.
2 A few manuscripts and versions read 'by the love of the Spirit'.
3 Marcion replaced 'in one word' by 'among you'; only among Christians could the law conceivably have been fulfilled.
4 There is a nice word play in the Greek between the final imperative of verse 13 and the first verb of verse 15 (Borse 193), which could be brought out thus: 'serve one another . . . but if you savage one another' (*douleuete allēlois . . . allēlous daknete*).

Liberty once gained might easily become the occasion for the licence of self-indulgence. History had already shown this often enough in the Greek city states in the corruption of democracy into demagoguery. And no doubt also at the individual level in the lapse of sophisticated Epicureanism into egoistic hedonism. Paul cannot have been unaware of such dangers: he may already have been all too conscious of criticisms of his own teaching to similar effect – free grace means free sin (cf. Rom. iii.8; vi.1; see also on ii.17), 'all things are lawful' (1 Cor. vi.12; x.23); and it may well have been concern about lack of clear guidelines for daily conduct which gave life under the law an added attraction to many of the Galatians (Betz 273; Barclay, *Obeying* 60–74). Hence the need to spell out how freedom once granted and preserved should conduct itself without the old constraints. How could freedom be prevented from lapsing into licence, from falling into the new servitude of self-indulgence? If the Jewish way of life was not to be accepted as the life-style for his Gentile converts, if it was rather to be regarded as equally unacceptable as their old pagan ways, what then? If the law, taken straightforwardly as the other missionaries argued, did not provide the blueprint for daily conduct, what did? This is the burden of what follows (v.13–vi.10).

There is no difficulty, therefore, in understanding the 'why' of the transition from the exposition and appeal of iii.1–v.12 to the exhortation of v.13–vi.10. It is simply a particular instance of a natural pattern which we find elsewhere in Paul anyway – exposition followed by exhortation (cf. particularly Rom. i–xi and xii–xv). We need not assume use of fixed or established catechetical material. On the contrary, here the terms of the paraenesis seem largely to have been determined by the circumstances addressed – with freedom as the appropriate link word (v.13), and Spirit as the dominant category (v.16–18, 22, 25; vi.1, 8) replacing law. This was precisely the challenge with which Paul was faced: having made so much of his appeal to the Galatians depend on their experience of the Spirit (iii.2–5), it was now incumbent on him to explain how the Spirit functioned to provide a viable pattern of living. A theology of freedom, particularly freedom from the law, which did not explain how that theology translated into daily living would have been a theology of irresponsibility.

It is quite unnecessary therefore, and betrays a lack of appreciation of the practicality with which Paul sought to live out his theology, to argue that v.13ff. can only be explained as Paul turning to take on a second front – Galatian enthusiasts (as again particularly Lütgert and Ropes). An over-enthusiastic tendency is a natural recoil from long constraint. It was the *same* people who, if they resisted the logical attractiveness of life under the law, might rebound into a too indiscriminate lawlessness. That is to say, we need not assume that a condition of enthusiastic lawlessness already existed in Galatia; Paul would have attached more rebukes to his exhortations and warnings had that been the case. No doubt there were some in the Galatian congregations with a greater propensity to over-enthusiasm, as there were others with a greater propensity to the orderedness of the traditional Jewish life-style. But that there were two clear factions or fronts is an unnecessary hypothesis (so most; see also Introduction §5).

V.13–15 provide an effective introduction to the complete section (v.13–vi.10), with v.13 in particular striking an opening chord which is then elaborated in what follows:

v.13–15 – a thematic statement contrasting (a) freedom for
the flesh and (b) love of one another briefly elaborated;
v.16–24 – (a) the contrast between freedom of the flesh and
freedom of the Spirit set out in fuller detail;
v.25–vi.5 – (b) love of one another given practical exposition;
vi.6–10 – a concluding, more general paraenesis.

To be noted is the way in which reference to the Spirit provides the key statement at the beginning of each of the two major paragraphs (v.16; v.25; note also vi.8), and how the whole section revolves round and hangs upon the three thematic terms – Spirit (v.16–18, 22, 25; vi.1, 8), law (v.14, 18, 23; vi.2) and love (v.13–14, 22) – the first two in particular serving as a reminder of how much Paul's exhortation was conditioned by the particular crisis confronting him in Galatia.

13 The continuity of thought with the appeal just made (**For**) expresses itself in the continuing passion with which Paul turns to look at the other side of freedom: **you** (in the place of emphasis), *you*, whatever may be true of the trouble-makers, **were called** (that is, by God, emphasizing once again the divine initiative, the basis of all moral effort – see on i.6 and v.8) **to freedom** (see on ii.4 and v.1). We should also note that he addresses the same complete constituency as before – **brothers** (iv.31; v.11; see on i.2 and 11). All this suggests that it is the same freedom which Paul had in mind, that he was all too conscious of the dangers of the theme, and that it was the roundedness of his readers' freedom which he sought to safeguard and promote. The point he now wished to bring out was that the call to freedom was a call not merely *from* the older enslavement, but also a call *to* a new responsibility. The freedom of God has both aspects, otherwise it is not God's freedom. The liberty which does not ask, Liberty for what?, is a dangerous commodity.

Paul saw this clearly – **only not the freedom for opportunity to the flesh.** According to an old Greek saying, 'the free man is one who lives as he chooses'. The thought that such freedom could be dangerous is hardly unexpected or surprising (cf. 1 Pet. ii.16; 1 Cor. viii.9). The word translated 'opportunity' (*aphormē*) means literally 'the starting point or base of operations for an expedition', and so 'occasion, pretext or opportunity' (BAGD, *aphormē*). Only Paul uses it in the NT. In itself it is not a negative metaphor (cf. 2 Cor. v.12), though in Paul's other usage it denotes an opportunity deceitfully gained and used for discreditable or evil purposes (Rom. vii.8, 11; 2 Cor. xi.12; so also 1 Tim. v.14).

By 'flesh', as usual, Paul means the human condition in its belongingness to this world – that is, the weakness of the human being in contrast to the power of the divine, the dependency of the creature on the satisfaction of bodily appetites, and the tendency of the physical body to decay and corruption (see on ii.16, 20). Translations like 'lower/unspiritual nature' (NEB/REB) lose the wholeness of the concept, and 'sinful nature' (NIV, Fung 244) implies an innate sinfulness of the human condition rather than a propensity towards what is sinful or weakness before the power of sin (Rom. vii.14–25); 'flesh' needs to be retained as an important theological concept (so also Barrett, *Freedom* 71–2). Paul did not think that this human condition can be escaped (ii.20; iv.14). His fear was rather that life would be lived solely on that level, that satisfaction of bodily appetites (self-indulgence in all its forms) would become the chief·factor in living, that freedom from the clear guidelines of a nomistic life-style would result in a casting off of all restraint. It is a sad commentary on the human condition that what is human *weakness* regularly becomes the *dominant* factor in determining life-style. That 'egocentrism' (Schlier 242) is in view is also indicated by the antithetical 'serve one another'. The continuity of his thought is confirmed when we recall that Paul also saw his fellow Jewish opponents as also putting too much stress on the flesh (see on iii.3; iv.23, 29; vi.13): too much dependence on or priority to the flesh either way (ethnic identity, or self-indulgence) were dangers equally to be avoided. This typically Pauline range of reference for 'flesh' strongly suggests that it is his word, here as elsewhere, rather than that of his opponents.

The safeguard against giving too much scope to the flesh was not to look at once to a system of regulations embracing the whole of life, in all its eventualities, **but through love** (literally 'the love', referring, presumably, back to v.6) **to serve one another**. 'The person who loves is the free person' (Mussner 369). Paul had already indicated that love, not law or particular blanket requirements, was the key corollary to grace and faith (see on v.6) − continuity with the preceding section being thus again underlined. Now he begins to spell out more fully what 'faith working effectively through love' means in practice. The implication of the contrast − love as the fundamental energizing principle rather than law − is that moral living and communal harmony require a depth of personal engagement and motivation welling up from passion deeply felt which no external rule or ritual can provide of itself. Such love also makes possible a spontaneity and adaptability to the demands of each specific situation which rules applied whatever the circumstances can never match. In so saying, of course, Paul was simply putting into his own words the insight of earlier teachers of Israel, as for example, Deut. x.16 and Jer. xxxi.33–4.

The use of the verb, literally, 'to perform the duties of a slave', would be intended to have some shock effect, since in Greek thought slavery was the complete antithesis of freedom (*TDNT* ii.261–4; see on i.10), and his earlier use of the same verb had reflected such negative feelings (iv.8, 9, 25); Paul would strive for the same shock-effect with fuller elaboration in Rom. vi.16–23 (also 1 Cor. vii.22). The expression of true (or Christian) freedom is not self-indulgence but subordination of mere self-assertiveness to meeting the needs of others. For the moment the others in view are the 'one another' of the Galatian congregations − truly to put themselves at the disposal of each other would be challenge enough; but Paul is about to fill out the challenge with the more open-ended concept of the 'neighbour' (see on v.14). Since Paul is about to cite a passage given prominence by Jesus (see again on v.14) it is quite likely that his teaching here too was influenced by the tradition of Jesus' urging on the same point (Mark ix.35 par.; x.42–4 pars) − the greatness of discipleship as symbolized in the slave rather than the ruler.

14 **For the whole law**, the law seen as a whole rather than as an aggregation of individual commandments (see BDF §275(7)), **is fulfilled in one word** − most translations render 'word' here by 'command(ment)', perhaps reflecting the traditional reference to the ten commandments as 'the ten words' (Exod. xxxiv.28;

Deut. x.4; Philo, *Heres* 168; Josephus, *Ant.* iii.138). Again the implication is clear that Paul is continuing to address the same people as before, those 'who desire to be under the law' (iv.21). What he is calling for is *not* an abandonment of the law ('"Fulfilled" does not mean "replaced"' – Schrage 207), far less an abandonment of all restraint, but for a different way of 'doing' the law. 'Fulfilled' here (perfect tense) probably has the sense of 'has been brought to full expression, shown to have its real or complete meaning' (BAGD, *plēroō* 3, 4b), a rendering thoroughly acceptable in Jewish circles (as James ii.23 confirms), which at least overlaps with the 'is summed up' in the parallel formulation of Rom. xiii.9. The implication is either that this was always true of the law, as some other teachers of the law also argued – the 'one word' being, after all, an OT text (see next paragraph). Or that the meaning of the law (what it really requires) has been made clear in the new age introduced by Christ, and, made clear, presumably, by Christ himself (see below and on vi.2; cf. particularly Matt. v.17).

The possibility of summing up the law in a single formulation emphasizing the prime importance of love was not a new or distinctively Christian claim. The tradition of Hillel summing up 'the whole law' in the negative form of the golden rule (*b. Sabb.* 31a) is well known. According to both Mark and Luke, Jesus was by no means alone in focusing the law in the double command to love God and the neighbour (Mark xii.32–3; Luke x.26–8). And Rabbi Akiba (early second century) is said to have described Lev. xix.18 as 'the greatest general principle in the Torah' (*Gen. Rab.* xxiv.7; *Sipra* on Lev. xix.18) (see further SB i.353–64, 907–8; also Thielman 55–9). Paul repeats the point with still greater emphasis in Rom. xiii.8–10. In neither instance can he be said to be making an anti-Jewish point. On the contrary, his claim here is part of his continuing debate with the Jewish-Christian missionaries in Galatia on what it means to 'fulfil the whole law'.

But how could Paul thus claim a fulfilment of 'the whole law', or even think that such fulfilment was even desirable? The contrast with v.3 is obvious and cannot have been unintentional: there is a 'doing the whole law (*holon ton nomon*)' which is to be avoided, and a 'fulfilling the whole law (*ho pas nomos*)' which is desirable. How could Paul make both assertions without falling into complete contradiction? On this contrast many an attempt to exegete and expound Paul's thought has run aground. The problem arises principally from dubious exegesis of v.3, with the resultant inference that the argument here cannot mean what it seems to mean or is 'anti-Jewish'. It needs to be said, therefore, that neither here nor in v.3 was Paul thinking of a perfect keeping of every individual commandment ('fulfil' here in the sense of 'exhaustively complete'), as though seeking to counter a teaching which insisted on a legalistically aggregated notion of 'doing the law' (see also on iii.10 and 12). Nor can 'the whole law' here be readily distinguished from 'the whole law' in v.3, as though the phrase here did *not* refer to the Mosaic law (so particularly Hübner 36–40; cf. SB i.907);[1] the 'one word' is from the Mosaic law, the parallel in Rom. xiii.9 (not to mention James ii.8) points unmistakably to the Mosaic law, and the Matthean parallel to v.14 uses *holos ho nomos* as in v.3 (Matt. xxii.39–40). Nor is it likely that Paul intended a clear distinction between 'doing' the law and 'fulfilling' it (as Betz 275; Westerholm 203; Barclay, *Obeying* 139–41; Longenecker 242–3; but see Thielman 51–2), since elsewhere he can talk of 'doing the law' in a wholly positive sense (Rom. ii.14; cf. Gal. vi.9; see also on iii.12; and cf. again James ii.23). What was in view in v.3, rather, was a whole life-style (see on v.3) – a life-style within ethnic or national Judaism, a life-style which could therefore be focused in the demand for circumcision, *the* rite which gave the Gentile right to a share in the heritage of 'the circumcision'. In contrast, Paul calls here for a life-style which could best be summed up in love of neighbour.

The difference, then, is not that one called for obedience to every last rule and regulation (legalism in that sense), and the other disregarded the law completely or called only for a selective obedience as such. Recognition of the need to obey God's law was common to *both* sides. Paul was as desirous to obey the *whole* law as his opponents; in Rom. xiii.9 he took care to list specific commandments (contrast the 'over-the-top' assertion of Bruce 240 – 'the principle of law was so completely opposed to spiritual freedom that it could never be enlisted in defence of that freedom'). *Both* sides saw that this desire to keep God's law could be summed up in a single focal command. Both sides no doubt recognized that some commandments had to be given lower priority than others; for diaspora Jews in particular, distance from the Jerusalem temple meant a *de facto* sitting light to the bulk of the law governing the cult.

The real difference came in the practical working out of the common desire, in the attitudes which came to expression in the different focal points (circumcision, the love command). For the one, 'doing the whole law' meant a complete package, a life

---

1 Drane 112–3 effectively ignores v.14 when he argues that 'the devaluation of the Old Testament, and, therefore, the rejection of the law in any sense for the Christian community, was an inevitable outcome of Paul's teaching'.

within Judaism, a life-style marked out by the Jewish distinctives; so Hillel, having summed up the whole law in the negative golden rule, goes on immediately to require that the rest of the law should be learnt. For the other, 'fulfilling the law' meant an obedience not simply exemplified by, but conditioned throughout by love of neighbour, where the relative importance of other laws is determined by the love-command. In the latter case, other laws continued to illustrate how the love-command would come to expression in particular situations (Rom. xiii.9), but since fulfilment of the law was no longer a matter of simply conforming to Jewish life-style, it required its own guidelines ('the law of Christ' – see on vi.2) and a greater sensitivity to the Spirit (v.16, 18, 25; see on v.16).

Paul, be it noted, was claiming a better, more complete fulfilment of the whole law than was possible for the typical Jewish covenantal nomism. At this point v.14 answers to iii.10 and confirms that Paul understood covenantal nomism ('those whose identity emerges from works of the law') as a failure to 'remain in everything written in the book of the law' (iii.10). In other words, he understood his insight here *not* as an abandoning of the law, nor as 'a radical *reduction* of the law to the love command' (Räisänen, *Paul* 27), but as the key to what the law (the whole law) was all about (cf. Rom. ii.15), as the *only* way to 'fulfil the just requirement of the law' (Rom. viii.4). Which also means that he wrote as a Jew anxious to fulfil the covenant obligations of his people. His position at this point has rarely been appreciated, least of all by those who can only understand Paul's theology as an out and out rejection of the law as a still important yardstick for Christian conduct.

Paul's claim, then, is that the real or complete meaning of the law is given **in the well-known** (literally 'the', but thus clearly referring to something familiar, as in Rom. xiii.8–9), **'You shall love your neighbour as yourself'**. The quotation, of course, is from Lev. xix.18 LXX – itself part of the law! Explicit references to Lev. xix.18 are lacking in Jewish literature before Paul, and allusions to it are given no particular prominence (see e.g. O. Wischmeyer, 'Das Gebet der Nächstenliebe bei Paulus', *BZ* 30 [1986] 161–87, here 162–8). In contrast, Lev. xix.18 is the Pentateuchal passage most often cited in the NT (Mark xii.31 pars; xii.33; Matt. v.43; xix.19; Rom. xiii.9; James ii.8; also Did. i.2). The stimulus to focus thus on Lev. xix.18 must therefore be peculiarly Christian and is best explained as deriving from Jesus himself, as the Synoptic traditions indicate. James (cf. particularly James v.12) confirms what we might have guessed anyway from the echoes of the Jesus-tradition in Pauline paraenesis, that the tradition recalling Jesus' teaching had become often absorbed into Christian paraenesis without there being any felt need to cite Jesus explicitly as the authority (see e.g. my 'Paul's Knowledge of the Jesus Tradition. The Evidence of Romans', *Christus Bezeugen*, W. Trilling Festschrift, ed. K. Kertelge *et al.* [Leipzig: St Benno, 1989] 193–207).

Once again the citing of this passage should not be taken as anti-Jewish in intent. It is true that Lev. xix.18 itself refers to the fellow Israelite; Qumran use of Lev. xix.17–18 is even more restrictive (CD ix.2–8); and Matt. v.43 and the parable of the good Samaritan (Luke x.25–37) imply rebuke of their fellow Jews from the side of Jesus or the first Christians to the same effect (see also A. Nissen, *Gott und der Nächste im antiken Judentum: Untersuchungen zum Doppelgebot der Liebe* [Tübingen: Mohr, 1974] 304–29). But a more open attitude is already indicated in Lev. xix.34, and is confirmed by such passages as Exod. xxiii.5, Prov. vi.1, Sir. xiii.15, *1 Enoch* xcix.15, and Philo, *Spec. Leg.* ii.63 (see also K. Berger, *Die Gesetzesauslegung Jesu I* [Neukirchen: Neukirchener, 1972] 100–15); whereas in the NT the Johannine literature reflects a more restricted outlook (John xiii.34; xv.12, 17; 1 John iii.11, 14, 23; iv.7, 11, 21). Once again it is the attitude which comes to expression in and through such a singular summing up of the law which is decisive: whether one loves one's neighbours by keeping the law and encouraging them to do likewise (cf. *m. Abot* i.12 – ' . . . loving mankind and bringing them nigh to the Law'), or one keeps the law by means of loving one's neighbour.

It should not be thought that 'loving one's neighbour' is an easier option than 'doing the whole law'. On the contrary, just because it is less prescribed beforehand what love of the neighbour demands, and depends on who the neighbour is and his/her situation in each particular instance, it is all the more demanding. Moreover, the demand is open-ended: we do not know beforehand who our neighbour might be at any one time (see also on vi.10). At the same time it is important to realize that the demand is not unlimited: it is the *neighbour* one is called to love, not a multitude, far less everyone (1 Thess. iii.12 is hyperbole); and the call is to love the neighbour *as oneself*, no less, but no more. That is to say, it is a call for a practical love, a concentrated love, not a vague feeling for humankind stretched so thin as to be non-existent at particular points of need, but one which utilizes the resources which one actually has in specific 'Jericho-road' situations (see also vi.10).

15 Demanding as the ideal of Christian conduct is, the

alternative is too fearful to contemplate – **But if you bite and tear** (generalizing statements, rather than descriptions of the actual situation in Galatia) **at one another, look out**, in the sense, 'beware', envisaging as usual a possible undesirable outcome (Mark xiii.5 pars; Acts xiii.40; 1 Cor. viii.9; x.12; Col. ii.8; Heb. xii.25), **lest you are consumed by one another**. The imagery is of dogs or animals of prey biting and snapping at each other, perhaps while also tearing at and devouring their victim (LSJ, *daknō, katesthiō;* cf. Ignatius, *Rom.* v.2) – 'snapping at one another and tearing one another to pieces' (NJB). It may be sustained into the second half of the verse, since the last verb too can be used for animals devouring one another (Plato, *Protagoras* 321b). 'Comparisons of bad conduct with the behaviour of wild animals were a commonplace in the diatribe literature' (Betz 276–7). If allowance is made for its rhetorical character, the language need not imply that such was already happening among the Galatian congregations; the exhortations of v.16–21 indicate more a danger to be warned against (v.21) than a situation to be rebuked. On the other hand, the teaching of the other missionaries must have caused tension and considerable disagreement within the Galatian churches; in which case the call for neighbour-love was also a call for love towards those who disagreed 'savagely' with Paul! However, the imagery would have been inviting enough for anyone who was familiar with the way political groups, united in their struggle for freedom under some tyrant, can turn on each other once the tyrant is overthrown and lose the advantages gained, in bitter factional infighting (in modern times the French Revolution is a classic example). Paul would no doubt be familiar with the history of his own people, and how in the wake of the Maccabean revolt in the 160s BC, Judaism itself had been riven with sectarian disputes and bitter recriminations (1 Macc., *1 Enoch* 1–5, *Jub., Pss. Sol,* CD and 1QS, *Test. Mos.* 7); worse still was to happen in Jerusalem in the Jewish revolt of 66–70. And he would hardly need further proof in Galatia that the freedom of the Spirit can easily degenerate into the same back-biting power struggles (cf. ii.4, 12; the dangers of 'Enthusiasm'/Schwärmerei). This is the lot of those who throw over the law without a principle as penetrating as love of neighbour to guide them and without a genuine commitment to serve one another. Without that the call to freedom can open a floodgate which sweeps away every foundation (see also on v.26).

2 WHAT IT MEANS TO BE LED BY THE SPIRIT v.16–24

(16) I tell you, walk by the Spirit and you will[1] not satisfy the desire of the flesh. (17) For the flesh desires against the Spirit, and the Spirit desires against the flesh; for these are opposed to one another, to prevent you from doing those things you want to do. (18) But if you are led by the Spirit, you are not under the law. (19) And the works of the flesh are plain, which are[2] unlawful sexual intercourse, impurity, debauchery, (20) idolatry, sorcery, hostile feelings and actions, strife,[3] jealousy,[3] displays of anger, selfish ambitions, dissensions, factions, (21) envyings,[4] drunkenness, excessive feasting, and such things as these. I tell you in advance, as I told you before, that those who behave in such ways shall not inherit the kingdom of God. (22) But the fruit of the Spirit is love, joy, peace, patience, kindness, goodness, faith, (23) gentleness, self-control[5]. Against such as these there is no law. (24) And those who belong to the Christ Jesus[6] have crucified the flesh with its passions and desires.

Having defined freedom in terms of love, Paul now reintroduces talk of the Spirit. This would be no surprise to his readers, since he had made so much of their experience of the Spirit in his earlier appeal (iii.2–5, 14; iv.6, 29; v.5). Moreover, it was precisely the contrast between 'beginning with the Spirit' and 'being completed in the flesh' (iii.3; cf. iv.29) which had been at the heart of this appeal. The mistake he was seeking to counter was the persuasive teaching (of the other missionaries) that the new life begun with the Spirit was brought to its completion by conforming to the requirements laid down by the law for Jews and proselytes, that the only sure means of gaining direction on how to live was by reference to the law. This Paul saw as just another form of pandering to the flesh, by over-evaluation of

1 To take the clause as an imperative, as RSV/NRSV, would be an unusual but possible rendering.
2 Some witnesses insert 'adulteries'.
3 Some manuscripts have made these words plural, in order to fit with the otherwise consistent plurals of the second half of the list.
4 A strong tradition adds 'murders' (*phthonoi, phonoi*), perhaps by accident, perhaps by conscious or unconscious echo of Rom. i.29 (Metzger 597–8).
5 A few witnesses add 'chastity' – an understandable addition in the patristic period when virginity became over highly prized; see also Metzger 598.
6 The absence of 'Jesus' from p^{46} and other manuscripts and versions, strengthens the possibility that the definite article was intended to retain its earlier titular significance – 'the Messiah, Jesus'.

physical rite and ethnic identity, and amounted to an abandoning of the Spirit (iii.3). Consequently it was necessary for Paul now to spell out what life in accordance with the Spirit really meant and how it contrasted with life lived on the level of the flesh. In both cases, the other missionaries and Paul, we should note the centrality of ethical concern: that inward reality of faith should express itself in an appropriate manner of life.

The section falls fairly naturally into an abccba pattern:

a	16–17	assurance against desire of flesh
b	18	led by Spirit, not under law
c	19–21	works of flesh
c	22–23a	fruit of Spirit . . .
b	23b	. . ., law not against
a	24	assurance against flesh and its desires

16 **I tell you** (the same opening formula as in iv.1, indicating an important statement), **walk by the Spirit**. The choice of metaphor – walk = conduct oneself, Christianity seen as a 'way' to be 'walked' (cf. Acts ix.2; xix.9, 23; xxii.4; xxiv.14, 22) – is no doubt deliberate. For the metaphor is typically Jewish (e.g. Exod. xviii.20; Deut. xiii.4–5; Ps. lxxxvi.11; Isa. xxxiii.15; the repeated use of the metaphor in 1QS iii.18–iv.26 makes a fascinating comparison with Paul here) and untypical of Greek thought (*TDNT* v.941). Paul, therefore, is deliberately using the language of OT moral obligation, precisely with a view to its impact on those familiar with or attracted to the Jewish life-style (as in Rom. vi.4; viii.4; Phil. iii.17–18; see also on v.25). Moreover, Paul would be well aware of the typical OT use of the metaphor: the conduct looked for was 'to walk in (God's) law(s)/statutes' (as in Exod. xvi.4; Lev. xviii.4; Jer. xliv.23; Ezek. v.6–7; BDB, *halak* 3; hence halakah = legal ruling – see also on i.13). By speaking instead of a 'walk by the Spirit' Paul is deliberately posing an alternative understanding of how the people of God should conduct themselves – not by constant reference to laws and statutes, but by constant reference (the verb is present continuous) to the Spirit; and not to the Spirit as norm, but to the Spirit as resource. The active force of the verb, however, should not be lost sight of, as in NJB and REB, 'be guided by the Spirit', which then loses the point of the balancing passive in v.18, 'led by the Spirit'.

The emphasis on the Spirit is consistent with Paul's emphasis in iii.3 – that the Galatians should continue as they began. This means that he is putting considerable weight on what they had experienced – as an experience of acceptance by God (iii.14), of sonship to God (iv.6), of liberty (v.1, 13), and now of guidance for daily living. He must therefore have been envisaging a life-style and decision-making which constantly referred back to that inward fact or consciousness of the Spirit's presence, and which sought to bring it to expression in daily life (so v.25). The contrast with 'walking in God's laws' likewise implies an inward rather than an outward reference point in matters of ethical decision. This is presumably what Paul had in mind when he spoke confidently of a discerning of God's will by virtue of a renewed mind (Rom. xii.1–2), in contrast to traditional Jewish confidence of discerning what matters by instruction from the law (Rom. ii.18); so too particularly Rom. xiv.22 and Phil. i.9–10. In other words, this counsel reflects Paul's assumption (as in 2 Cor. iii.3) that those who had been given the Spirit thus also knew the eschatological experience looked for in Jer. xxxi.33–4 – an immediate knowledge of God, an enabling to know what God's will was in particular instances. This is the basis of a charismatic ethic, depending more on inward apprehension of what is the appropriate conduct than on rule book or tradition. Paul 'may well have been the first to see the indwelling Spirit as the abiding guide and enabler of Christian moral behaviour' (Westerholm 213). See also my *Jesus* 222–5.

At the same time it should not be thought of as simply a 'situation ethic' or inner-light ethic. Paul was well aware elsewhere of the need to 'test the spirits', to discern what the 'manifestation of the Spirit' was in particular instances (1 Cor. xii.10; xiv.29; 1 Thess. v.21), and in 1 Cor. 12–14 he made conscious use of several criteria to do so (see my *Jesus* 233–6, 293–7, 318–38). Here it is clear that there are at least three controlling factors. (1) The echo of iii.3 indicates that walking by the Spirit will be consistent with the initial receiving of the Spirit (so again v.25), and thus also be an expression of the same faith which received the Spirit. (2) The context indicates that walking by the Spirit is another way of saying, Fulfil the law by loving the neighbour as oneself (v.14) – an expression of the same freedom into which they were released by faith. The paradigm of Jesus is not far in the background here (see on v.22 and vi.2). (3) And here, not least, 'walking by the Spirit' is the antithesis of 'completing the desire of the flesh', the opposite, that is, of all selfish grasping and self-promoting display (see also on vi.1). Yet, however qualified, we should not lose the point of Paul's exhortation here: that the key to moral effort and acceptable conduct lies in the prompting of the Spirit from within, not in the constraints of the law from without; that moral living springs from inward engagement and motivation enabled from God rather than from outward compulsion. 'The Christian ethic is no longer a law-ethic but a Spirit-ethic!' (Mussner 365).

The other side of the same coin is what 'walking by the Spirit' prevents: **and you will not** (a double and thus strengthened negative, 'assuredly not' – BDF §365) **satisfy**, literally 'bring to an end', so 'complete, accomplish, carry out' (BAGD, *teleō*; the simpler form of the verb used in iii.3) **the desire of the flesh.** 'Desire' (*epithumia*) can be neutral in meaning, but more often has a negative sense – desire for something forbidden, in Greek (particularly Stoic) as well as Jewish thought (*TDNT* iii.168–70). It is a key word in Paul's analysis of human sinfulness, as indicated by its prominence in Romans (i.24; vi.12; vii.7–8; xiii.14). Given this already negative note, the association with 'flesh' (see on ii.16 and v.13) is particularly appropriate (as again in v.24; also Rom. xiii.14; Eph. ii.3; 1 Pet. ii.11; 1 John ii.16). The singular ('desire' rather than 'desires'; contrast v.24) indicates the characteristic of the flesh – almost 'the desiring flesh'. The active role attributed to the flesh (still more in verse 17) need occasion no surprise, as though Paul was treating the flesh as a spiritual power ('personified like Gnostic aeons'! – Oepke 174; but see particularly *TDNT* vii.132–3). What is evidently in view is the craving of the mortal for satisfaction of its mortality, the reduction of the human creation of God to the feeding of its ephemeral appetites, the forever unfulfillable coveting of others' success, the turning in upon itself of humankind as though self-gratification was what mattered most of all. The *power* of the flesh is the enticement it engenders to pander to its *weakness*. Philo, no doubt in common with most thinking Jews of the time, saw circumcision as symbolizing 'the excision of pleasure and all passions' (*Migr.* 92). But over against the Galatian 'agitators' Paul saw that symbol as effectively realized (and thus rendered redundant) by the 'circumcision' of the Spirit (cf. Phil. iii.3). Only the Spirit from God is strong enough to overcome and withstand the power of the flesh's weakness. For a brief comparative study of flesh and spirit in Paul's time and the apocalyptic character of the antithesis in Paul see Barclay, *Obeying* 182–91, 203–9.

17 Now follows one of the most realistic and psychologically insightful observations made by Paul. **For the flesh desires** (the verb equivalent to the noun) **against the Spirit, and** (set in chiastic parallel) **the Spirit desires** (the repetition of the verb implied; to supply 'fights', as NEB/REB, is unwarranted) **against the flesh** (NRSV gives a very wooden translation by using 'opposed' three times in this verse). The condition described is one of inward contradiction, of an individual pulled in two different directions. It will be true of any who recognize that this life is not limited to the flesh and its sphere, who look beyond the satisfaction of their merely bodily appetites and human desires; to that extent *pneuma* could be referred to both divine Spirit and human spirit (Lagrange 147 refers it to human spirit, but most to divine Spirit; for bibliography on Hellenistic and Jewish parallels see Betz 279, nn.69, 70; in the DSS cf. particularly 1QS iv.23). But Paul clearly sees the condition as true in particular of those who have received the Holy Spirit; the description fills out the appeal of v.16, which itself looks back to iii.3. That is to say, it is precisely the coming of the Spirit, and the Spirit's action within the believer which sets up or exacerbates the experience of inward contradiction. For the Spirit desires something quite different from the flesh; that is, by implication, for a quality of life which recognizes the spiritual nature of the human creature and seeks for satisfaction on that higher or deeper level. Where life previously could be lived on the level of the flesh with little or no self-questioning, now the presence of the Spirit brings with it a profound dis-ease with the reduction of humanity to the level of animal appetites.

It is important to recognize that Paul sees this as a Christian condition. Sometimes, it is true, he seems to envisage 'in the flesh' as denoting a condition which the Christian has left behind (Rom. vii.5; viii.9). But since he also talks of believers as still 'in the flesh' (see ii.20), the former passages probably mean '*solely* in the flesh', where 'satisfying the desire of the flesh' was the dominant feature in conduct and life-style. Here the reality is clear: 'in the flesh' is an inescapable aspect of the human condition, so that believers too cannot escape it so long as this mortal life continues. There is no perfection for the Christian in this life; the desires of flesh as well as of Spirit characterize the ongoing process of salvation. It was precisely because the flesh was a factor of continuing importance in the Galatian situation, both as a factor of ethnic identity and as a factor of self-serving desire, that Paul knew it was necessary to write as he did. This is presumably why he focuses on the flesh here, whereas in Rom. vii his fuller analysis of the condition separates out the power of sin as the chief culprit.

More surprising is the description of this condition not merely as an unresolved tension between two dimensions of the human, particularly Christian state, but as outright opposition, even warfare between the two tendencies — **for these are opposed** (the substantive denotes 'the opponent, adversary', as in Phil.

i.28; see BAGD, *antikeimai;* Martyn's 'Antinomies' 415–6, 'these two powers constitute a pair of opposites', is too static) **to one another, to prevent you from doing those things you want to do.** The surprise comes in the conjunction: the conflict takes place *'hina* you may not do what you want to do'. *Hina* normally has a final sense ('in order that'), though many prefer to take it in a consecutive sense ('so that' – as NEB/REB), which is quite possible (BAGD, *hina*). But Paul may indeed have intended the final sense, in order to bring out the character of the tension between flesh and Spirit precisely as an adversarial contest; the *hina*, in other words, expressing intention rather than accomplished fact (so e.g. Burton 301–2 and Schlier 249). After all, the thought is hardly likely to be that of two forces (flesh and Spirit) acting in effect together to prevent the self (as a third party) from doing what it wants; that would run counter to verses 16 and 18. Nor that they neutralize each other and leave the self free to choose (Betz 281 n. 83 criticizes Mussner 377–8 for maintaining this view), nor that the Spirit–flesh conflict makes it 'impossible for the believer to remain neutral' (Fung 251), both of which are too remote from the sense of the Greek. Nor that the self is identified with the one rather than the other, as though Paul meant to say *only* that the Spirit seeks to prevent the flesh-incited will having its way (Duncan 167–8 and Barclay, *Obeying* 112, 115–6 have verse 17 in effect say the same as verses 16 and 18), or *only* that the flesh seeks to prevent the Spirit-incited will from having its way (as Beyer-Althaus 48 and Cole 209); but the opposition of flesh and Spirit is mutual. So the implication must be rather that 'those things you want' are associated with the desirings of *both* flesh *and* Spirit (Burton 302; Rohde 234–5; Longenecker 246).

The point then seems to be to underline the extent to which the individual, including here particularly the believer, is on *both* sides of the conflict. (S)he as flesh is opposed to the Spirit; (s)he as recipient of the Spirit (or as spirit) is opposed to the flesh. Believers (Paul states it as a general truth) experience in themselves a real unwillingness and antagonism against the Spirit as much as against the flesh. They know all too well desires in themselves to oppose what they also know and desire in themselves as God's will, to prevent them from doing what *they* want. Just as they know desires in themselves from the Spirit to oppose the will of the flesh, to prevent their doing what *they* (as flesh) also want. That is why the call to 'walk by the Spirit' is so important: there must be that inward resolution and determined discipline to side with the Spirit *against oneself* in what is an ongoing and inescapable inner warfare, so long as the flesh continues to be a factor (that is, for the duration of this earthly life). 'The Christian is at the same time stage and object, battlefield and trophy of the contest between flesh and Spirit' (Schlier 250). The classic expression of this tension, warfare and resolution is Rom. vii.14–viii.30, which thus can be seen as a fuller treatment of the theme, rather than as a marked development or divergence from what Paul wrote here; the exegesis of Rom. vii in particular, however, is much disputed (see *Jesus* 312–18; also my *Romans*).

18 **But** (introducing the resolution to the problem of verse 17) **if you are led by the Spirit**. The choice of verb underlines the charismatic character of Paul's paraenesis. For the idea of being 'led' by feelings (desire, anger, pleasures), as in 2 Tim. iii.6, was familiar in Greek thought (BAGD, *agō* 3). And when used with the Spirit the sense of being constrained by a compelling inner force, or of surrendering to a powerful inner compulsion is hard to escape (cf. particularly Luke iv.1; Rom. viii.14; 1 Cor. xii.2). Again the understanding of the Spirit is of a power which works like a deep-rooted passion or overmastering compulsion; God, as it were, recognizing the power of human desire, gives to those who open themselves to him a power (the Spirit) which is stronger than human desire. To surrender to that power is to be enabled to rise above and overcome the baser human instincts and appetites (see further on v.17). It is presumably important to note that the passive here is balanced by the active in verse 16: those who wish to walk by the Spirit have to be led by the Spirit; those who wish to be led by the Spirit have the responsibility to conduct themselves accordingly (see further on v.16 and 25).

Those who are so led **are not under the law**. The reference to the law once again is no accident. Paul's exhortation here is aimed precisely at those who were being persuaded that the Jewish law provided the necessary directions and rules for their daily conduct, now that they had believed in Messiah Jesus. His concern, therefore, has been to show that a life-style determined by the Spirit gives them all that they need and more. No external constraint or rule-book is capable of countering 'the desire of the flesh' adequately. What is needed is the Spirit, or, alternatively expressed, the law written within (Jer. xxxi.33–4), to provide an inner drive of greater and more enduring strength, the supplanting of one motive centre (selfish desire) by another of greater power (the Spirit).

But Paul's concern here goes further. The point here is to reinforce the message that such a Spirit-led life is quite other in character from one 'under the law'. The re-emergence of the phrase which featured so strongly in the middle section of the main exposition (iii.23; iv.4–5, 21) is no doubt deliberate. For it denoted for him the space of the nation Israel, the Jewish people under the law as their guardian angel (see on iii.23); reference to legalistic self-righteousness (as Oepke 176), or the condemnation of the law (as Borse 196), is uncalled for and excluded by iv.4 (Barclay, *Obeying* 116 n. 24). To put oneself thus 'under the law' was to look once again for an answer to 'the desire of the flesh' in a written code, an outward constraint; whereas in the age of fulfilment introduced by Christ, it was the circumcision of the heart, an effective inner force which was now available. To put onself 'under the law', in other words, was to look in the wrong direction for salvation. Worse still, to assume that only 'under the law' could salvation be found was to deny the reality of Gentile as Gentile having received the Spirit. No! The reality of being led by the Spirit, that is, the Spirit of Jesus (iv.6), was independent of being 'under the law' and should not therefore be identified with the ethnic Jewish identity which that phrase encapsulated. In short, their experience of the Spirit thus far should be enough to convince them that to take the step of becoming a proselyte (through circumcision) was unnecessary. Implicit here also is a clear distinction between being 'under the law' and 'fulfilling the law' (v.14); the law is 'fulfilled' by those who are 'led by the Spirit' (Thielman 53), not by putting oneself 'under the law'.

19 Paul does not hesitate to press the logic of his argument strongly. By implication, to put oneself 'under the law', to become a proselyte, to accept circumcision, is to think and act on the level of the flesh (see on vi.13), on that level of visibility and outwardness which is the very opposite of the inward reality of the Spirit's work (the contrast is explicit in Rom. ii.28–9). And to put oneself on the level of the flesh is to put oneself on the same level as so many of the very things which Jews (and all those of goodwill) hated and despised – **the works of the flesh**, the outworking of the flesh, those things which express the character of the flesh and its desires; the echo of the earlier repeated phrase, 'works of the law' (ii.16; iii.2, 5, 10) is no doubt intentional. The challenge to the other missionaries is as sharp as it could be, and may well have seemed to them outrageous. Judaism, after all, was more opposed to these things than others were (particularly idolatry and sorcery), and the very thought that desire for circumcision was even on the same plane as them must have seemed ridiculous. But this is precisely Paul's challenge: to put such weight on the fleshly rite of circumcision and on ethnic identity was actually to pitch the theological principle into the same realm as these things so widely despised; to make circumcision the test-case of eligibility for a share in Abraham's inheritance was to make the effective working of the Spirit dependent on a work of (done in) the flesh. By linking 'under the law' (v.18) with 'works of the flesh' (both in antithesis to what the Spirit produces) Paul thus presumably hoped to jolt his readers into a recognition of the level they were thinking on and of what they might lose (see also on v.22).

To bring out his point Paul presents a catalogue of vices. Such catalogues were widely familiar in the ancient world, particularly among the Stoics. But, as we might expect, Judaism, with its strong sense of ethical obligation, used such lists too (e.g. Wisd. Sol. xiv.25–6; *4 Macc.* i.26–7; ii.15; 1QS iv.9–11; Philo, *Sac.* 32; *2 Enoch* x.4–5). So also did earliest Christianity (see particularly Mark vii.21–2; Rom. i.29–31; 1 Cor. vi.9–10; 2 Cor. xii.20; Col. iii.5, 8; 1 Tim. i.9–10; 2 Tim. iii.2–5; 1 Clem. xxxv.5; Did. v.1–2; Barn. xx.1–2) (see further particularly Longenecker 249–52; bibliography in Betz 282 n. 93). The degree of diversity in these lists indicates that it was the pattern which was common more than the content; but also that Paul in particular probably attempted to make his catalogue on each occasion appropriate to his readers' situation (contrast Betz 282–3 – 'the conventional morality of the time'; 'the seemingly chaotic arrangement of these terms is reflective of the chaotic nature of evil').

In this instance Paul's list is very artfully contrived. It begins and ends with items which would receive disapprobation from most ethically concerned people ('unlawful sexual intercourse, impurity, debauchery . . . drunkenness, excessive feasting'); and the middle section picks out two items which were particularly hateful to Jews ('idolatry, sorcery'). Paul's intention was evidently to compile a list to which his readers could not help but give assent. It was the other missionaries and those influenced by them who would be the first to agree that such things **are plain**, that is, are manifestly what they are – 'works of the flesh'. But the bulk of the list is given over to items which were particularly apposite for the situation in Galatia ('hostile actions, strife, jealousy, displays of anger, selfish ambitions, dissensions, factions, envyings'). The implication is that these features had become, or were in danger of becoming, in Paul's view, all too characteristic of the Galatian churches. That is, the Galatians were in danger of surrendering to the power of the flesh precisely as a result of the agitators' insistence on another fleshly requirement – circumcision. For the view that by 'are plain' Paul was referring to well-known characteristics of the religious, political and social life of the region, see Ramsay 446–54 ('overstated' – Lagrange 149).

Unlawful sexual intercourse, or more explicitly, 'prostitution, unchastity, fornication' (BAGD, *porneia*). The typical Greek attitude to sexual relations was very libertarian, though Stoicism sought to reform sexual morality (*TDNT* vi.582–4). Judaism however was uniformly strict on the subject, as indicated not least by the use of the imagery of adultery to express Israel's unfaithfulness to Yahweh (classically in Jer. iii.1–iv.4 and Hos. i–iii). The NT is likewise uniform in following the OT emphasis (Matt. v.32; Mark vii.21 – the Markan vice-catalogue; Acts xv.20, 29 – 'the apostolic decree'; 1 Cor. v.1; vi.13, 18; 2 Cor. xii.21; etc.). The fact that cult prostitution was widespread throughout Asia Minor, including not least the regional cult of Cybele, would make the inclusion of this item at the head of the list particularly appropriate, and particularly fitted to win his readers' assent: it was precisely in order to escape such immorality that the Galatians had been attracted to the Nazarene sect of Judaism, and still more (now) to Judaism. We may compare Rev. ii.14, 20–1, where 'immorality' is linked with another Jewish *bête noire*, eating food sacrificed to idols; here, as there, we are dealing with boundary issues, what marked (Christian) Jews off from surrounding paganism.

Impurity, *akatharsia*, uncleanness, was commonly understood to indicate a negative state requiring to be rectified, particularly in cultic terms (e.g. *TDNT* iii.427; Lev. xv). But it was also used in a moral sense, without particular reference to the cult (e.g. Prov. vi.16; Wisd. Sol. ii.16; *Aristeas* 166; 1 Thess. ii.3), and especially in close connection, as here, with sexual immorality (e.g. Plutarch, *Othone* 2; *1 Enoch* x.11; Philo, *Leg. All.* iii.139; *Test. Jud.* xiv–xv; 2 Cor. xii.21; Col. iii.5; Eph. v.3). The fact that Paul uses this word of more general disparagement, rather than the more distinctively Jewish word for what is impure (*koinos* – Rom. xiv.14; cf. Mark vii.20–3), confirms that Paul was casting the net of his appeal as widely as possible. But he would also want to avoid the word (*koinos*) which in Jewish-Greek vocabulary had come to denote unclean food in particular (1 Macc. i.47, 62; Mark vii.15; Acts x.14; Rom. xiv.14).

In wider usage **debauchery** could denote 'wanton violence', or 'insolence' (LSJ, *aselgeia*). It is a natural third element in such a sequence (as in 2 Cor. xii.21), and so probably has the overtone of 'sexual excess' (as in Wisd. Sol. xiv.26; Rom. xiii.13; 1 Pet. iv.3; cf. Mark vii.22); in 2 Pet. ii.7 it characterizes the sin of Sodom and Gomorrah; for Josephus's characteristic use in similar vein see Longenecker 254–5. Characteristic of Jewish analysis of the human condition was the insight that rejection of God regularly, and probably inevitably, results in the sexual appetite's becoming one of the 'desires of the flesh' which dominate existence and relationships, and which, if not checked, can lead all too quickly to dehumanizing excesses (cf. Rom. i.21–7). 'In nothing did early Christianity so thoroughly revolutionize the ethical standards of the pagan world as in regard to sexual relationships' (Duncan 171–2).

20 Although the word **idolatry** (worship of idols) itself is a Christian formation (Paul our earliest attestation – 1 Cor. v.10–11; vi.9; x.7,14; Col. iii.5; also 1 Pet. iv.3), the attitude is thoroughly and peculiarly Jewish. It was precisely Judaism's attack on idolatry which distinguished Jewish monotheism from the typically tolerant syncretism of Hellenistic religiosity. Hence the classic polemics of Isa. xliv.9–20, Wisd. Sol. xii–xv, Epistle of Jeremiah, and *Sib. Or.* iii.8–45. Typically Jewish too was the conviction that idolatry and sexual licence were closely related – not unnaturally in view of the prevalence of cult prostitution (hence Wisd. Sol. xiv.12–27; Rom. i.23–7; also 1 Cor. vi.9; Eph. v.5; Col. iii.5; 1 Pet. iv.3; Rev. xxi.8; xxii.15). The insight that idolatry is a projection of human desire, as seen by the degree to which it gives free rein to the desire of the flesh, was not a nineteenth-century discovery.

Sorcery comes from the word meaning 'drug' (*pharmakon*, from which the English 'pharmacy' is derived); hence also Ignatius, *Eph.* xx.2 – the Eucharist as a *pharmakon* of immortality. But because drugs were so often used in witchcraft and to administer poison the word regularly had a sinister meaning; so in its other earliest Christian use (Rev. ix.21; xviii.23; Barn. xx.1; Did. v.1); see BAGD and LSJ, *pharmakeia*. Although sorcery/poisoning was a serious offence under Roman law (Bruce 248), magic was a regular element in Hellenistic syncretism (see e.g. *OCD*, 'Magic'), but was strictly forbidden in Jewish law (Exod. xxii.18; Lev. xix.26, 31; xx.6, 27; Deut. xviii.9–14). The implication of the last of these texts is that the raising up of a prophet like Moses would render unnecessary any need to try other channels of other-worldly knowledge. Note the similar contrast (black magic vs. Spirit) in Mark iii.22 pars.

To this list of vices, which would evoke warm assent in any Jewish or God-fearing audience, Paul now adds a sequence of items which were probably intended to strike nearer home, as characterizing more closely their own situation or the danger in which they stood. First, **hostile feelings and actions**. The word denotes antagonistic feelings or actions across a divide – in the only other NT usage, between God and humanity (Rom. viii.7; James iv.4), or, interestingly, between Jew and Gentile (Luke xxiii.12; Eph. ii.14, 16). The implication would be plain enough: the troublemakers, for all their protestations, were acting out of a spirit of hostility to Gentiles as such; and their teachings were encouraging the Galatians to regard Paul as an enemy (iv.16). They should recognize this as evidence that in following the agitators they were actually 'gratifying the desire of the flesh'.

Strife, rivalry, is also a natural member of such a list (Rom. i.29; xiii.13; 2 Cor. xii.20; 1 Tim. vi.4; Tit. iii.9; 1 Clem. xxxv.5), but again was peculiarly appropriate to the Galatian situation. So too **jealousy** (obviously here in a bad sense, 'envy'; see also on i.14 and iv.18) and **displays of anger** (passion uncontrolled, so 'rage', or in the plural, as here, 'outbursts of anger'). Again, all three were a natural association (so Sir. xxx.24; xl.5; Rom. xiii.13; 1 Cor. iii.3; 2 Cor. xii.20; 1 Clem. vi.4; BAGD, *zēlos* 2, *thumos* 2). Paul, having stressed the importance of an experiential dimension in Christian conduct (being led by the Spirit – see on v.18), makes it clear that he was well aware of the dangers of uncontrolled emotion.

Eritheiai probably means **selfish ambitions**, rather than 'factious ambitions' (BAGD; cf. particularly Phil. ii.3–4), but the association with the two following words suggests that the difference does not amount to much. Note the link with 'jealousy' in James iii.14 and 16, and with 'outbursts of anger' again in 2 Cor. xii.20. **Dissensions** (elsewhere in biblical Greek, only 1 Macc. iii.29, Rom. xvi.17 and a quite strongly supported variant reading in 1 Cor. iii.3) and **factions** (*haireseis*, not yet = 'heresies'), the word used both in Josephus and NT to describe the different sects or schools within the Judaism of that time (e.g. Josephus, *Ant.* xiii.171; Acts v.17; xv.5; the Nazarenes were also seen as such a 'sect' – Acts xxiv.5, 14 and xxviii.22), are the two words which stand out in the list as most unusual in comparison with other vice-catalogues. The implication again is clear, that Paul saw these as dangers particularly confronting the Galatian churches. His concern, we may say, was that the factionalism which disfigured late second-Temple Judaism might be imported into the new movement by the activities of the other missionaries. Since that factionalism was characteristically exclusive and judgemental of other Jews, discounting them as 'sinners' and as those whose actions effectively put themselves outside the covenant people (see on ii.15), Paul had every reason to resist such censorious factionalism in his own churches. Elsewhere, where the particular threat of Jewish factionalism was less strong, his attitude could be rather more relaxed (1 Cor. xi.19).

21 Envyings, 'jealousy' (Rom. i.29; 1 Tim. vi.4; Tit. iii.3; 1 Pet. ii.1; 'the grudging spirit that cannot bear to contemplate someone else's prosperity' — Bruce 249), probably belongs with the preceding items — the last of the items particularly directed at the situation in Galatia.

Having thus made his main thrust, Paul reverts to more obvious elements in such vice-lists — **drunkenness** (Luke xxi.34; Rom. xiii.13) and **excessive feasting** (Rom. xiii.13; 1 Pet. iv.3). The last item (*kōmoi*) originally denoted a festal procession in honour of Dionysus, hence the overtone of uninhibited revelry to excess, as in the only other biblical usage (Wisd. Sol. xiv.23; 2 Macc. vi.4; note also Philo, *Cher.* 92). The last two words could be taken almost as a hendiadys — 'drunken revelry, bouts of eating and drinking to excess'. Here 'the desires of the flesh' are writ large. **And such things as these**; Paul could have gone on (Philo's vice-list in *Sac.* 32 contained more than 140 items), but his point was made. By 'topping and tailing' his list with items which he could be sure his Galatian audiences would echo warmly, his hope no doubt was that the items in the heart of the list directed more *at* them themselves would strike home with greater impact.

Without hesitating he runs on — literally, 'these things which' **I tell you in advance, as I told you before**. We need not assume either that Paul is exaggerating here, or that he had predicted what would happen in the Galatian churches. He evidently made a point of passing on to his churches a large amount of ethical paraenesis (Phil. iv.9; 1 Thess. iv.1; 2 Thess. ii.15; iii.6; 2 Cor. xiii.2 has the same formula as here) (bibliography in Betz 285 n. 124). It would be the absence from such catechesis of instruction regarding the distinctively Jewish practices which would have left the door open for the other missionaries to point out a (to them) important gap in the instruction provided by Paul. Here, however, the reference is specifically to the following saying — **that those who behave in such ways** (literally 'practise such things', the phrase relating back to the vice-list, as in Rom. i.32) **shall not inherit the kingdom of God**. The language is formulaic: both the talk of 'inheriting the kingdom' (Mark x.17 par.; Matt. xxv.34; Luke x.25), and the specific thought, as here, that certain conditions and conduct would be unable to inherit the kingdom (1 Cor. vi.9–10; xv.50; Eph. v.5; James ii.5). This range of texts strongly suggests that the Christian usage was dependent on the memory of how Jesus himself had spoken (we recall the vice-catalogue of Mark vii.21–2), and particularly the memory of how much he had spoken of the kingdom of God – part, in other words, of the treasured memory of Jesus' teaching which was imparted to newly established churches (cf. particularly Acts xiv.22).

What is striking, in that case, is the fact that the Christian usage placed such an emphasis on this aspect of the kingdom theme, on the kingdom as yet to be inherited, and that this forward-looking concept of the kingdom is the only one which has been thus enshrined in such a formula. In comparison, the idea of the kingdom as having *already* come is not really or so clearly evident (cf. Rom. xiv.17; 1 Cor. iv.20; Col. i.13). In fact, any emphasis on the presentness of the kingdom to be found in the Synoptic tradition (Matt. xii.28/Luke xi.20; Luke xvii.21), has been replaced in the letters of Paul by talk either of Christ's resurrection, or of the Spirit, or both (see on i.1 and iii.2). In particular, it is important, not least in this context, to appreciate that for Paul the gift of the Spirit to the believer is the beginning of the inheritance of the kingdom, the first instalment and guarantee, the beginning of the process which will climax in the kingdom harvest of the resurrection (Rom. viii.14–17; 1 Cor. vi.9–11; Gal. iv.6–7; also Eph. i.13–14; Tit. iii.6–7). If this was part of his earlier teaching when he founded the Galatian churches, he would not need to spell out the implication that this sort of conduct, including the factionalism they were in danger of falling into, was the very antithesis of the life of the Spirit.

But there is another reason why Paul has reached for this familiar phraseology. For the theme of 'inheritance' was fundamental to Jewish self-identity. Israel could only understand itself as the people who inherited the covenant promises made to Abraham, the land of Israel in particular (Gen. xii.7; xiii.15–16; xv.5, 18; xvii.7–8, 19; xxii.17–18). By picking up the theme of inheritance again (see on iii.18) and by putting it in this context, Paul once again underlines the fact that inheritance of God's promises (or the kingdom, it comes to the same thing) is now primarily a matter of the Spirit and not of the flesh (including the fleshly rite of circumcision). Once again, then, he says in effect to the Galatians, Your inheritance of the promises given to Abraham is already sure: the decisive event has already happened (iii.14; iv.6–7), you need do no more to ensure your standing with God; and the conduct of those who will enter into the full inheritance in the end is conduct motivated and enabled by the Spirit, not conduct determined by desires of the flesh or by activities on the level of the flesh.

22 In contrast (**but**) to the works of the flesh there is **the fruit of the Spirit**. 'Fruit' is a natural metaphor to indicate the consequence or result of actions or lives, whether good or evil; so particularly in Stoic writings (*TDNT* iii.614), in the OT (e.g. Prov. i.31; xxxi.31; Jer. xvii.10; Amos vi.12 and *Aristeas* 232 – 'the fruit(s) of righteousness'), in Philo (see Betz 286 n. 138), and elsewhere in the NT (e.g. Matt. iii.8 par.; xxi.43; John xv.2–8; Rom. vi.21–2). The closest parallels to the phrase here are Eph. v.9 ('the fruit of light'); Phil. i.11 and James iii.8 ('fruit of righteousness'). The recognition that fruit was a clear demonstration of the nature of the tree which bore it was proverbial (*Proverbs of Aesop*, in BAGD, *karpos* 2a; Matt. vii.16, 20). Paul's point then is that the nature of God's Spirit (see on iv.6) is demonstrated in the quality of character exemplified in the following list.

To be noted is the fact that Paul once again reverts to what was a matter of firm agreement between himself and his Galatian audiences – that their Christian experience began with the gift of the Spirit (iii.2–3). In part this is a continuation of the warning of v.13ff.: the Spirit is *not* to be understood in terms simply of miraculous acts (iii.5) and casting off restraints (v.13); Christ-like character (see below) is the principal product of the Spirit. But the contrast between 'works of the flesh' and 'fruit of the Spirit' almost certainly is intended also to echo that earlier contrast of iii.2–3 ('works . . . Spirit . . . flesh'): 'works of the law' belong with the flesh, belong with 'works of the flesh' (see also on v.19). That is to say, the life of the Spirit does *not* manifest itself or come to complete expression in such works but in character formation. Moreover, if Paul intended to evoke the imagery of fruit-bearing Israel (classically Isa. v.1–7), his point would be that the fruit for which God looked in Israel was being produced (only) by those (Galatian Gentiles included) who walked by the Spirit (Barclay, *Obeying* 120–2).

The contrast between 'works' (v.19) and 'fruit' also invites some elaboration. The flesh *demands*, but the Spirit *produces*. Where the one list breathes an air of anxious self-assertiveness and frenetic self-indulgence, the other speaks more of concern for others, serenity, resilience, reliability. The one features human manipulation, the other divine enabling or engracing, reinforcing the point that inner transformation is the source of responsible conduct (cf. Rom. xii.1–2). Perhaps too the plural, 'works', in a list where factionalism is a prominent feature, is intended to contrast with the singular, 'fruit' (though the undisputed Paulines always use the singular): life lived primarily on the level of the flesh promotes divisiveness; life lived primarily at the prompting of the Spirit produces that quality of character without which community cannot be sustained. The contrast between 'fruit of the Spirit' and 'charisms (of the Spirit)' (1 Cor. xii.4–11) should not be exaggerated (as Guthrie 139): both are manifestations of the Spirit, expressions of grace (*charis*); but the former are more deep-rooted and character-forming (cf. 1 Cor. xiii), while the latter are more typically visible (in word and deed) and given for particular occasions.

As with lists of vices, so it was quite common for lists of virtues to be compiled (see e.g. 1QS iv.2–8; Philo, *Sac.* 27; *Virt.* 182; Josephus, *Ap.* ii.146; for bibliography see again Betz 282 n. 93); though there are less of the latter in the NT, they are normally not so extensive, and the range of items is less diverse. Human sin is more complex than human goodness.

Gal. v.22–3	2 Cor. vi.6	1 Tim. iv.12	1 Tim. vi.11	2 Tim. ii.22	2 Pet. i.5–7
love	love	love	love	love	love
joy					
peace				peace	
patience	patience		steadfastness		steadfastness
kindness	kindness				
goodness					
faith		faith	faith	faith	faith
gentleness			gentleness		
self-control					self-control
	purity	purity			
	knowledge				knowledge
			righteousness	righteousness	
			godliness		godliness
					virtue
					brotherly love

The items are listed in the order of Gal. v.22–3; see also Phil. iv.8, Col. iii.12, Eph. iv.2 and 2 Tim. iii.10.

Most prominent in the list here (as in 1 Cor. xiii.13, 1 Tim. iv.12 and 2 Pet. i.5–7), and the only regular feature in the other NT lists, **is love** (see on v.6; my *Jesus* 294–5). In addition, whereas all the other items are common in Hellenistic philosophy, the focus on love is distinctively Christian (Betz 281; though Mussner 385 draws particular attention to 1QS iv.5). Moreover, Paul has already focused his rejection of the need for circumcision in the reality of 'faith operating effectively through love' (v.6; as fruit of the Spirit, cf. particularly Rom. v.5 and xv.30), and in love of neighbour as fulfilment of the whole law (v.14). These considerations give some weight to the suggestion that all the following items are to be seen from a Christian perspective as expressions of the one all-embracing grace of love (cf. Col. iii.14); 'love is not one virtue among a list of virtues, but the sum and substance of what it means to be a Christian'

(Cousar 131). In view also of the clear echo of Jesus' characteristic teaching on the theme (see on v.14), and the immediately following description of those who bear this fruit as 'those of Christ Jesus' who have patterned themselves on Christ's passion (v.24), and who are to 'fulfil the law of Christ' (vi.2), the suggestion is also very inviting that Paul had in mind here a kind of 'character-sketch' of Christ. This would certainly tie in with his characteristic understanding, and indeed definition of the Spirit as the Spirit of Christ, who reproduces the prayer and status of Christ in the believer (see on iv.6), and who transforms the believer into the image of Christ (see on iv.19). The piety thus inculcated ('imitation of Christ') may sound naïve and simplistic, but it is the more easily graspable as an ideal than other ethical ideals; when Christ's passion is included it has a critical power of profound depth, and it ensures that the Jesus-tradition retains the central place in Christian theology, practice and devotion it probably always had from the beginning of Christianity.

As with 'love', so with **joy**, the emotive dimension is prominent – 'joy' as the felt experience of being joyful; elsewhere regularly in the context of religious or cultic festival celebrations (Rohde 246). Such experiences were evidently a feature of the earliest Christian movement (e.g. Acts viii.8; 2 Cor. vii.4, 13; viii.2; Phil. i.4; ii.29; Phm. 7; 1 Pet. i.8). Here again the contrast with 'works of the flesh' is noteworthy: joy by its nature is something uncontrived, often with an unexpected element in it; in this case a consequence of the believer's openness and responsiveness to the leadings of the Spirit, affording new experiences of fellowship and new insights into the working out of the gospel (cf. Acts xiii.52; Rom. xiv.17; xv.13; 1 Thess. i.6). Its infrequency in other comparable NT lists suggests that here Paul once again harks back to the vividness of the Galatians' initial experience of the Spirit.

Peace too is an infrequent member of such lists, though Paul elsewhere links 'joy and peace' or 'love and peace' as natural associates (Rom. xiv.17; xv.13, 32–3; 2 Cor. xiii.11; also Eph. vi.23); cf. also the near sounding 'grace and peace' (see on i.3). It is important to recall that in Jewish thought 'peace' was not reducible to an individualistic inner tranquillity, but included also a corporate dimension, all that makes for social well-being and harmonious relationships (see again on i.3). Its inclusion here therefore is to highlight still more sharply the contrast between 'the works of the flesh' and 'the fruit of the Spirit', since divisive factionalism was such a feature of the former. Moreover, in Jewish thinking 'peace' was also bound up with covenant faithfulness (e.g. Num. vi.22–7; xxv.12–13; Isa. xlviii.18; Mal. ii.4–5; 2 Macc. i.2–4) and with covenant 'righteousness' (e.g. Ps. xxxv.27; Isa. xxxii.17; xlviii.18). So the sub-text of Paul's inclusion of 'peace' at this point is a further reminder that one of the great blessings promised to the people of the covenant is a direct consequence of the Spirit's activity in individual and community life.

Having made his principal thrust in the first trio of items, Paul lets the list run on to include more generally recognized virtues: **patience**, literally 'long-tempered' (prominent in *Test. Jos.* ii.7, xvii.2, xviii.3, and linked with other virtues in 2 Cor. vi.6, Eph. iv.2, Col. iii.12, 2 Tim. iii.10, 1 Clem. lxii.2 and Barn. ii.2); **kindness** (the twinning with 'patience', as again in 1 Cor. xiii.4, 2 Cor. vi.6 and Col. iii.12, presumably reflecting God's 'patience and kindness', as in Rom. ii.4, fruit of the same divine Spirit; cf. Eph. iv.32); and **goodness** ('fruit of the light' in Eph. v.9, an exclusively biblical word, rendered 'generosity' by BAGD, *agathōsunē;* cf. its only other NT occurrences, Rom. xv.14 and 2 Thess. 1.11). These would be generally recognized as virtues of the genuinely or thoroughly 'good' person (on the first two see *TDNT* iv.375, 378 and ix.489–90). Lightfoot 212–13 sees an ascending scale, from the passive 'patient endurance', through the neutral 'kindly disposition towards one's neighbours', to the active 'goodness, beneficence' as an energetic principle.

In contrast to the list of vices, where the 'sting' comes in the middle, in the list of virtues the points where Paul was seeking to exert greatest pressure come at the beginning and the end. **Faith** is the other most common member of the above lists. In Hellenistic ethics 'faith' in the sense of 'good faith, trustworthiness' (LSJ, *pistis* I.2; BAGD, *pistis* 1a), was highly valued; it is linked with 'meekness' in Sir. i.27 and xlv.4. But its appearance here probably reflects the prime importance Paul placed on faith (see on i.23 and ii.16). And here in particular Paul will have included it, no doubt, in order to reinforce the central and immediate link (for him) between the Spirit and faith. Just as it was through (hearing with) faith that they received the Spirit, so his readers should recognize that the fruit of the Spirit is not something other than that same faith. What the Spirit produces is not dedication to works of law or flesh, which was what the demands of the other missionaries amounted to, but the continued expression of that same faith which they as Gentiles had first experienced and exercised when they responded to the gospel Paul had preached (see also on iii.2).

Paul does not reflect here on the relation between 'faith' as human response to the gospel, and 'faith' as that which manifests the presence and activity of the Spirit in a human life. He would presumably see no great distinction between the two or insist on some strict order of salvation (gospel -> faith -> Spirit); after all, it was a Spirit-inspired preaching which incited the response of faith (cf. iii.2 with 1 Cor. ii.4–5 and 1 Thess. i.6). This also implies that he would not want to make any sharp distinction between 'justifying faith' (as in Rom. v.1; see on ii.16) and 'charismatic faith' (1 Cor. xii.9; xiii.2), or indeed between 'faith' as accepting God's grace and 'faith(fulness)' as the continuing response to that grace (most commentators take it in the latter sense here; but cf. 1QS iv.3 and 1 Cor. xiii.7, cited by Mussner 388; see also on i.23 and iii.9). 'Faith' consistently in Paul denotes unconditional trust in God alone – that reliance on God expressed first in receiving the gospel, but continuing to be expressed in the Christian's walk (hence iii.3, 16), in responsiveness to the leading of the Spirit alike for ministry as for moral decision (Rom. xii.3, 6; xiv.22–3).

23 Gentleness was another widely prized virtue, though in Greek thought it was recognized that, as with most other virtues, gentle friendliness could be taken to extreme (*TDNT* vi.646). The Hebrew sense and high evaluation of humility or meekness are particularly clear in the Psalms (xxv.9; xxxiv.2; xxxvii.11; xlv.4; etc.), Zech. ix.9 (Zion's king) and ben Sira (i.27; iii.17–18; iv.8; x.14, 28; xxxvi.23; xlv.4), and is reflected in the NT by the close association with the near synonym, 'humility' (Matt. xi.29; 2 Cor. x.1 – 'gentleness of Christ'; Eph. iv.2; Col. iii.12). It is particularly important for a theology which takes the fact of creation seriously and the obligation and need of the creature to honour and worship the Creator (cf. Rom. i.21). Here, no doubt, the word has a polemic nuance, as with 'peace' earlier in the list: such meekness was in some contrast to the insistent claims made by the 'agitators' (see also on vi.1).

Self-control was still more characteristic of philosophical ethics in the Greek world, reckoned, for example, a cardinal virtue by Socrates, and given a full treatment in Aristotle's *Ethics* (*TDNT* ii.340; Bruce 255). The concept is almost wholly absent from the Hebrew Bible, though it appears (chiefly) in the Wisdom literature of Hellenistic Judaism, and Josephus claims that it was held in high regard by the Essenes (*War* ii.120). NT usage reflects the same feature: the word appears nowhere in the Gospels, and the noun elsewhere only in Acts xxiv.25 and 2 Pet. i.6 (verb in 1 Cor. vii.9 and ix.25; adjective in Tit. i.8), though it appears more regularly in second-century Christian writings

(BAGD, *enkrateia*; Bruce 255). Here it will certainly have been Paul's intention to weigh it against the 'works of the flesh' appearing at the beginning and end of the vice-list. In some contrast to Greek thought, however (*TDNT* ii.342), it is not as an ideal in itself that Paul lauds 'self-control', but because of its importance in community relations, in contrast to the unrestrained emphasis placed on the flesh both by the other missionaries and by any who over-indulged their human appetites. To that extent, Paul's striving for the happy mean between the extremes is very Greek in character. 'The gift of the Spirit and the "fruit of the Spirit" reach their climax in the fulfilment of the old Greek ideal of self-control' (Betz 288).

To make clear that his line of thought is still on the main theme of the challenge posed to his gospel by the other missionaries in Galatia, Paul adds, **Against such as these** (neuter, as with most commentators) **there is no law**. The precise meaning is unclear. Presumably he meant more than that he knew of no law which forbids such virtues (cf. 1 Tim. i.9); Barrett takes it as an *'ad hominem* dig . . . "You want to observe the law, don't you? You will not find any law that forbids these things"' (*Freedom* 77). At all events, a reference to the Torah is probably inescapable in the context of this letter, particularly since in the abccba structure of the passage this clause answers to verse 18b. And the overall thrust of the argument would seem to point to a sense like this: no law is required in order to produce such virtue. That is, in order for the fruit of the Spirit to flourish in the lives of the Galatians it was *not* necessary to refer to or put oneself 'under the law'; 'a life under law is not the only alternative to a life of self-indulgence' (Duncan 176); the Spirit writing on the heart (2 Cor. iii.3) was compulsion enough; 'the Spirit, not the law, is the sole "moral principle"' (Mussner 389); 'a vine does not produce grapes by Act of Parliament' (S. H. Hooke, cited by Bruce 255).

The choice of preposition, however, is puzzling (why 'against'?). The awkwardness of the clause, if this is what Paul intended to say, may simply reflect the sense of opposition which the activities of the 'agitators' sharpened – the opposition between Spirit and law, between faith and law, and, not least here, between the appropriate conduct expected of those who had received the Spirit and the law. To be noted is the fact that Paul does not promote or insist on that opposition: rather his protest is precisely against a missionary policy which set the experience of the Galatians in opposition to the claims of covenantal nomism, which in effect put the law above the Spirit, by insisting that the fruit of the Spirit was impossible for those outside the law.

24 Paul now rounds off this section of paraenesis by reverting to and rewording the opening assurance (v.16): **and those who belong to the Christ Jesus**, the phrase with its titular resonance (the Christ/Messiah; see above p. 294 n. 6) recalling, no doubt deliberately, the conclusion of iii.29 and the argument leading up to it (see on iii.29), **have crucified the flesh with its passions** (used negatively here, as in Rom. vii.5, contrast iii.5 above, and so a near synonym with the following word – see Burton 320–1 and *TDNT* v.930) **and desires** (see on v.16, here in the plural to indicate particular expressions or instances). As the talk of freedom in v.1–12 required the cautionary reminder that freedom can be all too easily abused, so the last two nouns provide a warning that feeling and emotion, important as they are (v.22), can easily be degraded into mere passion and self-indulgence.

The talk of crucifying the flesh is striking. So to use crucifixion as a metaphor was unheard of at the time. Crucifixion was such a horrific punishment (see M. Hengel, *Crucifixion* [London: SCM, 1977]) that the use of it in any kind of positive sense would probably have seemed almost obscene, 'gallows humour' of the lowest kind (contrast the negative force in the nearest parallel in Philo, *Som.* ii.213). The Christian usage is thus entirely dependent on the Christian evaluation of Jesus' death on the cross. The metaphor means, to do to the flesh precisely what was done to Jesus by crucifying him (the challenge of Mark viii.34–5 pars). Implicit also, therefore, is the further echo of ii.19: what is in view is the being-crucified-with-Christ there spoken of. That is to say, Paul doubtless had in mind the whole theme of the believer's sharing in Christ's sufferings and death (see on ii.19 and vi.14). It is another way of expressing the eschatological significance of Christ's death, as an act which broke the power of 'the present evil age' (see on i.4), as expressed not least in the power of fleshly weakness in captivating and dominating with its 'passions and desires'. The only way that power could be broken was by putting the flesh on the cross, that is, by bringing it to its natural end in death, that is, by killing it! But that could only be achieved safely (without finally destroying humanity) and effectively (for more than the one or two) by participation in the one death of flesh which had broken through the cul-de-sac of death in the present evil age, that is, the death of Christ.

What Paul adds at this point is (1) the important emphasis on human responsibility in thus participating in Christ's crucifixion. Here the single metaphor answers to the double exhortation-and-assurance of v.16: as there is a responsibility to 'walk by the

Spirit', so there is a responsibility actively to participate in the killing off of the flesh, or, more precisely, 'the flesh with its passions and desires' (even here the flesh is not seen as wholly negative; cf. particularly Rom. viii.13); as there is an assurance that such commitment will ensure that the desire of the flesh will not be satisfied, so the active force of the metaphor of crucifixion here presupposes the passive use already in ii.19 and again in vi.14.

(2) Equally significant is the use of the aorist tense at this point, in contrast to the perfect tense of ii.19. What is being emphasized here is the decisive act taken at the beginning of their Christian experience (not subsequent moral decision, as *TDNT* vii.583); that is, when they were baptized (iii.27; baptism as an act of commitment and self-mortification) and received the Spirit (iii.2 – as usual, the primary focus of such recall to beginnings). The initial event by which they became members of the covenant people was a mysterious blend of divine initiative and enabling, and human response and commitment. Once again Paul directs his readers back to the decisiveness of that event: it was not lacking in anything decisive for their participation in the new age introduced by Christ. That did not mean, and Paul would hardly expect so to be taken, that the Galatians had thereby achieved a quasi-docetic state, wherein the flesh could exert no more influence; such an interpretation, of course, would make nonsense of the exhortations of v.13 and 16 (though some have unwisely interpreted the parallel aorists of Rom. vi.6 in such an extreme way). As the overall balance of divine initiative and human response is clear, so also is the balance in Paul's understanding of the process of salvation between the 'already' and the 'not yet'. For further treatments of the theme of the indicative and imperative in Paul's ethics see Schlier 264–7, Fung 278–83, Schrage 167–72 and my *Romans* 301–3.

3 WHAT IT MEANS FOR MUTUAL
RELATIONSHIPS   v.25–vi.6

(25) If we live by the Spirit, let us also follow the Spirit.
(26) Let us not become conceited, provoking one another,
envying one another.[1] (vi.1) Brothers,[2] if however a person[3] is
detected in some transgression, let you who are spiritual
restore that person in a spirit of gentleness, keeping an eye
on yourself lest you also be tempted. (2) Bear one another's
burdens and thus you shall fulfil[4] the law of Christ. (3) For if
anyone thinks he is someone important, when he is not, he
deceives himself. (4) Let each evaluate his own work, and
then he will have reason for boasting with reference to
himself alone and not with reference to the other person. (5)
For each will have to bear his own load. (6) But let the one
who is taught the word share in all good things with the one
who teaches.

Having described what it means to be led by the Spirit in broad
generic terms of character formation, Paul now indicates how
this will work out in the practical terms of everyday relationships
within the community and the mutual responsibilities which love
will lay upon its members. The sequence of thought is simply an
elaboration of the thematic call of v.13: having filled out the
contrast between the freedom of the flesh and the freedom of the
Spirit (v.16–24), he now seeks to elaborate what is involved in
serving one another through love. The style, form and in large
measure content of the ethical maxims used by Paul are familiar
elsewhere in the Greco–Roman world (Betz 291–3; but see
Barclay, *Obeying* 170–7), but the source of motivation (the Spirit
– v.25) and the norm of behaviour (Christ – vi.2) are
distinctively Christian. On the applicability of the maxims to the
Galatian Christians see particularly Longenecker 268–71.

1 The more strongly attested accusative may reflect the original, since in
classical usage *phthoneō* was followed by the dative, to which more stylistically
sensitive scribes were likely to have altered their texts.
2 See on p. 23 n. 3.
3 Again later manuscripts indicate that some scribes thought it desirable to
make clear that the 'someone' in view was a member of the Christian
community – hence 'someone from among you'.
4 A natural variant was to read the imperative ('and thus fulfil'), treating the
second half of the verse as a continuation of the exhortation rather than as a
promise attached to the imperative of the first half; see Metzger 598.

Paul has a technique of summing up a phase of his argument
or exhortation in a tightly structured sentence which serves to
introduce the next point he wishes to make (cf. e.g. Rom. iii.20,
31; iv.25; viii.17); so here, v.25, which by its very form reflects
the indicative-imperative structure of Paul's ethics. The
exhortation is then elaborated, first negatively (v.26) and then
positively (vi.1–6), echoing the similar structure of v.13, and thus
helping to bind the whole section (v.13–vi.6) together.
Fundamental to v.25–vi.6 is the thought that the order of the
Spirit is marked both by sympathy towards others and readiness
to criticize oneself – not the other way round! That the
exhortations are concrete but general and not prescriptive in
close detail marks the difference between an ethic of Spirit and
an ethic of law. For discussion on where the paragraph break
should come see e.g. Longenecker 265; but the address 'brothers'
in vi.1 need not indicate a new section (cf. iv.28, 31 and v.11).

25 As at the beginning of the previous section (v.16), Paul
sums up what he wants to say with a thematic statement (as in
v.1, without a conjunction). And as at v.16 he does so in terms of
the Spirit – **If we live by the Spirit, let us also follow the
Spirit**. The first verb is evidently intended as an all-embracing
description of character and direction of life, as in its earlier uses
(ii.14, 19, 20; iii.11–12). But not so all-embracing as to render the
second half of the verse meaningless. The implicit contrast
between the two halves is evidently that between principle and
working out, or between beginning and continuation. In other
words, this is a further variation on one of the major themes of
the letter: what is involved in the 'second phase' of salvation (see
Introduction §6.3); and on Paul's insistence that the second phase
must be consistent with the first. That is also to say, Paul here,
once again, must be recalling his readers to their initiating
experience of the Spirit (iii.2–3). We could paraphrase, 'Since we
now experience a wholly different quality of life as a
consequence of our reception of the Spirit, . . .'; there is, of
course, no doubt expressed by the 'if' (BDF §371.1); hence the
NEB/REB translation – 'If the Spirit is the source of our life'.

The second verb, on which the emphasis falls, is not simply a
synonym for 'walk' (as RSV/NRSV; see on v.16), but presumably
is intended by Paul to retain something of its basic sense of
'stand in line' (Zahn 267; Oepke 186); hence to 'keep in step
with' (NIV), 'hold to, agree with, follow' (BAGD, *stoicheō*), 'be in
harmony with' (*TDNT* vii.668–9). As in its only other occurrence
in this letter (vi.16), the verb carries with it a sense of order
imposed by an external authority or in accord with a recognized

standard (elsewhere in Paul only Rom. iv.12 and Phil. iii.16). Paul, in other words, does not see the Spirit as an anarchic power disruptive of all order, and continues to warn against treating the freedom given by the Spirit as a licence for self-indulgence. As the elaboration of this thematic exhortation indicates (v.26–vi.6), the distinction between the well-ordered life of the Spirit and the nomistic life-style to which so many of his readers were attracted is not to be reduced simply to a sharp antithesis between Spirit and law. At the same time, the difference from a life ordered in accord with the elemental forces (iv.3) or nature is clear.

26 What it means to follow the Spirit is elaborated first in negative terms – **Let us not become conceited, provoking one another, envying one another.** The concern for mutual relationships ('one another'), so strong in v.13–15, re-emerges with force. It is here that the life and leadership of the Spirit, or claims regarding them, are brought to the acid test; the fruit of the Spirit is nothing if it does not appear in genuine practical concern for one another. The three clauses are obviously linked. Those who are (self-)conceited, who are preoccupied with (literally) empty glory, and who in consequence are boastful (cf. e.g. *4 Macc.* ii.15; elsewhere in the NT only Phil. ii.3), will also tend to provoke or challenge others by their empty pretensions, and to envy those whom they perceive as a threat to their sense of self-importance (the last two verbs appearing only here in the NT). Once again Paul exhibits a shrewd insight into human psychology, as confirmed repeatedly in spiritual awakenings in the history of Christianity: those who claim to have been specially graced by the Spirit often assume an importance and authority well beyond even their Spirit-enhanced abilities, encouraging a spirit of competitiveness in charismatic manifestations and provoking schism within the larger community (see also on v.15).

vi.1 Within a community such a degeneration of spiritual life into self-glorifying flights of fancy can be prevented only by a thoroughgoing and realistic emphasis on the 'one-another', that is, by a concern for others which displaces or rises above self-concern. So Paul turns to the positive working out of the 'order of the Spirit', and envisages a quite different scenario. **Brothers** (as usual, this would be recognized as embracing all members of the congregations where the letter was read out; see on i.2), **if, however, a person is detected in some transgression . . ..** The meaning is ambiguous. The form of the verb implies some element of surprise or unexpectedness – literally 'taken beforehand', though the weight of the prefix ('beforehand') is in dispute (BAGD, *prolambanō*). What is unclear is whether the person in view has been caught off guard by a 'false step or blunder' (LSJ, *paraptōma*) ('do something wrong on a sudden impulse', NEB; cf. Wisd.Sol. 17.17 – 'seized' by sudden and unexpected fear); or has been discovered (unexpectedly) in the act of some 'transgression' (e.g. Lightfoot 215; Lagrange 155; Schlier 270). The weight placed upon the example by Paul suggests the latter: the test of spiritual maturity is dealing kindly not just with the unwitting (and regretted) mistake, but with the fellow Christian whose deliberate unacceptable conduct has come to light despite his or her attempts at concealment; but Paul may have been content to leave his meaning ambiguous. Paul does not specify the 'transgression', but in the moral climate within which these first Christian congregations had to exist he would presumably have in mind any one of the range of sins listed in such catalogues as v.19–21. That he takes it for granted that there will be such occasions is a reminder that Paul did not assume the possibility of sinless perfection in this life.

Let you who are spiritual restore that person in a spirit of gentleness. To whom is Paul addressing himself? (1) Does he mean all members of the Galatian congregations, since all are embraced by the references of iii.2 and v.25 ('you who have received the Spirit', NRSV)? That at first seems less than likely, since 'you who are spiritual' seems to imply a group within the whole, and presumably Paul did not expect the whole congregation to descend on the guilty fellow member.

(2) More likely, Paul has particularly in mind those who happened to catch the person in the act; the close conjunction of the two clauses may point that way, and the closest parallels elsewhere in the NT certainly do (Matt. xviii.15; James v.19). In effect he appeals to those who detected the person in transgression: a test of your spirituality is how you handle that situation.

(3) A third possibility is that Paul could be referring to a leadership group, such as may be implied in James v.14–15 and John xx.23. The difficulty here is that Paul would then be giving dangerous hostages to fortune, by encouraging the idea that there were some within a congregation who could be designated more spiritual than the rest. Of course, Paul himself could be falling into the trap of over-emphasizing manifest experience or overt displays of the Spirit as a mark of maturity (cf. the thesis of Drane); and it could be that he learned only by later experience how badly wrong such an emphasis could go (1 Cor. ii.13–iii.1);

that is, had he written Galatians after he wrote 1 Corinthians he would not have expressed himself as he does here! But the thrust of v.13ff. has surely been sufficient to indicate that Paul needed no lessons on the danger of a too enthusiastic emphasis on the Spirit.

(4) On the possibility of there being a pneumatic faction in Galatia, see the Introduction §5 – 'a group who claimed the title for themselves' (Barrett, *Freedom* 79); but the reference here is neither sarcastic nor disapproving. At the same time, Rom. xv.1 is a reminder that Paul could envisage congregations in which some were more mature (in his view) than others in their appreciation of the gospel, and indeed that he could count himself as one of the strong (Rom. xiv.14, 20), or, by implication, one of the 'spirituals' (cf. 1 Cor. ii.6–16; vii.40). In which case he would be appealing in effect to his own supporters within the Galatian congregations and indicating how that maturity/ spirituality should be displayed (but Lightfoot 215 rightly notes that there are 'no very distinct traces of such a party in the Galatian churches').

(5) A less specific variation is that Paul is appealing to those convinced by his own arguments in the letter, over against those more attracted by the clear rules and regulations ('works') of the law. Paul, in other words, expected those who were led by the Spirit and who were not succumbing to the clearer cut attractions of the Jewish way of life (cf. iii.2–3; iv.6–10; v.2–6) to provide the spiritually sensitive leadership (rather than rule-book formalism) which such delicate situations require.

(6) A further variation, closer to (1), is that Paul is laying a more general challenge before all his readers ('brothers'), which he expects at least some of them to respond to (cf. particularly Schweizer, *TDNT* vi.424, n.605). That is, he gives an example of what a life ordered by the Spirit will mean in mutual relationships, and expects that as the congregation as a whole seeks the leading of the Spirit, some will be directed to deal with the case in question, thus demonstrating the character of their spirituality, but as a responsibility recognized by all those acknowledging the Spirit's leadership (cf. 1 Cor. xiv.37; Phil. iii.15). A decision between these possibilities is not easy, but the immediate context and the implicit challenge implies some combination of (2), (5) and (6).

At all events it is significant that the test of spirituality indicated is one involving delicate personal relationships, where the spirituality is marked by the character of the objective and means: to restore the erring fellow member to his former condition and mend the injured relationships (BAGD, *katartizō* 1;

cf. 2 Cor. xiii.11; the tense implies that it might be a lengthy
task); and to do so in a spirit (the ambiguity is probably
deliberate) which expresses the gentleness which is part of the
fruit of the Spirit (see on v.23; cf. 1 Cor. iv.21; 2 Cor. x.1). It is
striking that such concern should be Paul's immediate response
to such a 'transgression', rather than the thought of discipline
and punishment (contrast 1 Cor. v; Lightfoot 215 refers appropriately to 2 Cor. ii.6–8). Moreover, it is important to note that,
once again, Paul has no thought of the Spirit's operating in
anarchic terms (see also on v.16). On the contrary, a community
of maturing spirituality is one where there are clear moral
guidelines ('transgression'), and where there are those with
pastoral and counselling skills able to deal in a sensitive manner
with such as ignore these guidelines, and without wholesale
recourse to the law. The contrast with the attitudes warned
against in v.26 is very marked.

The contrast, however, is pushed further. For those addressed
can only maintain such pastoral ministry if, all the while they
are engaged in it, you **keep an eye on yourself lest you**
(singular, to bring home the individual application) **also be
tempted** or be put to a test similar to that which proved the
undoing of the erring fellow member. The first verb has the
force of 'look at carefully or critically' (LSJ, *skopeō*; *TDNT*
vii.414–15; cf. Rom. xvi.17; Phil. ii.4). Paul sees the ability to
maintain a critical self-scrutiny as equally a mark of the Spirit
(see on vi.4); the spiritual person lives out the old Greek proverb,
'Know thyself' (see also Betz 298). Here too Paul draws on the
wisdom of sound pastoral experience: those who become involved
with a person guilty of some (presumably) moral failure (cf.
1 Cor. vii.5; x.9; James i.13–14) become vulnerable to the same
failure precisely because of their genuine sympathy with that
person in that failing. It is this very sense of human frailty
which helps maintain the dependence on the Spirit which marks
out 'those who are spiritual'. Again the contrast with the self-
assertiveness described in v.26 is strongly marked.

2 A life ordered by the Spirit will be able not only to handle
occasional lapses of fellow members, but also to accept the more
humdrum daily responsibility of helping out those fellow
members whose load is too heavy for them to bear alone – **Bear
one another's burdens** (not a distinctively Christian exhortation
– Betz 299). A reference to the burden of the law's commands
(Lightfoot 216) is unlikely; that burden he wanted to exempt the
Galatians wholly from (v.1–4). It is possible, however, that by
'burdens' Paul was still thinking of the sort of moral lapses

alluded to in vi.1 (BAGD, *baros* 1; *TDNT* i.555; cf. Rom. xv.1); and it could be that Paul envisaged both the (now repentant) transgressor experiencing the transgression as a burden, and some regular practice of mutual confession of sin. But it is more likely that the word 'burden' has a broader meaning. Elsewhere it is regularly used to denote the burden of suffering, but also the burden of responsibility (Matt. xx.12), or the burden of taxation (*TDNT* i.554). So here Paul is probably thinking of a whole range of illnesses and physical disabilities, of responsibilities borne by slaves or widows, scruples of fellow members (Rom. xv.1 – not sins), and so on; though the particular thought of bearing financial responsibility for another (J. G. Strelan, 'Burden-Bearing and the Law of Christ: A Re-examination of Galatians vi.2', *JBL* 94 [1975] 266–76) is probably reserved for vi.6. At any one time all members of a Christian congregation would have such burdens to shoulder, and when such burdens outgrew the individual's strength, it was important that there should be a supportive family-community to help out. This too and particularly this was the mark of the Spirit-led community – concern to restore the transgressor and to sustain the too heavily burdened, not concern to keep particular rules which excluded the 'sinner'. It was such mutual concern and support which caused not a few in the ancient Mediterranean world to exclaim, 'See how these Christians love one another!'

Not least of importance for Paul was the fact that **thus**, through such concern and conduct, **you shall fulfil the law of Christ**. Almost certainly Paul refers in this shorthand way to the Jesus-tradition as indicating how Jesus interpreted the law in his teaching and actions. (1) It can hardly be doubted that much of what now makes up the Synoptic accounts of Jesus' ministry was passed on to new churches, as part of their founding traditions; any group identifying itself by reference to a particular individual (Christians) would want to know enough about that individual in order to inform their own identity and to enable them to explain who they were to others (see also on vi.6). That Paul saw it as one of his priorities to pass on such ethical traditions is clearly enough indicated in passages like 1 Cor. xi.2, 1 Thess. iv.2 and 2 Thess. ii.15. (2) The clearly discernible echo of not a few Synoptic sayings equally indicates a common pool of shared knowledge of Jesus' teaching to which allusion could be made without further identification (e.g. Rom. xii.14; xiv.13–14; xvi.19; 1 Thess. v.2, 5, 13). (3) Even more significant is the fact that in v.14 Paul had almost certainly intended to draw upon one of Jesus' most important teachings (see on v.14), and that verses v.13–14 serve as a heading for the whole section to be elaborated in what follows: what Paul calls for here is an expression of neighbour love (it has been common among commentators to limit the reference to the love command).

(4) Most striking of all, is the parallel between Rom. xiii.8–10, xv.1–2 and Gal. v.14, vi.2; note not least the common theme of 'fulfilling' the law (Rom. xiii.8, 10; Gal. v.14; vi.2; see on v.14). In both cases the call for love of neighbour, in echo of Jesus' teaching, is followed by a series of practical exhortations illustrating this love. In Romans the climax comes with clear allusion back to xiii.8–10 and with explicit evocation of the example of Christ (xv.2–3). In Galatians the climax comes by referring to the law of Christ at the equivalent point and with the equivalent function: fulfilling the law of Christ (Gal. vi.2) means following the example of Christ in seeking the good of the neighbour (Rom. xv.2–3). Thus, to refer the phrase 'simply to the way of life characteristic of the church of Christ' (Räisänen, *Paul* 77–82) is inadequate; we must speak at least of Christ's self-giving treated as a paradigm for Christian relationships (R. B. Hays, 'Christology and Ethics in Galatians: The Law of Christ' *CBQ* 49 [1987] 268–90, here 289–90). (5) The phrase looks like a Christian formulation, and not an adaptation of a Jewish belief in 'the Torah of the Messiah' (Oepke 188; Schlier 272) for which there is insufficient evidence at this time.

It is significant, not least, that Paul speaks of *the law* of Christ (an exceptional phrase in the NT). If the above reasoning is correct, this does not mean a law other than the Torah, the (Jewish) law. It means that law as interpreted by the love command in the light of the Jesus-tradition and the Christ-event (so particularly H. Schürmann, '"Das Gesetz des Christus" [Gal. vi.2]: Jesu Verhalten und Wort als letztgültige sittliche Norm nach Paulus', *Neues Testament und Kirche*, R. Schnackenburg Festschrift, ed. J. Gnilka [Freiburg: Herder, 1974] 282–300, here 289). Thus it is in line with the important sequence of positive references to 'the law' which pepper Paul's major writings (particularly Rom. iii.27, 31; vii. 12, 14; viii.2, 4; ix.31; xiii.8–10; 1 Cor. ix.20–1; Gal. v.14), but which are usually discounted or interpreted differently in view of the (seemingly) overwhelmingly negative view of the law elsewhere (with reference to ii.19, iii.19–21, 24 and v.4). In contrast, the fact that Paul does not call for an abandonment of the law, but retains it (reinterpreted through Christ) as a norm for ethical behaviour and relationships among Christians, is an important reminder that Paul did not see Christianity as constituting a complete break with the religion of Israel, but as its mature form (see again iv.1–7). It also means that Christian theologies which work from a fundamental gospel/law antithesis require rather more careful nuancing of their basic principle.

So far as Paul's ethical paraenesis is concerned, it is also important that he calls upon an external norm (the law of Christ), as well as the inward principle of the indwelling Spirit. It is precisely such norms which are necessary to prevent a too exclusively focused Spirit-ethic from degenerating into the attitudes illustrated in v.13a and 26; precisely the example and teaching of Jesus which provide essential guidelines and illustrations of what counts as Christian conduct; only so can the interdependence of Paul's theology and the teaching of the (Synoptic) Gospels be held in proper balance. At the same time, we should recall that at the head of both of the main paragraphs in this section Paul puts the first emphasis on the leading of the Spirit (v.16, 25): it is only the Spirit which can make the norm a dynamic motivating power, only the Spirit which can enable that sustained love of neighbour so fully illustrated by Jesus (see also on v.16).

3 Having made his point positively, Paul, in good teaching style, underlines it by warning against the opposite – **for if anyone thinks he is someone important** (literally 'something'), **when he is not** (literally 'being nothing'), **he deceives** (a rare word, but with clear meaning; cf. Tit. i.10) **himself**. In fact, Paul reverts to the warning of v.26 – 'mind-deceiving' as equivalent to 'empty glory' – with perhaps a further echo of the distancing description of the Jerusalem apostles in ii.6. The maxim may be of widespread use (Betz 301), but similar warnings are a feature of Paul's paraenesis (e.g. Rom. xi.20, 25; xii.3, 16; 1 Cor. i.30; iv.8; viii.1–2; xii.21; 2 Cor. xii.11; Phil. ii.3); many refer to the parable of the Pharisee and the Tax-collector (Luke xviii.9–14), but still more apposite is a reference to 1 Cor. xiii.2. Evidently Paul himself was familiar with Christians who, delighting in their experience of the Spirit, assumed airs and responsibilities which they were manifestly unfit to discharge. He does not name names, but the attitude of superiority and inflated self-esteem were a sufficiently common occurrence for Paul to express himself in blunt terms.

4 The remedy is for each to have a sober estimate of the abilities, gifts and responsibilities bestowed by God and through the Spirit (Rom. xii.3). This includes the important responsibility of critically examining what one accomplishes – **Let each evaluate his own work**. The verb has the force of 'make critical discrimination, test'. It describes one of the most desirable gifts, as recognized by contemporary philosophers as well (Betz 302; Bruce 262) – to be able to discriminate what is of real importance (Rom. ii.18; xii.2; Phil 1.10). But even more to be coveted is the gift of self-discernment (1 Cor. xi.28; 2 Cor. xiii.5). Elsewhere Paul makes it clear that the near synonym (cf. 1 Thess. v.21 with 1 Cor. xiv.29) is itself a gift of the Spirit (1 Cor. xii.10; cf. 1 Cor. ii.13). Such critical self-appraisal, not least as measured by the love command and the law of Christ, is the essential antidote to the danger of empty glory (v.26–vi.1; see on vi.1) and uncritical self-esteem (vi.3). The use of 'work' meaning conduct or actions is common and would not be confused with the more technical 'works of the law' (see on ii.16).

The next sentence sounds odd – **and then he will have reason for boasting with reference to himself alone and not with reference to the other person**. For elsewhere Paul regards the boasting which at first seems to be in view here in a very negative light (Rom. iii.27; iv.2; 1 Cor. i.29; v.6; ix.16; 2 Cor. v.12). Mussner 401 and Rohde 262 indeed suggest there is a note of deep resignation here: an honest self-appraisal will show that one's own work is mostly affected by sin, so that such self-boasting is only empty glory (v.26). The key, however, is probably to be found in the preposition – *eis*, 'towards, in reference to', rather than *en*, 'in' (as in Rom. ii.17, 23; v.3, 11; etc.). That is to say, what is in view is not the object of which boast is made ('boasting in/of oneself'), but, as it were, the target of boasting, the direction and purpose of the boasting. It is a boasting which emerges from the process of self-evaluation (the act of critical self-comparison of oneself as though a spectator of one's own conduct), and which reflects a positive result; not a boasting which is concerned to compare oneself with another and to demonstrate superiority to the other. In other words, Paul envisages his audiences as being confident in their conduct and relationships as a result of careful self-discernment; the thought is close to Rom. xiv.22–3, and the thought of critical self-assessment allowing some boasting is present also elsewhere in Paul (Rom. xv.17; 1 Cor. ix.15; 2 Cor. i.12; x.9–10, 13–17; xi.10, 30; xii.5–6, 9; Phil. ii.16). Verses 4–5, in fact, are all about taking proper responsibility for oneself; and that includes an appropriate self-respect – the other side of the love command ('. . . your neighbour *as yourself*' – v.14).

5 This is evidently the balance Paul attempts to maintain as he rounds off this section of paraenesis – **for each will have to bear his own load**. The verb is the same as in vi.2 – thus underlining the complementary character of the two exhortations. But the noun is different, and unlike *baros* may refer simply to the load of inescapable and everyday responsibilities (cf. LSJ, *phortion*) – the adjective strengthening the point ('his own' and not anyone else's). This also is a product of discriminating self-evaluation of one's situation: the recognition that there are responsibilities which cannot be shelved or passed on to others. The mature spiritual community (and political society) is one which is able to distinguish those loads which individuals must bear for themselves, and those burdens where help is needed.

It does not follow from Matt. xxiii.4/Luke xi.46 that the burden of the law is in view here. Though if it is, the thought is still more close to that of Rom. xiv.22–3, and indeed of Rom. xiv as a whole: each should decide what is the burden of the law in his or her own case, and not by comparison with others (Rom. xiv.3–6) (BAGD, *phortion*). On the other hand, the complementary character of vi.2 indicates that the thought is not simply that of the philosophical ideal of *autarkeia*, 'self-sufficiency' (despite Betz 304). If, alternatively, the two words denoting 'burden' are synonyms, and if there is thought of the burden of sin in the former (see on vi.2), then part of the point here is that one should take responsibility for one's own sins, but be willing to interpret the failings of others in a generous spirit. However, it is less likely that the future tense looks to the final judgement, despite the parallel of Rom. xiv.12.

6 Having struck a fine balance between taking responsibility for others and bearing responsibility for oneself, Paul seems to have had a sudden thought. To end this sequence on mutual relationships thus could have one unfortunate result. For some might take the exhortation, to bear one's own burden (vi.2), as applicable to those members of a church who were called and gifted for a ministry which prevented their earning enough to maintain themselves. So he hastens to qualify his last exhortation – **But** (the lightness of the adversative perhaps indicating that Paul had mixed views on the point – see below) **let the one who is taught the word share** (BAGD, *koinōneō* 2) **in all good things with the one who teaches**. An allusion to a particular problem among the Galatian churches is less likely, since the exhortation receives no particular emphasis.

Paul uses the language of 'sharing' which was a feature of the new movement from its earliest days (Acts ii.42, 44–5; iv.34–5), and which was the main motivation behind Paul's own commitment to the collection for the poor (Christians) in

Jerusalem (Rom. xv.26–7; 2 Cor. viii.4; ix.13). But that was a sharing more in line with the exhortation of vi.2 – the responsibility of the (relatively) rich for the poor (as also Rom. xii.13; Did. iv.8; probably also Barn. xix.8), itself an extension of the strong tradition of Jewish social concern for the poor, the widow and the orphan (as in Philo, *Spec. Leg.* ii.107), which helped mark out the Jewish ethos within the wider world of the time (*TDNT* iii.803). Here, however, what is in view is more in line with Rom. xv.24, Phil. i.5 and iv.15 – that is, the financial support necessary to maintain missionary work or other ministry on behalf of the Christian community. The principle that those who taught something of value should be supported by followers or sympathizers was, of course, well established in the ancient world (see Betz 305) and could be underpinned by a dominical word (Luke x.7; 1 Cor. ix.14). Elsewhere in Paul's ministry it caused a good deal of controversy – not least because Paul, though recognizing his right to such support, usually refused to take it (1 Cor. ix.3–18; 2 Cor. xi.7–11; 1 Thess. ii.9; 2 Thess. iii.7–10)! But here he states the principle clearly and without qualification, from which an obvious deduction is that financial support was not an issue with the other missionaries in Galatia (in contrast to the later controversy in Corinth). The 'all good things' presumably covers all that was generally agreed to be necessary to material well-being (cf. Luke i.53, xii.18–19 and xvi.25); some, like Duncan 183–5 and Oepke 191–3, think that a moral and religious exchange of 'spiritual goods' is primarily in view (but see Schlier 275 and Rohde 264), though this is less obvious since Paul is referring to the responsibility of the taught.

The verb ('taught', 'teach') denotes only religious instruction in early Christian literature (Acts xviii.25; 1 Cor. xiv.19), and from it comes the English transliteration 'catechesis'. But at this stage a distinctively pre-baptismal catechesis should not be thought of (as perhaps already in 2 Clem. xvii.1), since baptism seems to have been administered without delay in the NT period (e.g. Acts xvi.15, 33). What is probably more in view is the responsibility to instruct new Christians in the things which distinguished them as Christians, within and in relation to the wider Jewish and Greco-Roman communities – including the Jesus-tradition (see on vi.2), the ramifications of the gospel, and Christian interpretation of the Jewish scriptures (all embraced within 'the word' – cf. particularly Luke i.4, Acts xvii.11, 1 Cor. xiv.36 and Col. iii.16; but NJB's 'in doctrine' is too narrow). This is certainly in line with the other, confirmatory evidence that teachers and teaching played an important role within the earliest Christian groups (Acts xiii.1; Rom. xii.7; 1 Cor. xii.28;

Eph. iv.11); and it is what we would have expected anyway — that is, that such new formations within first-century Mediterranean society would require to be instructed in the founding traditions which gave them their identity.

This text provides the earliest evidence of what we might call a 'professional' Christian ministry, although we should note that it was dependent on the sense of obligation (and ability to pay) of the one taught, rather than on a more formal organization. To absorb the range of material already part of a church's founding traditions, to master it and to be responsible for retaining it within the community (in oral form), for recalling it in church gatherings, and for giving instruction in it as occasion demanded, was a considerable and time-consuming responsibility. Probably only freedmen or citizens could engage in it (Epictetus only began to teach philosophy after he had been freed from slavery). And while almost certainly the majority of the teachers were men, such references as Acts xviii.26 and the prominence of such women as Phoebe, Junia and Nympha (Rom. xvi.1–2, 7; Col. iv.15) suggest that women (though usually not wives — 1 Cor. xiv.34–6) could also have filled this role. At all events the fact that teaching was the first Christian 'professional' ministry is an important reminder of the extent to which the first churches were built round 'the word' (see BAGD, *logos* 1bβ) and were distinguished by the importance they placed on instruction in it.

4 REAPING THE REWARD vi.7–10

(7) Be not deceived: God is not mocked! For whatever a person sows, that is what he or she shall also reap. (8) For those[1] who sow to their own flesh shall from the flesh reap corruption; but those who sow to the Spirit shall from the Spirit reap eternal life. (9) Let us not become weary in well-doing, for in due time we will reap, if we do not lose heart. (10) So then, as we have[2] opportunity, let us work for the good of all, especially the members of the household of faith.

---

1 The Greek is singular, as in verse 7b, but the general assertion can be rendered equally well using the plural.
2 Two important manuscripts read the subjunctive ('as we may have'), but the sense is more or less the same.

As in other letters (Rom. xiii.11–14; Phil. iii.12–21; cf. 1 Cor. xv) Paul brings his more general paraenesis to a climax and conclusion by looking to the future. Since his eschatological expectation was both a spur and a constraint in his own work (e.g. Rom. xi.13–15; 1 Cor. ix.27), it was natural that he should expect it to exercise the same effect on his churches (hence Phil. iii.12–16). The paragraph is constructed round the imagery of sowing and reaping, and once again takes its starting-point from the fact of the Spirit's activity in their own lives (vi.8).

7 Be not deceived! Such abruptness is quite typical of Paul's paraenesis; there is no transitional particle, but of itself that would not exclude a continuity of thought with vi.6. This particular challenge may be something of a rhetorical trick, intended, in part at least, to retain (or regain) attention, and one he may have learned from the use of the diatribe among Stoic teachers (*TDNT* vi.244–5; cf. 1 Cor. vi.9; xv.33; also Luke xxi.8 and James i.16). The implication is not that anyone was deliberately trying to deceive the Galatians, simply that they could be holding an opinion or following a course of action which amounted to self-deception. The abruptness of the challenge is rather an attempt by Paul, following a section which could have lulled his Galatian audiences into a false sense of security, to startle them back into an awareness of the danger of their current situation.

God is not mocked! NIV's 'God cannot be mocked' does not change the sense. The imagery is of 'turning up one's nose' and so treating contemptuously, though the verb could be taken in the sense 'let oneself be deceived' – 'Don't let yourselves be deceived; God doesn't!' (*TDNT* iv.796; Rohde 265–6). The language is Jewish, though the thought of humans mocking or despising God is rare (only in Prov. i.30 and Ezek. viii.17), and the sentiment would be hardly distinctive to Jewish monotheism (see Betz 306–7). Again the implication is hardly that anyone in the Galatian situation was trying to do so. It is simply a way of bringing home the folly (in Paul's eyes) of the present trend in Galatia. The thought is more of the certainty of judgement, rather than of its imminence.

For whatever a person sows, that is what he or she shall also reap. The correspondence between what is sown and what is reaped was a natural image for human action and its (inescapable) consequences and gave the metaphor widespread proverbial currency; see particularly Job iv.8, Prov. xxii.8 ('he who sows injustice will reap calamity'), Jer. xii.13, Hos. viii.7, Sir. vii.3, Philo, *Legat.* 293, *Test. Levi* xiii.6 ('If you sow evil, you

THE EPISTLE TO THE GALATIANS

will reap every kind of trouble and tribulation'); also Plato, *Phaedrus* 260D and Aristotle, *Rhetorica* 3.3.4 (BAGD, *therizō* 2; Bruce 264). A modern equivalent is that we are free to choose, but we are not free to choose the consequences of our choice. What is significant here is the way Paul turns this common proverb to his own account by adapting it to his own characteristic Spirit–flesh contrast.

8 For those who sow to their own flesh shall from the flesh reap corruption. The reference once again back to the 'flesh', a theme so prominent in this letter (see on ii.16, 20 and below), is a neat attempt on Paul's part to pull together and intertwine the main threads of both his theological argument and the following paraenesis. For the 'flesh' in view is certainly that described in v.13, 16–19, 24, but also the 'flesh' of ii.16 and iii.3, as also that of iv.23 and 29 (and again of vi.12–13). That is to say, Paul clearly intended his readers to understand that the concentration which his opponents were placing on the flesh would reap the consequences outlined in v.19–21. To make so much of their own physical descent (cf. iv.23, 29) and so much of the act of circumcision, a cutting of the flesh (see on vi.12–13), was to focus the challenge of the gospel on that which was by nature given to weakness and decay and which could end only in corruption and dissolution to dust. The very concentration on ethnic identity as alone giving legitimate part in the inheritance of Abraham put the other missionaries in direct antithesis and opposition to the Spirit of God. And those who followed them would reap only the benefit of corruption, the only end even for Abraham's flesh (evoking the horrifying image of a decayed and rotted harvest). The train of thought is similar to both Rom. viii.12–13, 17–23 and 1 Cor. xv.42–50, where Spirit-inheritance and flesh-corruption are likewise set in juxtaposed antithesis. Once again the attempts by modern translations to avoid 'flesh' as a translation only succeed in obscuring a major part of Paul's meaning (NEB – 'lower nature'; REB – 'unspiritual nature'; NIV – 'sinful nature'; NJB – 'self-indulgence').

But those who sow to the Spirit shall from the Spirit reap eternal life. Again the intertwining of theology and paraenesis is evident, since the Spirit/flesh antithesis recalls the earlier expressions of the same antithesis – not only iii.2–3 and iv.29, but also v.16–24. The fact that Paul disturbs the closeness of the parallel between the two clauses by omitting 'his own' in the second (the Greek is singular; see p. 328 n. 1) makes it clear that a reference to the Spirit of God (not human spirit) is intended, and so also prevents any suggestion that purely human effort is in view or any contrast to v.25. In thus recalling his readers once again to their starting-point as Christians (iii.2–3) Paul offers a further expression of his 'second-phase' theology: that only a continued (present tense) attending to the Spirit will ensure the harvest of the Spirit (see Introduction §63). So too the implied exhortation provides an effective summary of the preceding thematic statements which opened the preceding two paragraphs: 'walk by the Spirit' (v.16); 'let us follow the Spirit' (v.25). NIV's 'sows to please the Spirit' is an unnecessary and ham-handed elaboration of a simple metaphor; such metaphors are only blunted by attempting to give 'sowing to the Spirit' (the Spirit, as it were, the field in which the seed is sown) some precise or allegorical meaning, or by treating the aphorism as a condensed version of Mark iv.3–8, 13–20 pars.

Paul is quite comfortable with the concept of 'eternal life, life without end' (Rom. ii.7; v.21; vi.22–3), although it is only a relatively late entrant to Jewish thought (Dan. xii.2; 2 Macc. vii.9; *Pss. Sol.* iii.12; the thought here is quite close to that of 1QS iv.7; see also Philo, *Fuga* 78; *4 Macc.* xv.3). As the first three references just cited indicate, the language emerged in Jewish theology in connection with the hope of resurrection. Hence Paul's preference elsewhere to pose the contrast with 'corruption' in terms of the resurrection of the body (Rom. viii.21–3; 1 Cor. xv.42–50; also 2 Cor. iv.16–v.5), since it is precisely the resurrection of the body which provides the only final answer to the decay of the flesh into dust and nothingness; the resurrected body ('spiritual body', 'eternal dwelling') is the harvest of the Spirit. The metaphor of the Spirit's harvest is obviously different from 'the fruit of the Spirit' in v.22, but the two are complementary; Paul can vary the metaphor without any sense of inconsistency, precisely because he sees a positive complementarity between the divinely produced fruit and the corresponding human responsibility (in vi.10 he does not even avoid the verb 'work' as a Christian responsibility). Consequently he can continue –

9 Let us not become weary in well-doing (see Burton 344–5), **for in due time** (see BAGD, *kairos,* and on vi.10; cf. 1 Tim. vi.15) **we will reap, if we do not lose heart**. The exhortation is somewhat stereotyped (2 Thess. iii.13), natural in a context of battle or athletic contest (cf. Deut. xx.3; 1 Macc. ix.8; Heb. xii.1–6). But the continuance of the harvest metaphor ties it to the preceding verses – the thought being of the sustained hard work required of the farmer between sowing and reaping if the harvest (of 'eternal life', vi.8) is to be won. It thus reflects the particularly eschatological tension in the Christian understanding of the process of salvation: that is, of a decisive initiating act of God (sowing in them the seed of the Spirit), followed by a lengthy period (imminent expectation is hardly marked here) of germination and growth, characteristically in adverse conditions, in which the human participants have a responsibility not to slacken in their own (co-operative) efforts (cf. the other NT uses of the first verb – Luke xviii.1; 2 Cor. iv.1, 16; Eph. iii.13; 2 Thess. iii.13). The two verbs ('become weary', 'lose heart') are near synonyms, the latter however evoking the image of an unstrung bow or of a tunic unbelted (Did. xvi.1), that is, of a state of relaxation unprepared for sudden challenge or demand (thus neatly NEB/REB – 'if we do not slacken our efforts'). It is a striking fact that Paul can re-express his exhortations to 'walk by the Spirit' and 'follow the Spirit' (v.16, 25) in such general terms ('well-doing, doing what is good'; as in Rom. vii.21, 2 Cor. xiii.7, and in equivalent terms in Rom. ii.10, vii.19 and xiii.3). The growth of spiritual life shows itself not in idiosyncratic behaviour but in conduct which all those of good will recognize to be good.

10 Consequently, Paul can round off his paraenesis with a final, unthreatening injunction – **So then, as we have opportunity**, the same word as in verse 9 ('in due time'), denoting a favourable time to be recognized or a suitable time to be seized, usually with eschatological overtones in Paul (cf. Rom. xiii.11; 1 Cor. vii.29; 2 Cor. vi.2; Col. iv.5; Eph. v.16), **let us work for the good of all** (more literally, 'do what is good for all'). It is notable that Paul in his concluding summary chooses to repeat the same non-specifically Christian exhortation as in verse 9, that is, to do what others would recognize as 'the good'. Still more notable that the concern and outreach are not to be limited to the Christian community, thus confirming that the 'neighbour' of v.14 is not to be confined to the fellow Christian (see on v.14). For all his sense of imminent eschatological denouement, Paul did not seek to encourage his churches to turn in upon themselves or to hide away from the world. On the contrary, his sense of mission to the wider community necessarily involved a considerable degree of interaction with that wider community (cf. particularly Rom. xii.14–xiii.7); hence the tensions he had to deal with later in Rom. xiv and 1 Cor. viii–x.

Nevertheless, and without diminishing that wider obligation, Paul expected his audiences to have a special care for one

another – **especially the members of the household of faith**.
The more general obligation comes to practical daily expression
in the 'love of neighbour', not as a narrowing of the general
obligation, but as the most immediate way of giving it effect (see
again on v.14). The possibility of a reference to the collection
cannot be excluded (cf. vi.6–10 with 2 Cor. ix.6–9; see
particularly L. W. Hurtado, 'The Jerusalem Collection and the
Book of Galatians', *JSNT* 5 [1979] 46–62, here 54–6) but is
hardly evident from the text. Be that as it may, the sense of
mutual obligation and responsibility is certainly heightened by
depicting the Christian community as a family, that is, in the
broader sense of household/family, including slaves (cf. the house
churches of Rom. xvi.5; 1 Cor. xvi.19; Col. iv.5; Phm. 2). The
household in view is the family of God (cf. particularly Eph.
ii.19, 1 Tim. iii.15 and Heb. iii.5–6), or in the context of
Galatians, the family and heirs of Abraham (iii.7; iii.29–iv.7;
iv.21–31; hence the repeated reference to his audiences in
Galatia as 'brothers' – see on i.2). But if the latter, it is more
precisely defined as 'the household of faith', that is, those who
are bound together by the shared experience of believing in
Christ Jesus, rather than by a common corpus of belief (see on
i.23, ii.16 and iii.2). The phrase is presumably constructed in
conscious contrast to the typical OT 'house of Israel' (e.g. Num.
xx.29; 2 Sam. i.12; Ezek. iii.4; Judith iv.15; *Pss. Sol.* xvii.42), or
some such sectarian variant as we find in the DSS – 'the house
of truth in Israel' (1QS v.6), 'the house of holiness for Israel'
(1QS viii.5), 'the house of perfection and truth in Israel' (1QS
viii.9), 'the sure house in Israel' (CD iii.19, alluding to 1 Sam.
ii.35, 2 Sam. vii.16 and 1 Kings xi.38), and 'the house of the law'
(CD xx.10, 13). In which case it will be significant once again
that the bonding characteristic of this household is faith, and not
membership of ethnic Israel, and not the Torah. Paul maintains
to the last his opposition to any attempt to change the basis and
constitution of this house to anything other than faith.

If this line of exegesis is valid, we should again note that here
too Paul finds no difficulty in conjoining faith with talk of
'doing' good and 'working' good (vi.9–10). This confirms and
underlines the earlier conclusion that Paul was not hostile to the
idea of 'doing' (as in iii.12) or to the idea of '(good) works'. The
contrast between faith and 'works of the law' is differently and
more specifically focused (see on ii.16 and iii.10, 12).

E   Postscript vi.11–18

(11) See with what large letters I have written to you in my own hand. (12) It is those who want to make a fair showing in the flesh, they are trying to compel you to be circumcised, but only to avoid being persecuted for the cross of Christ. (13) For even those who have themselves circumcised[1] do not themselves keep the law, but want you to be circumcised in order that they might boast in your flesh. (14) But as for me, God forbid that I should boast except in the cross of our Lord Jesus Christ, through whom[2] the world has been crucified to me and I to the world. (15) For[3] neither circumcision counts[3] for anything, nor uncircumcision, but a new creation. (16) And as many as will follow this rule, peace be on them and mercy, as also on the Israel of God. (17) From now on let no one cause me trouble. For I bear the marks of Jesus[4] on my body. (18) The grace of our Lord Jesus Christ be with your spirit, my brothers.[5] Amen.

It would appear that Paul regularly followed the practice of adding a concluding paragraph in his own hand at the end of his dictation (vi.11; 1 Cor. xvi.21–4; 2 Thess. iii.17; so probably also Rom. xvi.17–20; Col. iv.18); for the convention of an epistolary postscript see Lietzmann 43, Oepke 198 and Betz 312 n. 4. In this case in particular it was clearly an opportunity to underscore his special concerns in the letter and to leave no doubt as to where Paul's own emphases lay. Hence the final impassioned

---

1 Important manuscripts read the perfect passive tense, 'those who have been circumcised, in the state of circumcision'. But this is obviously explained as a change introduced by scribes who thought Paul must be referring to the other missionaries in Galatia and who wished to remove any possibility that the text be understood as referring to some of the Galatians themselves. See also Metzger 598.

2 So NJB, Borse 221. RSV/NRSV, NEB/REB, NIV and almost all commentators translate 'through which', treating 'cross' as the antecedent, even though it is separated from 'through' by the five words, 'of our Lord Jesus Christ'; Lightfoot 223 and Lagrange 165 observe that a reference to Christ would more likely have been expressed by 'in whom' or 'with whom'. But it comes to the same thing, since 'through whom' must mean 'through the crucified Christ', or 'through Christ on the cross'.

3 It would appear that some scribes introduced 'in Christ Jesus' at this point, probably under the influence of v.6; see Metzger 599. The attempt also to conform the verb to v.6 is still more obviously secondary.

4 The personal name, Jesus, on its own is sufficiently remarkable to have prompted scribes to replace it by the more common 'Christ' or to elaborate it by adding 'Lord' or 'Lord Christ' in various combinations.

5 See above p. 23 n. 3.

plea regarding circumcision (vi.12–16), involving a repeated
contrast between circumcision and the cross (vi.12, 14–15), and
the abrupt request for no more trouble on this issue (vi.17), with
a further implicit contrast between circumcision and the cross,
before the brief farewell (vi.18). The postscript thus echoes in
rough chiastic form the abrupt personal introduction and
greetings in i.1–5, followed by the similarly fervent rebuke of
i.6–9. The absence of any personal greetings is presumably an
indication of Paul's irritation at the news from Galatia (cf. vi.17).

**11 See with what large letters I have written to you in my
own hand**. The aorist tense is probably an 'epistolary aorist'
(written from the time perspective of the recipients, which could
therefore be translated 'I am writing'; as in Phm. 19 and 21). It
is more likely that Paul is referring to what he was about to
write (vi.12ff.) than that either he had written the whole letter
himself, or was referring only to the preceding paragraph. The
reversion to the theme of circumcision in vi.12ff., the subject of
the most impassioned section earlier (v.1–12), confirms the very
personal character of the plea that is to follow; hence the 'in my
own hand', giving these final utterances the indisputable stamp
of his own authority.

The 'large letters' could indicate that Paul had sustained some
injury to his hand (Zahn 278); or that his short sight (or perhaps
his sight in general) was weak – strengthening the possible
implication of iv.13–15 that he had defective eyesight (see on
iv.15). But why should he remind his audiences of that at this
point? As an attempt to win their sympathy it would jar with the
rather dismissive and peremptory tone of the following verses. It
is more likely that he wrote in large letters to emphasize the
importance of what he was about to write (see particularly Oepke
199–200), perhaps either as taking up more expensive papyrus
than would otherwise be necessary, or as large enough for the
reader to hold up so that the various congregations could read his
words for themselves (see also Bruce 268).

12 With stylus firmly in hand Paul takes the opportunity to
reinforce the primary and urgent message of his letter, directed
clearly once more (as in i.7–9, iv.17 and v.7–12) against the
other missionaries who were insisting that the Galatian converts
be circumcised, that is **those who** (literally 'as many as, all who')
want to make a fair showing in the flesh. The subordinate verb
is not attested anywhere else in literary Greek till well after our
period, but the equivalent noun ('fair appearance') is used by

Dionysius Halicarnassus (first century BC), the corresponding adjective is well enough known (LSJ, *euprosōpos* – once in LXX, Gen. xii.11), and the verb occurs in a second-century BC papyrus (MM & LSJ, *euprosōpeō*). The meaning, however, would have been clear from the construction of the word (literally 'to have a good face'). As that part of the body which most visibly registered character, feeling and personal response, *prosōpon* ('face') could indicate also the impression made on another, as well as the mask used by actors to project a character (*TDNT* vi.769–70).

There is something ironic here, however, in the talk of making such a good impression 'in the flesh'. For in typical Greek understanding such talk would naturally be taken to refer to the pleasingness of the human body, as, typically, stripped for athletic contest (such 'fair showing in the flesh' is still evident in the countless statues, part or whole, preserved from the Hellenistic period). But in this instance the 'fair showing' clearly refers to circumcision (literally 'in the flesh'), which most Greeks would regard as a form of mutilation (see on v.12): **they are trying to compel** (as in ii.14, the tense is presumably conative – BDF §319) **you to be circumcised**. As in Paul's earlier talk of 'compulsion' (ii.3, 14), then, the thought is entirely Jewish (only Jews would regard circumcision as 'making a fair showing in the flesh') and reflects the emphasis put on ethnic identity (physical descent) as most distinctively attested by the rite of circumcision ('the circumcision' = Jews; see on ii.3); the point is again obscured by failure to translate *sarx* as 'flesh' ('outwardly in good standing' – REB; 'a good impression outwardly' – NIV). That Paul can thus once again sum up the goals of his Galatian opponents in the single objective of having Paul's Galatian converts circumcised confirms the tremendous symbolic power which this one ritual act had for Jews in general. This from-inside-Judaism perspective confirms the Jewish identity of the Galatian 'trouble-makers' and Paul's ability to express his point from that perspective.

The motive Paul gives for this continued pressurizing of his converts is also notable: they do so **only** (the adverb is, of course, the exaggeration of polemic) **to avoid being** (literally, 'in order not to be') **persecuted for the cross of Christ**. That Paul had in mind fear of losing the protection of Judaism's status as a *religio licita* (Oepke 201) is unlikely: it was not Rome's policy to suppress or persecute ethnic or national religions; and Roman persecution could hardly be described as 'for the cross of Christ'. The persecution in mind is much more likely to be that also referred to in iv.29 and v.11; that is, 'persecution' by (some) Jews or Christian Jews, such as Paul both had carried out before his conversion (i.13, 23) and himself experienced (2 Cor. xi.24; see on iv.29 and v.11). The implication is clear enough: if they (the other Jewish missionaries) succeeded in circumcising those Gentiles drawn into the Nazarene movement, they would escape such persecution, presumably because their success in thus drawing these Gentiles fully within the covenant people (as proselytes) removed the reason for the persecution. This straightforward deduction seems to confirm the earlier conclusions (see particularly on i.13–16, ii.15–16 and iii.13–14): that at the heart of the problems confronted in this letter was a characteristic Jewish conviction that faithfulness to their covenant God necessarily involved the distinctiveness of the Jewish people and a marked degree of separateness from Gentiles; that it was precisely this separateness and thus withholding of the covenant inheritance from Gentiles as Gentiles which Paul was resisting so fiercely; and that pressure was being exerted by Christian Jews on Paul's converts in turn to maintain these Jewish prerogatives (see also Introduction §6.2).

That Paul should describe the persecution as 'for the cross of Christ' is also significant. This in fact is the fourth, but not last time (vi.14–15) that Paul explicitly contrasts the demands of the other missionaries with the cross (ii.18–21; iii.1–2, 10–13; v.2–6, 11). If the deduction drawn immediately above is correct, Paul does not mean that these Jewish-Christian missionaries were persecuted (by other Jews) simply because they preached a crucified Jesus as Messiah; that message was clearly at the heart of the gospel for the Christian Jews in Palestine also, and they remained relatively undisturbed. Nor can we infer that the 'different gospel' of i.6 denied the cross in any direct or overt manner. Paul must mean rather that the policy of insisting on circumcision was a way of removing that which in the common preaching of a crucified Messiah constituted an offence to most other Jews (v.11). And that must refer to the claim of Paul (and others) that the cross was a sufficient basis for acceptance into the inheritance of Israel – that is, the cross alone or, to be more precise, faith in the cross as wholly sufficient to remove sins (i.4) and neutralize the curse of the law so that the promise of Abraham might be extended to Gentiles as well (iii.13–14). By adding circumcision (= membership of the Jewish people) to the cross, the other Jewish-Christian missionaries avoided the persecution suffered by those who preached faith in the cross alone as the ground of acceptance (iii.1–2); but in so doing they also in effect made the cross of no effect (ii.21; see further on ii.21, iii.13–14 and v.11).

13 It is not clear whether Paul at this point slightly shifts his attack or continues to direct it against the other missionaries. **For even those who have themselves circumcised** would seem most naturally to refer to those in the process of being circumcised. That is, Paul may have in mind that group (probably still small) within the Galatian churches who had already succumbed to the propaganda of the other missionaries and who with the zeal of converts were now trying to persuade others to follow suit (cf. iv.21; see e.g. those cited by Bruce 269; Munck 89 and Gaston 81 build their theses that the 'Judaizers' are Paul's own Gentile converts on this verse). The alternative is to suppose that Paul's language is rather loose and that he means simply 'the circumcised' (so NRSV, NJB, NIV), those for whom circumcision is important (e.g. Zahn 280; Mussner 412, n.23; Longenecker 292); or that he uses the middle voice with causative significance (Jewett, 'Agitators' 202–3; Bruce 270; Lightfoot 222 – 'the advocates of circumcision'); that is, he continues to attack the other missionaries directly (see also p. 334 n. 1 above).

The point of critique is also surprising: they **do not themselves keep the law**. (1) If Paul was referring to a small group of Galatians who had already accepted circumcision, the point would be clearer: by accepting circumcision they have only begun to keep the law (echoing v.3; so Burton 352 and Lietzmann 44–5), and still fall well short of characteristic Jewish observance (see on v.3). Such a criticism, however, would seem to be self-defeating, since it would play into the hands of those who wanted the Galatians to become fully observant proselytes.

(2) If alternatively, Paul had in mind the Christian-Jewish missionaries in Galatia, the proper deduction might well be that such Christian Jews were not themselves wholly consistent: although more rigorous than Paul, they were not so rigorous as, for example, Pharisees and Essenes (so Howard, *Crisis* 15–16; Longenecker 293). In other words, this would be of a piece with the intersectarian polemic characteristic of Palestinian Judaism during this period (see above on ii.14–15; cf. also Acts vii.53). Such a criticism, however, would also seem to be dangerously double-edged; and by insisting on circumcision, despite the agreement at Jerusalem (ii.1–10), the other missionaries were presumably already at the extreme conservative end of the Jewish-Christian spectrum.

(3) The only other obvious solution lies along the lines of Rom. ii.12–29 (the only other context in his letters where Paul speaks about 'keeping the law' – Rom. ii.26); that is, Jewish loyalty to their covenant prerogatives and practice of covenantal nomism are not sufficient to counter the breaches of the law of

which they are guilty (Rom. ii.21–4); and the very assumption, that 'having the law' puts them in a position of advantage over those who do not (Rom. ii.12–14), is itself a sign of the pride and presumption which the law was meant to undermine (Rom iii.9–20). This last solution also makes good sense of iii.10: that those who rely on their practice as Jews (covenantal nomism, 'works of the law') are not in fact doing what the law demands (see on iii.10).

(4) As most agree, the difficulties of exegesis are not sufficiently serious to commend the suggestion that Paul is attacking here a second or different group, of libertines or Gnostics (Lütgert 20; Schmithals, *Gnostics* 33–43). That such should seek circumcision for themselves or for others is much less plausible than any of the above alternatives (see also Introduction §5).

Whatever Paul meant by the first half of the verse, the second half is reasonably clear: they **want you to be circumcised in order that they might boast in your flesh.** Again this could refer to an initial group of Galatians won to the 'other gospel' and now sharing the ethnic attitudes of the other missionaries. But it is more naturally taken as referring to those attacked in vi.12, since the evaluation of the flesh is the same in both cases. Certainly the talk of 'boasting' receives most illumination from the similar talk in Rom. ii.17, 23 and iii.27 (echoed in Phil. iii.3 and Eph. ii.9). That is, the boasting in view is almost certainly that of Jews confident in their standing before God and within the law (marked not least by circumcision). In other words, the boasting here in view, 'boasting in the flesh', is boasting in ethnic identity and prerogative, the boast of a Jew confident of acceptance by God over against the 'Gentile sinner'.[1] In particular, here, it is 'boasting in your flesh', because for Gentiles thus to affirm that their acceptance by God was dependent on their becoming Jews, by taking on the fleshly identification mark of the Jew (see on ii.3), was tantamount to affirming the Jewish claims to have a distinctive prerogative over against the Gentiles. When Gentiles thus subjected *their* flesh to the *Jewish* rite of circumcision, they gave *Jews* grounds to boast in *their* flesh thus subordinated to and incorporated within distinctive Jewish identity. Here again the force of 'flesh' is regularly missed: Paul is not simply protesting against submission to circumcision as such (NEB/REB), or thinking in terms of outward appearance (NJB); his thought is more of flesh as a corporate and

1 Wholly implausible is the argument of Schmithals, *Gnostics* 55, that what is in view here is a gnostic '*contempt* for the flesh' (emphasis added).

incorporative category (as in iv.23 and 29; cf. 1 Cor. x.18 – 'Israel according to the flesh'). Nor, it should be added, is there any thought of a boasting in human potential (Bonnard 129), or self-achieved merit (as in Betz 318 and Bruce 271), or 'merely human attainments' (Longenecker 294); in the nearest parallel (Phil iii.3), the contrast to boasting in Christ Jesus is 'trusting in flesh', where the context makes clear that 'trusting the flesh' (repeated twice in Phil. iii.4) is trusting in ethnic identity (iii.5) and covenantal nomistic zeal (iii.5–6; see on i.13–14).

14 The (typically Jewish) attitude just described is one which Paul himself could no longer share: **but as for me, God forbid** (see on ii.17) **that I should boast except in the cross of our Lord Jesus Christ**. The point is presumably the same as in vi.12: what the other missionaries sought to avoid, Paul gloried in. That is, a focusing of the gospel in the cross as alone sufficient basis for acceptance by God and the gift of the Spirit (ii.21–iii.2; iii.13–14), the very thing which was so disturbing for those who sought to maintain distinctive Jewish identity, was the very thing in which Paul boasted. It was precisely this shift in the ground and cause of boasting which marked Paul's transition from persecutor to apostle: from a boasting in the covenant prerogatives given to ethnic Israel, to a boasting in a gospel which relativized these prerogatives within the longer-term promise and purpose of God; from a boasting which focused the principle of covenant grace in God's choice of (ethnic) Israel, to a boasting which focused the principle of grace in a crucified and cursed Messiah – a shocking thought, given the horror and disgust with which crucifixion was regarded in the ancient world (see on v.24). Characteristic of Paul's theology is the fact that it is the death of the Christ which has become the primary ground of boasting before God (Rom. v.11; xv.27; 1 Cor. i.31; xv.31; Phil. ii.16; iii.3). As he draws the letter to a close, the convention of giving the full title, 'Lord Jesus Christ', becomes operative (as in vi.18; cf. i.3).

The significance of the cross is not simply the revaluation of Jewish prerogative over Gentile, for that revaluation means a revaluation of the whole world – **through whom** (see p. 334 n. 2) **the world has been crucified to me and I to the world**. As regularly in Paul, 'the world' denotes the totality of the whole creation (human as well as non-human) in its distance from God, and as yet unredeemed state (e.g. Rom. iii.6, 19; v.12–13; 1 Cor. i.20–1; ii.12; vi.2; vii.311–34; 2 Cor. v.19; vii.10; see *TDNT* iii.892–3). Here it is equivalent to 'the present evil age' (i.4; so also e.g. 1 Cor. ii.6–8 and 2 Cor. iv.4; see on i.4). What Paul means is that every rationale for individual and corporate existence which is independent of God (as in Rom. i.21–2), together with its system of beliefs and values and corresponding life-style, has been condemned and put to death so far as he is concerned; and that he himself has likewise been rendered inoperative so far as the attractions of such rationales, belief and value systems and life-styles are concerned. The language is given fuller resonance by modern talk of an individual's 'social world' or 'world of meaning', but to hear its full resonance, the cosmic and eschatological overtones have to be given full weight (Martyn, 'Antinomies' 412–13).

The imagery is particularly vivid and contains within it several key features of Paul's theology. (1) The imagery itself, of course, is derived from the central gospel fact of Christ's crucifixion: the world has been 'crucified', not merely killed or destroyed. What has happened has happened 'through him' (the phrase having the same force as in Rom. iii.24; v.1, 9–11, 18–19; vii.4; etc.). The cross on which the world is crucified to Paul and Paul to the world is the cross of Christ – none other. The implication is that on the cross the world was crucified to *Christ* and Christ to the world, that Christ's crucifixion is the paradigmatic example of what it means to refuse to be conformed to this age (Rom. xii.2). It is this which gives the claim its cosmic and eschatological power: in Christ's death the whole world has been put to death and a new world of possibilities come to birth (cf. 2 Cor. v.14–17).

(2) The thought, then, is part of Paul's understanding of the process of salvation as one of identification with Christ, particularly Christ on the cross (see further on ii.19–20). Only here it is not simply a matter of an interchange between Christ and the individual believer (or believers as a whole) (see also on iv.5); the world is also involved in this interchange – a unique example in Paul of a double 'interchange in Christ' (Hooker). As in Rom. vi.3–8, the dying *with* Christ includes a dying *to* the world, that is, the dying of individuals in their belongingness to the world, what Paul describes as 'the old me', 'the body of sin' (Rom. vi.6; Col. iii.9; also Eph. iv.22).

(3) Elsewhere it is important to appreciate the decisiveness of that past event, reflected in the aorist tenses of Rom. vi.3–4, that initial identification with Christ through baptism (Rom. vi.4), and/or in the reception of the Spirit of Christ (as in Gal. iv.6). But here, as in ii.20, the tenses are perfect – denoting a continued state resulting from that initial act of nailing to the cross. Paul's whole Christian life was spent in a state of the world having been crucified to him and him to the world. Which

is also to say (since crucifixion was a long-drawn-out execution) that the dying on both sides was not yet complete; until which time his belongingness to the world (his old nature) was not yet ended (see again on ii.20).

(4) Most striking of all for the present context is the line of thought running from verse 13 to verse 15 through verse 14. Thus read in context, it becomes clear that boasting in the flesh (vi.13) is an example of the worldly attitude renounced in vi.14; and that over-evaluation of the significance of both circumcision and uncircumcision (vi. 15) is an indication of an uncrucified state, in which the significance of the cross has not been adequately appreciated or entered into (see further on vi.15).

15 For neither circumcision counts for anything, nor uncircumcision, but a new creation. The message of the previous verse is explained ('for') by being rephrased. The attitude under attack is clearly Jewish, since only a Jew would categorize conditions of humanity in these terms (Gentiles would not normally think of themselves as 'uncircumcised' or 'the uncircumcision'; see on ii.3). Moreover, since 'new creation' clearly stands in antithesis to '(old) world' (vi.14), the implication is reinforced that such an over-evaluation of ethnic identity and ritual marker is an example of thinking which belongs to the old age of minority (iii.23–iv.11), prior to the coming of Messiah Jesus (see also on vi.14). Here too the irony of Paul's critique should not be missed: the very appraisal of circumcision by which Jews typically saw themselves as marked out *from* the wider world (as special to God) was itself a mark of their belongingness *to* the world in its distance from God and deserving of God's judgement. The line of thought is, of course, close to that of v.6, but the similar phrasing of 1 Cor. vii.19 comes in a different context and serves a different purpose. The brevity of the expression does not necessarily imply an already established maxim (Betz 319 n. 79), far less a Jewish-Christian one (Longenecker 296), since it belongs to the terseness of the final summary (vi.12–17) and summarizes the distinctive emphasis of the letter (see again v.6). On the other hand, Betz's claim that Paul 'in fact announces the establishment of a new religion' (p. 320) is also overstated, since the 'new creation' is the fulfilment of the Abrahamic promise and the 'coming of age' of the (Jewish) heirs (iii–iv).

'World' is a term Paul confines to the present age, but 'creation' (like 'age') can also be used for the age to come (cf. Rom. viii.19–22 and 2 Cor. v.17 – 'new creation'). By 'new creation' he presumably means the world of existence made new, recreated, to serve as a fitting context for God's children (Rom. viii.21; for bibliography see Betz 319 n. 79); the word can mean 'creature', but the contrast with 'world' suggests the larger meaning (cf. Isa. lxv.17; lxvi.22). Paul in fact speaks in apocalyptic terms of 'two different worlds' (Martyn, 'Antinomies' 412; this verse provides the basis for Martyn's exegesis of iv.21–5 and v.16–17). The thought, in other words, is of a piece with Paul's eschatology in general. With Christ's death the exclusive rule of sin and death has been broken; with Christ's resurrection the new age/creation has already begun (Rom. vi.9–10; see also on i.4). In so far as believers are identified with Christ in his death (see on ii.19 and vi.14) and have begun to share in the last Adam, life-giving Spirit (1 Cor xv.45), they have begun to share in that new creation, which is to say, have begun a process of being 'conformed to the image of the creator' (Col. iii.10; see also on Gal. iv.19). Since the process is not yet complete, 'the new creation', in practical terms, means a life oriented both to the past (Christ's death and resurrection as paradigmatic, for relationship to the world as well – see again on vi.14), and to the future triumph of God in Christ (what will be in God's intention as creator, as providing norms and goals for life in this world).

16 Paul has now shot his bolt; further argument and pleading would be unlikely to make any difference. All that remains, therefore, is to give a final blessing, a final warning and to say farewell. He turns first to those who, in his fond hope at least, will take seriously what he has written and draw back from any thought of accepting circumcision – **and as many as will follow this rule, peace be on them and mercy.** By 'rule' (*kanōn*) Paul means clearly the norm by which he lives and the standard by which he judges the 'other gospel' (*TDNT* iii.597–8). As in v.25, 'follow' signifies an orderly 'falling in line with'. As a summary of his own teaching, verse 15 provides the norm and standard by which he hopes the Galatians will judge and act in response to the pressure from the other missionaries. His hope is that, like him, they will sit loose to issues of ethnic identity and ritual distinction, and that such issues will be seen to be of irrelevant significance beside the gospel of the cross. That Paul can reduce the gospel to this 'rule' is a reminder of how central to his understanding of the gospel was the Jew–Gentile issue.

The blessing is, in part, the same as the opening greeting, 'peace' (see on i.3), reinforced now by its appearance in the list of fruit produced by the Spirit (v.22) which they had all received (iii.2). But of course, it is also the characteristic Jewish salutation (*salom*); particularly noteworthy here are Pss. cxxv.5, cxxviii.6

and 11QPs^a xxiii.11 – 'Peace be upon Israel'. And this Jewish character of Paul's blessing is reinforced by his use of 'mercy'. For the word itself is one of the most evocative for Jews that he could have chosen, the Greek (*eleos*) being the normal translation of the Hebrew *hesed*, '(God's covenant) faithfulness and kindness' (*TDNT* ii.479–80; as in the much echoed Exod. xxxiv.6–7 – see my *Romans* 552). Particularly noteworthy are the regular appeals to God to remember his mercy or invocations of God's mercy in *Psalms of Solomon* (iv.25; vi.6; viii.27–8; ix.8; xi.9 – 'The mercy of the Lord be upon Israel for ever and ever'; xiii.12; xvi.6; xvii.45 – 'May God hasten his mercy upon Israel'; xviii.5). The association of 'mercy and peace' is also to be found in Ps. lxxxv.10 and Isa. liv.10, in the greeting of the letter in *2 Bar.* lxxviii.2, in the Babylonian recension of the *Shemoneh 'Esreh* (18 Benedictions) 19, and in variant readings at *1 Enoch* v.5 and Tobit vii.12. Given also the exceptional character of the usage in Paul (only here as part of his introductory and concluding pleasantries; though, cf. 1 Tim. i.2 and 2 Tim. i.2), the conclusion is unavoidable: at this point Paul has deliberately introduced a strongly Jewish benediction, whose very Jewish character would be unmistakable to all the Christian Jews in Galatia and to those most influenced by them.

It will be significant, then, that Paul evokes this very *Jewish* blessing precisely on 'as many as follow' the very rule that diminishes Israel's most distinctive identity marker (vi.15) – as though to emphasize, for those with ears to hear, that Israel's covenant blessings were no longer tied to ethnic Israel = that people marked out precisely by circumcision, 'the circumcision'. This must also explain why Paul adds the otherwise puzzling and unique phrase, **as also on the Israel of God**. The precise referent has been a source of unresolved debate. 'Israel', it should be remembered, is a specifically Jewish self-designation: whereas 'Jew' characteristically denotes the view of an outsider (see also on ii.13), 'Israel' expresses the Jewish people's sense of identity as the covenant people of God (*TDNT* iii.359–65, 369–72). Paul, therefore, is doing one of two things.

(1) He is reinforcing the complete redrawing of definitions already implicit in his argument. This blessing is also for the 'Israel of God' understood as believers in Christ, particularly Gentile believers, and including, not least, those just exhorted (vi.16a) (e.g. Lightfoot 225; Borse 223; Hansen 161) – that is, 'Israel' understood as other than ethnic Israel. This would certainly fit with the overall thrust of the letter, and constitute a final abrupt warning to the other (Jewish) missionaries: God's covenant peace and mercy is only for that Israel which

recognizes the rule of vi.15! The point would be reinforced if we translated '. . . even on the Israel of God' (identifying 'the Israel of God' with the 'as many as'; so REB and NIV). It would be a fierce parting shot, but no fiercer than the repeated anathema of i.8–9. In that case, we would have to say that Paul modified his position (when his exasperation cooled) in Rom. ix–xi.

(2) Alternatively, Paul has recoiled a little from the implication that (Israel's) peace and mercy are only for those who follow his rule; and so he adds, 'as also on the Israel of God'. We could even translate, 'Peace on them (the "as many") and mercy also on the Israel of God' (cf. Burton 357–8; P. Richardson, *Israel in the Apostolic Church* [Cambridge University, 1969] 84). The reference would then presumably be to the Jewish people as a whole (Mussner 417; W. D. Davies, 'Paul and the People of Israel', *NTS* 24 [1977–8] 4–39, here 9–10 and n. 20; elsewhere Paul never calls Christians 'Israel' as such). But, in the light of his earlier argument, that would have to mean the Jewish people precisely in their covenant identity, 'Israel' rather than 'the Jews'. That is, an Israel understood in terms of the promise to Abraham (and Jacob/Israel), the very promise which included blessings for the Gentiles (chs. iii–iv) – in other words, Israel understood *not* as excluding Jews as a whole, but as *including* Gentile believers (cf. Rom. ix.6; xi.17–26; 1 Cor. x.18).

This latter alternative is probably to be preferred, since both the Greek here and the earlier theology allow, if not encourage, that kind of ambiguity – Israel consisting of all Abraham's seed and heirs, including both those still 'minors' and those who were seed as being 'in Christ' (iii.29–iv.3). Paul's prayer would then be that God's covenant mercy be fully sustained and achieve its end for *all* the seed. In that case, and even in the heat of his exasperation, Paul deliberately refrains from driving a (different) wedge between ethnic Israel and the new movement among Gentiles. For his own theology it remained fundamental that the gospel was the working out of the original promise to Abraham (iii.8); with the corollary that the development of thought between Galatians and Romans is not so great as is often claimed. It also means that, somewhat surprisingly, even in his final curtness Paul holds out an olive branch to his opponents – though only (implicitly) on his terms: 'the Israel of God' is the seed of Abraham understood in terms of the argument of chs. iii–iv. Despite N. A. Dahl, 'Der Name Israel: Zur Auslegung von Gal. vi.16', *Judaica* 6 (1950) 161–70, such a concession would no more invalidate Paul's argument in Galatians than his earlier description of his fellow Jews as heirs still in their minority (see again iii.23–iv.3); the attempt by the other missionaries to impose the 'other gospel' on the Gentile Galatians did not *ipso facto* nullify the Jewish people's status as heirs not yet entered upon their inheritance. At all events, however precisely the phrase is to be understood, Paul's use of it here certainly underlines the strong sense of continuity which he saw between the religion of Israel and faith in Messiah Jesus, and undermines Watson's thesis that Paul called for 'the separation of the church from the Jewish community' (p. 65).

17 Even if an olive branch has been thus extended to the trouble-makers in Galatia (vi.16), Paul at once retreats back into an impatient grumpiness: **From now on** (BAGD, *loipos* 3aβ) **let no one cause me trouble**. In secular Greek the noun (*kopos*) denotes a 'beating', or 'weariness as though one had been beaten', and so also the 'exertion' or 'trouble' which causes this state (*TDNT* iii.827); in Jewish literature cf. particularly Ps. cvii.12 and 1 Macc. x.15; in Paul of. 2 Cor. vi.5 and xi.23, 27 with 2 Thess. ii.9, iii.5 and 2 Thess. iii.8. The idiom ('cause trouble') appears in the papyri, and elsewhere in biblical Greek in Sir. xxix.4, Mark xiv.6 par., Luke xi.7 and xviii.5. Paul indicates that the troubles caused among the Galatian churches had been almost like a physical assault on himself (because of his concern for his converts and the degree to which he had personally invested himself in the Gentile mission) which left him weary in mind and spirit. The brevity of these final 'courtesies' equally indicates the extent of his weariness and exasperation.

To this half-command, half-plea Paul adds an explanation – **for I** (emphatic) **bear the marks of Jesus on my body**. The idea of his troubles as a kind of beating reminds him that his body bears the marks of a far more important event. That is to say, the 'for' introduces the reason why they should refrain from causing him any more trouble, not the explanation for his beaten, weary state. What Paul means by 'the marks (Greek, *stigmata*) of Jesus' has been long debated. That some sort of branding is in view is generally agreed (hence NRSV, NEB/REB, NJB – 'branded on my body'). The older view is that the image was drawn from the practice of branding slaves (so still Bruce 275 and Rohde 279–80); the fact that such branding was regarded as a disgrace (*Ps. Phoc.* 225 – 'Do not brand your slave, thus insulting him'), need not be decisive, given Paul's love of such paradox (e.g. 1 Cor. i.23–5; 2 Cor. xii.9–10). More popular now, however, is the view that Paul had in mind the practice whereby in the ancient orient one might indicate one's dedication to a god and thus come under his protection (cf. Gen.

iv.15; Ezek. ix.4; *3 Macc.* ii.29–30; Rev. vii.2–4; see further BAGD and MM, *stigma; TDNT* vii.657–63; Oepke 205–8).

There is a strong consensus that by 'the marks of Jesus' themselves Paul means the scars and physical effects of the various beatings and severe hardships (including being stoned) which Paul had already experienced in the course of his missionary work (2 Cor. xi.23–7; for a brief review of other alternatives see Mussner 418–20). The thought, in other words, links up with his talk elsewhere of sharing Christ's sufferings and death (Rom. viii.17; 2 Cor. i.5; iv.8–10; Phil. iii.10; Col. i.24; see on ii.19). The allusion to the death of the man Jesus is probably heightened by the unusual use of Jesus' personal name, without any title (Lord or Christ); cf. particularly 2 Cor. iv.10–11, and the echo of an early resurrection formula in Rom. viii.11, 1 Thess. i.10 and iv.14. Paul sees his own sufferings as a missionary as a working out of that identification with Jesus on the cross of which he had just spoken (see on vi.14). The marks of his identification with Jesus' sufferings and death should be sufficient proof of the genuineness of his apostleship in the eyes even of the most conservative and trouble-making Christian Jew. For the third and final time within this short, highly personal section, Paul, by implication, sets in contrast an identity defined in terms of circumcision and one focused in the cross of Christ.

18 All that remains is to take farewell of his several audiences in Galatia: **the grace of our Lord Jesus Christ be with your spirit**. The benediction is typical of Paul's parting words in his letters: some are longer (1 Cor. xvi.23–4; 2 Cor. xiii.13), but others are briefer (Rom. xvi.20; Col. iv.18), with 1 Thess. v.28 and 2 Thess. iii.18 very similar, and Phil. iv.23 and Phm. 25 almost the same. Since the last two mentioned are Paul's friendliest letters we cannot read anything into the brevity here (as implying a final flourish of irritation). On the contrary, Paul uses his usual favourite word, 'grace' (the characteristic Christian term replacing the normal epistolary 'farewell'), with its full overtone, no doubt, of wholly generous divine initiative (see on i.3); as also the normal full sonorous title, 'our Lord Jesus Christ' (as again i.3). The prayer that this grace should be with their 'spirit' (only here in Galatians for the human spirit) is perhaps a gentle reminder that what bonded them all together was the Spirit of God working in their spirit (cf. Rom. viii.16), rather than ethnic identity as marked out by circumcision; but otherwise the language is unremarkable. But the most unusual feature is the final, **my brothers** (nowhere else in any other Pauline farewells, Eph. vi.23 apart), as Paul makes a final appeal to their common belonging to 'the household of faith' (vi.10; see on i.2 and vi.10); 'the severity of the whole epistle is thus softened' (Bengel). The concluding **Amen** (see on i.5) no doubt likewise was an echo of Paul's fervent hope for a good outcome in Galatia – 'may it be so!' – one in which he must have hoped the Galatian congregations would join (cf. 1 Cor. xiv.16).

INDEX OF MODERN AUTHORS

SUBJECT INDEX

INDEX OF ANCIENT SOURCES

Barnabas
2.2, 311
3.6, 226
4.9, 281
9.4, 191
16.5, 34
19.8, 327
20.1, 304
20.1–2, 302

Ps. Clem.
Epistula Petri
1.1, 76
2.3, 237

Homilies
17.13–19, 54
17.16.6, 69
17.19, 125

18.10, 50
19.6, 125
Recognitions
1.43, 76
2.42, 192

Didache
1.2, 291
1.3, 46
4.8, 327
5.1, 304
5.1–2, 302
6.2, 263
11–13, 233
16.1, 332

Eusebius
HE
2.1.2–5, 76

2.23, 76
2.23.4–7, 108
3.1.1, 109
3.23, 109
3.24, 109
7.19, 76

Praep. Evan.
9.22.5, 15, 129, 266

Ignatius
Ephesians
12.2, 131
18.1, 281
20.2, 304

Magnesians
8.1, 226
10.2, 276

10.3, 57, 226

Philadelphians
6.1, 57

Romans
3.3, 275
5.2, 293

Justin
Dialogue with Trypho
47.4, 226

Gospel of Thomas
96, 275